NEW PERSPECTIVES ON GLOBAL GOVERNANCE

Global Finance Series

Edited by
Michele Fratianni, Indiana University, USA, John J. Kirton, University of Toronto, Canada, and Paolo Savona, LUISS Guido Carli University, Italy

The intensifying globalisation of the twenty-first century has brought a myriad of new managerial and political challenges for governing international finance. The return of synchronous global slowdown, mounting developed country debt, and new economy volatility have overturned established economic certainties. Proliferating financial crises, transnational terrorism, currency consolidation, and increasing demands that international finance should better serve public goods such as social and environmental security have all arisen to compound the problem.

The new public and private international institutions that are emerging to govern global finance have only just begun to comprehend and respond to this new world. Embracing international financial flows and foreign direct investment, in both the private and public sector dimensions, this series focuses on the challenges and opportunities faced by firms, national governments, and international institutions, and their roles in creating a new system of global finance.

Also in the series

Sustaining Global Growth and Development:
G7 and IMF Governance
Edited by Michele Fratianni, Paolo Savona and John J. Kirton
ISBN 0 7546 3529 5

Global Financial Crime:
Terrorism, Money Laundering and Offshore Centres
Edited by Donato Masciandaro
ISBN 0 7546 3707 7

Governing Global Banking:
The Basel Committee and the Politics of Financial Globalisation
Duncan Wood
ISBN 0 7546 1906 0

Elements of the Euro Area:
Integrating Financial Markets
Edited by Jesper Berg, Mauro Grande and Francesco Paolo Mongelli
ISBN 0 7546 4320 4

New Perspectives on Global Governance

Why America Needs the G8

Edited by

MICHELE FRATIANNI
Indiana University, USA

JOHN J. KIRTON
University of Toronto, Canada

ALAN M. RUGMAN
Indiana University, USA

PAOLO SAVONA
LUISS Guido Carli University, Italy

LONDON AND NEW YORK

First published 2005 by Ashgate Publishing

2 Park Square, Milton Park, Abingdon, Oxfordshire OX14 4RN
711 Third Avenue, New York, NY 10017

Routledge is an imprint of the Taylor & Francis Group, an informa business

First issued in paperback 2017

British Library Cataloguing in Publication Data
New perspectives on global governance : why America needs
the G8. - (Global finance)
1.Group of Eight (Organization) 2.International economic
relations 3.International cooperation 4.United States -
Foreign economic relations
I.Fratianni, Michele
337.1

Library of Congress Cataloging-in-Publication Data
New perspectives on global governance : why America needs the G8 / edited by Michele
Fratianni ... [et al.].
p. cm. -- (Global finance)
Includes bibliographical references and index.
ISBN 0-7546-4477 4
1. International organization--Congresses. 2. International cooperation--Congresses. 3. International finance--Congresses. 4. Group of Eight (Organization)--Congresses. I. Fratianni, Michele. II. Global finance series

JZ1318.N489 2005
341.2--dc22

2005041991

ISBN 13: 978-0-7546-4477-4 (hbk)
ISBN 13: 978-1-138-26683-4 (pbk)

Contents

PART II: PROSPERITY AND SECURITY

PART III: FINANCE AND SECURITY

PART IV: THE G8 AND INTERNATIONAL TRADE POLICY

CONCLUSION

DOCUMENTARY APPENDICES

List of Tables

List of Figures

List of Contributors

T. Taylor Aldridge is a Master's student at the School of Public and Environmental Affairs at Indiana University in Bloomington. He is also a Fellow at the Max Planck Institute for Entrepreneurship, Growth, and Public Policy in Jena, Germany.

David B. Audretsch is the Ameritech Chair of Economic Development, Director of the Institute for Development Strategies and Director of the Center for West European Studies at Indiana University. He is also Director of the Max Planck Institute for Economics Research, Growth, and Public Policy in Jena, Germany.

Sir Nicholas Bayne, KCMG, is a Fellow at the International Trade Policy Unit of the London School of Economics and Political Science.

Michele Fratianni is the W. George Pinnell Professor and Chair of Business Economics and Public Policy at the Kelley School of Business at Indiana University in Bloomington, Indiana.

Jeffrey A. Hart is Professor of Political Science at Indiana University in Bloomington, Indiana.

Heejoon Kang is Professor of Business Economics and Public Policy at the Kelley School of Business at Indiana University, Bloomington, Indiana.

John J. Kirton is Director of the G8 Research Group, Associate Professor of Political Science, Research Associate of the Centre for International Studies, and Fellow of Trinity College at the University of Toronto. He was principal investigator for 'Strengthening Canada's Environmental Community through International Regime Reform' (the EnviReform project) at the University of Toronto.

Donato Masciandaro is Professor of Monetary Economics at the Paolo Baffi Centre at Bocconi University and in the Department of Economics, Mathematics, and Statistics at the University of Lecce.

Bernhard May is a resident fellow at the Research Institute of the German Council on Foreign Relations (DGAP) in Berlin, where he is responsible for the U.S./Transatlantic Relations programme, and is Secretary General of the German Group of the Trilateral Commission.

Sylvia Ostry is the Distinguished Research Fellow at the Centre for International Studies at the University of Toronto. She was a co-investigator for 'Strengthening Canada's Environmental Community through International Regime Reform' (the EnviReform project) at the University of Toronto.

Victoria Panova is a doctoral candidate in the Department of International Relations and Foreign Policy of Russia at Moscow State University of International Relations.

Risto E. J. Penttilä is Director of the Finnish Business and Policy Forum EVA, a think tank based in Helsinki. He is also Secretary General of the European Business Leaders' Convention. At the time of writing, he was also a fellow at Saïd Business School at the University of Oxford.

Alan M. Rugman holds the L. Leslie Waters Chair in International Business at the Kelley School of Business at Indiana University in Bloomington, and is Director of Indiana University's Center for International Business Education and Research (CIBER). He was a co-investigator for 'Strengthening Canada's Environmental Community through International Regime Reform' (the EnviReform project) at the University of Toronto.

Paolo Savona is Professor of Political Economy at LUISS Guido Carli University in Rome, and chair of Impregilo Group.

Richard M. Stazinski is a Research Fellow at the Max Planck Institute for Research into Economic Systems, Growth, and Public Policy in Jena, Germany.

Heidi K. Ullrich is a visiting lecturer at the London School of Economics and Political Science, where she also completed her Ph.D. She is Director of the London office of the University of Toronto's G8 Research Group and serves as editor of *G8 Governance*.

George M. von Furstenberg is the J. H. Rudy Professor of Economics at Indiana University in Bloomington, specialising in international financial policy.

Preface and Acknowledgements

This book is the sixth in Ashgate Publishing's Global Finance series. It continues a tradition, begun in 1998, of using the annual G7/8 summit as a catalyst for edited volumes that explore the central themes in the emerging dynamic of global governance with a particular relevance to the field of global finance. This volume continues its central concern with core finance issues, notably those related to combating money laundering and terrorist finance. But it broadens the focus to deal with related economic issues such as trade, the cyberspace economy, energy supply, and the new human capital and knowledge drivers of economic growth. Even more broadly, it addresses a trilogy of thematic areas at the centre of the June 2004 Sea Island Summit — security, prosperity, and freedom, and the complex interconnections among the three. Given this complexity, and the fact that Sea Island marked the 30th anniversary of G7/8 summitry, this book offers new perspectives on the performance and work of the G8 as a whole.

This volume is based on a research project designed by the University of Toronto's G8 Research Group with Indiana University's Kelley School of Business, with support from Indiana University Center for International Business Education and Research (IU CIBER) and Office of the Vice-President for Research, West European Studies National Resource Center, and Office of International Programs. Significant additional funding came from the Research Group on Global Financial Governance, the Guido Carli Association, and 'Strengthening Canada's Environmental Community through International Regime Reform' (the EnviReform project) at the University of Toronto. Consultations with the Center for Strategic and International Studies (CSIS) and the Woodrow Wilson Center for International Scholars, led by Lee Hamilton and involving scholars from these institutions as well as from the University of Georgia's Center for International Trade and Security, were also particularly valuable.

For this project, scholars and policy makers from the G8 countries examined how best the United States, with its G8 partners and through the G8, could meet its vital security needs in ways that enhance the prosperity of America and its partners. Coming from a diverse set of disciplines in economics, political science, management, these scholars addressed this question in the context of how America's G8 partners and institutions could best align their policies and interests. This book is a strong example of the new thinking and useful policy advice that can result from such interdisciplinary research.

Acknowledgements

In producing this volume, we have enjoyed the exceptional support of those who contributed in many different ways. Our first debt is to Antonio Fazio, Governor of the Bank of Italy, who as Chair of the Guido Carli Association provided part of the funding that made our conference possible. We are also grateful to David Dodge, Governor of the Bank of Canada, and Jonathan Fried, Jim Wright, and Gordon Venner and his G8 team in the Department of Foreign Affairs and International Trade for their ongoing support and wise counsel. We also received significant support from several key officials involved in the G8 process in the U.S. State Department and government as a whole.

We have a special debt to Indiana University, and the many outstanding individuals who came forward to help: Louise Siffin, Walteena Albright, and Paula Scherschel at the Kelley School in particular were endlessly helpful; Mildred Harris was equally patient and ready to lend a hand; George Vlahakis did an excellent job promoting the project; Michael Jasiak and Steven Egyhazi and their team, particularly Sharlyn Deglow, James Scott McGookey, and Alexis Androni, handled the technical requirements effortlessly.

We also gratefully acknowledge the important contribution of Christopher Sands and Andre Belelieu at CSIS, David Biette and Lee Hamilton at the Woodrow Wilson Center and their colleagues John Tyler and Paul Graphow, and Gary Bertsch and Igor Kripinov at the University of Georgia.

We also acknowledge the financial support of the Social Sciences and Humanities Research Council of Canada, through the EnviReform and After Anarchy projects. We further appreciate the willingness to take a major role in our project of several members of the G8 Research Group's Professional Advisory Council, notably Nicholas Bayne and George von Furstenberg.

In Toronto, we owe a very special word of thanks to Madeline Koch, the Managing Director of the G8 Research Group. Her managerial and editorial skills were essential in helping organise the project and ensuring that initial thoughts and rough drafts were transformed into a polished integrated book. Her devoted professionalism and personal dedication to getting this book into press in accordance with a demanding schedule at a difficult time is a contribution we will always cherish as a source of inspiration in our work.

We are also grateful to Helen Walsh, president of Think Content, for her vital role in ensuring that our project's findings were made available in electronic format to the world at large. More broadly, we note with deep appreciation the indispensable contributions of Ella Kokotsis, Director of Analytical Studies of the G8 Research Group, of Sandra Larmour, the Director of Development of the G8 Research Group, and of Shinichiro Uda, Director of the G8 Research Group's office in Japan.

At the University of Toronto, we are grateful to President Robert Birgeneau and his colleagues for their support. We also acknowledge the continuing support of our colleagues at the Centre for International Studies: its director, Professor Louis Pauly, who oversees our research activities, and Professor Peter Hajnal, who assumed the vital task of securing the anonymous referees who reviewed our draft manuscript and who collectively approved it for publication. We owe much to the comments of our referees, whose astute and supportive comments have been taken fully into account. At Trinity College, we acknowledge the critical support of provost Margaret MacMillan, bursar Geoffrey Seaborn who manages the G8 Research Group's accounts, head librarian Linda Corman, who oversees the development of the G8 Research Library Collection, and Professor Robert Bothwell, Co-ordinator of the International Relations Programme. At the Department of Political Science, Professor Robert Vipond, the Chair, provided important support. At the University of Toronto Library, we remain grateful, as always, to chief librarian Carole Moore.

As always, we reserve a special word of thanks for Kirstin Howgate, and her colleagues at Ashgate, especially Alexandra Polson, for recognising the virtue of producing this volume and for working so effectively to ensure the smooth adoption and speedy publication of the manuscript. Finally, we acknowledge the understanding, patience, and support of our families as we laboured to convert raw drafts into publishable text. We are also indebted to the alumni of the G8 Research Group and our students at universities throughout the G8 and beyond. They provide a constant source of inspiration and constructive criticism as we pursue our work. It is to this next generation of scholars on G8 governance, and their new perspectives on the subject, that we dedicate this book.

Michele Fratianni, John J. Kirton, Alan M. Rugman, and Paolo Savona
November 2004

List of Abbreviations

ABM Treaty	Anti-Ballistic Missile Treaty
ADEN	Appui au désenclavement numérique (network of public internet access points, proposed by France for Africa)
ANZCERTA	Australia-New Zealand Closer Economic Relations Trade Agreement
APEC	Asia-Pacific Economic Cooperation
APR	Africa Personal Representative (of a G8 leader)
ARPA	United States Department of Defense Advanced Research Projects Agency
ASEAN	Association of Southeast Asian Nations
BaFin	Bundesanstalt für Finanzdienstleistungen
BaKred	Bundesaufsichtsamt für Kreditwesen
BMENA	Broader Middle East and North Africa
CACM	Central American Common Market
CAP	Common Agricultural Policy
CARICOM	Caribbean Community and Common Market
CERT	computer emergency response team
CIA	United States Central Intelligence Agency
CIS	Commonwealth of Independent States
COMECON	Council for Mutual Economic Assistance
CTAG	Counter-Terrorism Action Group
CTBT	Comprehensive Test Ban Treaty
CU	customs union
DFEN	Dot Force Entrepreneurial Network
Dot Force	Digital Opportunity Task Force
DPRK	Democratic People's Republic of Korea
EC	European Community
ECSC	European Coal and Steel Community
EEC	European Economic Community
EPIC	Electronic Privacy Information Center
EURATOM	European Atomic Energy Community
FATF	Financial Action Task Force on Money Laundering
FBI	U.S. Federal Bureau of Investigation
FDI	foreign direct investment
FEAT	features
FIPs	Five Interested Parties

FIU	Financial Intelligence Unit
FSA	firm-specific advantage
FTAA	Free Trade Agreement of the Americas
G7	Group of Seven (France, United States, United Kingdom, Germany, Japan, Italy, and Canada, with representatives from the European Union)
G8	Group of Seven plus Russia
G20	Group of 20 finance ministers and central bank governors of emerging economies (G8 plus Argentina, Australia, Brazil, China, India, Indonesia, Korea, Mexico, Saudi Arabia, South Africa, and Turkey)
GATT	General Agreement on Tariffs and Trade
GDP	gross domestic product
GEOSS	Global Environment Observation System of Systems
GII	Global Information Infrastructure
GIIC	Global Information Infrastructure Commission (of the World Bank)
GMEI	Greater Middle East Initiative
HIPCs	heavily indebted poor countries
IAEA	International Atomic Energy Agency
ICAO	International Civil Aviation Organization
ICC	International Chamber of Commerce
ICT	information and communications technology
IDA	International Development Association (World Bank)
IEA	International Energy Agency
IFC	International Finance Corporation
IFF	International Financial Facility
IFI	international financial institution
ILO	International Labour Organization
IMF	International Monetary Fund
IMO	International Maritime Organization
L20	Leaders 20 (the heads of state and government of the G20 countries)
MANPADS	man-portable air defence systems
MDB	multilateral development bank
MDG	Millennium Development Goal
MERCOSUR	Common Market of the South (Mercado Común del Sur)
MNC	multinational corporation
MNEPR	Multilateral Nuclear Environmental Programme in the Russian Federation
MU	monetary union
MVT	money/value transfer

NAFTA	North American Free Trade Agreement
NATO	North Atlantic Treaty Organization
NCCTs	Non-cooperative Countries and Territories
NEPAD	New Partnership for Africa's Development
NGO	nongovernmental organisation
NIEO	New International Economic Order
NORAD	North American Air Defense Command
NSFNET	National Science Foundation Network (United States)
NTIA	National Telecommunication and Information Administration (of the United States Commerce Department)
ODA	official development assistance
OECD	Organisation for Economic Co-operation and Development
OPEC	Organization of the Petroleum Exporting Countries
OSCE	Organization for Security and Co-operation in Europe
P5	Permanent Five members of the United Nations Security Council (United States, United Kingdom, France, China, and Russia)
PATCRA	Australia and Papua New Guinea
PPP	purchasing power parity
PRC	People's Republic of China
PSI	Proliferation Security Initiative
Quad	Quadrilateral Trade Ministers
R&D	research and development
RTA	regional trade agreement
SAFTI	Secure and Facilitated International Travel Initiative
SME	small and medium-sized business
SPARTECA	South Pacific Regional Trade and Economic Co-operation Agreement
UMP	Union pour un Mouvement Populaire
UNDP	United Nations Development Programme
UNSC	United Nations Security Council
UNSCR	United Nations Security Council Resolution
USIS	United States and Israel
USTR	United States Trade Representative
WFP	World Food Programme
WHO	World Health Organization
WMD	weapons of mass destruction
WTO	World Trade Organization

INTRODUCTION

Chapter 1

Introduction

Michele Fratianni, John J. Kirton, Alan M. Rugman, and Paolo Savona

The G8 Summit held at Sea Island, Georgia, in June 2004 marked the 30th anniversary of an institution that started in 1975 at Rambouillet, outside of Paris, as a result of an initiative by French president Valéry Giscard d'Estaing, German chancellor Helmut Schmidt, and U.S. secretary of state Henry Kissinger. On such an anniversary, it is appropriate to ask a few fundamental questions. Has the summit been successful? Has it served its members well, including its most powerful member, the United States? Is the world a better place because of its existence?

This volume answers those questions. It assesses the latest summit, hosted by U.S. president George Bush in 2004. It also projects what is in store for the summit, its members, and the world in the years to come. It seeks to go beyond the existing arguments about G8 effectiveness to offer new perspectives on an institution that has now stood the test of time, but that some think is overdue for fundamental change.

Why the G8?

There is virtually a consensus that international co-operation is superior to independent national policymaking. In a complex and interdependent world, many actions taken by one nation directly and indirectly affect other nations. But there are serious impediments to international co-operation. The first is the difference in national preferences that may make agreements impossible. The second is the ever present incentive that some nations may deviate from a commonly agreed position. The third is the incentive for small nations to free ride on large nations. As a result of these limitations, it is necessary to ask in what specific areas co-operation is feasible, and what international governance structure is best suited to achieve intended results with a minimum degree of cheating and free riding.

Democracy purists prefer all-encompassing international organisations such as the United Nations because they have the legitimacy that comes from universal membership (Held 1995). Institutions such as the G8 are viewed as representing the narrow interests of a small club of industrialised countries. But legitimacy and effectiveness are more substitutable than complementary. The UN is not effective in delivering co-operation because of the size and heterogeneity of its membership and the confines of its formal, legalised principles, rules, decision-making procedures, and organisational culture.

On many important issues, conflicts among members are so numerous and intense that the UN can be no more than a talking shop. Resolutions tend to converge toward the lowest common denominator. The occasional resolutions that rise above this level are prone to a considerable degree of free riding, as in troop contributions to fight a war, and cheating, as in the embargo on Iraq.

In contrast, the G7 and now G8 is sufficiently small, homogeneous, and informal that it has a higher chance to achieve co-operation and agreements that are less prone to cheating and free riding. In essence, the theoretical effectiveness of a small club derives from its exclusiveness. Should the club transform itself into an all-inclusive institution, it would lose effectiveness (Fratianni and Pattison 2001). In sum, legitimacy and effectiveness are substitutes: more of one implies less of the other. Calls for enlarging the G8 need to be analysed in this context (Kirton 2004).

Given these advantages, what would the world be like without the G8? According to Nicholas Bayne, in Chapter 2, the world without the G8 would be more brutish and riskier than it is now. The great merit of the G8 is that 'brings together the leaders of eight of the world's most powerful nations and reminds them of their responsibility to co-operate internationally, rather than giving way to domestic pressures'. In essence, these leaders together make decisions that they would not make if they were on their own. Without the G8 they would overweight the domestic impact of policy actions and underweight the foreign impact. In isolation, they would have too narrow a focus. But to co-operate, the G8 members must have sufficiently similar preferences. If those preferences were to diverge too much, the G8 would break up. Bayne notes that this was about to happen at the 2003 Evian Summit when Bush was so upset with French president Jacques Chirac that he contemplated showing up for the meetings at Evian but spending the nights next door in Switzerland.

How can one measure the success of the G8? One measure of success is survival. Since the G8 competes with other groups and international organisations, the survival test is an objective criterion of positive value (Kirton 2004). A second measure of success is media attention. The G8 summits receive a great deal of attention from the media, more than comparable events organised by other international organisations. A third measure of success is civil society attention and participation. Civil society increasingly wants its voice heard by the G8 summiteers. The carefully planned and bloody demonstrations of the antiglobalists at the 2001 Genoa Summit were, in a perverse way, an indicator of the importance of the G8. In contrast, the reaction of the media and civil society to UN sessions tends to be lethargic. One problem is that the G8 has recently been devoting many resources to isolate itself from the attention of the media and protestors.

A large formal literature exists on the performance of the G8, to which many of the authors in this volume have contributed (Bailin 2005; Bayne 2005; Penttilä 2003; Hodges, Kirton, and Daniels 1999; Putnam and Bayne 1987). Summits are scored either by overall grades, in a method pioneered by Robert Putnam and Nicholas Bayne, or in terms of carefully measured statements, commitments and compliance, as John

Kirton shows in Chapter 3. While there is inevitable disagreement on the measurement of output and achievements, few scholars would label the G8 only a 'talk and picture show'. The early years of summitry focussed on economics and in particular on co-ordination of fiscal and monetary policies and on trade liberalisation. Bernhard May in Chapter 5, Sylvia Ostry in Chapter 13, and Heidi Ullrich in Chapter 14 recall this legacy and its recent results. The topics in the summits became more diversified in the 1980s, with the disintegration of the Soviet Union, the rising menace of international terrorism, nonproliferation of weapons of mass destruction (WMD), and the wars in the Persian Gulf, Balkans, Afghanistan, and Iraq crowding out the traditional staple of economic issues. Yet the summits focussed on economic issues where co-ordination was sorely needed, such as the reform of the international financial architecture, currency and banking crises, debt relief for poor nations, health, and economic development. In early the 1990s, the economic transformation of the Soviet Union and then of Russia took pride of place.

The G8 is a small but unspecialised club. There is no limit to the topics that may be put on its agenda. Its output touches that of many other international organisations. It overlaps the domain of the International Monetary Fund (IMF) when it deals with currency crises, banking crises, and reforms of the international financial architecture. It overlaps the domain of the World Bank when it deals with economic development. It overlaps the domain of the Paris Club when it restructures or forgives foreign debt. It overlaps the domain of UN agencies when it tackles health and food assistance to developing countries. Yet the G8 countries are important members in the IMF, World Bank, Paris Club, and UN agencies.

Why would the leaders of the G8 countries spend scarce resources to work out deals at the G7/8 summits instead of instructing their finance ministers or foreign ministers to work out the same deals in the appropriate specialised international organisations? One answer is that the summits are unique settings for the G8 leaders to appear leader-like and international, and they are a photo opportunity forum or 'bully pulpit' from which to exude effective moral suasion. Although of some significance, the photo opportunity hypothesis cannot explain the persistence of the institution, the attention it receives from civil society, and the calls for making the G8 more representative of the world community.

An alternative explanation is that the G8 facilitates co-operation. The deals struck by the eight leaders are signals to the IMF, the World Bank, the Paris Club, and UN agencies that similar agreements should also be struck within their respective organisations. The strength of the signals varies from case to case and from institution to institution. The signal is stronger on international financial matters that fall under the jurisdiction of the IMF than on political issues that are the domain of the UN. The G8 members are critical, decisive shareholders of the IMF but not of the UN. In sum, the value of the G8 is in discovering, defining, and catalysing co-ordination opportunities, which are unwieldy tasks for large international organisations to perform. The process is enhanced by the intimate setting, the familial atmosphere, the one-to-one chats of the G8 summits, and the authority and power of the leaders at them. Once achieved, the discovery is transmitted to other international agencies, which then work on expanding the range of consensus, developing the details of the new G8-mandated and more widely accepted policies and programmes, and formally implementing them.

Would the discovery process improve if the G8 were to become a G11, with Brazil, China, and India added, or the G20 meeting at the leaders level (L20), as May discusses in Chapter 5? It is difficult to answer precisely. As membership enlarges, members' preferences are more likely to diverge and organisational and decision-making costs rise. That likelihood in itself tends to reduce the number of co-ordinated deals. On the other hand, larger representation gives more legitimacy to the decisions taken by the club and, thus, increases the strength of the signal to the larger and more specialised international organisations. Without quantitative knowledge of the added costs and benefits of enlargement, it is difficult to conclude whether a G11 or L20 would be superior to the G8. The reluctance of existing members to enlarge the club suggests that the costs outweigh the benefits. This assessment, however, may change if the world were to become more turbulent.

The United States is *primus inter pares* in the club, yet it has been less enthusiastic about the value of the G8 than the other members. May calls this the principle of participation without support:

> As a superpower, the U.S. depends less on the other major industrialised countries and is, therefore, less interested in policy co-ordination. Its priority has always been to strengthen bilateral relations, because it would always be the stronger partner and would be able to decide and rule. Summit meetings — and multilateral negotiations — are much more difficult for the U.S. to manage and it is therefore less interested in participating. But in a globalising world, the U.S. must learn to co-operate.

Kirton in Chapter 3 raises the issue of who needs whom in the club. The traditional school sees the survival of the G8 depending on the leadership of the U.S. (Putnam and Bayne 1987). That is, it is the G8 that needs America. But America is neither big nor powerful enough to carry out a unilateralist policy. The limitations of the latter are evident in the so-called war on terror, as Michele Fratianni and Heejoon Kang discuss in Chapter 8. So, despite his dislike of multilateralism, George Bush found it to his own advantage to rediscover that America needs the G8. As Kirton puts it:

> Amid all this scepticism, however, there were good grounds for believing that George Bush might make the Sea Island Summit a success. These grounds flowed from the concert equality model, which highlighted — not 'America the victorious' in the long Cold War — but 'America the vulnerable' to shocks from elusive enemies everywhere, who kill Americans anywhere and require the full co-operation of America's G8 allies to defeat. Getting the collaboration of this highly capable, continuing 'coalition of the willing', containing countries all committed to democratic principles and leaders allowed by their citizens to act in their defence, required an America willing to adjust at the summit to what its now necessary G8 allies want.

The U.S. President succeeded at the Sea Island Summit because he was forced to accept the reality that America gains by being more engaged and more collegial with its allies. May goes even further: the United States needs the G8 to achieve 'good global governance'.

Nations, even the largest, would be more isolationist without the G8. With lesser co-operation, economic and political shocks would reverberate more powerfully at home, especially as even the largest nations become more open to global flows.

The Contributions

'Part I: The G8 in the Past and in the Future' examines the historical contributions of the G8 summits and likely developments to come. This examination begins in Chapter 2, with Nicholas Bayne's 'Do We Need the G8 Summit? Lessons from the Past, Looking Ahead to the Future'. Bayne, in particular, looks at British prime minister Tony Blair's seven-year summit cycle starting with Birmingham of 1998 and ending with the 2005 Summit in Gleneagles, Scotland. The innovation in Birmingham was a concise economic agenda, with politics playing a marginal role. After 11 September 2001, the weight of the summit agenda shifted dramatically in favour of politics. The Gleneagles Summit is expected to return to a lean economic format.

In Chapter 3, 'America at the G8: From Vulnerability to Victory at the Sea Island Summit', John Kirton explores how George Bush achieved an unexpected success at the 2004 Summit. The preparation for Sea Island had started in a climate of skepticism about the value of the G8, but as the deadline approached the Americans changed their tune dramatically because external events — especially the war in Iraq, terrorism, and rising oil prices — had shown the U.S. to be vulnerable. The Middle East and Africa were the highlights of Sea Island. The spotlight on the Middle East was a direct response to the war in Iraq. The interest of the Sea Island Summit in promoting economic development in Africa goes back to the 2001 Genoa Summit, and this interest is likely to continue in the future.

In Chapter 4, 'Russia in the G8: From Sea Island 2004 to Russia 2006', Victoria Panova deals with the newest member of the club, Russia. Her key message is that the G8 with Russia is more effective and more representative than the old G7. Russia will host its first G8 meeting in 2006. Its format will likely follow the model of the 2000 Okinawa Summit, with the G8 leaders interacting with leaders of other countries and civil society. The agenda will emphasise economic development and security issues.

In Chapter 5, 'The G8 in a Globalising World: Does the United States Need the G8?', Bernhard May makes two central points. The first is that the U.S. has been a reluctant player in the G8. The second is that it needs the G8 to achieve its foreign policy objectives.

'Part II: Prosperity and Security' addresses the relationship between counterterrorism and economic performance. In Chapter 6, 'Advancing American Security Interests through the G8', Risto Penttilä explores whether the United States has used the G8 to advance American interests in counterterrorism, arms control, and regional security. He concludes that while there are cases of the U.S. doing so, the G8 has not been utilised to its full potential. This is due to the reluctance of the U.S. to use multilateral forums, and to policy differences among the G8 member states. Above all, immediately after the 11 September 2001 terrorist attacks, the U.S. saw the G8 only as a narrow instrument in the fight against the financing of terrorism. However, by the time of the Sea Island Summit in June 2004, the United States was willing to give the G8 a much broader role, mobilising the Summit for policy co-ordination with its allies and for launching major initiatives at the heart of U.S. foreign policy.

In Chapter 7, 'Economic Growth and National Security', David Audretsch, Richard Stazinski, and Taylor Aldridge explore the tradeoffs between economic growth and homeland security that restrict the crossborder flows of human capital. In the endogenous growth literature, knowledge generates spillovers and is responsible for increasing returns to scale. Reflecting the importance of knowledge workers, the United States has historically practiced an open-door policy with respect to 'brain' immigration. Homeland security has changed all that. Inflows of human capital have been drastically curtailed. The consequence on economic growth is bound to be negative.

In Chapter 8, 'Borders and International Terrorism', Michele Fratianni and Heejoon Kang analyse how terrorism affects national border policies and transnational flows of goods. The U.S. reaction to 11 September 2001 was to unleash a mostly unilateralist war on terror and to harden national borders. Over time, other industrial economies will have incentives to stop free riding on U.S. actions and adopt similar border security. The multilateral approach to counterterrorism, while appearing to be a co-operative solution, will in fact emerge because private costs of international terrorism will progressively shift from the United States to the other members of the club. One likely effect of counterterrorism is the trade diversion to countries with softer borders. Another effect is the thickening of economic borders and the consequent rise in the home bias of intra-national trade. The main premise of the chapter is that international transactions are more prone to international terrorism than domestic transactions. If the opposite were the case, the main effect of counterterrorism will fall on total factor productivity and ultimately on economic growth.

In Chapter 9, 'The G8 and the Governance of Cyberspace', Jeffrey Hart reviews the history of the G8 on cyberspace policies. In the early phase, the G8 concentrated on governance issues, such as the regulation and taxation of e-commerce, the protection of individual privacy and security, the maintenance of infrastructure security, and the promotion of broadband infrastructure. Then, the discussions focussed on ways to bridge the global digital divide. Since 11 September, the concern has shifted to cybersecurity. Hart's main conclusion is that 'the G8, especially relative to other international regimes, [has been effective] in creating solutions to collective action problems in cyberspace'.

In Chapter 10, 'U.S. Energy Security and Regional Business', Alan Rugman launches the bold idea that the United States does not need Middle Eastern oil and, consequently, can disengage politically and militarily from the hot spot of the world. Data on oil imports indicate that the United States relies primarily on North American oil; only 11.5 percent of the imported oil comes from the Persian Gulf nations. This pattern reflects a broader phenomenon of the regionalisation of trade and foreign direct investment (FDI). The chapter ends with an assessment that runs counter to the rest of the book: that is, the U.S. 'does not need the G8 as much as the G8 needs the United States' and that 'the G8 will continue its slide into irrelevancy in the face of increasing regionalisation pressures'.

'Part III: Finance and Security' looks at the role of the G8 in constraining hidden money flows, in general, and money laundering in particular. In Chapter 11, 'Combating Black Money: International Co-operation and the G8', Donato Masciandaro looks at the determinants of financial centres that engage in money laundering. He uses a simple benefit/cost model in which policy makers balance the expected revenues from money laundering against the expected cost of running such an activity, the collateral cost connected with money laundering — such as organised crime and terrorism — and the expected sanctions applied by the international community. The optimal level of money laundering depends positively on the expected return from it and, negatively, on the probability of being blacklisted and sanctioned as well as on the reputational cost and the cost of dealing with the negative externalities of money laundering. One policy conclusion is that the 'name and shame' approach may be counterproductive in two fundamental ways. It may signal the comparative advantage of the blacklisted country and, at the same time, it may raise the cost of an exit strategy. These two effects may give added incentives to the blacklisted country to invest further in money-laundering activity.

In Chapter 12, 'Terrorist Finance: Within the Grip of the G8?', George von Furstenberg argues two points. The first is that an exclusive focus on the supply side is inadequate. The supply of black money, like that of illegal drugs, is resilient and capable of finding alternative sources. Money laundering is not limited to official blacklisting: a great deal of it goes on in industrialised countries. Second, money laundering and terrorist financing have different methods of recycling. Money launderers tend to recycle contaminated funds into clean funds, whereas terrorists can first substitute goods and services for contaminated money and then clean money for goods and services. The difference between the two methods lies in the technology of transfer. Money laundering specialises in technology and financial intermediation. Terrorist financing specialises in human networks, for example the hawala system. The probabilities of detecting the two types of recycling are different. Governments that specialise in detecting money laundering may not be successful in detecting terrorist financing.

'Part IV: The G8 and International Trade Policy' assesses the historical record of the summits with respect to international trade policy. In Chapter 13, 'Summitry and Trade: What Sea Island Could Do for Doha', Sylvia Ostry scores the early summits of the 1970s as very successful in facilitating trade liberalisation; in contrast, the summits of the 1980s and '90s were not. Among the reasons for this decline in effectiveness,

Ostry cites higher paper output and the rising complexity of the issues. There is now a divide between the North and the South, with the South determined not to see a repeat of the 'bum deal' of the Uruguay Round. In that round, the industrialised countries captured most of the net benefits. Developing countries, once more, were denied open access to markets where they have a comparative advantage — namely, agriculture and textiles. It looks now as though now the South is capably led by Brazil, India, and China, and Doha may deliver what previous agreements failed to do. Ostry concludes that the G8 is no longer a suitable organisation to handle trade conflicts between North and South, and proposes a larger and more representative institutional setting, a group of 20 on each side of the divide.

In Chapter 14, 'Effective or Defective? The G8 and Multilateral Trade Negotiations', Heidi Ullrich provides a more detailed account of the G8 record on trade liberalisation. Her conclusions are consistent with Ostry's on the historical record. But Ullrich is less pessimistic than Ostry on the institution of the G8 delivering a good deal for both sides.

The concluding chapter, 'New Perspectives on the G8', summarises a broad literature, as well as many of the contributions in this volume, on the critical question of whether the world is a better place because of this institution. It also puts the American-hosted Sea Island in perspective and links it prospectively to the next two summits, hosted by the British and the Russians respectively. The overall judgement is that

> as the global community moves into the 21st century, the G8 is increasingly becoming the global governor of first resort. It is not merely the catalyst steering difficult issues to existing organisations. It is now the creator and developer of a new generation of global governance that includes both the innovative ideas and international institutions that the world now needs.

References

Bailin, Alison (2005). *From Traditional to Group Hegemony*. Ashgate, Aldershot.

Bayne, Nicholas (2005). *Staying Together: The G8 Summit Confronts the 21st Century*. Ashgate, Aldershot.

Fratianni, Michele and John C. Pattison (2001). 'International Organisations in a World of Regional Trade Agreements: Lessons from Club Theory'. *World Economy* vol. 24, no. 3, pp. 333–358.

Held, David (1995). *Democracy and the Global Order: From the Modern State to Cosmopolitan Governance*. Stanford University Press, Stanford.

Hodges, Michael R., John J. Kirton, and Joseph P. Daniels, eds. (1999). *The G8's Role in the New Millennium*. Ashgate, Aldershot.

Kirton, John J. (2004). 'Getting the L20 Going: Reaching Out from the G8'. Paper prepared for a workshop on 'G20 to Replace the G8: Why Not Now?', sponsored by the Brookings Institution, Institute for International Economics, and the Centre for Global Governance, 22 September. Washington DC.

Penttilä, Risto E.J. (2003). *The Role of the G8 in International Peace and Security*. Oxford University Press, Oxford.

Putnam, Robert and Nicholas Bayne (1987). *Hanging Together: Co-operation and Conflict in the Seven-Power Summit*. 2nd ed. Sage Publications, London.

PART I:
THE G8 IN THE PAST AND IN THE FUTURE

Chapter 2

Do We Need the G8 Summit? Lessons from the Past, Looking Ahead to the Future

Nicholas Bayne

The underlying aim of this chapter is to examine whether the G8 summit serves a useful purpose in the 21st century and whether the world would miss the summit if it were not there. The chapter approaches this enquiry from two directions. First, it will draw lessons from the history of the summits and apply them to the 2004 Sea Island Summit. These lessons will sometimes be taken from the full 30-year perspective since the summits began. But the main focus will be on the sequence of summits since Tony Blair inaugurated the current 'heads-only' model at Birmingham in 1998, which also marked the change from G7 to G8 (see Table 2-1). Second, it will look forward into the future. Sea Island in 2004 concluded the first G8 sequence of seven summits, each hosted by a different country.[1] Blair now gets the chance to host a second summit, the first British prime minister to do so, and to start a new sequence. The chapter will assess the outlook for the 2005 Gleneagles Summit, for Russia's first summit in 2006, and beyond.

The lessons from the past try to capture the recent evolution of the G8 summit in three respects: how well the heads-only format is working, the integration of politics and economics in the summit's themes, and the operation of collective management of the international system by North America, Europe, and Japan (see Bayne 2004). The following conclusions can be drawn from this analysis:

- the new format has worked well, especially up to the Kananaskis Summit of 2002, although important elements are now being eroded;
- the new format has also encouraged outreach to non-G8 countries and to non-state actors such as civil society;
- the G8 summits have developed a new capacity to introduce combined economic and political initiatives;
- contrary to the conventional wisdom, G8 collective management has survived under U.S. president George Bush and gained some ground in 2004.

The forecast for the future considers whether the summit will continue much as now, whether it will shift toward more economics or more politics, and whether outreach to non-G8 countries will change the summit itself. The conclusions from this analysis are as follows:

- the present focus on combining economics and politics could persist through 2005 and 2006, but will eventually run out of material;
- the United Kingdom is seeking to revive the G8 economic agenda, while Russia may prefer more politics;
- converting the G8 to the G20 (or the 'Leaders 20' or 'L20' of heads of state and government) would change the summit's nature and the current G8 heads are not attracted by the idea;
- there are strong grounds for a G9, embracing China, but it is not clear how to get there at summit level (as opposed to at lower ministerial levels).

Both the past record and the future prospects confirm the utility of the G8 summit. Thanks to the new format, the summit has been able to achieve results that would not have been possible in other forums: by innovating, by striking deals not available at lower levels, by mending deep divisions among the heads, and by developing new

Table 2-1 The Summits of the First G8 Sequence

Year	Site	Host and Country
Sixth Summit Series: Globalisation and Development		
1998	Birmingham	Tony Blair, United Kingdom
1999	Cologne	Gerhard Schroeder, Germany
2000	Okinawa	Yoshiro Mori, Japan
2001	Genoa	Silvio Berlusconi, Italy
Seventh Summit Series: Fighting Terrorism and Its Causes		
2002	Kananaskis	Jean Chrétien, Canada
2003	Evian	Jacques Chirac, France
2004	Sea Island	George Bush, United States
Start of Second G8 Sequence		
2005	Gleneagles	Tony Blair, United Kingdom
2006	Site not known	Vladimir Putin, Russia

Note: A summit 'sequence' denotes a run of seven summits, each chaired by a different country. Thus the sequence that began at Birmingham in 1998 concluded at Sea Island in 2004. A summit 'series' is a group of summits focussed on a particular set of issues. The sixth series began with reforms to the format and concentrated on the G8 response to globalisation. The seventh series took over in 2002, when the summit began paying more attention to terrorism and related political issues after 11 September 2001.

capacities to integrate politics and economics. Although it now works with non-G8 countries and wider institutions in a more co-operative manner than before, the summit provides a source of collective management that cannot be replicated elsewhere. For the future, the G8 is well positioned not only to maintain these capacities, but also to revive its economic vocation, which had gone a bit into abeyance, and to develop the outreach that is essential in a globalising world. The G8 summit could dissolve itself with very little trouble and is subject to various pressures to do so, both external and internal. But a world without the G8 would be a more fractious and dangerous place.

Lessons from the Past

The Heads-Only Format

The Birmingham reforms to the summit format were intended to limit the numbers, the agenda, and the documentation.[2] The first of these reforms has worked well throughout the sequence. The regime whereby only the heads of government come to the G8 summit, without supporting ministers or large delegations, is often presented as a return to the original vision of the summit as an informal, personal encounter. In fact, that early vision was never achieved, even at the very first summit at Rambouillet in 1975.[3] Today's summits are indeed more intimate than those of the 1970s. There are fewer people at the summit table, even as G8. Delegations are kept small and all housed close together at the summit site. Everything is done to encourage a personal rapport between the leaders during the time that the summit lasts.

The latter objectives — shorter agenda and documents — were also well maintained from Birmingham 1998 to Kananaskis 2002 (with a slight lapse at Okinawa 2000). The summit hosts chose a short agenda of precise topics well in advance and stuck to it, and the documentation from those summits was kept within limits. All these summits produced innovative initiatives or struck deals only available at the level of head of government. These embraced, for example, new financial architecture, debt relief, settling Kosovo, the digital divide, fighting infectious diseases, help for Africa, and the nonproliferation of weapons of mass destruction (WMD).

For Evian 2003, however, France preferred an agenda of broad themes that could accommodate almost anything. The consequence was that, by the time the summit arrived, the agenda had become something of a Christmas tree. This in turn inflated the documentation, so that the Evian Summit produced a record number of action plans.[4] The G8 recognised that Evian was over-ambitious and in 2004 the Americans promised a much more austere summit. But they too preferred broad themes — freedom, security, and prosperity — that set no limits to the agenda. In consequence, by the time of Sea Island, more and more items had crowded on to the agenda and the copious and confusing summit documentation sacrificed quality to quantity. Despite these lapses, Evian and Sea Island were vital in restoring agreement among the G8 heads over the approach to Iraq and made advances on Africa, nonproliferation, and the Middle East.

Because the new format limits the official participation at the summit, it has allowed the G8 to reach out to other circles, such as non-G8 countries and non-state actors including business and civil society. The real breakthrough here came in 2000. The Japanese hosts consulted civil society worldwide and provided facilities for them at Okinawa.[5] They invited selected non-G8 leaders to join the G8 over dinner before the summit. Both practices have developed further at subsequent summits. For example, a strong representative gathering with non-G8 leaders (including China) took place at Evian in 2003. In 2004, however, the American hosts resisted both trends, at least at first. There was no engagement with civil society. There was originally no intention to invite non-G8 leaders. But as the summit approached, Middle Eastern countries were involved in the preparatory meetings of finance and foreign ministers and leaders from the 'broader Middle East' region were invited to the summit itself. Since it was unclear whether enough of them would come, the African leaders who had been at previous summits were also invited to Sea Island. Outreach from the summit is thus well established, although no permanent pattern has emerged.

Many civil society bodies are equally ready to sit down and make suggestions to G8 governments on summit issues and then to mobilise massive demonstrations against the summit when it is held. The riots associated with these demonstrations at Genoa in 2001 caused the Canadians to decide to hold the next summit in a remote Rocky Mountain resort, well away from the public eye. Fears of terrorist attacks after 11 September 2001 reinforced this isolation, which also determined the choice of summit sites by France in 2003 and the U.S. in 2004. Yet isolation has its drawbacks: the G8 leaders are closer to each other, but cut off from the outside world, including the media, who are increasingly sceptical of the value of the summits.

Economics and Politics

The early summits were meant to be exclusively economic, with politics excluded. But politics began to encroach on the agenda very early on and gathered strength during the long U.S. presidency of Ronald Reagan. The end of the Cold War revived the economic agenda, with help first for Central Europe and then for Russia, while new issues arrived such as the environment and money laundering. But the political component was always present, and Russia's growing involvement made it stronger.

Blair's Birmingham reforms were intended to focus the summit on a concise economic agenda, with politics only on the side. The next three summits kept to that pattern, except for Cologne 1999, where the Kosovo crisis required a combined political and economic response and generated a new interest in conflict prevention (Kirton and Stefanova 2004). But after the terrorist attacks of 11 September, it was inevitable that political issues, such as terrorism and nonproliferation, would move up the G8 agenda, driven especially by the United States. Since the Kananaskis Summit of 2002, political issues have had at least equal weight in the summit agenda with economic ones. The 2004 Sea Island Summit, with George Bush as host, had two political themes to one economic.

Heads of government can deal equally well with economic issues and political issues; they can also integrate the two. In earlier years the summits dealt with economics and politics separately. Since Birmingham, however, they have learned how to combine political and economic components, starting with their treatment of Kosovo at Cologne in 1999. The most enduring example of this practice is the summit's involvement in Africa, where the G8 Africa Action Plan combines provisions on security, governance, and economic growth, matching the content of the New Partnership for Africa's Development (NEPAD) in this respect. But the Global Partnership against the Spread of Weapons and Materials of Mass Destruction to clean up chemical weapons and nuclear installations also integrates politics and economics, as does transport security; both issues, first treated at Kananaskis, returned to the agenda in 2004. These combined political and economic initiatives are new to the G8 summit but also play to its strengths, because only heads of government can integrate all the aspects involved.

The principal topic chosen by the Americans for the 2004 Summit — the Broader Middle East and North Africa (BMENA) Initiative — fitted these criteria precisely. The region it would cover, from Morocco to Afghanistan, was marked by both political unrest and economic sluggishness, with each feeding on the other. A programme of linked political and economic reform, to enhance democracy and stimulate market economies, would be a very suitable subject for the G8 leaders. The American proposals were new, but they had the same objective as the Barcelona process launched by the European Union in 1995 to enhance political and economic development around the Mediterranean. That programme survived, although it had made only very slow progress. There was therefore the basis for a common G8 agreement, comparable with what has been done over Africa.

The great difference, however, was that in Africa the G8 were responding to an initiative that came from the African leaders themselves. The Africans had clear ownership of NEPAD and the G8 took care to preserve this. In the Middle East, however, as word of American intentions leaked out early in 2004, leading regional powers, such as Egypt and Saudi Arabia, reacted strongly against them. These countries insisted that they must be in control of their own reforms — they could not accept dictation from outside. The Arab League tried to launch its own reform process, but had great difficulty in agreeing what that should be.

The difficulties facing this topic at Sea Island were therefore formidable. But thanks to intensive preparatory work, the Summit was able to agree on a programme to encourage political and economic reform in the Middle East. This was based on universal values of freedom, democracy, and human rights. It embodied specific principles: reform could not be imposed from outside; each country was unique; governments, business, and civil society would be involved as full partners; and reform was a long-term effort, which required 'a generational commitment'. On that basis, the programme proved acceptable to the regional powers that attended the Summit and was not disowned by any of the absentees, such as Egypt and Saudi Arabia. A full turnout of regional states (except Iran and Syria) later attended joint meetings with G8 foreign and finance ministers to prepare for the first meeting of the Forum for the Future in Morocco in December 2004.

Collective Management

One original aim of the G7/8 summit, right from 1975, was to bring about a transition from American hegemony to a regime of collective management of the international system, with responsibility shared between Europe, North America, and Japan. But U.S. hegemony continued to cast a long shadow. For the first 15 years or so, the G7 process depended heavily on U.S. initiative. If the Americans took the lead, with one or more G7 partners, there were good results. If the Americans tried to lead alone, the outcome was disappointing. If the Americans did not lead, nothing much happened (Putnam and Bayne 1987, 272–273).

During the 1990s, as the summit revived after the end of the Cold War, this pattern changed and became much closer to real collective management. While the Americans usually led on monetary and financial issues, the Europeans began to take the lead in other areas: the environment, debt relief for poor countries, and even, by the late 1990s, international trade. Japan and Canada were also initiators, especially in the years when they chaired the summits. Genuine shared initiatives emerged, for example on drugs, crime and money laundering, and employment (Bayne 2000, 194–198).

When George Bush became president of the United States in 2001, there were fears that he might draw back from the concept of collective management and insist that only U.S. initiative counted. There were some backward moves, for example on climate change. But in many G8 subjects the Americans proved ready to follow the lead of others, as on Africa, or to work for joint initiatives, as shown by the strong alliance on trade between Bob Zoellick and Pascal Lamy. After the terrorist attacks of 11 September 2001, the Americans initially developed a strongly multilateral strategy in response and this attracted strong G8 and worldwide support.

On many of the issues on the agenda for the Sea Island Summit, the impetus for collective management was strong. This applied to nonproliferation, the leading political topic. The initiative usually came from the Americans, but other G8 members made substantive contributions, for example, in dealing with Libya, Iran, and North Korea. It also applied to the cluster of economic issues that were discussed at Sea Island focussed on development: food security, HIV/AIDS, engaging the private sector, and transparency in government operations. G8 members might have different approaches to these issues, but all, including the Americans, agreed on the merits of a collective strategy.

The greatest uncertainty was over the Middle East. In 2003, the G8 was painfully split over the U.S. invasion of Iraq and only came together again at Evian. A year later the Americans needed the support of their G8 partners if they were to convince the states of the broader Middle East to buy into their reform proposals. Before the Summit, this support looked hard to win. The problem lay not so much with the BMENA Initiative, which fit in well with earlier EU policies, but with U.S. policies on Palestine and Iraq. The Europeans had not denounced the outcome of Bush's meeting with Ariel Sharon in April 2004, but had grave reservations about it. They were also deeply disturbed by recent trends in Iraq, which tended to confirm their earlier anxieties, although they welcomed the growing involvement of the United Nations.

In the event, Bush was able to win the support of the rest of the G8. The emergence of the interim government in Iraq and the unanimous adoption of the UN Security Council (UNSC) resolution, just before the Summit opened, created one essential foundation for agreement. The G8 gave a strong commitment to helping 'the fully sovereign Iraqi interim government' to rebuild Iraq and make it peaceful, democratic, and prosperous. France, Germany, and Russia, while still critical of the U.S. invasion, rallied behind the new Iraqi government and were satisfied by the safeguards in the UN resolution. On the Israel and Palestine conflict, the G8 Summit essentially brought the peace process back on track again and sought to stimulate forward movement, based on the 'Road Map' and the work of the 'Quartet' (U.S., EU, Russia, and the UN). Agreement on Iraq, Israel and Palestine, and the broader Middle East was possible because the Americans showed greater readiness than before to accept collective, rather than sole, management in this area.

Prospects for the Future

Persistence of Past Trends

In the three aspects of summitry treated so far in this chapter, the early summits of the next G8 sequence are likely to move forward along lines established in the first.

Summit Format The British will be determined in 2005 to return the summit, as far as possible, to the austere format pioneered by Blair at Birmingham seven years before. The agenda will be short and specific. Blair has identified two key items well in advance — Africa and climate change. The UK will also revive the tradition, interrupted in 2004, of involving civil society as closely as possible. African leaders will be invited, and there is also likely to be a larger outreach meeting on the lines of the Evian gathering. Security reasons have dictated the choice of another secluded summit location — Gleneagles in Scotland — but the media will not be banished as far away as they were in 2002 or 2004.

When the Russians' turn comes in 2006, they will have to cope with the demands of this unusual format. There are signs that they will not try to innovate, but will stick to established custom as closely as they can. Vladimir Putin by then will be a veteran of six previous summits. The Russians would be wise to choose a limited agenda of items where they can contribute — possible items are discussed below. Finding a secluded location should cause no problem for them, although they may find it easier to revert to the American tactic of keeping civil society at a distance. Russia would also have its own ideas about G8 outreach (see Chapter 4).

Politics and Economics For the 2005 Gleneagles Summit, it is already clear that Blair will give priority to Africa, where the G8 needs to maintain its involvement in this deprived and unstable continent. In preparation for the Summit, Blair has created the Commission for Africa, with leading members from both G8 and African countries. This is intended to maintain public interest in ending the international marginalisation of sub-Saharan Africa. Gordon Brown, the British finance minister, is promoting the 100 percent reduction of multilateral debt owed by poor countries, especially in Africa, and an International Finance Facility (IFF) that will double the amount of aid flowing to them, and hopes that this will win G8 backing by the time of the Gleneagles Summit in July 2005. As with all the G8's African initiatives since Genoa 2001, the Summit will make use of both political and economic instruments. But while Evian and Sea Island made their main advance in politics, especially peacekeeping, Gleneagles will give more attention to the economic component.

What would be an innovative topic for the Russians in 2006 that would combine politics and economics? One subject clearly stands out: energy policy. To the G8 economic agenda, the Russians have little to contribute on trade or finance or development. But on energy matters they are world players — and the summit has not had a serious discussion on the economics of energy policy for decades. Politically, energy issues would fit squarely into the ongoing Middle East programme. The 2006 Russian Summit could, in any case, come back to the Middle Eastern reform initiative, to enable the G8 heads and regional leaders to build on whatever progress has been made since Sea Island, again combining economics and politics.

Beyond 2006, however, the supply of themes worthy of G8 treatment but requiring a combination of economics and politics may begin to run dry.

Collective Management In 2004, there were doubts, right up until the G8 met, over whether the American host would move back toward collective management in the Middle East, including Iraq and Israel and Palestine. Looking forward to 2005, such anxieties appear less serious. The British hosts, being enthusiastic promoters of the concept of collective management, would try to build bridges among all the participants. If transatlantic tensions again cast a shadow over the Summit, the British would be the best equipped of the G8 to engage the Americans in the process. Indeed, in 2003 Blair angered his French and German colleagues, Jacques Chirac and Gerhard Schroeder, by leaning too far toward the U.S. But in 2004 he moved to mend his fences with France and Germany. At Gleneagles in 2005 he would be even more concerned to show the benefits of Britain's EU membership, as Britain holds the EU presidency and prepares for a referendum on the new European Constitution.

The British would also aim to act as mentors to the Russians, for when they host the Summit in 2006. For Russia, the idea of being part of the world's collective management is very appealing. While their old superpower instincts might incline the Russians to seek bilateral deals with the Americans, this would be offset by the enlarged EU being by far their biggest trading partner, while Japan is important for their Asian interests. During 2004, the rest of the G8 expressed growing concern about its attitudes toward democracy and human rights. Putin reacted sharply against such criticism, but he would be more inclined to respond if he thought his presidency of the G8 summit was at risk.

Evolutionary Change

So far this forecast has identified likely elements of continuity, including efforts to restore the post-Birmingham format in the rigorous version that largely prevailed up to Kananaskis 2002. But there are indications of more extensive shifts in the future, as regards agenda and participation.

More Economics The second agenda item already chosen by Blair for Gleneagles 2005 is the global environment, specifically climate change. This is a pure economic item, which does not combine with political elements. It is, furthermore, a subject that requires G8 (and other) governments to reconcile domestic and international pressures, which was one of the original purposes of the summit. There will be other economic items of this kind on the Gleneagles agenda, because they are relevant to the treatment of Africa. One is trade, in the context of market access for the products of low-income countries; another is financing for development, covering both debt relief and the proposed IFF.

This suggests that the British are seeking to turn the G8 summit back to its initial economic vocation and its original purposes. This could determine the subject matter of future summits when the G8 runs out of issues requiring combined economic and political treatment. This approach has many merits, but it also faces obstacles. The summits of the first G8 sequence have not been very successful at reconciling domestic and external pressures (Bayne 2004, 2005). This has been evident in development finance, because of budgetary constraints everywhere, and in international trade, where Genoa 2001 was the only summit to make a worthy contribution (see Chapter 14). On the environment, the G8 has failed to reach worthwhile agreements for more than a decade, because of deep divergences that set the United States (sometimes joined by Canada) against the European Union and Japan. On climate change in particular, the U.S. under Bush has been unresponsive to international pressure. So the UK faces a Sisyphean task, despite Russia's welcome ratification of the Kyoto Protocol. The British must hope that the progress made at Gleneagles encourages not only Russia but also Germany and Japan (summit hosts in 2007 and 2008) to maintain the priority given to the environment and other mainstream economic subjects.

More Politics If the UK favours economics, Russia is likely to favour politics. There are a few items on the G8's broad economic agenda in which Russia can take part on equal terms, such as energy, as noted above, and debt relief. But in many other areas Russia is not in the same class as the rest of the G8. Even though its accession negotiations are making progress, it is not clear that Russia will be a member of the World Trade Organization (WTO) by the time of the 2006 Summit. Russia's economy is now booming, thanks to oil and gas export earnings, but its troubles with the International Monetary Fund (IMF) are still a recent memory.

This could well incline the Russians to focus the agenda in 2006 on political issues, building on the trend at work since Kananaskis 2002 and reverting to the American priorities in 2004. If this, for example, reinforced responsible Russian policies in nonproliferation subjects, this would be welcome to the rest of the G8. The long Russian border also gives them an interest in a very wide range of regional issues, in which they and the rest of the G8 could find common interests. But if this trend were continued beyond the 2006 Summit, the prolonged focus on politics could make the G8 heads lose the capacity to resolve economic disputes among themselves, which was the original rationale for the summits.

From G7 to G20 There is broad agreement among the G8 members about developing outreach to major non-G8 countries, such as China, India, and Brazil. But there is less consensus on how this could be combined with the regional links the G8 has developed with Africa since Genoa 2001 and with the Middle East at Sea Island 2004. Chirac, following an established French line of argument, would like to see the large outreach meeting at Evian become an annual event. Canadian prime minister Paul Martin has called for meetings at head-of-government level of the G20, the group of finance ministers and central bank governors created in 1999, of which he was the first chair.[6] But Bush had no large outreach meeting at Sea Island, giving priority to regional links.

As long as the G8 determines which non-G8 powers to invite each year, it retains the initiative of the development of outreach. But once the G8 heads have established a recurrent link with a broader group with fixed membership, such as the G20, there would be cumulative pressure for the G8 itself to be absorbed into the wider grouping. Many commentators already call for this, arguing that this would create a group that is much more representative of today's globalised world.[7] In particular, converting the G8 into a L20 summit is gaining outside support (for a discussion of the merits and obstacles, see Bradford Jr. and Linn 2004; English, Thakur, and Cooper 2005; Kirton 2004). But the process of creating a representative group, whatever its merits, would undermine the present advantages of personal contact and informality, which enable the G8 to strike deals that are not attainable elsewhere.

Recent evidence suggests that the current G8 heads value the intimacy of their exclusive grouping. When they decided at Kananaskis 2002 to allow Russia to host a summit for the first time, they also laid down a cycle of G8 presidencies for the rest of the decade. This showed no sign of wanting to expand the participants further. All the G8 heads present at Kananaskis were still there at Sea Island, except that Canada's Martin had replaced Jean Chrétien, and all should meet again at Gleneagles 2005.

G8 to G9—Admitting China The G8 wants to develop outreach to non-G8 countries, without being absorbed into a larger grouping of heads of government that might be more representative. But there is a separate question of whether the G8 could admit a further member, to become the G9. Since the G8 had their conversation in Kananaskis, the case for admitting China has become much stronger. The Chinese economy has grown so big that it alone can have an impact on the world trading and monetary system. China is now an active member of the new grouping of major developing countries in the WTO. On the margins of the IMF; the G7 finance ministers have begun inviting China to their meetings (Balls 2004). There are outside proposals for a new 'key currency group' composed of the U.S., the Eurozone, Japan, and China (Kenen et al. 2004).[8] Politically, China is increasingly influential both in Asia, where it co-operates with G8 members, for example over North Korea, and in the world at large, especially as a permanent member of the UNSC.

On economic and foreign political grounds, therefore, China has a strong case, which puts it well ahead of other aspirants such as India or Brazil. The problem is that China does not meet the standards of democracy that are an implicit criterion for summit membership, even for Russia. The G8 will hesitate to admit China until this problem has been resolved by domestic change within the country itself. The idea has been floated of inviting China to attend on condition that it moves to become more democratic (Goodman 2004; see also Kirton 2001a). But conditional membership of this kind is like the long apprenticeship served by Russia. China is unlikely to find such conditions acceptable and for that reason is showing no enthusiasm to join the summit. If the G8 maintain the democracy test rigorously, this stand-off could persist for some time.

Do We Need the G8 Summit?

In the light of this examination of past and future, fundamental questions can now be asked: Do we need the G8 summit? Would it be missed if it were not there? These are not unrealistic questions. Unlike established institutions, such as the IMF or the EU, the G8 could disappear very easily. It has no founding charter or treaty and no organisation distinct from its members. If the G8 members, or even one leading member like the United States, should decide no longer to take part, the G8 summit could simply cease to exist.

The achievements summarised earlier in this chapter, especially since the reforms introduced at Birmingham in 1998, provide evidence of the abiding value of the G8 summit. The lessons from the past reveal that:

- by virtue of the authority of its component heads, the summit can launch wide-ranging and innovative initiatives beyond the reach of other institutions;
- by bringing the heads together in a compact and informal setting, the summits can produce agreements that are not available at lower levels;
- the direct, personal contact provided by the summits has served to reconcile deep divisions among the heads themselves;
- despite some setbacks, the summit has preserved the concept of collective management of the international system;
- the new format has broken down the exclusive nature of the summits and made them more open to non-G8 and non-state forces.

The future prospects for the summit suggest that the G8 members are determined to maintain these merits in the years ahead. In addition, the Gleneagles Summit seeks to strengthen the G8's capacity to strike deals on mainstream economic issues such as trade, finance, and the environment, which have been slipping off the summit's agenda. As globalisation advances, the summit needs to recapture its ability — not shared by other institutions — to reconcile domestic and international pressures. In 2006 the experience of hosting a summit for the first time will further embed Russia in the G8 process and encourage the Russians to adopt open and responsible policies that respect democracy and human rights.

Despite these merits, the summit faces both external and internal threats, which could lead to its disappearance. Would this matter? One external reason would be that the G8 summit became too costly and difficult to organise, because of the high level of security required. This reason is regularly suggested by the media, who are in fact the people who suffer most from the unreal seclusion forced upon the summit (see, for example, Chaffin 2004). But if this happened, it would hand a victory to the hostile demonstrators and the terrorists who want to stop the G8 from meeting. This makes it most unlikely that the heads themselves would abandon G8 meetings for this reason.

A more serious external reason would flow from the argument that the G8 is no longer a rational grouping, because no serious decisions can be taken without involving a wider circle of countries. This has developed from the criticism, which goes back to 1980, that the summit undermines established institutions with worldwide membership.[9] Today, the G8 heads understand perfectly well that their decisions become effective only if they are accepted by the international community at large. This will only happen if they devote time and effort to persuading other countries, starting with the major non-G8 powers. But the G8 members still value the summit as a vehicle for resolving disputes among themselves or for launching new collective ideas, without which no progress will be possible in a wider circle. If the G8 disappeared or was absorbed into a L20, a valuable source of international initiative and conciliation would be lost.

The third reason for the dissolution of the G8 would be internal: a complete breakdown in co-operation among the participating heads. This is not inconceivable. In the spring of 2003 relations between Bush and Chirac were so bad that they were not speaking to each other.[10] The Americans let it be known that while Bush would come to the Evian Summit in 2003, he would rather stay in Geneva than be lodged on French soil. In the event, Bush stayed in Evian and the Summit was the beginning of a slow reconciliation between Bush and the leading opponents of the invasion of Iraq. By the 2004 Sea Island Summit, the rapprochement among Bush, Schroeder, and Putin was essentially complete. Although Chirac still persisted on being the grit in the G8 oyster, this did not prevent far-reaching agreement on issues related to the Middle East ('A Bit of Gallic Grit: U.S. and France Inject Useful Tension into G8 Summitry' 2004). Where Bush and Chirac still disagreed, it was better for them to do so openly and face to face than for real and imagined slights to fester at a distance.

The greatest value of the G8 summit lies in its personal quality. It brings together the leaders of eight of the world's most powerful nations and reminds them of their responsibility to co-operate internationally, rather than giving way to domestic pressures. The results are often oversold in advance and disappoint in practice. But without the discipline of this regular encounter, it would be very easy for tensions and disputes to spread and to poison the underlying relationships between the G8 members. A world that did not have the safety valve of the G8 summit would be an increasingly fractious and dangerous place. As German chancellor Helmut Schmidt, joint founder of the original summit, commented: 'the economic summit conferences ... did not bring about much, but what they avoided was of enormous importance' (*The Economist*, 29 September 1979, cited in Putnam and Bayne 1987, 33–34).

Notes

1. Russia, which has not yet hosted a summit, will do so in 2006. Thereafter the summit sequence will consist of eight summits.
2. For an account of the Birmingham reforms and of the later G7 summits of the 20th century, see Nicholas Bayne (2000). For a new analysis of the G8 summits of the 21st century, which overlaps with this chapter, see Bayne (2005).
3. For an analysis of the early summits, from Rambouillet 1975 to Venice II 1987, see Robert Putnam and Nicholas Bayne (1987).
4. There is a difference between Bayne's (2004) assessment of Evian and that of John Kirton (2004). Kirton argues that the volume of documentation and the number of commitments made at Evian are a sign of the G8's growing role in global governance.
5. Peter Hajnal (2002) charts the development of the G8's relations with civil society.
6. The G20 is sometimes referred to as the L20, to differentiate between the leaders (L20) and the finance ministers and central bank governors (G20). Although the participants in the Evian meeting and the G20 both include the leading non-G8 powers, such as China, India, Brazil, Mexico, and South Africa, their membership is not identical. For an early analysis of the G20, see John Kirton (2001b). His later analysis suggests that the performance of the G20 has dropped back since Martin ceased to chair it (Kirton 2005).
7. The idea that the G8 should be replaced by a wider more representative grouping has been advocated by outside commentators for several years, such as Jeffrey Sachs (1998) and Michel Camdessus when he was at the IMF (Chote 1998; Bardacke 2000). Similar changes

are proposed by Jim O'Neill and Robert Hormats (2004); Hormats is a former U.S. sherpa.

8. Peter Kenen, Jeffrey Shafer, Nigel Wicks (a former UK sherpa and G7 deputy), and Charles Wyplosz (2004) also argue for a new Council for International Financial and Economic Co-operation, going wider than the G7 finance ministers. But they envisage the survival of the G8 summit (101).
9. This was first developed by J. Robert Schaetzel and Harald Malmgren (1980).
10. When Chirac spoke by telephone to Bush on 15 April 2003, after the fall of Baghdad, it was their first direct contact since 7 February of that year (Graham and Spiegel 2003).

References

Balls, Andrew (2004). 'G7 Invites China to Discuss Fixed Exchange Rate'. *Financial Times*, 1 October.

Bardacke, Ted (2000). 'Camdessus Seeks Broader G8'. *Financial Times*, 14 February.

Bayne, Nicholas (2000). *Hanging In There: The G7 and G8 Summit in Maturity and Renewal*. Ashgate, Aldershot.

Bayne, Nicholas (2004). 'G7/8 Performance from Birmingham to Evian and Beyond'. In M. Fratianni, P. Savona and J. J. Kirton, eds., *Corporate, Public, and Global Governance: The G8's Contribution*. Ashgate, Aldershot. Forthcoming.

Bayne, Nicholas (2005). *Staying Together: The G8 Summit Confronts the 21st Century*. Ashgate, Aldershot.

'A Bit of Gallic Grit: U.S. and France Inject Useful Tension into G8 Summitry'. (2004). *Financial Times*, 12 June.

Bradford Jr., Colin I. and Johannes F. Linn (2004). 'Global Economic Governance at a Crossroads: Replacing the G7 with the G20'. Brookings Institution Policy Brief 131. <www.brookings.edu/comm/policybriefs/pb131.htm> (November 2004).

Chaffin, Joshua (2004). 'Trapped Inside the Summit's Trouble-Proof Bubble'. *Financial Times*, 3–4 July.

Chote, Robert (1998). 'Camdessus Urges G8 to Embrace Other Countries'. *Financial Times*, 9 May.

English, John, Ramesh Thakur, and Andrew Fenton Cooper (2005). *A Leaders 20 Summit: Why, How, Who, and When?* United Nations University, Tokyo. Forthcoming.

Goodman, Matthew (2004). 'The G8 Should Start Opening to China'. *Financial Times*, 3 June.

Graham, Robert and Peter Spiegel (2003). 'Chirac Talks to Bush but Chilly Relations Remain'. *Financial Times*, 16 April.

Hajnal, Peter I. (2002). 'Civil Society Encounters the G7/G8'. In P. I. Hajnal, ed., *Civil Society in the Information Age*. Ashgate, Aldershot.

Kenen, Peter B., Jeffrey R. Shafer, Nigel L. Wicks, et al. (2004). 'International Economic and Financial Cooperation: New Issues, New Actors, New Responses'. Centre for Economic and Policy Research, London. <www.cepr.org/pubs/books/cepr/booklist.asp?cvno=P171> (November 2004).

Kirton, John J. (2001a). 'The G7/8 and China: Toward a Closer Association'. In J. J. Kirton, J. P. Daniels and A. Freytag, eds., *Guiding Global Order: G8 Governance in the Twenty-First Century*. Ashgate, Aldershot.

Kirton, John J. (2001b). 'The G20: Representativeness, Effectiveness, and Leadership in Global Governance'. In J. J. Kirton, J. P. Daniels and A. Freytag, eds., *Guiding Global Order: G8 Governance in the Twenty-First Century*, pp. 143–172. Ashgate, Aldershot.

Kirton, John J. (2004). 'Explaining G8 Effectiveness: A Concert of Vulnerable Equals in a

Globalizing World'. Paper prepared for the International Studies Association conference. Montreal, 17–20 March. <www.g8.utoronto.ca/scholar/kirton2004/kirton_isa_040304.pdf> (November 2004).

Kirton, John J. (2005). 'Towards Mulitlateral Reform: The G20's Contribution'. In J. English, R. Thakur and A. F. Cooper, eds., *A Leaders 20 Summit: Why, How, Who, and When?* United Nations University, Tokyo. Forthcoming.

Kirton, John J. and Radoslava Stefanova (2004). *The G8, The United Nations, and Conflict Prevention*. Ashgate, Aldershot.

O'Neill, Jim and Robert Hormats (2004). 'The G8: Time for a Change'. Global Economics Paper No. 112. Goldman Sachs, New York. <www.gs.com/insight/research/reports/report15.html> (November 2004).

Putnam, Robert and Nicholas Bayne (1987). *Hanging Together: Co-operation and Conflict in the Seven-Power Summit*. 2nd ed. Sage Publications, London.

Sachs, Jeffrey (1998). 'Global Capitalism: Making It Work'. *Economist* 12 September.

Schaetzel, J. Robert and Harald B. Malmgren (1980). 'Talking Heads'. *Foreign Policy* vol. 39, no. 2, pp. 130–142.

Chapter 3

America at the G8: From Vulnerability to Victory at the Sea Island Summit

John J. Kirton

From 8 to 10 June 2004, President George W. Bush hosted the 30th annual summit of the G8 major market democracies at Sea Island, Georgia. As he prepared to do so, there were few outside observers who thought he was likely to produce a significant success. Most scholars of American foreign policy focussed on the bitter two-year-long divisions between America and many of its G8 partners over the war in Iraq, and on the President's dislike of multilateralism and international institutions in achieving American goals in the world. Students of the G8, following the conventional American leadership tradition, wondered whether the forum could survive the absence of an America willing to lead and able to secure the support of a strong second in the summit club (Putnam and Bayne 1987). They also knew that among G8 leaders, U.S. presidents were historically the last to plan and prepare for the annual summit, and that only once before, under Gerald Ford in 1976, had a U.S. president hosted a summit in an presidential election year. It was one of the least successful summits of all.

Similarly sceptical were most scholars who had analysed America's G8 contribution to G8 summits past. The dominant school, of discretionary dominance, saw a G8 that needed an America capable of leading, but an America that was finding the G8 less useful in a post–Cold War, rapidly globalising world (Putnam and Bayne 1987; Smeyser 1993). A second school saw the G8 as an increasingly useful instrument of American influence, but still not an essential institution for a self-confident, unilateralist president leading an America at war (Owen 1997; Putnam 1994; Antholis 2001). A third school argued that the G8 could and should become America's central future institution in a post–Cold War, globalising age, but only if it were reformed or transformed into a full-fledged, highly legalised international organisation such as the United Nations or European Union (Ikenberry 1993; Lewis 1991–92; Bergsten and Henning 1996). Few felt that America would, out of necessity, regularly adjust to the members and the institutions of the G8 (Stephens 2000).

Amid all this scepticism, however, there were good grounds for believing that George Bush might make the Sea Island Summit a success. These grounds flowed from the concert equality model, which highlighted not America the victorious in the long Cold

War but America the vulnerable to shocks from elusive enemies everywhere. Those enemies kill Americans anywhere and require the full co-operation of America's G8 allies to defeat them (Kirton 2003, 2004). Getting the collaboration of this highly capable, continuing 'coalition of the willing', containing countries all committed to democratic principles and leaders allowed by their citizens to act in their defence, required an America willing to adjust at the summit to what its now necessary G8 allies want.

Pushing the Sea Island Summit toward success were the rising performance of the G8 and America in it over the past 30 years, the momentum from the Evian Summit of 2003, and a Sea Island preparatory process in which America increasingly listened to, learned from, and adapted to its G8 partners. Pulling the Sea Island Summit toward high performance were intensifying energy and terrorist shocks that reminded America and its allies of their common vulnerability, and the failure of the UN or U.S. alone in response. Also important were the still predominant and equalising capability of G8 countries and the fidelity of Sea Island's central agenda to the core G8 principles of globally promoting open democracy, individual liberty, and social advance. Yet the diminished domestic political capital of Bush and most of his potential strong summit supporters, and the large number of visitors and issues to be dealt with at a very short summit, severely tested the ability of these leaders to make the right deals in the little time they had alone.

They met the challenge. America adjusted to make the Sea Island Summit one of substantial achievement on poverty reduction in Africa, the nonproliferation of weapons of mass destruction (WMD), regional security, and the world economy. At the same time, America's partners backed Bush's bold vision and historic beginning to bring democracy, reform, prosperity, security, and sovereignty to Iraq and the Broader Middle East and North Africa (BMENA). Yet whether Sea Island would become a summit of historical significance still depended ultimately on the willingness of America's allies to make Bush's brave beginning toward a democratic Middle East a permanent, expanding, well-financed priority at G8 summits in future years.

The Push from the Promising Past

The first push toward success at Sea Island came from the rising trend in G8 (formerly G7) performance over the previous 30 years. As shown by Table 3-1, since its 1975 start, the G8 had become increasingly effective in performing most of its major functions (Kirton 2004). The duration of its deliberations jumped to three days in 1982, and to four days in 2003. Its directional function of setting new principles and norms, measured roughly by the number of words in the leaders' concluding communiqués, jumped in 1996 to a high, generally sustained level. Its decisional function of making collective commitments also did so, reaching a new peak of 253 commitments at Evian in 2003. Since 1992, the delivery of these commitments through compliance by G8 members also rose, even if their intended impact in the

Table 3-1 G8 Summit Performance by Function, 1975–2004

Year	Site	Bayne Grade	# of Days	# of Stmts[a]	# of Words	# of Commit.[b]	Compl. Score[c]	# of Minist. Created[d]	# of Remit Mandates	# of Leaders Bodies Cr[e]	Ttl[f]
	Ldg[g]	A–	3	1	1129	14	+57.1	0	1	1	1
1976	*Res[h]*	*D*	*2*	*1*	*1624*	*7*	*+08.9*	*0*	*1*	*0*	*1*
1977	Cap[i]	B–	2	6	2669	29	+08.4	0	1	0	1
1978	Cap	A	2	2	2999	35	+36.3	0	0	2	3
1979	Cap	B+	2	2	2102	34	+82.3	0	1	3	5
1980	Prv[j]	C+	2	5	3996	55	+07.6	0	1	0	3
1981	Ldg	C	2	3	3165	40	+26.6	1	1	2	4
1982	Ldg	C	3	2	1796	23	+84.0	0	1	3	3
1983	*Res*	*B*	*3*	*2*	*2156*	*38*	*–10.9*	*0*	*1*	*0*	*2*
1984	Cap	C–	3	5	3261	31	+48.8	1	3	1	4
1985	Cap	E	3	2	3127	24	+01.0	0	1	2	5
1986	Cap	B+	3	4	3582	39	+58.3	1	1	1	3
1987	Prv	D	3	6	5064	53	+93.3	0	1	0	2
1988	Prv	C–	3	2	4872	27	–47.8	0	1	1	3
1989	Cap	B+	3	11	7125	61	+07.8	0	1	1	2
1990	*Prv*	*D*	*3*	*3*	*7601*	*78*	*–14.0*	*0*	*3*	*2*	*5*
1991	Cap	B–	3	3	8099	53	00.0	0	3	0	2
1992	Prv	D	3	4	7528	41	+64.0	1	2	1	2
1993	Cap	C+	3	2	3398	29	+75.0	0	5	0	2
1994	Prv	C	3	2	4123	53	100.0	1	2	0	4
1995	Prv	B+	3	3	7250	78	100.0	2	6	2	3
1996	Prv	B	3	5	15 289	128	+36.2	0	2	1	6
1997	*Prv*	*C–*	*3*	*4*	*12 994*	*145*	*+12.8*	*1*	*10*	1	6
1998	Prv	B+	3	4	6092	73	+31.8	0	3	1	4
1999	Prv	B+	3	4	10 019	46	+38.2	1	3	1	2
2000	Res	B	3	5	13 596	105	+81.4	0	5	2	5
2001	Prv	B	3	7	6214	58	+49.5	1	4	1	6
2002	Res	B+	2	18	11 959	187	+35.0	1	6	3	8
2003	Prv	C	3	14	16 889	206	+51.0	0	4	2	9
2004	*Res*		*3*	*16*	*29 658*	*253*			*12*		
Av. All		C+			6197	26	+.37	.38	2.6	1.1	3.5
Av. Cycle 1		B–			2526	29	+.32	.14	1.0	1.1	2.6
Av. Cycle 2		C–			3408	34	+.32	.29	1.0	1.3	3.1
Av. Cycle 3		C+			6446	56	+.48	.57	3.1	0.9	2.9
Av. Cycle 4		B			10 880	106	+.41	.57	4.7	1.4	5.3
Av. Cycle 5		C			16 889	206	TBA	.00	4.0	2.0	9.0

Notes:

- a. Number of statements; b. Number of commitments; c. Compliance score (1990–1995: compliance with commitments selected by Ella Kokotsis; 1996–2003: compliance with commitments selected by the G8 Research Group); d. Number of ministerials created; e. Created; f. Total; g. Lodge (outskirts of capital city); h. Remote resort; i. Capital city; j. Provincial city.
- U.S.-hosted summits are in italics.

wider world was less clear (Kokotsis 1999; Baliamoune 2000). The G8 had also been more active since 1995 in the development of global governance, notably by creating and directing G8 bodies of its own. Not surprisingly, higher overall scores were awarded to most summits in recent years (Bayne 2000).

To be sure, these grades suggest that the U.S. performed poorly as a summit host, and that America's best effort had come when Ronald Reagan hosted at Williamsburg way back in 1983 (Nau 2004). But a broader look across all the individual summit functions shows that American-hosted summits had been on a rising trend, through George H. Bush's Houston Summit in 1990 and Bill Clinton's Denver Summit in 1997 (Fauver 2003; Brainerd 2004).

This long-term rise in G8 summit performance had generally intensified since the French-hosted Evian Summit of 1–3 June 2004. Evian had produced a record high number of commitments, across a wide array of issues, and mobilised modest amounts of new money to help put them into effect. The priority commitments made at Evian proved to be complied with +51 percent of the time during the following year, with both France and the United States complying at an above-average rate. Evian created three new G8 bodies: for fighting terrorism, for WMD nonproliferation, and for science and technology for sustainable development. The Evian leaders also issued several instructions to other international institutions. Above all, they recorded their common determination to respond together through the G8 to the external shocks they collectively recognised — WMD proliferation, terrorist attacks, and sinking oil tankers polluting ecologically fragile shores. Evian also requested reports at the 2004 Summit on terrorism and transport security. It left a report on Africa to the British-hosted Summit in 2005.

In the year after Evian, the G8 countries continued to co-operate, in ways that diminished the deepened political divide among them that had arisen over the spring 2003 American-led war against Iraq. To be sure, by late spring of 2004, the old divisions reappeared over the premature leak of America's Greater Middle East Initiative (GMEI), Bush's pledges to Israeli president Ariel Sharon over the Middle East Peace Process, revelations of the abuse of Iraqi prisoners by American guards, and ongoing demands for the U.S. to hand over authority to a sovereign Iraqi government and the UN. But those divisions were increasingly overwhelmed by several stronger processes of G8 co-operation, arising in several 'coalitions of the willing' containing G8 partners in their core. These included the progress made by U.S. emissary James Baker on Iraqi debt relief, commitments of new money from G8 partners outside the Iraq war coalition to reconstruct Iraq, co-operation among several G8 partners in the Asia-Pacific Economic Cooperation (APEC) forum, and the admission of all G8 countries to America's Proliferation Security Initiative (PSI).

Also important was the cadence of co-operative, institutionalised plurilateral summitry the Americans orchestrated when they chose in the summer of 2003 to hold their G8 summit on 8–10 June 2004. In this plan, the month started with Bush's 4 June visit to Silvio Berlusconi and the Pope in Rome, a 5 June visit with Jacques Chirac in Paris, and a 6 June encounter in Normandy with all G8 leaders except Japan's Junichiro Koizumi to celebrate the 60th anniversary of D-Day. Soon after the Sea Island Summit, Bush was scheduled to attend the U.S.-EU Summit in Dublin, and then the summit of the North Atlantic Treaty Organization (NATO) in Istanbul on 28–29 June. These four major summits were well designed to show that George Bush was indeed an effective allied global leader. The month would begin by featuring Chirac thanking Bush for sending American troops to fight and die for freedom in his country, before there even existed a UN to issue 'permission slips'. It would end with Turkey — the great democratic, secular Muslim country and NATO ally — helping America get NATO to take responsibility for securing the liberation of Iraq after the 30 June transition of authority. With these well-choreographed reminders that the U.S., France, and most G8 partners were fighting together for freedom on so many different global fronts (including Afghanistan and Haiti), memories of the UN-magnified divisions of early 2003 would fade, while those of the common fight for freedom in the greater Middle East would come to the fore.

Accompanying this architecture was a major American accommodation of its G8 partners as the Sea Island preparatory process advanced. Bush, disappointed with his first summit encounter at Genoa in 2001, had begun Sea Island preparations sceptical of the value of the G8 summit, and of the need to hold it every year. During the summer of 2003, some Americans indicated a preference for a very short summit, in an informal setting at Sea Island on Georgia's coast. At the last French-hosted sherpa meeting in November 2003, the Americans signalled that they wanted no lead-up G8 ministerial meetings (apart from those for Finance and Home Affairs), no new money pledged, and probably no invited outsiders — or at least very few and no one who had been there before. As themes for their summit, the Americans offered 'security, prosperity, and freedom', the latter based on Bush's speech to the National Endowment for Democracy on 6 November 2003 and its vision of democratising the Middle East (Bush 2003). The central agenda that had fuelled the success of the last three summits — Africa and ecologically sustainable development — were virtually absent from this initial American game plan.

Once America assumed the G8 chair on 1 January 2004, the U.S. began to move away from this stark vision. Bush employed his ministers in G8 forums on his priorities of terrorism (Home Affairs), finance (including terrorist finance), and GMEI. For the latter, he reinstated the lead-up G8 foreign ministers meeting, held on 14 May in Washington, and he visited the foreign ministers assembled there.

Within the sherpa process, American adjustment was apparent as well. At their first sherpa meeting, the Americans presented an agenda composed of four major deliverables: GMEI and its integrally linked issues of the Middle East Peace Process and Iraq; transport security and terrorism, featuring the Secure and Facilitated International Travel Initiative (SAFTI); further action on WMD proliferation; and action on private sector-led development.

The centrepiece was GMEI, renamed the 'BMENA Initiative' on the Summit's eve. As the second and third sherpa meetings passed, GMEI took the shape of a general G8 political statement of principles, a list of existing G8 members' programmes in this area and new G8 initiatives, on issues such as literacy, women's education, freedom of the press, and finance. G8 members moved closer to consensus that GMEI must be accompanied by progress on Middle East peace, as America's G8 and Middle East partners demanded, but that the two would be done simultaneously, as America insisted. A similar spirit of convergence pervaded the equally delicate and integrally linked issue of the political transition to sovereignty, security, development, and democracy in Iraq.

The second major deliverable, on transport security and terrorism, included initially divisive issues such as the forward deployment of immigration and customs personnel, and full airside screening to ensure that those who worked in the airline industry faced the same thorough screening as their passengers every time they boarded or serviced a plane. Also included were the Evian remit mandates on counterterrorism capacity-building assistance, a progress report on man-portable anti-aircraft missiles (MANPADS), and an overall terrorism review.

The third major deliverable, keeping WMD from falling into the hands of terrorists and other enemies, included an American proposal to deny potential enemies access to the specific components they needed for a full nuclear-fuel cycle and thus the ability to develop nuclear weapons of their own. Other American-driven proposals were expanding PSI; controlling chemical, biological, and radiological weapons; and expanding the Kananaskis Global Partnership against the Spread of Weapons and Materials of Mass Destruction to include new money for the dismantlement of WMD in Libya, which had now suddenly joined the camp of co-operating states. Progress here would depend on adjustment by Germany, which insisted it would make no new serious spending commitments at Sea Island at all.

The fourth deliverable, private sector-led development, was inspired by the recently released report, 'Unleashing Entrepreneurship: Making Business Work for the Poor', co-chaired by Canadian prime minister Paul Martin and Mexican ex-president Ernesto Zedillo (Commission on the Private Sector and Development 2003). To flesh it out, the Americans sought to foster the flow of remittances from those in the rich North to their families in the poor South. They also considered creating growth index bonds, which would reward rich investors placing money in poor countries according to how much the recipient country grew each year. All G8 members endorsed the first initiative, while only Germany, very grudgingly, gave the second any support.

As the spring progressed, America's partners and parts of the American administration and society expanded the list. A fifth item, peace support primarily in Africa, signalled by the Americans in November 2003, was outlined in a paper co-authored by Italy and the United States. Here the now free-spending United States was prepared to put US$660 million of its own money for programmes in Africa and another US$200 million elsewhere. America invited its G8 partners to contribute as well. The G8 members, many with programmes of their own for training heavy police and experience in the civilian policy component of the G8's conflict prevention programmes, urged the U.S. to reinforce existing mechanisms, rather than reinvent the wheel (Kirton and Stefanova 2004). The U.S. seemed willing to do so, although again Germany remained reluctant to spend.

A sixth item, famine and food security, first floated in a fragile form by the Americans in the early spring, received an enthusiastic push by the partners. It aroused the familiar intra-G8 debate about how the issue would be framed, what it would include, and what geographic areas it would focus upon. The G8 partners found an expansive solution, and the combined category of 'Famine/Food Security' jumped onto the Sea Island agenda for discussion with the African leaders who were later invited for a session on the Summit's last day.

A seventh item, which received similarly expansive accommodation, was global health. From the very beginning, all G8 members, including the frugal Germans, agreed that they would act to eliminate polio by providing the funds necessary to ensure its eradication and intervening with those countries, such as Nigeria, where the disease was breaking out again. Added on was action against HIV/AIDS and tuberculosis, and the future of the Genoa Summit–financed Global Fund to Fight AIDS, Malaria, and Tuberculosis.

The issue of global economic growth saw a major shift in emphasis as the preparations proceeded. An initial American desire to focus strongly on delivering the Doha Development Agenda of the World Trade Organization (WTO) by its intended completion date of 2005 shrank as the months went by. Volatile oil prices were rising rapidly, an issue of particular of concern to voters in both the United States and Canada, where elections loomed.

The political-security agenda centred on the regional priorities of Iran and North Korea. The Summit was also arranged to deal with any late-breaking political-security crises, in response to Japan's request that one session be kept free for the leaders to discuss any issues they might want.

American accommodation did have its limits, however. France pushed to return to Evian's science and technology for sustainable development. Several sought to upgrade the Global Environment Observation System of Systems (GEOSS) that a G8-centred group was advancing at lower levels. Japan proposed an initiative on 'reduce, reuse, and recycle'. Tony Blair wished to address climate change directly. But the division of labour initially established in autumn 2003, under which sustainable development and Africa would be left almost entirely to Britain's 2005 G8 Summit, seemed to hold.

By the end of May 2004, with all the ministerials and all but the final sherpa meetings concluded, American accommodation had produced a wide-ranging agenda. Here the priorities of America's partners — led by their African agenda — featured as strongly as those of America alone. This result reflected an American desire both to have fallback successes should its GMEI centrepiece not spring to life and to adopt its partners' priorities in return for their support for the initiative itself.

This drive toward the expansive, big-package, synergistic solution was reinforced by the particular configuration of priorities America's partners brought. Few had strongly entrenched demands on key issues that were anathema to the others. Most made modest efforts within the bounds of the possible or, in the case of GMEI, made a serious shared attempt to find a solution to the big divisions among G8 partners that flourished outside the G8 club.

Second-ranked Japan, an American ally with armed forces in Iraq, was highly supportive of the U.S. At an early stage, Koizumi publicly stated that Sea Island would allow all G8 partners to express their commitment to the democratic reconstruction of Iraq. Privately he worked to have them do so with the approval of the UN. He also showed Japan's continuing concern with the return of Japan's abductees and their children still in North Korea, and with North Korean nuclear proliferation, including the Korean sale of enriched uranium to Libya. Within the preparatory process, Japan was happy to let the U.S. set the agenda, offering as its only real initiative one on the environmental three R's of reduce, reuse, and recycle.

Third-ranked Germany joined France in showing the greatest interest in shaping GMEI into something that all could accept and that might work. They continued to insist on no new spending, beyond the low-cost polio front. They also stood alone in supporting American ideas on growth index bonds.

France approached Sea Island as the guardian of the Evian legacy, with a desire to end the transatlantic divide over Iraq. This led it to join Germany in the quest to make GMEI work, especially on the immediate imperative of securing the UN resolution required to hand over authority to a new, genuinely sovereign Iraqi government on 30 June. France also sought to add the Evian priorities on African famine and food security, peace support, private sector development, and HIV/AIDS. The French were further tempted to bring to the summit table the issues of financing for development, since Chirac had become attached to the idea of a tax on international transactions such as oil to raise the necessary funds, and sustainable development — an Evian highlight that Sea Island threatened to erase completely.

Britain, the ranking American ally in Iraq, focussed on preparing for its presidency the following year. It thus sought to lay a strong Sea Island foundation for the centrepiece themes of Africa and sustainable development that it had signalled in 2003 to feature in 2005. Thus the British were interested in famine, development finance, and sustainable development, including climate change and water. They tried to keep environmental issues alive at the working level and thus available for an upgrade to the leaders level should the occasion arise.

Italy, another American ally in Iraq, had less well-defined priorities. But it was highly active at the working level, weighing in across the board on technical concerns. Its one big initiative was peace support for nearby Africa, where it co-authored the paper with the U.S.

Canada continued to emphasise its 2002 Kananaskis legacy (Fowler 2003). Its new prime minister, Paul Martin, had an election looming on 28 June, burning domestic political issues, and an established international and G8 reputation. He thus largely left the Americans alone to add Canada's core concerns on their own. Martin was a pioneer on the polio issue, where early victory came, and on private sector–led development, where the Martin-Zedillo report served as the lens through which the issue would be addressed. On the campaign trail at home, Martin promised he would raise the issue of world oil prices. There remained the possibility that he would also try to advance his pet project of creating a leaders-level G20, or L20, to reinforce the work of the G8, even knowing that the other G8 leaders — the same individuals who had been gathering annually since 2001 — quite liked the G8 membership the way it was.

For Russia, the big issues were terrorism and how to accommodate its G8 partners' desires for reduced oil prices and for nuclear nonproliferation in North Korea and Iran. Russia, with one eye to its hosting of the G8 in 2006, was also anxious to secure G8 support for its membership in the WTO and fully at the G7 finance ministers forum.

The Pull from the Pressures Outside

As Sea Island approached, several powerful outside pressures pulled the G8 leaders toward making their summit a success. The first force was the combination of recent shocks that reminded all of their individual vulnerabilities and thus common aversion to severe threats to basic national interests.

Rearing its well-recognised worrisome head was the major vulnerability that had always reliably induced a repeatedly shocked and now hyper-sensitive G8 to co-operate in the past (Kirton and Stefanova 2004; Keohane and Nye 1989; Ikenberry 1988). World oil prices in nominal dollars rose to new and potentially sustained new highs, just as American and Canadian voters began their summer driving seasons and as the sustained economic expansion of the U.S., Japan, and now China promised to keep demand and oil prices high. Even with most members of the Organization of the Petroleum Exporting Countries (OPEC) co-operating with the G8, an unprecedented and ominous new version of the old vulnerability came from angry non-state actors in a politically troubled, troubled, terrorist-ridden Middle East.

A second, closely connected, shock-driven vulnerability came from an upsurge in terrorist attacks against G8 nationals and targets. The first five months of 2004 delivered an unusually steady and deadly succession of terrorist attacks against the G8. Russia again bore the brunt. But the March bombing of the Madrid train system brought terrorist mass murder to continental Europe and to a member of the EU. Even though the Madrid bombing led middlepower Spain to pull its troops out of Iraq, all G8 members with troops already in Iraq, as responsible great powers, kept theirs in. America, Britain, and Italy continued to take casualties, as terrorists increasingly targeted foreign nationals working for the oil industry in Saudi Arabia and Iraq.

A second pull came from the poor performance of the United Nations system and of America acting alone (cf. Ikenberry 2001, 1998/99). In the shock-scarred field of energy, neither the UN nor the U.S. on its own (even with its Strategic Petroleum Reserve) was particularly relevant in mounting an effective response. In sharp contrast, oil-exporting G8 allies Russia and Canada promised relief. In response to the shocks of terrorism and threats to transport security, neither the multilateral International Civil Aviation Organization (ICAO), the International Maritime Organization (IMO), Interpol, nor America alone could offer the effective response that came from the G8-centred Container Security Initiative, PSI, or programme against MANPADS (Flynn 2004). On WMD proliferation, on the eve of the Sea Island Summit the head of the International Atomic Energy Agency (IAEA) spoke eloquently of the failures and weakness of his organisation in Iran, North Korea, and elsewhere. The discovery of extensive WMD caches in a now co-operative Libya showed that, short of a major military invasion and occupation, America acting alone could not do the job.

Even in Iraq, as casualties and costs mounted, the United States became eager to hand over responsibility to a UN-approved sovereign Iraqi government on 30 June. But neither America nor its G8 partners were under any illusions, after the previous twelve years, that the UN could cope without major support in many forms from the G8 great powers themselves. Only on the issue of development could the UN claim a level of normative and epistemic effectiveness that the G8 could use as a foundation for action to move ahead.

A third pull came from changes in G8 capabilities. When outside vulnerabilities flow through the inadequate defences of the UN multilateral system or a hegemonic, unilateralist America to seriously threaten G8 members, they often encounter a G8 club with the collective capabilities in the world, and the equal capabilities among members, to inspire an effective response. In 2004, the G8 — with the now enlarged European Union — still collectively dominated the global economy, despite the recent rise of communist China and democratic India. Within the G8, the growth of gross domestic growth (GDP) in the first quarter of 2004 showed that an oil-rich Russia and a now strongly recovering Japan stood in first and second place (Morse and Richard 2002). Similarly, the strong decline in the value of the U.S. dollar against other G8 currencies since Evian made America sufficiently modest about its capabilities to search for co-ordinated solutions with its G8 friends.

A fourth pull came from the fidelity of Sea Island's GMEI centrepiece to the G8's core principles of 'open democracy, individual liberty and social advance' (Kirton 2003). Summits succeed when they focus on issues that directly invoke these core principles, and when all G8 members have internalised them as part of their political practice and identity at home. Here one impediment arose from worries that Vladimir Putin's Russia was backsliding from the G7 standards in respecting freedom of the press and renouncing arbitrary arrest. However, all G8 members were aware of the need to defend open democracies against Islamist-linked terrorism and to build democratic societies on the front lines of Afghanistan and post-Saddam Iraq. The remaining challenge was whether the G8 could get leaders from the greater Middle East to embrace the democratic path, for many were very embryonic democracies at best.

Compounding the challenge was the G8 leaders' limited freedom at home to adjust to the demands of their partners abroad, for the leaders' political capital and control were collectively weak. Exceptional American weakness was juxtaposed against Russian strength. Host George Bush had a very old and razor-thin electoral mandate, a looming election five months after the Summit, and a minority personal and party approval rating plummeting in the polls. Canada's Paul Martin was even more electorally preoccupied, as he faced a general election less than three weeks after the Summit and party voter intention ratings that promised him a minority government at best. Britain's Tony Blair had a party behind in the polls, even if his next election was at least a year off. Germany's Gerhard Schroeder was also domestically unpopular. So was France's Jacques Chirac, whose party was routed by the Socialist opposition and its allies in regional elections in March. Japan's Junichiro Koizumi was in better shape, but faced upper house elections in July.

The only experienced, legislatively confident, electorally secure leader with political capital in domestic public opinion was Russia's Putin. His recent re-election by a 71 percent majority, a massive majority in his legislature, and very high approval ratings were the inverse of those of Bush. The Sea Island Summit thus promised to do well in areas where Russia was a major player — such as terrorism, transport security, WMD, and energy — if Putin proved to be a full member and leader of the G8 club.

A final challenge was the absence of the constricted participation and the considerable time that allowed G8 leaders to be alone to bond as leaders and thus lead the world to great achievements and historic change. The Americans' chosen setting at informal, isolated Sea Island was well suited to bring out G8 leadership at its best. But the Americans had designed one of the shortest summits in G8 history, and had further compromised it with extensive ceremonial, bilateral, and social components. Furthermore, on their first full day of summitry they would meet at noon with several invited leaders from the greater Middle East, and would have a similar meeting again with six invited African leaders on the final day.

These outreach sessions and guest lists did demonstrate American skill in adding Africa as an equal emphasis, and in attracting the leaders of several consequential Middle East countries to come to Sea Island and give GMEI a chance. Yet they left very little time for the G8 leaders to go beyond what their sherpas and ministers had already decided on their behalf. Moreover, on the critical issues of democratic development in the Middle East and of Africa, these sessions required G8 leaders and their outside partners to all come together in the same way, at the same time. This format, added to the difficulties in the Middle East and Africa outside, made it extraordinarily challenging for the Sea Island Summit to be the historic success in spreading freedom that Bush so much desired. As the Summit started, it was very much up to him, as a statesman, as a political leader, and as a person, to make it all work.

The Performance at Sea Island

This he largely did. As it unfolded from 8 to 10 June, Sea Island proved to be a summit of substantial achievement for its many accomplishments across the broad array of issues it had come to include. It also had the potential to be a summit of historical significance if its bold beginning to bring democratic reform to the Middle East would be kept alive by the G8 at subsequent summits, starting in Britain in 2005.

On many of the standard dimensions of summit performance, Sea Island set new highs, as Table 3-2 shows. As a deliberative institution, the G8 issued a record 16 often very lengthy and detailed documents covering ten separate issue areas. In setting normative directions and principles, it highlighted the theme of freedom and democracy throughout. As a decisional institution, it generated a record 253 concrete, future-oriented collective commitments.

The Summit further specified twelve 'remit mandates' for reports to be submitted to the 2005 Gleneagles Summit or for work to be completed by then. It also mobilised an estimated US$2.77 billion in new money, a sum more than four times as much as Evian in 2003. It created or importantly directed 17 G8 or G8-centred institutions, at the ministerial, official, and, importantly, civil society levels. And it issued more than 500 instructions, of both guidance and support, to a vast array of other international institutions. On all dimensions save money mobilised, Sea Island saw a major advance from the performance of virtually all summits past.

The centrepiece for the Summit was the democratic development of the Middle East, its integrally linked component of the Middle East Peace Process (or 'Road Map'), and the immediate imperative of the sovereignty, security, development, and democratisation of a new Iraq. Here history was made. One hour before the Summit opened, and due to its strong 'pull' effect, the United Nations Security Council (UNSC) unanimously passed a resolution transferring sovereignty to a new Iraqi government at the end of the month. In doing so, it reunited G8 members after their often bitter divisions over Iraq during the previous year and a half. During and — importantly — due to the eight months' preparatory process for the Sea Island Summit, the issue of democratic development in the Middle East was put on the international agenda, adopted as a goal by the Arab League Summit, and affirmed by the seven invited leaders from the region at a lunchtime dialogue with the G8 on the Summit's second day. The Summit's signature moment came when Ghazi Mashal Ajil al-Yawer, the newly installed president of a soon-to-be sovereign Iraq, sat beside George Bush and thanked him and the American people for the sacrifices they had made in freeing Iraq from Saddam Hussein. The G8 followed with a bold political declaration promising support for the principles of democracy, the rule of law, and human rights in the Middle East. It backed these words with the Plan of Support for Reform containing specific projects embracing political, economic, and social reform, well targeted to the priorities of the region, and financed by US$100 million in new funds. To make this down payment permanent and expansive, G8 leaders created the Forum for the

Table 3-2 The Policy Summit

	Document	Wds[a]	Par[b]	Cmt[c]	Mob[d]	Amt (US$)[e]	Remit (hard)[f]	Remit (soft)[g]	G8 Inst[h]	Instr[i]
1	G8 Leaders Statement on Trade	679	8	4						13
2	G8 Action Plan: Applying the Power of Entrepreneurship to the Eradication of Poverty	2512	50	39					1	38
3	Partnership for Progress and a Common Future with the Region of the Broader Middle East and North Africa	1590	23	8	3				1	42
4	G8 Plan of Support for Reform	4359	130	38	1	100 m			5	69
5	G8 Action Plan on Nonproliferation	2147	28	23	2			1		61
6	G8 Secure and Facilitated International Travel Initiative (SAFTI)	1549	46	35				5		34
7	G8 Statement on Sudan	345	5	1						1
8	G8 Statement: Gaza Withdrawal and the Road to Mideast Peace	504	6	3						8
9	G8 Action Plan for Expanding Global Capacity for Peace Support Operations	1435	18	14	1	961 m		1	1	13
10	G8 Action to Endorse and Establish a Global HIV Vaccine	791	11	4		15 m 360 m	1	1	1	15
11	G8 Commitment to Help Stop Polio Forever	460	9	5	1	200 m		1		6
12	Fighting Corruption to Improve Transparency[j]	11 013	255	18			1		3	111
13	Debt Sustainability for the Poorest (HIPC)	163	4	4	1	1 b		1		4
14	Ending the Cycle of Famine in the Horn of Africa, Raising Agricultural Productivity, and Promoting Rural Development in Food Insecure Countries	365	56	49						47
15	Science & Technology for Sustainable Development: "3r" Action Plan & Progress on Implemention	687	21	8					5	29
16	Chair's Summary	1059	29							23
	Total: Sea Island 2004 (16 docs)	29 658	699	253	9	2.77 b	2	10	17	514
	Total: Evian 2003 (14 docs)			206	10	500 m	5		3	

Notes: a. Number of words; b. Number of paragraphs; c. Number of concrete, forward-looking commitments; d. Number of commitments of new money by the G8 in the lead-up to or at the summit; e. Amount of money committed; f. Number of specific commitments for leaders to deal with the subject at a subsequent summit mobilised (remit mandates); g. Number of specific commitments to deal the subject at a future specified date or by the time of the next summit (remit mandates); h. Number of G8 or G8-centred institutions created or directed; i. Number of instructions issued to other international organisations; j. Includes the four Compacts to Promote Transparency and Combat Corruption between the G8 and Nicaragua (4 institutions), Nigeria (4 institutions), Peru (3 institutions), Georgia (4 institutions). *Other documents issued:* G8 Global Partnership Annual Report, G8 Global Partnership Consolidated Report.

Future for G8 and Middle East ministers of foreign, economic, and related affairs. They also established several similarly inclusive bodies for civil society stakeholders in strategic sectors.

The second big winner at Sea Island was Africa. It secured a new programme to build capacity for peacekeeping and peace support, backed by almost US$1 billion from the U.S. and the EU. It obtained another new programme, containing 49 specific commitments, to end the cycle of famine in the Horn of Africa and provide food security beyond. Poor countries in Africa and elsewhere also received a promise, potentially worth another US$1 billion, that G8 leaders were prepared to extend the debt relief programme for heavily indebted poor countries (HIPCs), due to expire by the end of 2004, for another two years, and to top up the HIPC Trust Fund to write off bilateral debt. They also obtained a commitment, worth up to US$200 million, to eradicate polio by 2005, and a programme, backed by approximately US$375 million, to develop vaccines and otherwise act against HIV/AIDS. More broadly, Africans benefited from a G8 action plan to apply entrepreneurship to eradicate poverty, featuring an initiative to lower the cost of the remittances sent by those in the rich North to family and friends in the poor South. To receive these promises and discuss their future, African leaders attended the G8 for the fourth year in a row, with the veterans from South Africa, Nigeria, Senegal, and Algeria joined by newcomers from Uganda and Ghana for a lunchtime session with G8 leaders on the Summit's third day. Africa's prominence on the Sea Island agenda, above or equal to that of the Middle East in many respects, was due to the strong, skilful pressure from many sources, notably American-supportive Blair, Berlusconi, and Koizumi, as well as Canada and France as past summit hosts, the institutional nest of the G8's African personal representatives (APRs), pressures from African advocates within the U.S. administration, and a transnational coalition inspired by South Africa's Thabo Mbeki, supported by Blair, and delivered by the Council on Foreign Relations in the United States (Atwood, Browne, and Lyman 2004).

A third area of accomplishment was WMD proliferation. Here the G8 imposed a one-year moratorium on the export of materials that recipient states could use to acquire nuclear weapons, and a promise to modernise the leaky nonproliferation regime to close such loopholes for good. The G8 also expanded its 2002 Global Partnership to include Iraq and Libya.

A fourth area of major movement was regional security. The discussion at dinner on the second day focussed on the Middle East, and dealt with Iran, Israel and Palestine, Iraq, Afghanistan, and North Korea. It produced a G8 statement, much sought by America's G8 partners and those in the region, on Gaza Withdrawal and the Road Ahead to Mideast Peace. Showing the Summit's flexibility and political responsiveness, the leaders also discussed Haiti, where American, French, and Canadian troops were involved in democratic nation-building. They issued a strong statement to stop ethnic cleansing in Sudan.

In other areas of traditional G8 summit action, however, the results were more modest. The discussion of the energy component of the world economy saw the G8 start to explore solutions within the G8, including energy efficiency, conservation, and alternatives to oil. Moreover, the leaders expressed their unscripted concern with how the threat of terrorism could hurt or end the strong economic recovery, not just through its impact on energy prices, but in adding uncertainty and transactions costs across the G8 and global economy as a whole. In doing so, these leaders drew from their memory of past energy vulnerabilities, melded them to terrorism, and came together to confront the much broader threat posed by this deadly combination in the post–11 September world.

On trade, the leaders invited G8 ministers establish a framework by the end of July for the deadlocked negotiations for the Doha Development Agenda. But they refused to acknowledge the outstanding commitment to complete the Doha negotiations by 2005. On terrorism, the G8 produced the SAFTI with 28 action items. But it omitted a contentious proposal for full airside screening or measures to deal with small airports and aircraft or ground transportation on subways and trains. The action plan for science and technology largely approved existing work but also endorsed Japan's initiative on the three 'R's'.

Most strikingly, the Sea Island summiteers, meeting on the 60th anniversary of the founding of the Bretton Woods institutions, devoted no attention to modernising the international financial system to meet the needs of the 21st-century world. Nor did they address any current international financial crises, such as that in Argentina, or those that might arise if U.S. and G8 interest rates were to rise too much too fast.

If the policy summit had some disappointments, the physical summit had very few, at least for those seeking a flawlessly executed, completely safe, and peaceful experience, well designed to let George Bush get his preferred message out. The many bilaterals, the opening dinner with the spouses, the four sessions among the G8 leaders, and the three outreach sessions (with the leaders of the Middle East, Iraq, and Africa) all flowed smoothly, and won public approval and praise from both the G8 leaders and their guests. As Table 3-3 shows, no more than 500 civil society activists arrived, for activities that produced only 15 arrests on minor charges and no bodily injury or physical damage at all. The 20 000 security personnel kept any potential terrorist threats at bay. And a cost-conscious U.S. government, which spent only one third as much to mount the Sea Island Summit as had the French the previous year, reaped the reward of having only 1492 media members present to scrutinise the G8 leaders and report the event, largely from the information the U.S. administration constantly dispensed. The obvious losers were the locals, who, with much of the media missing, lost some of their one chance in a lifetime to showcase their city and state to the world.

As a domestic political event, Sea Island also proved its value. Bush had been plunging in the polls for the previous two months, to the point where his presumptive Democratic presidential rival, John Kerry, had a six- to seven-point lead on the Summit's eve. Sea Island allowed Bush to show that he could work with the allies, solve the Iraq problem before it became a Vietnam-like nightmare, and globally forward the value of freedom that most Americans recalled they so cherished, especially as they honoured the memory of the recently deceased Ronald Reagan during the week the Summit began. A Fox News poll released on 13 June, three days after the Summit ended, showed that Bush had cut Kerry's lead to a statistically insignificant 2 percent from a margin of 6 percent to 7 percent just before the Summit's start.

Canada's Paul Martin, whose personal and party's standings in the polls had been slipping, stopped this trend and then started moving upward as his performance at Sea Island dominated the airwaves back home. Outside North America, however, Japan's Koizumi saw his approval and his party's sink back to where they had been before the strong surge brought by his pre-Summit trip to North Korea. In Britain, Blair returned home to a devastating defeat in local and European elections, as his Labour Party's 22.3 percent of the vote in the latter was the lowest since before World War I. Elsewhere in the European parliament elections, France's ruling Union pour un Mouvement

Table 3-3 The Physical Summit

Dimension	2004
G8 leaders present	10
Early departures	01
Outside leaders invited	13
Outside heads of international organisations invited	00
Sessions at eight (all G8 leaders present)	04
Hours alone at eight	10
Media accredited[a]	3100
Media arrived[b]	1492
Security personnel	20 000
Civil society activists[c]	500
Arrests[d]	15
Personal injury	0
Property damage	0
Security spending	US$37 million

Notes:

Numbers are the most reliable and mean estimates derived from news accounts or, where possible, direct evidence from G8 officials.

a. Number of media representatives who successfully completed the accreditation process and had credentials available to them.

b. Number of media representatives who picked up their credentials when they arrived to cover the Summit.

c. Includes those at the Summit and the International Media Centre sites, and those taking part in protests and demonstrations and educational forums such as The Other Economic Summit.

d. Includes those for minor charges such as blocking a highway or providing a false name.

Populaire (UMP) received only 16 percent, Germany's ruling Social Democrats 21 percent, and Italy's ruling Forza Italia 20–23 percent of the vote.

Despite their poor standing back home, the leaders at Sea Island largely resisted the temptation to play to their domestic audiences by garnering quick popularity at the expense of their G8 colleagues abroad. While divisions did emerge over how much a soon-to-be sovereign Iraq would receive in debt relief from the Paris Club and security support from NATO, these questions were left for different forums to deal with at a later time. The most discordant note came, safely, from Chirac, who emphasised at the end that the concluding Chair's Statement did not reflect his views, without specifying in what manner.

As the leaders left Sea Island, it remained unclear how large the legacy of the Summit's centrepiece — Bush's bold beginning on Middle East democratisation — would be. Blair reiterated that he would focus his 2005 G8 Summit on Africa and climate change, without adding the Middle East to the list. He implied that he would again invite outsiders, without suggesting the Middle East leaders themselves would return. The onus thus shifted to the American effort to use vigorously the second, post–Sea Island Summit half of their year as host to get as much as possible done. Beyond that, a strong surge forward would wait until it was clear who would be the U.S. president in 2005, and how those in the Middle East would decide to proceed.

Conclusion

To the surprise of many, amid the continuing divisions among G8 members over America's spring 2003 invasion of Iraq, the apparently unilateralist American president George Bush hosted a successful G8 summit at Sea Island in June 2004. Indeed, by some measures, it was the highest performing G8 summit of all time. Bush delivered a Sea Island success in large part because America had now become vulnerable to the fused threats of energy scarcity and terrorism, was bogged down in Iraq, and needed a big bold initiative to bring democratic development to the Middle East in response. To get this initiative from his sceptical allies, Bush's America adjusted to give full summit attention and action to their priorities, notably democratic development in Africa, the peace process in the Middle East, and the transfer of power in Iraq to the UN and the Iraqis themselves.

Bush was able to do on the road to and at Sea Island because the G8 summit system was available to force and facilitate the conversion of these outside pressures into a balanced, expansive package deal. Mutual accommodation was made much easier by the momentum of 30 years of successful summitry, the beginning of Franco-American accommodation at Evian in 2003, four years of summit familiarity among the Sea Island leaders, and the G8's 21st-century legacy of success on Africa, WMD proliferation, and terrorism, whatever the ongoing strains over the war in Iraq. Also important was the failure of the multilateral UN organisations to cope with America's new vulnerabilities, the close fit between the G8's core mission, and Bush's chosen priority of democratically developing the Middle East, as well as his need to show voters that he could work with his allies to forward his vision in the Middle East.

Without the G8, George Bush and the world would have been left with only the UN system, where the mutual veto of the great powers of 1945 on the Security Council routinely bred distrust, division, and collective inaction over Iraq, Iran, the Middle East, and beyond. They would have been forced to rely on unilateral American leadership in forming ad hoc coalitions of the willing to meet each particular threat as it arose. By spring 2004, it was evident that this formula was failing, in Iraq as well as in response to many of the other challenges America faced. Fortunately, the G8 was readily available to allow George Bush, as its host, to use it for his Middle East vision, to accommodate and adopt his allies' priorities, to show his voters that he could lead the democratic community, and to forward freedom through democratic development in the world as a whole.

References

Antholis, William (2001). 'Pragmatic Engagement or Photo Op: What Will the G8 Become?' *Washington Quarterly* vol. 24, no. 3, pp. 213–226.

Atwood, J. Brian, Robert S. Browne, and Princeton Lyman (2004). 'Freedom, Prosperity, and Security: The G8 Partnership with Africa, Sea Island 2004 and Beyond'. May. Council on Foreign Relations, New York.

Baliamoune, Mina (2000). 'Economics of Summitry: An Emprical Assessment of the Economic Effects of Summits'. *Empirica* vol. 27, pp. 295–315.

Bayne, Nicholas (2000). *Hanging In There: The G7 and G8 Summit in Maturity and Renewal*. Ashgate, Aldershot.

Bergsten, C. Fred and C. Randall Henning (1996). *Global Economic Leadership and the Group of Seven*. Institute for International Economics, Washington DC.

Brainerd, Lael (2004). 'Interview'. 6 February. <www.g8.utoronto.ca/oralhistory> (November 2004).

Bush, George W. (2003). 'Remarks by the President at the 20th Anniversary of the National Endowment for Democracy'. <www.whitehouse.gov/news/releases/2003/11/20031106-3.html> (November 2004).

Commission on the Private Sector and Development (2003). 'Unleashing Entrepreneurship: Making Business Work for the Poor'. Report by Paul Martin and Ernesto Zedillo to the United Nations Secretary General. United Nations Development Programme, New York. <www.undp.org/cpsd> (November 2004).

Fauver, Robert (2003). 'Interview'. 13 March. <www.g8.utoronto.ca/oralhistory> (November 2004).

Flynn, Stephen (2004). *America the Vulnerable: How Our Government is Failing to Protect Us from Terrorism*. HarperCollins, New York.

Fowler, Robert (2003). 'Canadian Leadership and the Kananaskis G8 Summit: Toward a Less Self-Centred Policy'. In D. Carment, F. O. Hampson and N. Hillmer, eds., *Canada Among Nations 2003: Coping with the Canadian Colossus*, pp. 219–241. Oxford University Press, Toronto.

Ikenberry, John (1988). 'Market Solutions for State Problems: The International and Domestic Politics of American Oil Decontrol'. *International Organization* vol. 42, no. 1, pp. 151–177.

Ikenberry, John (1993). 'Salvaging the G7'. *Foreign Affairs* vol. 72 (Spring), pp. 132–139.

Ikenberry, John (1998/99). 'Institutions, Strategic Restraint, and the Persistence of American Postwar Order'. *International Security* vol. 23 (Winter), pp. 43–78.

Ikenberry, John (2001). *After Victory: Institutions, Strategic Restraint, and the Rebuilding of Order after Major Wars*. Princeton University Press, Princeton.

Keohane, Robert O. and Joseph S. Nye (1989). *Power and Interdependence*. 2nd ed. HarperCollins, New York.

Kirton, John J. (2003). 'After Westphalia: Security and Freedom in the G8's Global Governance'. In T. Noetzel and M. Lerch, eds., *Security and Freedom: Foreign Policy, Domestic Politics, and Political Theory Perspectives*. Nomos, Baden-Baden.

Kirton, John J. (2004). 'Explaining G8 Effectiveness: A Concert of Vulnerable Equals in a Globalizing World'. Paper prepared for the International Studies Association conference. Montreal, 17–20 March. <www.g8.utoronto.ca/scholar/kirton2004/kirton_isa_040304.pdf> (November 2004).

Kirton, John J. and Radoslava Stefanova (2004). *The G8, The United Nations, and Conflict Prevention*. Ashgate, Aldershot.

Kokotsis, Eleanore (1999). *Keeping International Commitments: Compliance, Credibility, and the G7, 1988–1995*. Garland, New York.

Lewis, Flora (1991–92). 'The G7 1/2 Directorate'. *Foreign Policy* no. 85, p. 25–40.

Morse, Edward and James Richard (2002). 'The Battle for Energy Dominance'. *Foreign Affairs* vol. 81, no. 2, pp. 16–31.

Nau, Henry (2004). 'Interview'. 7 May. <www.g8.utoronto.ca/oralhistory> (November 2004).

Owen, Henry (1997). 'Defending the G7'. *International Economy* vol. 11, no. 1, pp. 30–34.

Putnam, Robert (1994). 'Western Summitry in the 1990s: American Perspectives'. *International Spectator* vol. 29, no. April-June, pp. 81–94.

Putnam, Robert and Nicholas Bayne (1987). *Hanging Together: Co-operation and Conflict in the Seven-Power Summit*. 2nd ed. Sage Publications, London.

Smeyser, W.R. (1993). 'Goodbye, G7'. *Washington Quarterly* Winter, pp. 15–28.

Stephens, Gina (2000). 'The Roots of the New Consensus: The United States and the Transformation of the G8 System'. In J. J. Kirton and J. Takase, eds., *New Directions in Global Political Governance: The G8 and International Order in the Twenty-First Century*, pp. 237–247. Ashgate, Aldershot.

Chapter 4

Russia in the G8: From Sea Island 2004 to Russia 2006

Victoria Panova

In the G8 'club' of the highly developed democratic countries, Russia stands slightly aside. Unlike the other members, it is a newcomer. Unlike the others, the process of its inclusion lasted for more than a decade. Indeed, many still question whether to call the group the G8 or the G7.

Russia's Evolution as a G8 Partner

The gradual development of the G7-Russia partnership began at the end of the 1980s between the former foes in the Cold War — the G7 partners as representatives of the West and the Soviet Union as the pillar of the communist bloc. In 1989, the first and the last Soviet president, Mikhail Gorbachev, sent a letter (labelled by the British foreign secretary as a 'cry for help') to the G7. Two years later, in 1991, Gorbachev was invited to the final part of the London Summit to discuss some of the G7 members' aid programmes to a reforming USSR. After the collapse of the USSR, discussions with the G7 continued with Russia. Starting in 1992, Russia was always invited to the summit as a guest.

At the 1994 Naples Summit, the situation changed somewhat. This time, President Boris Yeltsin was not present as an 'aid beggar', but as an equal partner to discuss world problems during the political part of the Summit. The following year, at the Halifax Summit, the main outcome for Russia was the considerable expansion of the Russia's participation in discussions about economic and global issues, confirming its status as an equal in the G8 political format.

The year 1996 was remarkable for Russia. In Moscow, a special summit, co-chaired by France and Russia, was held on nuclear security, in addition to the traditional G7 Summit in Lyon. Also, as proposed by the Russian Federation, the Lyon Summit was held in three sessions, with the first — devoted to economic issues — as a purely G7 event. The other two sessions, on political and global issues, were held with Russia as an equal partner.

Some experts and politicians consider 1997 the birth of the full-scale G8, with that year's encounter termed the 'Denver Summit of the Eight'. Russia was present virtually throughout the Summit.[1] Others mark the following year's summit in Birmingham as the first full-fledged G8. However, the G7 partners still took time to discuss — just among themselves — questions of economics and finance.

In 1999, at the Cologne Summit, political-security issues dominated the meeting, especially the Kosovo crisis. This summit marked a virtual defeat of the still very weak Russian Federation: it had to give in to the West's scenario for the Balkans. It also showed the importance that Russia attached to its membership in the G8. In recent summits, with Russia getting stronger, there has been a growing and real role for Russia in the G8 process, with compromises being made rather than Russia simply following its partners.

Still, to make the 1999 Cologne Summit sound, and to press for Russia's vision of its changing international relations, Yeltsin launched a number of wide-ranging initiatives. These included working out a concept of the world for the 21st century by the next summit, a plan for the G8 to consider the issue of legal aspects of the use of force in the international relations and their codification at the United Nations Millennium Summit in New York, and the creation of the Global Control System for the Nonproliferation of Missiles and Missile Technology.

The Okinawa Summit in 2000 and the Genoa Summit in 2001, with Vladimir Putin at the G8 table, both showed Russia's growing involvement in the global affairs, with the country no longer only as a marginal participant, timidly watching its 'elders'. The issue of Soviet and Russian debt restructuring not raised at all (as Putin claimed that Russia would never 'beg' — see 'Russian Leader Promises "No Begging" from IMF' 2000). Indeed, Russia confirmed its donor status for the poorest countries. Other interesting and important efforts concerned the Anti-Ballistic Missile (ABM) Treaty and mediation between the United States and North Korea, although in the end these efforts were fruitless.

However, the 2002 Kananaskis Summit can justifiably be considered the first full G8 summit. Only then was it confirmed that the Russian Federation would host its own summit, in 2006. It was at Kananaskis that a new eight-year cycle was first identified.

Thus, since the beginning of the 1990s much has changed. The Russian economy is booming, and the situation in the country is gradually improving. Among its fellow G8 members, Russia is now one of the best economic performers. In the 21st century, it has enjoyed dynamic economic growth, becoming the G8 leader in terms of growth rates of gross domestic product (GDP). Since the period of reform began, 2003 was one of the country's most successful years. Its macroeconomic accounts have all remained in surplus. The rate of economic growth in Russia is far greater than in many other countries in the world. Most of the economic indicators saw faster growth in 2003, compared to the previous year, and 2003 was marked by a significant GDP growth of 7.3 percent (with 65 percent of growth due to internal factors). This compares to 4.7 percent in 2002. It also compares in 2003 with the U.S. at just 2.9 percent, Japan at 2.6 percent, the Eurozone at only 0.5 percent, and the overall world economy at 3.8 percent. The rate of growth is expected to continue, with the rate for 2004 anticipated to be between 5.2 percent and 7 percent (mostly due to increased oil production and development in services) and 5.6 percent for 2005. Furthermore, the volume of the industrial production sector increased by 7 percent in 2003.

The situation regarding Russian and Soviet-era debt has also changed. In 2003 Russia paid US$15.9 billion of its debt. The process of economic integration of the country into the world community continues. Russia was first taken off the black list of the Financial Action Task Force on Money Laundering (FATF), and then became a member of the task force in 2003. In addition, the Organisation for Economic Co-operation and Development (OECD) has raised the credit rating of Russia to the fourth level from the seventh. Moody's has also put Russia's rate up to investment grade.

Nonetheless, not everything is sunny. There remain problems with dependency on natural resources, as economic growth is still largely a function of hydrocarbon prices. Moreover, reforms are not being implemented as rapidly as desired and needed.

The Goals and Purposes of G8 Membership

Politics is not moved by charity. What always lie behind politics are the geopolitical interests of any particular actor. Thus both the G7 and Russia had their own politically and economically justified interests for Russia's participation. Those reasons and ends have changed over the time.[2]

In the beginning of the 1990s, Russia was very weak. It was necessary to find the means to accomplish the reforms required to make Russia into a market economy, to minimise the negative effects of very rapid and not thought-through process of price liberalisation, and to stabilise the situation in the social sphere. An abrupt and significant deterioration in the quality of life for the majority of the population could have brought severe political problems.

Besides, being the successor of the Soviet Union and thus responsible for all the Soviet-era debts, Russia was in great need of foreign credit. The G7 members are the most influential in this regard due to their economic weight in the World Bank and the International Monetary Fund (IMF). Also, because the G7 countries were also the main players in the Paris and London Clubs, dialogue with the G7 could help to restructure Russia's debt.

The collapse of the communist bloc brought about still another problem. Not only did the military and security organisation of the Warsaw Pact disappear, but the Council for Mutual Economic Assistance (COMECON) was also destroyed. Building the new economy and the country's very survival demanded improved trade conditions with the rest of the world, primarily with the rich industrialised countries of the West. Dismantling the discriminatory trade barriers could have been reached only with the help and consent of the main players in the General Agreement on Tariffs and Trade (GATT). These problems remain with the successor to the GATT — the World Trade Organization (WTO). Russia has also not yet joined the OECD.

It has also been important for Russia to find its new place in the world, in terms both of geopolitics and of its psychological character. Losing superpower status abruptly is a very painful process. Thus membership in an elite club has helped Russia take its place in the international hierarchy and not feel as an outsider, tempted to seek revenge.

Mutual Benefits

Further Integration into the World Economy

As Russia integrates further into the world economy, its goals are bound to change. The country is no longer in dire need of foreign credits or debt restructuring. Indeed, at the 2000 Okinawa Summit Putin pleasantly surprised his counterparts by not even mentioning the topic. Today, according to World Bank president James Wolfensohn, friendship between Russia and his institution has matured since 'today all the programs are worked out together' (Russian National Internet Channel 2004a, 2004b). The World Bank has approved 53 credit projects for Russia for a total US$13.4 billion, but the Russian Federation has used only US$8.4 billion (Putin 2004).

Russian and the IMF used to co-operate on the basis of co-ordinated programmes, according to which financial aid was granted by the IMF in turn for certain macroeconomic measures being taken. Since 1992, Russia has used up those resources eight times, with the total sum coming to US$22 billion. Between 2000 and 2004, the country did not turn to the IMF for credits. Its debt had fallen to US$6.335 billion by 2003. It paid US$4.3 billion in 2001, US$1.6 billion in 2002, and US$2.1 billion in 2003.

One of the priority issues continued to be the need to find an acceptable resolution to Russia's debt problems, an issue that no longer exists. In 2003, the total debt to the Paris Club comprised US$43.6 billion (with about US$38 billion being the Soviet part of the debt). Talks about a possible debt reduction in return for investments were held with Germany, Italy, and Spain.

Russia's G8 membership allows it to create necessary conditions for implementing economic reforms at home. During the period of co-operation, Russia managed — thanks to help from its G7 partners — to restructure a total of approximately US$70 billion of its foreign debt. Furthermore, as a result of being in the G8, Russia promotes and raises its own credibility within the world business community. It is not surprising that after the decision was taken in Kananaskis to allow Russia to host the summit in 2006, the country's credit rating rose, and Russian business access to foreign financing eased. The decision also stimulated an increase in foreign investments into the Russian economy (although this was shattered after the Yukos-Khodorkovsky affair in 2004). The G7 countries take about one third of Russian exports and provide more than half of Russia's inward direct foreign investment (FDI).

Although G8 membership helps create better conditions for stronger economic growth and preserving economic stability, Russia is also working closely with its G8 partners to join some of the world organisations such as the WTO and the OECD. Official sources claim that the process of Russian accession to the WTO is in its final stages; the process of bringing Russian internal law into accordance with WTO norms is also almost complete. An agreement was reached with the European Union on 21 May 2004, which marked a considerable move forward in the negotiations. Analogous agreements were signed with Kyrgyzstan, New Zealand, Hungary, the Czech Republic, Bulgaria, and Israel. Talks with Japan and South Korea will conclude soon, and a consensus with the United States and China is also likely possible. Still, not all the problems have been solved. Even if the official prognosis is true, WTO membership with the usual admission procedures is not likely before 2007.

This does not seem to pose a real problem for Russia. First of all, it is a matter of honour for the other G8 partners as well for Russia to it be qualified for the status of hosting in 2006, since it was the G8 who agreed to manage the hosting cycle that way at Kananaskis in 2002. Not being a structured institution with a charter and strict rules, the G8 does not necessarily demand that all its members be part of all the world economic organisations (although this is highly desirable).

The OECD is another body in which Russia is not yet a member. The OECD has started paying more attention to Russia. It is even interested now in acquiring Russian experience in such fields as steel production, navigation and ship-building, and scientific research.

Co-operation dates back to 1992, when the first programme of co-operation between the Russian Federation and the OECD came into being. Russia announced its intention to join the OECD at the G7 Halifax Summit in 1995, and issued an official request in May 1996. In December, the OECD claimed that Russia joining it was an 'aim shared by the OECD' (State University Higher School of Economics 2004). In May 1997 in Paris, a protocol to establish the committee on ties between Russia and OECD was signed, along with regular high-level meetings between the representatives of the Russian Federation and the OECD.

Today Russia has the status of the observer in ten OECD commissions and four separate working groups. The current issue is Russia's accession to the OECD Anti-Bribery Convention in fighting corruption among foreign officials when conducting international commercial deal, and to the Declaration on International Investment and Multinational Enterprises.

Elimination of Poverty and Sustainable Development

Lately, Russia is eager to use its political potential, but it is one of the largest donor countries among the G8. Between 1998 and 2004, Russia wrote off US$35 billion of debt for the poorest countries, with US$5.5 billion falling under the category of official development assistance (ODA). That brings Russia to first place in relation to GDP and, in absolute figures, third place after Japan and France.[3] Special attention is given to Africa, especially to the Heavily Indebted Poor Countries (HIPC) Initiative. Between 1998 and 2002, Russia wrote off the debt to African countries for a total sum of US$11.2 billion, including US$3.4 billion in 2002. Considerable sums are also directed to the HIPC Trust Fund.

Bilateral intergovernmental agreements on debt management have recently been signed with several countries. African countries also enjoy trade preferences. Russian law provides that goods that are the traditional export of the least developed countries, including African countries, are not taxed. Such goods do not fall under quantity import restrictions and do not suffer antidumping, compensating, or special protective measures. More than 80 percent of Russian imports from Africa are under the preferential regime.

The Russian Federation is rendering significant assistance in the spheres of training of specialists and health. More then 700 Russian state stipends are given to African states. Russian teachers and doctors work on the African continent.

Russia has donated US$20 million to the Global Fund to Fight AIDS, Tuberculosis, and Malaria and US$11 million to the World Food Programme (WFP). In 2003, Russia contributed US$4 million to the World Health Organization (WHO) to eliminate polio in the world.

During the period of 2000–03, Russia offered humanitarian aid to mitigate the consequences of natural calamities to the populations of Algeria, Angola, Mozambique, Sudan, Ethiopia, and Eritrea. Voluntary contributions were made into the budget of the UN's High Commissioner for Refugees for financing humanitarian operations in Africa.

At the 2004 Sea Island Summit, the HIPC Initiative — due to end that year — was extended until 31 December 2006.[4] This announcement received a mixed response: official governmental bodies along with the African leaders present at Sea Island praised the results (not surprisingly, so as not to risk ending co-operation with rich countries), while numerous nongovernmental organisations (NGOs) viewed it as yet another hypocritical claim that led nowhere. Many hoped for the G8 to forgive the poorest countries' debts completely. Such a critical view has some weight, because if, for example, the U..S. spends considerable sums on the war in Iraq but continues to spend and even to ask other G7 members to write off the debt of an oil-rich but war-ridden country that has been devastated by the U.S. invasion, why not spend much smaller sums to forgive African debt?

But, however, that might not be the case. It would not be enough just to forget about the current debts. The G8 is taking other indispensable steps to help the marginalised continent, although it may not be moving fast enough. These steps relate to complex measures that involve financial and technical assistance in promoting higher standards of health, education, nutrition, and, of course, good governance. The actions of the G8 countries might in fact be slow enough, since Africa presents no immediate danger to them. Although it is an unstable, conflict-ridden continent suffering an HIV/AIDS pandemic, it poses a far less real threat to the security and high standards of living in the G8 and other Western countries than the one presented, for example, by the Middle East.

Global Security Sphere

Indeed, the security issue today dominates almost any gathering in the international arena. One of the greatest challenges to security remains the problem of the nonproliferation and elimination of weapons of mass destruction (WMD). The Global Partnership against the Spread of Weapons and Materials of Mass Destruction, which was launched at the 2002 Kananaskis Summit, allows some additional very important possibilities (if it is actually complied with). Russia's vital interests lie with the successful completion of the programme. The country has been quite active in dealing with the elimination of chemical weapons.

In 2002, when it was created, the Global Partnership committed to deliver up to US$20 billion over ten years, with the U.S. responsible for half of the sum and other half divided among the partners (US$750 million from the United Kingdom, US$650 million from Canada, US$200 million from Japan, €1.5 billion from Germany, €1 billion from Italy, €750 million from France, and €1 billion from the EU). The goal is to secure disarmament, nonproliferation, the fight against international terrorism, and nuclear security in the territories of the former USSR. However, the total claimed to be committed by the G7 comes only to US$15.85 billion. With Russia's US$2 billion, the total is US$17.85 billion, still under the US$20 billion goal. Of course, no legally binding documents were issued at the Kananaskis Summit. Perhaps it does not matter what sum was named, because the commitment will not honoured. Indeed, the Global Partnership has so far not been working properly.

Russia claims to have a vital interest in the programme because it concerns co-operation for eliminating chemical weapons and dismantling the decommissioned atomic submarines of the former Soviet fleet (which involves removing the highly radioactive reactor compartment and hermetically sealing it to prevent leakage). Other Global Partnership priorities include the use of the excessive fissile materials and employment of former weapons scientists.

The problem of implementing the Global Partnership has been related to the focus of Russian leadership from the very start. In accordance with the Kananaskis obligations, a co-ordinating mechanism was set up with the Russian prime minister at its head. It was decided that over ten years, Russia would invariably finance the Global Partnership programmes with no less than US$2 billion. In the previous financial year, more than US$204 million was directed to these efforts.

At the 2003 Evian Summit, the G8 Action Plan on Global Partnership was adopted. It built on the success of the May 2003 signing of the Multilateral Nuclear Environmental Programme (MNEPR), which was ratified in Russia in December 2003.

On the official level, things seem to be moving ahead substantially. During Putin's visits to Britain and Italy in 2003, intergovernmental agreements on implementing the Global Partnership were concluded (in June there was an additional agreement with Great Britain on co-operation in the nuclear sphere, and in November a framework intergovernmental agreement on the use of atomic submarines and the elimination of chemical weapons was reached with Italy). Both are expected to be ratified. And in October 2003, two inter-ministerial agreements were signed with Germany.

The Global Partnership is also spreading to the other non-G8 countries. Thus, according to an agreement reached in January 2004, Switzerland will deliver SF15 million to help implement programmes on eliminating Russian chemical weapons. Work continues on bilateral agreements with Canada and France.

Nonetheless, huge problems remain. More than a half of all the stockpiled fissile material is not protected by the necessary security measures, which leaves the door open for terrorists to acquire materials that can be used for making nuclear weapons. Despite all the agreements that have been signed, the G8 countries are often slow to deliver the promised sums. A serious gap remains between those sums and the monies actually destined for the Global Partnership ends. Furthermore, to take one example, Japan — which has the smallest share in the Global Partnership — has neglected to comply even with that commitment.

Prior to the Sea Island Summit, many experts claimed the Global Partnership to be a high priority, but with the Americans set on their problems in Iraq and Middle East not enough attention was paid to it. As a result, the only initiative in this sphere was one that froze the transfer of enrichment and reprocessing technology to Iran, North Korea, and other non-nuclear countries for one year. The issue of performance on the previous Global Partnership pledges was simply dropped.

With regard to Iran, Russia has a dubious stand. Joining its G7 partners in their concerns about Iran and North Korea, it still disagrees with them on Iran. Plans remain in place to construct an atomic station in Bushehr, which would be done under the control of the International Atomic Energy Agency (IAEA) with the waste fuel being sent back to Russia.[5] To be more specific, Russia suggested that Iran sign and implement the provisions of an additional protocol prior to ratification of the agreement. The protocol would allow expanded inspections on short notice, stop any activities to enrich uranium, and provide comprehensive information to the IAEA. Russia did reach an agreement with Iran that all fuel spent would be sent back to Russia for reprocessing and storage, which freed Moscow-Tehran relations from previous diversions, and in fact there might be a possibility of building a second reactor in Bushehr.

On the issue of North Korea, at Sea Island — unlike at the 2000 Okinawa Summit — Russia left the role of mediator between the Kim Jong Il and Bush regimes to Japanese prime minister Junichiro Koizumi. Koizumi had visited the North Korean leader just prior to the Summit. If Putin's achievement in talks with Kim had influenced the Okinawa Summit and brought the Russian president to the front lines, in 2004 there were no such breakthroughs. On the contrary, North Korea responded fiercely, accusing the G8 of conspiring against it to create a situation like the one with Iraq, which eventually provided them 'with a strong catalyst and ample justification for strengthening' their self-defensive nuclear deterrent (Choe 2004).

That brings to light still another problem with the way the G8 functions. Sometimes statements issued by the leaders bring about the opposite results than those expected. At times, not enough preparatory diplomatic work and analysis are done to address certain problematic issues, sparking defiance instead of the conciliatory and cooperation-based approach that is needed.

Another contradiction lies with the double-edged sword of open relations with the media. The G8 cannot possibly stay behind closed doors, or its meetings will be considered by the rest of the world to be even more of a conspiracy among the rich. Such accusations are often heard now, but would multiply considerably if media coverage were reduced. However, with true transparency, the leaders cannot engage in the truly sincere, open discussions with each other because any discord or difference in views would be presented by the media as a major conflict or even collapse of unity among the industrialised countries. This leads to the necessity of careful wording. Bush's claim at the Sea Island Summit to seek an expanded role for the North Atlantic Treaty Organization (NATO) in Iraq met with a reserved stance on the part of France's Jacques Chirac and, to some extent, Germany's Gerhard Schroeder, which caused the world's media to announce another rift in transatlantic relations — although the divergences might have been not so serious.[6]

The division among the G8 countries over the war in Iraq was considerable in 2003. However, at Genoa in July 2001, much attention was brought to the discord between the U.S. and Europe and Japan on the Kyoto Protocol, after the U.S. dropped the protocol. During the Summit, Chirac demanded changes to the wording of the final communiqué to repair the disagreement. There was also tension about the U.S. attitude toward its National Missile Defense programme. Both of these issues remain important, but they do not by any means indicate the break in unity so often perceived by the media. In 2000, there was much noise about the *Sedov*, the Russian sailing ship that was impounded by France, with the press following every glance between Putin and Chirac. The fact that there was no bilateral meeting on the sidelines of the Okinawa Summit between the two leaders was seen an indication of considerable deterioration in relations on the whole range of issues. Today, by contrast, there is the greatest degree of co-operation and partnership between Russia and France.

Russia was also the last G8 member to join the Proliferation Security Initiative (PSI), an international programme to stamp out the proliferation of WMD, including ballistic missiles. Since Russia is the world's second-largest nuclear power, its participation in the PSI was seen as vital in strengthening enforcement of joint activities such as inspections of ships and aircraft to block the illegal transport of WMD and the transfer of related technologies. There was much doubt that the agreement would be finally reached, since many in Russia believed that it could be abused by America, with the unilateral use of military force against suspicious or unwelcome vessels, which could interfere with Russia's own economic interests (as with the case of co-operation with Iran).[7]

Another very important issue in the fight against international crime and terrorism is money laundering. According to the UN statistics, each year around US$500 billion of assets are legalised in the world, which comprises 8 percent of international trade. This phenomenon endangers not only the stability of the financial systems, but also the national security of states.

On 1 November 2001, the Decree of the President of Russia Number 1263 led to the creation of the Russian Federation Committee on Financial Monitoring. This body is authorised to take measures to counteract money laundering and co-ordinate other federal executive agencies activities in this sphere. One of the priorities of international co-operation on money laundering is to repatriate the capital that has been obtained by criminal means and taken abroad illegally. To this end, on 9 December 2003 Russia signed the Convention of the United Nations against Corruption in Merida, Mexico.

The G8 is advancing the working out of principles of finding, arresting, and confiscating illegally obtained money. These principles will likely contribute significantly to improving the legal assistance mechanisms in this sphere.

The FATF is the key element of cutting terrorist networks of financing. It is a leading organisation in the fight against money laundering, and it is working on establishing and improving such standards and their implementation on the regional and global levels. The first signs of progress were evident when Moscow was taken off the FATF's black list. Russia has been working continuously with the task force, but was admitted as a member only recently. It took part as a full member in the October 2003 session.

Ecological Threat

Ecological issues are traditionally very contentious in Russia. Understanding the seriousness of those problems does not always lead to necessary measures being taken. But there are signs that Russia is not totally neglecting the issue. The World Conference on Climate Change was held in Moscow on the fall of 2003, at the initiative of the Russian President. At the opening session, Putin touched upon the problem of the ratification of Kyoto Protocol, but nothing specific was said at the time. The breakthrough in this issue came later, during the 2003 Russia-EU Summit in Moscow, when it was agreed that Russia would finally ratify it. Indeed, ratification happened in the Duma on 22 October 2004 and on 27 October in the upper chamber of the Parliament, and on 4 November Putin signed the protocol.[8]

But what is also important in terms of Russia contributing to resolving the problem is that due to structural changes in the Russian economy in the early 1990s, as well as the closure of many plants, greenhouse gas emissions have been reduced by 32 percent. This decrease has led to Russia compensating for almost 40 percent of greenhouse gas emission growth in other countries since 1990.

Over the years, the Kyoto Protocol has caused many heated discussions in Russia, among both its proponents and its adversaries, and it continues to do so. The critics believe that ratification will bring too many economic disadvantages to the country (with Andrei Illarionov, former sherpa and now economic advisor to the Russian President, the most consistent representative of the group). First of all, it will freeze economic growth, because investments will be diverted to the construction of purification facilities, which is not currently a priority in Russia. Moreover, the Kyoto Protocol will contribute to reduced hydrocarbon prices, which is one of the country's staple exports.

Kyoto supporters argue that the norms were fixed on the 1990s level, when Russian industries were much more active, so there is now a considerable gap to fill before Russia reaches its limit. One positive possible outcome is also the implementation of ecological problems in its framework that would attract foreign investment. For example, at least 70 small and medium-sized projects could be launched that could attract financing of approximatethe ly €580 million to €850 million. Other Kyoto-related investments could be directed to utilisation of the oil and gas and the reduction of losses that occur during methane transportation.

The Sea Island Summit, despite previous demands of the European members, barely discussed the environment, which is not surprising since the U.S. is the biggest opponent to the Kyoto Protocol. The American stance on Kyoto did not become any softer after it refused to sign. Europeans are traditionally the most avid proponents of environmental issues, and Britain's Tony Blair is sure to emphasise this when the UK hosts the 2005 Gleneagles Summit.

Why the G8 Is Better than the G7

Although Russia still does not have equal status with its G8 partners, there nonetheless exist very important reasons for all the members of the group to be together. Today, it is not Russia that is most interested in the G8 membership; the other G8 members are all equally interested in Russia's participation. There are several reasons for this. In recent years, globalisation has brought enormous risks and dangers, along with benefits. It is all but clear that all the major countries, especially the G8 members, are interested in solving all those problems together. No one can argue today that the goals of building a collective security system, achieving sustainable growth in the world economy, eradicating poverty, preventing the proliferation of WMD, managing conflict, mitigating ecological problems, and fighting international terrorism, crime, and drugs — and so on — can be achieved without Russia. Why is that? What follows is a brief list of the main reasons why Russia is a vital component of the G8 concert.

- The Russian Federation occupies a very important geopolitical position. It still controls the heartland due to historical, economic, and political reasons, and exerts the greatest influence on its neighbours in the Commonwealth of Independent States (CIS) — and mediates conflicts in the territory as well.

- It is the world's second-largest nuclear power, and is thus an important ally in the issues of nonproliferation and disarmament.
- It has huge economic potential, not only for further growth for the country itself but also for the G7 economies.
- It has ancient and close connections with many developing countries, from the USSR years when it was one of the world's largest donors and creditors, from which it still derives much authority (that is, the sums that Russia writes off are the largest among the G8 members).
- It is a huge exporter of oil and gas, which are essential during the current unstable situation in the Middle East, even with conquered, but not totally controlled Iraq; it has many other resources, such as minerals, timber, and water.
- It offers a balance (in certain situations) in the relations between the U.S. and Europe (since Western solidarity vanished after the end of the Cold War).
- It is closer to the instability arc than all the other G8 members, and has experience in waging anti-terrorist operations (which is especially important today not only for the U.S., but for European countries and Japan as well, as the developed world as a whole is under global terrorist threat). It is an important element in the international fight against drugs (being one of the most convenient routes for drug traffickers, especially from Afghanistan and other countries in the region).

Looking Toward the 2006 Summit

Russia's year as host in 2006 is fast approaching. All its major efforts will be mostly concentrated on preparing for this event and showing Russia's eagerness to do so at the expected level, to prove that it is ready for full membership and is no different from the rest of its G8 partners.

By 2006, the situation will likely not have changed much. The Russian Summit will probably be successful. Putin will be politically secure, since it would be mid term between elections, and he will be able to concentrate fully on the Summit (which, according to John Kirton's [2004] concert equality model, is one of the essential elements for a successful summit). The year as host will further help in terms of promoting Russia's national interests in the international arena, deepening the co-operation with the leading countries, and furthering the growth of Russian influence on world problems and affairs.

Other factors contributing to the Summit's success will be Putin's personal diplomatic abilities and a well-selected team of those responsible for the preparations. In 2000, as a newcomer, he managed to impress his partners and even the media, so that several journalists called him the star of the Summit. He fit well into the process. Another example is the 2003 Evian Summit. Just before it began, the celebrations of the 300-year anniversary of St. Petersburg — with leaders attending from all over the world — allowed Putin to be the first to bring together the divided leaders since the start of the Iraqi war, and thus to win the laurels of peacemaker and intermediary within the G8.

Since the social and economic situation in Russia is improving, no major economic or financial crisis is likely to happen today. Russia has been integrating successfully into the world's economic, financial, and trade infrastructures. Of course, some challenges remain, such as its WTO membership, which is not likely to happen by the Gleneagles Summit.

As for Russia's priorities for the G8 agenda, unless the world situation changes drastically due to some cataclysm or shock, those issues are not likely to differ much from the usual G8 agenda. Russia has a good record in helping the poor countries, so the traditional G8 topics of sustaining global growth and eradicating poverty will remain, with Africa and the Middle East at the top of the list.

Another priority topic should be security, especially with regard to WMD nonproliferation, the fight against international terrorism, and conflict management, with an emphasis on the Balkans and broader Middle East because of their neighbouring and vital strategic position for Russia. These issues connect well with the above-mentioned topics, as an integral part of the programmes for problematic conflict-ridden regions.

Russia is likely to follow the model of the majority of the G8 partners and arrange meetings prior to or after the 2006 Summit with the heads of other countries, such as the G8 partners on the Africa Action Plan, or major developing countries such as China and India, with the difference of inviting as well — unlike other G7 countries — the CIS heads.

Conclusion

Times have changed. Today, Russia's role and purpose in the G8, as well as the attitude of the other member countries toward it, are very different from what they were in the early 1990s. Russia may not yet be fully integrated into the world economic system, but it already stands firmly on its own feet, re-emerging as a strong democratic state and an equal player in the club.

The G8 is better equipped to respond well to the current world problems then the G7 was, because today no serious global problem can be solved without Russia. Moscow can now use its political, economic, military, and psychological potential to contribute to improving the situation in all the parts of the world that the G8 is concerned with.

When Russia hosts the G8 summit in 2006, it promises to be successful, with the traditional G8 topics such as development and security issues on the agenda. Moscow will probably follow the format first tried in Okinawa in 2000, with additional meetings with the leaders of other countries and, possibly, civil society representatives.

Notes

1. At the Denver Summit, journalists used a new formula to refer to the meeting: 'seven plus one' was replaced with 'eight minus one'.
2. Much has already been said by Western experts on the G7 members' reasons for allowing Russia into the club, with most agreeing that inclusion was purely a political gesture, since Russian economic potential is not comparable to the rest of the group. (According to the classification of the International Monetary Fund [IMF], Russia is in the third group of countries, with GDP per capita being less then US$10 000, and the rest of the G7 in the first group with GDP per capita over US$15 000.) Because this chapter intends to present the Russian view, it will not cover the Western perspective, which can be found elsewhere.
3. By the end of 1991, the developing countries' debt to the USSR totalled about US$176 billion, of which $7 billion were given in U.S. dollars with the rest in so-called foreign currency rubles. In 1997, a deal struck with Paris Club meant that all the debt of those countries was counted at the rate of 0.6 ruble per dollar (the official Soviet currency rate), which led some foreign experts to assume the debt was grossly overvalued. But that memorandum also forced Russia to forgive half of its assets (after they were re-evaluated according to the IMF's method of considering the average level of state income, GDP per capita, and other criteria). Thus Russia was forced to write off about US$60 billion when it signed the memorandum with the Paris Club. At that time, more than half of the developing country debt was even then considered to be irretrievable.
4. Other achievements include the intention to work more intensely on developing the HIV/AIDS vaccine, with the U.S. promising US$15 million. The G8 also pledged to halt the cycle of famine in the Horn of Africa by encouraging land tenure, the development of new drought-resistant crops, and credit schemes for small farmers. Also as part of its efforts to help private sector initiatives in the developing world, the G8 committed to cut the costs of remittances made by immigrant workers to their families, which are estimated roughly at US$100 billion annually, twice the ODA given to poor countries. Another commitment is to train and equip 75 000 peacekeepers primarily in Africa, but also globally by 2010, with the U.S. pledging US$660 million.
5. That these plans remain is not surprising considering the significant economic interests in Iran, which add to the necessity to preserve political stability and friendly relations with neighbouring Iraq. The other project that might bring substantial advantages to the country is the provisional north-south transport corridor linking Europe and Asia (which could be an alternative to the Suez Canal), which is likely to start in Mumbai across the Arabian Sea to the Iranian port of Bandar Abbas, by rail through Iran to the Caspian Sea, through Azerbaijan to Russia and then to the rest of Northern Europe. The route could be able to handle up to 20 million tonnes of freight a year, which might lead to an annual trade turnover of US$10 billion, with Russia and Iran the main beneficiaries.
6. Another example occurred in 2003 when Russia, without much consultation with its G7 partners, advertised its hosting of the G8 Summit. Although this did not signal a rift or conflict of interest within the G8, it was very embarrassing for Moscow and caused some ironic comments by G7 officials and media.
7. Russia finally decided to join the initiative for two purposes. One is because of shared threats and necessity to fight them, as proclaimed everywhere; the other one is to control and limit the activities of the U.S. and the other PSI signatories in this field. Nonetheless, Russia has certain reservations. First of all, the programme is seen as a supplement to existing nonproliferation mechanisms, rather than a replacement. Russia is also inclined to act on the PSI in accordance with international and national laws, as a part of the global strategy to

strengthen international nonproliferation regimes. It was also stressed that being part of the PSI can in no way hamper legal economic and technical co-operation among the states.

8. Russia decided the fate of the Kyoto Protocol, since the agreement could only come into force 90 days after Russia signed it. The protocol unites 127 countries, with only the U.S. and Australia having dropped it. Thus Russian participation predetermined whether the whole UN system would work or whether the U.S. refusal would bury all the international efforts in this area. Some experts believe that Russia's ratification, although lobbied by the Europeans, came unexpectedly for most of the other countries that had signed the protocol, and that it will cause many problems for them — after it became evident they would have to abide by its norms (with no exception for Europe and Japan).

References

Choe, Sang-Hun (2004). 'North Korea Threatens to Strengthen Nuclear Development after G8 Statement'. Associated Press, 12 June.

Kirton, John J. (2004). 'Explaining G8 Effectiveness: A Concert of Vulnerable Equals in a Globalizing World'. Paper prepared for the International Studies Association conference. Montreal, 17–20 March. <www.g8.utoronto.ca/scholar/kirton2004/kirton_isa_040304.pdf> (November 2004).

Putin, Vladimir (2004). 'Speech of Vladimir Putin at a Meeting with James Wolfensohn'. 20 January, Novo-Ogaryovo. <www.worldbank.org.ru/ECA/Russia.nsf/0/BFAB4D0DA 09470D4C3256E240038E659> (November 2004).

'Russian Leader Promises "No Begging" from IMF' (2000). 7 February. Russian Public TV (BBC Monitoring).

Russian National Internet Channel (2004a). 'James Wolfensohn: Vsemirny bank I Rissiya stali zrelymi druziami (James Wolfensohn: World Bank and Russia Are Mature Friends)'. 20 January. <www.rfn.ru/cnews.html?id=14802&tid=1503&sid=4> (November 2004).

Russian National Internet Channel (2004b). 'Rossiya ispol'zovala lish chast' kreditov Vsemirnogo banka (Russia Used Only a Part of World Bank Credits)'. 20 January. <www.rfn.ru/cnews.html?id=14806&tid=1503&sid=4> (November 2004).

State University Higher School of Economics (2004). 'Organizatsia ekonomicheskogo sotrudnichestva i razvitia (Organisation for Economic Co-operation and Development)'. Moscow. <www.hse.ru/science/isiez/texts/oesr.doc> (November 2004).

Chapter 5

The G8 in a Globalising World: Does the United States Need the G8?

Bernhard May[1]

In today's globalising world, nation-states must co-operate in order to fulfil their three main tasks: to protect their people, to produce wealth, and to guarantee the freedom of their people. Today, all countries face new security challenges, and even the most powerful nation-state cannot protect its people alone. The challenge of international terrorism can be dealt with successfully only when countries co-operate. This is also true for a long list of global challenges such as climate change, poverty, and HIV/AIDS, and security challenges such as the proliferation of weapons of mass destruction (WMD). No country, not even the superpower United States, is powerful enough to fight these challenges alone. What is needed in today's globalising world is good global governance. The annual G8 summit is an important event in respect to improving global governance — and, therefore, the G8 is more important than ever.

However, critics of the annual G8 summit argue that the G8 is obsolete and should be abolished. There has always been strong criticism of the G8, especially with regard to the question of legitimacy as well as the question of taxpayers' money wasted on an overblown photo opportunity for a few heads of state and government. This has been the position voiced by nongovernmental organisations (NGOs) and left-wing groups arguing that a democratic process is needed to legitimise the G8.

But now the criticism is also coming from American critics arguing that in today's world the U.S. no longer needs the G8 to co-ordinate national policies among the G8 countries. The question, therefore, is: Does the U.S. still need the G8?

This chapter argues that the U.S. needs the G8 more than ever. This same is true for all G8 countries. Indeed, the G8 is more important in global affairs as well. To support these claims, this chapter first briefly reviews the history of the G8 summit. Second, it evaluates the question of legitimacy of the G8. Third, it discusses why the U.S. needs the G8 as well as the importance of the G8 in today's globalising world. Fourth, it discusses some proposals to change the G8 to a G2 or leaders-level G20 (L20). Fifth, it concludes by arguing that the United States needs the G8 very much — as do all the other G8 countries. The Sea Island Summit in June 2004 is a case in point: even though the summit was not the kind of success many observers would have liked to see, neither was it the total failure that many critics expected.

The G8 Summit: Continuity and Change

The first energy crisis in 1973/74 and the global recession it caused convinced academics as well as politicians that closer economic, financial, and political co-operation of the Western nations would be needed. This was the time when the former German chancellor Helmut Schmidt and French president Valéry Giscard d'Estaing came up with the idea of regular meetings of a group of heads of states and governments. In 1975, the first summit took place at the castle of Rambouillet outside of Paris, with France, Germany, Italy, Japan, Great Britain, and the United States attending. At this meeting, the group decided to meet regularly once a year. One year later, Canada joined the group and the world economic summit of the 'Group of Seven' was born (Putnam and Bayne 1987). Since 1977, the European Union has participated in the annual summit.[2] The EU is not a full member of the G7/8 but an observer, and is represented at the summit by the president of the European Commission and the head of government of the country holding the presidency of the European Union.

Russia took part at the G7 summit for the first time in Naples in 1994. Three years later, in 1997, Russia became a member of the group and the G7 thus became the G8. But the G7 still exists in the realm of economic and financial issues. At the Kananaskis Summit in 2002, the G7 leaders decided that Russia will host the summit in 2006, and Russia will therefore become a full member of the group in 2006, participating in all G8 meetings. The split between the G7 and G8 will disappear.

From the beginning, the U.S. was a reluctant supporter of the annual summit. President Gerald Ford and secretary of state Henry Kissinger both distrusted the Franco-German summit proposal and consequently authorised former secretary of state George Shultz to hold preparatory discussions with the Europeans. In September 1975, Shultz first met Chancellor Helmut Schmidt in Bonn, then Prime Minister Harold Wilson in London, and, finally, President Valéry Giscard d'Estaing in Paris. In his memoirs, he later described his recommendations to Ford, recalling: 'My instructions had been to be "neutral" on this new summit idea, but my message to President Ford was that we should take a positive attitude' (Shultz 1993).

It seems as though this recommendation by Shultz would be implemented by almost all American presidents since 1975, with just one exception: Jimmy Carter pushed very hard to make the summit substantial and successful, as could be seen with the Bonn Summit in 1978. The summit at Williamsburg in 1983 could perhaps be seen as another exception, when Ronald Reagan managed to get a substantial declaration on missile defence against new Soviet missiles. But in all the other years, it seems as though George Shultz was sitting at the table reminding the U.S. participants to participate but not to invest political capital to make the summit a success.

Shultz's recommendation seems to be the strongest element of continuity in the U.S. summit policy over the last 30 years. There is an obvious explanation for this position, which could be called 'participate but do not support'. As a superpower, the

U.S. depends less on the other major industrialised countries and is, therefore, less interested in policy co-ordination. Its priority has always been to strengthen bilateral relations, because it would always be the stronger partner and would be able to decide and rule. Summit meetings — and multilateral negotiations — are much more difficult for the U.S. to manage and it is therefore less interested in participating. But in a globalising world, the U.S. must learn to co-operate.

The Structure of G8

The founders of the world economic summit deliberately refrained from institutionalising the meetings in order to avoid the bureaucracy of annual meetings and in order to maintain the informal character of the meetings. Summit meetings are still more about the participants agreeing on common measures toward global challenges than about drawing up and signing international agreements.

The summit as well as the ministerial meetings are prepared by the sherpas and sous-sherpas, the high-ranking governmental and ministerial staff who assemble several times per year. Additionally, expert groups are entrusted with extended studies on specific topics.

The G8 summit has become the tip of a long, detailed, complicated, and labour-intensive process. The actual meeting of the heads of government is preceded by numerous meetings of the sherpas and sous-sherpas as well as by several smaller G8 summit meetings of the foreign ministers, the ministers of finance, as well as the ministers of environmental and development policy. The finance ministers still meet as a G7 group, without Russia — and a G7 meeting takes place just before the G8 summit.

The G8 summit process being increasingly complex, the question arises whether a permanent office should be set up. A G8 office could add continuity and professional efficiency. So far, the idea has always been rejected with the argument that the G8 is an informal group of active states. The heads of the G8 governments accordingly make decisions for their own sake.

Summit Topics

In the 1970s, the main purpose of the summit was to co-ordinate the economic and monetary policies of the major industrialised states. But from the outset, the United States and Germany held fundamentally different views on three central political challenges for co-ordination. At issue was, first, the question of whether economic growth or price stability should take priority; second, the division of the responsibility for economic policy between countries with a trade deficit and those with a trade surplus; and third, the extent to which nations participating in the summit should assume regional or global responsibility. The discussion of these issues remained part of the summit process for many years (Bergsten and Henning 1996).

The summit agenda changed profoundly in the early 1980s, with economic issues replaced by political and security problems relating to the East-West conflict. With the end of the Cold War and the disintegration of the Soviet Union, the role of the G7/8 summit evolved dramatically. The range of topics was widely extended in the 1990s. For instance, subjects such as global energy supply were put on the agenda in the 1970s, but the agenda of the summit meetings became more diverse, including environmental and climate-related topics, international crime, international terrorism, the debt problems of developing countries, the fight against infectious diseases, the nonproliferation of WMD, international monetary and currency crises, the reform of international organisations, the challenges of the digital revolution, as well as the wars in the Balkans, Afghanistan, and Iraq as well as other regional crises. Today, the summit can be seen as two separate events. On the one hand, political issues are discussed. On the other hand, the participants deal with global economic questions. The latter issues are still dealt with only by the G7 members.

Participants at the Summit

The personalities involved in the annual summit meetings have had a decisive influence on individual summits and on the summit process as a whole. In the 1970s, the Franco-German partnership of Giscard and Helmut Schmidt was especially important. From the outset, one of the important goals of the summit process was to build mutual trust between heads of state and government in a situation free of the constraints of protocol inherent in official state visits. But direct contact at the summit did not always improve relationships, and sometimes tensions increased rather than diminished. Personal conflicts dominated a good number of summits, such as those between Schmidt and Jimmy Carter in the 1970s and between Ronald Reagan and François Mitterrand in the 1980s, as well as between Jacques Chirac and Gerhard Schroeder on the one side and George W. Bush on the other in more recent summits.

The summit process is marked by a great long-term continuity of the participating leaders. Schmidt took part in the first eight summits. Reagan and Bill Clinton each took part in eight summit meetings as well. Mitterrand participated in a total of 14 summit meetings. The German chancellor Helmut Kohl set a record, participating in 16 summit meetings between 1983 and 1998. From the current G8 participants, the most experienced are Jacques Chirac (since 1995), Tony Blair (since 1997), and Gerhard Schroeder, who first took part at the G8 Summit in Cologne in 1999, when Germany was the host.

In the last 30 years, the summit process has seen profound changes but also considerable continuity. On the one hand, the world economic summits of the 1970s and early 1980s, which focussed on global economic and financial issues, were replaced by G8 summits in the 1990s focussed above all on political and security issues. However, the concept and the structure have not changed, nor has the rationale for the summits.

The Rationale for G8 and the Democracy Deficit

The rationale for establishing the world economic summits in the 1970s was the recognition by politicians that the global economic and financial crises in the early 1970s would demand a new and more flexible forum to co-ordinate policies among the important countries of the world, along with the recognition by Schmidt and Giscard that structural changes in international relations would require new forms of co-operation between major industrialised countries.

For Schmidt and Giscard, three main factors were decisive. First, growing interdependence restricted national sovereignty and resulted in conflicts for the government and politicians being blamed by their voters for economic developments caused by international factors that they could not influence (May 2004). The second argument for intensifying international economic co-operation arose from the weakening of the American hegemony. Europe and Japan had evolved to become economic and partially political rivals of the United States, and both were increasingly unwilling to accept American dominance. At the same time, the U.S. grew more reluctant to pursue its costly and unpopular leadership role. The monetary crisis in 1971 and the first energy crisis in 1973 forced the major industrialised states to face these fundamental changes. The summit meetings were intended to help create a new international system.

Another argument has been to establish the summit as an attempt to counter the bureaucratisation of international relations. The existing organisations and mechanisms — such as the Organisation for Economic Co-operation and Development (OECD), the General Agreement on Tariffs and Trade (GATT), the International Energy Agency (IEA), the World Bank, and the International Monetary Fund (IMF) — seemed too bureaucratic. These organisations were run by bureaucrats and had failed to respond to the unfolding crises of the early 1970s. Giscard and Schmidt regarded this a serious shortcoming. For them, the world economic summits were meant to rectify the deficiencies of high-level multilateral economic co-operation.

From its beginning in the 1970s, the G7/8 summit was criticised because of a 'democracy deficit'. At issue is democracy versus efficiency. Schmidt and Giscard wanted to create an informal meeting of a small group of major industrialised countries, with the emphasis on small, informal, and efficient. The G7/8 is an intergovernmental process among democratic governments. In that sense, any democracy deficit of the G7/8 should not be the problem. However, the G7/8 is criticised for being an 'undemocratic global event' because only a few countries participate at the summit, where decisions with global consequences are made that force many countries to adapt, even though they were not involved in the decision making. Behind this criticism lies the United Nations model of 'one country, one vote'. Such a model may guarantee more democracy, but it certainly prevents effective decision making.

The G8 is not an international organisation, in the conventional sense. Unlike the United Nations, it has no mandate. But the G8 plays an increasingly important role in determining and implementing solutions for regional and global problems. This creates tension, because G8 meetings are important for the entire world and not only for the member states. The G8, therefore, is criticised for being a 'world government without legitimacy'. The facts are clear: 839 million people live in the G8 countries, which amounts to 14 percent of the world's population. But the G8 countries account for 68 percent of the global economy (World Bank 2004). There is a profound misperception: the G8 is not a kind of world government, but the G8 is becoming an important actor in terms of global governance.

The G8 in a Globalising World: Does the United States Need the G8?

In the 1970s when the annual summit was established, the Cold War dominated international relations and world politics. In economic terms, the OECD countries had to cope with a system of complex interdependence (Cooper 1968; Keohane and Nye 1977). In such a system, the industrialised countries had to co-operate more efficiently. The answer to this challenge was to establish the world economic summit. For the U.S. as the hegemon in this system, co-ordinating national policies was less important — and, therefore, the U.S. reluctantly supported the annual summit from the beginning.

The situation has changed profoundly for the U.S., at least in terms of the necessity for co-operation. In the today's era of globalisation, countries and continents and people are bound together more than ever before in history. Many people and countries are winners, but there are profound challenges as well. No country is any longer powerful enough to cope with these new challenges alone.

What is the difference to the system of complex interdependence in the 1970s, and what are the consequences for the G8? There are many definitions of globalisation. Robert Keohane and Joseph Nye (2001, 229) define it this way: 'Globalism [is a] state of the world involving networks of interdependence at multicontinental distances.' And globalism can increase or decrease — and they call this process globalisation. For Keohane and Nye, interdependence and globalism are both multidimensional phenomena; they define four equally important forms of globalism: economic, military, environmental, as well as social and cultural globalism.

The U.S. is an important part of this new international system of globalisation. The U.S. is — to put it frankly — both a winner and a loser. The U.S. is a winner because it can enjoy many of the new opportunities this globalising world offers. But the U.S. is also loser for three reasons. The first is that the U.S. depends more on other countries than it ever has before. The second is that the U.S. must co-operate and by doing so must give up some sovereign rights. The third is that the U.S. is faced with new security threats that it cannot cope with alone.

George Bush (2003) put it succinctly in his speech in the German Parliament in May 2002. He stated:

> Our generation faces new and grave threats to liberty, to the safety of our people, and to civilization, itself. We face an aggressive force that glorifies death, that targets the innocent, and seeks the means to matter — murder on a massive scale.
>
> We face the global tragedy of disease and poverty that take uncounted lives and leave whole nations vulnerable to oppression and terror.
>
> We'll face these challenges together. We must face them together. Those who despise human freedom will attack it on every continent ... By being patient, relentless, and resolute, we will defeat the enemies of freedom. ...
>
> By remaining united ... we are meeting modern threats with the greatest resources of wealth and will ever assembled by free nations. Together, Europe and the United States have the creative genius, the economic power, the moral heritage, and the democratic vision to protect our liberty and to advance our cause of peace.

Today's is, indeed, a globalising world with new opportunities, but also with new common challenges. The world community will have to work together to cope with those new challenges and especially to fight the new security threats in the age of globalisation. The most important new security threats are international terrorism, the proliferation of WMD, failing states, regional conflicts, and organised crime. But there are also global environmental problems, the challenges of climate change, poverty, and diseases such as HIV/AIDS and malaria.

All of these problems affect not only individual countries, as Bush put it correctly. And all of them require the major actors in international relations work together more intensely and more efficiently. No country, not even the most powerful United States, can protect its people alone or can fight these new challenges alone. That is a painful learning process, particularly for the United States — and for China or Russia or India or Brazil, for that matter.

The U.S. now faces a paradox: on the one hand, the U.S. is the richest and most powerful country in the world. It is the world's only superpower. On the other hand, not even the U.S. can cope with the new challenges of a globalising world alone — the U.S. must co-operate. Nye (2002) calls it the 'paradox of American power'. The subtitle of his important book offers a succinct summary: 'Why the world's only superpower can't go it alone.' This is a detailed analysis of why the U.S. will have to co-operate more than it has in the past and why the U.S. depends more than ever on its partners. This is, of course, a painful learning process for 'the world's only superpower', but there is no alternative. The neoconservatives in the Bush administration tried to tell the American people that the U.S. would be strong enough to take on any enemy and cope with any challenge alone. They failed miserably — not only in Iraq. The U.S. must now co-operate in order to protect the American people, to take care of American interests, to cope with global challenges, and to produce what is called for and what is needed: good global governance. The G8 is an indispensable element for the U.S. to achieve those goals.

For the U.S., this learning process is much more difficult than for other countries, not only because it is a superpower but also because the U.S. — as Robert Cooper (2003) argues — has yet to decide whether to embrace the post-modern world of interdependence or pursue unilateralism and power politics. It seems as though the U.S. is moving slowly but steadily into accepting the realities of today's globalising world.

This shift in the U.S. policy toward a more co-operative approach and toward becoming a more active supporter of G8 could be witnessed at the Sea Island Summit in June 2004, which was hosted by Bush. The U.S. tried very hard to make this summit a success and to co-operate on important issues with its fellow G8 countries. The Bush administration was quite satisfied with the summit, and Bush (2004) himself called it a very successful summit. In his closing press conference, he stated:

> We just completed a very successful summit. The nations of the G8 are united in our desire to help bring stability and democracy to Iraq. We came together to support reform in the broader Middle East. We pledged to work together to build a more secure, peaceful and prosperous world.

The Sea Island Summit focussed significantly on the situation in the Middle East. Bush was pleased that the G8 nations and Turkey had agreed to support momentum toward greater freedom throughout the region. The G8 established the Partnership for Progress and a Common Future with the Region of the Broader Middle East and North Africa, to work with regional leaders seeking to advance the values of human dignity, freedom, democracy, the rule of law, economic opportunity, and social justice. The G8 also approved the creation of the Forum for the Future to bring together senior government officials from the Middle East and their G8 counterparts along with representatives of business and civil society. The forum provides a venue for exchanging ideas that can help the nations of the Middle East create jobs, increase access to capital, improve literacy and education, protect human rights, and make progress toward democracy.

While Iraq and the broader Middle East dominated the summit, the G8 leaders also reached agreements on issues such as training 75 000 new peacekeepers to patrol war-torn countries over the next five years and co-ordinating efforts to find a vaccine against HIV/AIDS. The G8 agreed to extend by two years the debt relief programme for the world's poorest nations, which had been scheduled to expire at the end of 2004 and to provide for larger amounts of debt forgiveness.

As Vladimir Putin put it after the summit, the leaders at the Sea Island Summit spent 70 percent of their time on political and security issues and only 30 percent on economic issues. This is the striking difference between the G8 summit of today and the world economic summit in the 1970s and early 1980s.

At Sea Island, the leaders did not have enough time to discuss all the important issues on their agenda, not because there were too many, but because, more importantly, the leaders of the G8 also met with invited heads of state and government from several African and Middle East countries. Even though these meetings are significant in terms of bringing peace and stability to the Middle East and North Africa, they shortened the amount of time available for discussion among the G8 leaders.

After the Summit, Bush and other leaders left for Washington to attend the state funeral of former president Ronald Reagan, who had died just before the summit began. Consequently, the U.S. media focussed on his legacy and on his funeral, and not on the Sea Island Summit. For this reason, Sea Island was essentially a non-event in the U.S. But in terms of the substance and the atmosphere at the Summit itself, Sea Island was neither a big success nor a total failure. It was — as was to be expected — a difficult and special summit because of the election campaign in the U.S. as well as the continuing crisis in Iraq and the attendant disagreements between the G8 countries.

But the Sea Island Summit was important insofar as it helped to continue the process begun at the 2003 Evian Summit of bringing the leaders of the G8 countries together and creating confidence among them. Furthermore, Sea Island was successful insofar as the leaders worked out a better understanding of the role the U.S. should play in today's globalising world (Ferguson 2004).

From G8 to G2 or L20?

The G8 should not be abolished. In this era of globalisation, it is more important than ever. But should the G8 be reformed in terms of institutional structure or membership? Should the G8 be replaced by a G2 or a L20? Should the summit be democratised? Or should the summit remain focussed on efficiency and informal meetings among the heads of state and government of such a small group of important countries?

The annual summit has always been criticised either for being exclusive and non-democratic or for being too big and inefficient. The small informal gathering in Rambouillet in 1975 grew over the years into an annual meeting with thousands of journalists watching, and became, as some critics put it, an expensive photo-op for politicians (Antholis 2001).

Four criteria can be used to measure the G8: size, efficiency, democracy, and importance. With respect to efficiency and democracy, from the beginning the participants have supported a small and efficient informal meeting rather than a big UN-type summit. The founding members of the G7 argued against institutionalising the annual meetings to keep them informal. To increase the efficiency, there have been many proposals to create a G8 secretariat or to institutionalise the G8 process. But the G7/8 leaders have always opted for a smaller and informal meeting. Indeed, in the 1990s the G8 summit was cut back so that he leaders meet without their ministers present, and became once more an intimate meeting as it had been in the 1970s, especially after the changes implemented at the Birmingham Summit in 1998.

The second question is about the appropriate size for such an annual meeting. In the 1970s, four countries started the summit process that became the G8, with eight countries plus the EU. Should more countries be included? China is often suggested as a possible new member, for example (to create what is sometimes called the G9).

There are many reasons for inviting China, but at present only democratic countries can participate in the annual meetings. For the first time, however, China participated in the G7 finance ministers meeting on 1 October 2004 in Washington. Still, if democracy is the criterion that prevents China from becoming a full member of the G8, what about India, Mexico, or Brazil? What about South Africa? Should the G8 then be replaced by an L20, a meeting at the leaders level of the G20 finance ministers? Or is the G8 already too big, and a G2 is needed? C. Fred Bergsten and Caio Koch-Weser (2004, 237) propose

> the creation of a new 'G2' consultative mechanism through which the European Union and the United States would manage their own economic (and possibly some security) relations and informally steer the world economy. It would address a growing number of issues through different groups of officials from different ministries on both sides of the Atlantic.

Even so, Bergsten and Koch-Weser argue that 'the G2, in playing its global management role, would be an informal process that would not replace any of the existing institutional mechanisms (including, for example, the G7/8)'.

In that sense, such a G2 would become part of the current G8 and would help to make the G8 more efficient by preparing a transatlantic agenda for the G8 summit and by accepting a transatlantic leadership role within the G8 in terms of global governance.

The world does not need a G2 — it needs a G20 at the leaders level, according to Colin I. Bradford Jr. and Johannes F. Linn (2004a; 2004b). They point out that in the 1970s and 1980s, the G7 comprised the seven biggest economies in the world. Decisions taken by the G7 have been important and sometimes efficient for the member states with regard to economic issues, especially budget, trade, and currency problems. Bradford and Linn argue the world economy has changed fundamentally: the G7 countries are no longer in control. Emerging market economies such as China are much more important, but they are not included in the G8. Critics argue, therefore, that the G8 summit is now less important and less efficient than it was in its first 15 years (see, for example, Bergsten and de Montbrial 2003).

Bradford and Linn suggest the current G8 be replaced with an annual G20 summit of heads of state and government. They recognise, however, the G20 that was established in 1999 by the G7 finance ministers, and focusses on economic and financial issues discussed among the finance ministers and central bank governors of 20 countries. Those countries are nine industrialised countries (the G8 countries plus Australia) and the EU and ten emerging market economies, namely Argentina, Brazil, China, India, Indonesia, South Korea, Mexico, Saudi Arabia, South Africa, and Turkey.

This G20 should be upgraded to replace the current G8 summit of heads of state and government, to form the L20. Such a summit would have an advantage in that the participating group of countries would be much more diverse: there would be the current eight industrialised countries, but the new group would include four countries from Asia, three Islamic countries, three countries from Latin America, as well as one country from Africa. The L20 would once again focus much more on global economic issues.

An L20 would, on the other hand, face the challenge of being less efficient because the decision-making process would be more difficult, and would be less powerful because the group will be bigger but less coherent — and, in the end, this could lead to a less important annual summit. The G8 faces a familiar problem of whether to include more countries and become more inclusive and representative or to continue as a small group and be more efficient and powerful. It seems as if the G8 countries support a double-track approach: on the one hand, they could continue with their annual summit, and, on the other hand, they could continue to invite selected countries to attend the summit, as was done at Sea Island when the leaders from several African countries and Middle East countries met with their G8 counterparts. In that sense, the link between the current G8 and the current G20 will most likely be strengthened in the future — but the G8 will not be enlarged in the coming years.

Conclusion: The Role of the G8 in a Globalising World

Today, most of the countries in the world — with just a few exceptions, such as North Korea — are part of a global system of complex interdependence. Such a system creates benefits for the participants, but there are also costs involved. For example, countries lose sovereignty, inasmuch they no longer control all the decisions and developments within their own territory. A good example — and a painful lesson for many countries — is an external economic shock. Such an external shock creates domestic economic, social, and political problems. A government cannot avoid such an external economic shock, but it is nonetheless held responsible for any negative results. This is the situation in many areas, such as economic, financial, and energy issues that link countries together so they have to work together.

Countries must face global challenges and global threats that no one country can cope with alone. The situation worsened after 11 September 2001, but international terrorism and religious fanaticism existed long before. It is the combination of international terrorism and the proliferation of WMD that has created a new security challenge for the world, especially for the U.S. and the G8 countries. Indeed, there is a long list of global challenges, and more and more of these challenges are put on the agenda of the annual G8 summit — and rightly so. The G8 could and should play a more active role in respect to global governance. The leaders of the G8 must accept their responsibility for global governance.

If the G8 did not already exist, it would have to be established. But what is needed is a more efficient G8, a more active G8 that accepts its role in global governance — and what is needed most is a United States that actively supports the G8 process and accepts the importance of the G8 in today's globalising world.

Notes

1. This chapter was originally prepared as part of a project on 'Backlash against Globalization' supported by the Otto Wolff Foundation in Cologne and the German Marshall Fund of the United States in Washington DC.
2. The EU was created by the Maastricht Treaty in 1992, bringing together the three original organisations of the European Economic Community (EEC), founded in 1957, European Atomic Energy Community (EURATOM), founded in 1957, and the European Coal and Steel Community (ECSC), founded in 1951. Since May 2004, the EU has 25 member states.

References

Antholis, William (2001). 'Pragmatic Engagement or Photo Op: What Will the G8 Become?' *Washington Quarterly* vol. 24, no. 3, pp. 213–226.

Bergsten, C. Fred and Thierry de Montbrial (2003). 'Restoring G8 Leadership of the World Economy: Recommendations for the Evian Summit from the Shadow G8'. Institute for International Economics and Institut Français des Relations Internationales. <www.iie.com/publications/papers/g8-2003.pdf> (November 2004).

Bergsten, C. Fred and C. Randall Henning (1996). *Global Economic Leadership and the Group of Seven*. Institute for International Economics, Washington DC.

Bergsten, C. Fred and Caio Koch-Weser (2004). 'The G2: A New Conceptual Basis and Operating Modality for Transatlantic Economic Relations'. In W. Weidenfeld, C. Koch-Weser, C. F. Bergsten, W. Stützle and H. Hamre, eds., *From Alliance to Coalitions: The Future of Transatlantic Relations*, pp. 237–249. Bertelsman Foundation, Gütersloh.

Bradford Jr., Colin I. and Johannes F. Linn (2004a). 'Global Economic Governance at a Crossroads: Replacing the G7 with the G20'. Brookings Institution Policy Brief 131. <www.brookings.edu/comm/policybriefs/pb131.htm> (November 2004).

Bradford Jr., Colin I. and Johannes F. Linn (2004b). 'Ist die G8 noch zeitgemäß? Plädoyer für eine Reform der "Global Economic Governance" mit einer gestärkten G20'. *Internationale Politik* vol. 7, pp. 90–94.

Bush, George W. (2003). 'President Bush Thanks Germany for Support against Terror'. Remarks to a special session of the German Bundestag, 23 May. Berlin. <www.whitehouse.gov/news/releases/2002/05/20020523-2.html> (November 2004).

Bush, George W. (2004). 'Press Conference of President George Bush after the G8 Summit'. Savannah, GA, 10 June. <www.g8.utoronto.ca/summit/2004seaisland/bush040610.html> (November 2004).

Cooper, Richard N. (1968). *The Economics of Interdependence: Economic Policy in the Atlantic Community*. McGraw-Hill, New York.

Cooper, Robert (2003). *The Breaking of Nations: Order and Chaos in the Twenty-First Century*. Atlantic Monthly Press, New York.

Ferguson, Niall (2004). 'A World without Power'. *Foreign Policy* no. 143, p. 32–40.

Keohane, Robert O. and Joseph S. Nye (1977). *Power and Interdependence: World Politics in Transition*. 1st ed. Little, Brown, Boston.

Keohane, Robert O. and Joseph S. Nye (2001). *Power and Interdependence*. 3rd ed. Longman, New York.

May, Bernhard (2004). 'The World Economic Summits: A Difficult Learning Process'. In J. Detlev, ed., *The United States and Germany in the Era of the Cold War, 1968–1990: A Handbook*. Cambridge University Press, New York.

Nye, Joseph S. (2002). *The Paradox of American Power: Why the World's Only Superpower Can't Go It Alone*. Oxford University Press, New York.

Putnam, Robert and Nicholas Bayne (1987). *Hanging Together: Co-operation and Conflict in the Seven-Power Summit*. 2nd ed. Sage Publications, London.

Shultz, George P. (1993). *Turmoil and Triumph: My Years as Secretary of State*. Scribner's, New York.

World Bank (2004). 'Annual Report 2004'. World Bank, Washington. <www.worldbank.org/annualreport/2004> (November 2004).

PART II:
PROSPERITY AND SECURITY

Chapter 6

Advancing American Security Interests through the G8

Risto E. J. Penttilä

The G8 has a long and proud tradition in arms control, counterterrorism, and regional security. Whether it can advance American interests in these policy areas depends on whether the United States wants to use it as an instrument of foreign policy and whether other member states allow the G8 to be used for this purpose.

After the 11 September 2001 terrorist attacks on Washington and New York, the U.S. had an opportunity to make the G8 a central instrument in the fight against terrorism. It chose not to do so. It turned down an offer by the holder of the rotating presidency to convene an extraordinary summit. This was a mistake. The G8 could have been a pragmatic half-way house between a veto-wielding United Nations Security Council (UNSC) and a fragile 'coalition of the willing'. Since then the U.S. has sought to involve the G8 in the fight against terrorism, in arms control (especially with regard to the nonproliferation of weapons of mass destruction [WMD]), and in regional security (in particular with regard to the Middle East). These efforts have, however, been marred by a mismatch of expectations between the U.S. and the other G8 member states regarding the role of the G8 in these policy areas. The U.S. has seen the G8 mostly as a technical instrument for the co-ordination of efforts among the G8 member states. The rest of the G8 member states — especially Russia and Canada — have sought to make the G8 a forum for policy co-ordination or, at least, a forum for a meaningful policy debate.

The underutilisation of the G8 as a global security instrument flows from several factors. World leaders still see the G8 as an economic instrument and overlook its potential in questions of international peace and security. The Bush administration saw the G8 at least initially as just another international institution to be avoided. The falling out over Iraq prevented member states from finding a common ground. Structurally, a concert of great powers such as the G8 cannot function properly when there is an enormous difference of economic and military power between the hegemon and the second-tier powers.

This chapter asks whether the United States has used the full potential of the G8 in advancing its own interests in counterterrorism, arms control, and regional security. An overview of the U.S.-G8 security-policy relationship provides a mixed answer. While there are cases of the U.S. advancing its security interests through the G8, it seems clear that the G8 has not been utilised to its full potential. This is due partly to the reluctance of the U.S. to use multilateral forums, and partly to policy differences among the G8 members. However, since 2001 the U.S. has drastically changed its attitude about the usefulness of the G8. Immediately after the 11 September terrorist attacks, the U.S. saw the G8 as a narrow instrument in the fight against the financing of terrorism. By the time of the Sea Island Summit in June 2004, the United States was willing to give the G8 a much broader role. It used the summit for policy co-ordination with its allies and for launching major initiatives that were at the heart of U.S. foreign policy.

Concert Governance

The G8 can be seen as a global security concert: an instrument for the joint management of international relations by the most significant powers. Concerts are informal instruments: they 'rely on few informal rules and mainly serve to co-ordinate policy' (Schwegmann 2001, 94). Concert-based models have traditionally emerged — or gained in importance — after major wars. The Concert of Europe emerged after the Napoleonic Wars. There was a short-lived concert after both the first and the second World Wars. The end of the Cold War made it possible for the G8 to emerge as a global concert (see Penttilä 2003).

Concert diplomacy has a number of advantages (as well as some obvious disadvantages) over the UN system and over such international organisations as the North Atlantic Treaty Organization (NATO) and the Organization for Security and Co-operation in Europe (OSCE). Perhaps the most significant is the flexibility of concert diplomacy. Since there are no explicit rules, bureaucratic procedures or legalistic considerations do not hamper a concert. When conditions are right, a concert can be an adaptable and powerful tool for managing international security. A concert can provide a forum for policy co-ordination, but it can also make an important contribution to restraining its members' behaviour. By condoning some actions and condemning others, a concert sets norms and codes for international behaviour. If there is a compelling argument for action, it can function as a *de facto* decision-making body in regard to the introduction of sanctions or military intervention. In short, a great-power concert can provide leadership, thus enhancing the ability of the international actors (states and international organisations) to manage a crisis.[1]

These benefits are offset by serious shortfalls. Not being based on international treaties, concert diplomacy is often seen as lacking legitimacy. Due to its restricted membership, it is often disliked by small states and aspiring powers: the former fear a great power condominium, while the latter would like a seat at the top table themselves. Owing to its emphasis on personal contacts between world leaders, it is detached from the normal decision-making apparatus and from the normal democratic process.

While the G8 is the only permanent global concert of great powers, there have been several recent cases of *ad hoc* concerts shouldering the responsibility for finding a solution to a regional crisis. The most conspicuous contemporary *ad hoc* concert is the Middle East Quartet, which consists of the United Nations, the European Union, the U.S., and Russia. Another example is the contact groups that were set up to resolve crises in Bosnia-Herzegovina, Kosovo, and Namibia.

During the Kosovo war, the G8 members were able to act together and find a solution at a time when the UNSC was not able to make any progress. This feat was not repeated in the lead-up to the war in Iraq. The disunity of the G8 members over the war in Iraq incapacitated the G8 as a security concert. As a result, the G8 did not play a significant role in the diplomacy preceding the war or in the management of the occupation. It remains to be seen whether the occupation of Iraq will qualify as a 'major war' that leads to a more concert-based approach. While the occupation of Iraq does not qualify as major war in a military sense — it was a limited campaign in both military and geographic sense — its political and diplomatic consequences may be so far-reaching that in terms of its political repercussions it may qualify as a major war: a war that has a radical impact on the future of international relations. As such it may usher in a new era of concert-based approaches to the questions of arms control, counterterrorism, and regional conflicts.

Historically, concerts have functioned well when their members have been of approximately equal weight. Considering the present disparity of economic and military power between the United States and second-tier G8 member states, one may be tempted to conclude that concert-based solutions cannot possibly work as long as the present disparity continues. Such a conclusion would be premature.

William Wallace (1984) has noted that a concert-based model of international governance may work if both the hegemon and the second-tier countries see mutual benefits in a concerted approach.[2] More specifically, a concert-based governance model can function in a situation that is characterised by a disparity of power between a hegemonic power and second-tier powers provided that first, the hegemonic power needs the added legitimacy that a concerted approach brings; second, the second-tier powers acquire influence in exchange for providing legitimacy; and third, international organisations are incapable of making progress toward resolving problems at hand without outside leadership.

Nicholas Bayne (2004) has divided decision making in the G7/8 system into three categories: the contribution of the heads themselves, the contribution of the supporting apparatus, and the contribution of other actors, both state and non-state. Only the first category qualifies as a concert of great powers. The supporting apparatus of the G8 ministerial and expert meetings, as well as the preparatory meetings, have begun to mimic a standard international bureaucracy, while the contribution of the state and non-state actors can best be seen as an expression of global public policy networks that today are connected to nearly all international institutions.[3] Because of its multilayered structure, the G8 can be seen as a 'meta-institution': it is able to direct the work of other international institutions.

The United States and the G8: A History of Discontinuity

Perhaps the most striking aspect of the U.S. attitude toward the G7/8 is its lack of continuity. One administration will see it as a key part of its global strategy, while another will practically forget that it exists.

At first glance, it seems that Democratic administrations take the G8 more seriously than their Republican counterparts. Jimmy Carter was eager to use the G7 for the joint management of the world economy, but he did not see the group merely as an instrument of economic policy. He also pushed for the inclusion of the issue of nuclear proliferation on the agenda, and also insisted on discussing regional security issues at summits. His Democratic successor, Bill Clinton, made the G7/8 fundamental to integrating Russia into the West. In Clinton's view, the G7/8 was important as an instrument of economic policy (it could influence the policy of the International Monetary Fund [IMF] *vis-à-vis* Russia). But, more significantly, it was a way for Clinton to manage the security aspects of the Russian transition from the removal of nuclear weapons from Ukraine to the pulling out of Russian troops from the Baltic states (Talbott 2002). During Clinton's tenure, the G8 also performed its most significant crisis management role to date, by orchestrating an end to the conflict in Kosovo.

A closer look, though, reveals that the G7/8 has not been an exclusively Democratic presidential passion. Republican Henry Kissinger played a central role in creating the G7 — he can be considered one of the founding fathers, together with Helmut Schmidt and Valéry Giscard d'Estaing. Gerald Ford surprised everyone by inviting heads of state and government to the second G7 summit only a few months after the first G7 gathering at Rambouillet. Ronald Reagan, who initially did not think much of the group, managed (together with Margaret Thatcher) to turn the 1983 Williamsburg Summit into a significant security-policy meeting. Indeed, he became so enthused by the security-policy potential of the group that he later called an extraordinary meeting to discuss nuclear arms control.

George H. Bush did not award the G7 a central place in his initial foreign policy formulations, nor did he become a convert during his tenure. For his Republican administration, the G8 was an important forum for top-level discussion, but it was not an instrument for the joint management of international affairs. George W. Bush started with an even cooler attitude toward the G8 than his father's. For example, in 2003 he left the Evian Summit early to attend to more pressing foreign policy concerns. However, he changed his attitude greatly in the lead-up to the 2004 Sea Island Summit — even if he did not become a convert as had Reagan.

John Kirton (2000) has argued that there is a long-term trend toward more reliance on the G8 on the part of the United States. If such a trend exists, it has been dormant during most of the presidency of George W. Bush.

Election-Year Considerations

In 2004, the U.S. presidency of the G8 coincided with the presidential elections. (In 1976, the Summit had been hosted by Gerald Ford, who was also running for re-election.) The campaign was visible in the staging of the Sea Island Summit: photo opportunities and declarations emphasised the commitment of the member states to work together. Unsurprisingly, Bush declared Sea Island a success. Whether this declared success will lead to a more robust role for the G8 in international peace and security will depend on three questions: First, does the United States need the added legitimacy that a concert leadership can bring? Second, do other member states agree sufficiently with U.S. policies on some of the central regional security issues, such as Iraq and the Israel-Palestine conflict, to intensify co-operation with the U.S.? And third, is the G8 the optimal forum for agreeing on new meaningful policy initiatives on international security?

The answer to the first question seems to be affirmative in the aftermath of the Sea Island Summit. The difficulties that the U.S. has encountered in Iraq, together with a sharp upturn in anti-American sentiment in the Muslim world, in Europe, and in many other parts of the world, suggest that it would be easier for the U.S. to advance its interests in arms control, counterterrorism, and regional security if it were able to work together with other leading nations.[4] Indeed, recently there has been a marked turn toward a more multilateral rhetoric in U.S. foreign policy.

The answer to the second question seems to be negative. In May 2004, Bush urged his partners in the G8 to set aside past differences over Iraq and back U.S.-led security and reconstruction efforts. The issue was discussed in Washington, where the G8 foreign ministers met to prepare for the Sea Island Summit. Bush's proposal was rejected by France, Germany, Russia, and Canada, each of which refused to send even a small contingent of troops to help protect UN personnel in Iraq, as the administration had requested (Deans 2004). The fact that Bush spoke to the foreign ministers for only eight minutes and took no questions indicates that the amount of genuine policy debate was limited. At Sea Island, Bush made another attempt to recruit new troops to Iraq, but to no avail. French president Jacques Chirac reiterated his opposition to the use of NATO troops in Iraq. Chancellor Gerhard Schroeder of Germany stated he would not send troops, although he also noted that he would not block a decision within NATO, if Iraq requested such help. Bush conceded defeat, telling reporters: 'I don't expect more troops from NATO to be offered up. That is an unrealistic expectation' (Raum 2004).

The answer to the third question — whether the G8 would be ideally suited for taking a more significant role in promoting arms control, counterterrorism, and regional security in the present international situation — appears to be affirmative. The G8 has clear advantages with regard to two established institutions that traditionally play a significant role in promoting arms control, counterterrorism, and regional security: the UNSC and NATO.

The UNSC has unrivalled legitimacy in issues of war and peace. Yet it is not an ideal place for the search of common ground. In the aftermath of the failure to reach a decision in the UNSC concerning the war in Iraq, the threshold for taking new initiatives to the UNSC became higher than before the start of hostilities. In the past, the G8 has been helpful in helping heads of state and government overcome their differences. It could conceivably play such a role again.

It is also possible to see the G8 as a noteworthy second-best option if the UNSC route is blocked for one reason or another. For the international community, the G8 is a more acceptable vehicle than unilateral action. The ending of the Kosovo conflict demonstrates the point. After it proved impossible to find a solution within the UN setting, the G8 became a *de facto* decision-making forum. Having reached a consensus, the G8 members consulted China. With the assurance that China would not veto a resolution, the matter was passed to the UNSC for approval.

With regard to arms control negotiations conducted under the auspices of the UN — such as nuclear nonproliferation negotiations — the G8 can provide leadership and direction in the same way it has in many cases provided negotiations with the General Agreement on Tariffs and Trade (GATT) and the World Trade Organization (WTO). This will not always be easy. The United States and other G8 members have disagreed sharply in the recent years on such issues as the Comprehensive Test Ban Treaty (CTBT) and the Anti-Ballistic Missile (ABM) Treaty. However, there are other areas on which consensus among the G8 member states will be possible to achieve. One of them is the reconstruction of better transatlantic relations.

Transatlantic Relations

The G8 is broader than NATO both in scope and in the geographic extent of its membership. Yet, at the same time, the transatlantic relationship forms the core of the G8. The two countries that are not members — Russia and Japan — have much at stake in the future of the transatlantic relationship. The fact that the G8 deals with a variety of issues makes it better suited for rebuilding transatlantic relations than NATO, which is focussed on security issues. In 'Renewing the Atlantic Partnership', the report of an independent task force established by the Council on Foreign Relations, co-chairs Henry Kissinger, Lawrence Summers, and Charles Kupchan (2004) argue that in addition to security issues, a renewed emphasis must be based on the broader agenda. This agenda includes many of the same issues that the G8 has dealt with for years, but it also has a few points that the G8 has not touched so far. Because of the interdependence between the health of transatlantic relations and the vitality of the G8, the key items are as follows.

First, the U.S. and Europe should establish new guidelines for the use of military force. Second, the EU and the U.S. should develop a common policy toward irresponsible states. Third, Atlantic partners should agree on the role of multilateral institutions. Fourth, the Atlantic partners should build a common approach to the broader Middle East. In addition, 'Europeans and Americans must work together, not just to liberalize U.S.-European trade, but also to ensure the successful completion of the current round of world trade negotiations' (Kissinger, Summers, and Kupchan 2004, 26).

The task force's recommendations bear a very close resemblance to the agenda of the G8. Indeed, the only existing forum that allows heads of state and government and relevant ministers to discuss these issues is the G8. Iraq, Iran, and the Israel-Palestine conflict are regional issues that have featured in the G8 agenda. The G8 has been the main driver for completing various world trade negotiations in the past. Furthermore, all the items listed here would benefit from the participation of Russia and Japan in the discussions. Disputes over the CTBT, the Kyoto Protocol, the International Criminal Court, and the ABM Treaty have not only strained transatlantic relations. They have also had a negative impact on great power relations at large. Russia is a member of the Middle East Quartet, while Japan's reliance on imported oil makes it a natural stakeholder in the future of the Middle East.

The G8 offers the United States an opportunity to kill two birds with one stone. The G8 can be a forum for the reconstruction of transatlantic relations and a vehicle for the advancement of U.S. interests in counterterrorism, arms control, and regional security. However, this requires the U.S. to take the interests of the other G8 member states seriously.

Counterterrorism: In Search of a G8 Role

The G7/8 has dealt with terrorism as well as other asymmetric and non-military security threats since the 1970s. Yet the G8 was not awarded a central place in the 'war on terror' that was launched after the terrorist attacks on 11 September in 2001. Instead, the group was initially given a more limited role: countering the financing of terrorist operations.

The decision to confine the G8 to a technical role reflected the view of the United States that a loose coalition of like-minded countries would be sufficient to guarantee a sufficient degree of international will to mount an open-ended war on terrorism. Since that time, the U.S. has come to recognise that the G8 can play a more significant role in the war against terror than it initially envisaged. Indeed, after encountering problems in maintaining the unity of the coalition of the willing, the U.S. has sought to use the G8 for the purpose of building both will and capacity. One can only speculate whether the war against terror would have taken a turn for the better if it had been anchored in the multilateral framework of the G8 from the very beginning.

The War on Terror

François Heisbourg was the first analyst to suggest that the G8 should be given a central role in the war on terror: 'It offers an opportunity for a counterterrorist vote by the world body and then also a policy commitment by G8 leaders essentially the West, Russia and Japan to the new rules of the game that will be needed for any effective attempt to throttle modern hyperterrorism' (quoted in Fitchett 2001).

The Italians were quick to follow, suggesting that a special G8 summit should be called to co-ordinate efforts to stamp out international terrorism. The Italians may have been motivated by a desire to have a second chance after clashes between protestors and the police overshadowed the less than successful Genoa Summit in 2001. Nevertheless, they also showed a profound understanding of the group's potential in dealing with different aspects of the problem, ranging from terrorist financing to redirecting the attention of international organisations.

The Bush administration dismissed the Italian proposal. Secretary of state Colin Powell declared that he was so impressed with the establishment of the *ad hoc* anti-terrorist coalition that saw no reason to engage the G8 at the top level. Instead, the U.S. was ready to rely on the G8 in combating the financing of terrorism. The G7/8 was well suited for this: in addition to having paid occasional attention to the terrorist threat since 1978, it had organised annual ministerial meetings on the subject since 1995. In December 1998, there was a virtual meeting of G8 justice and interior ministers that analysed the links between organised crime and terrorist funding. The G8 had also organised several meetings of counterterrorist experts.

Terrorist financing was the main focus of the G7 finance ministers meeting in New York on 6 October 2001. In the Action Plan to Combat the Financing of Terrorism, the finance ministers (2001) stated: 'We stand united in our commitment to vigorously track down and intercept the assets of terrorists and to pursue the individuals and countries suspected of financing terrorists. We will implement UN sanctions to block terrorist assets.' They lent their support to the Financial Action Task Force (FATF). At an extraordinary plenary meeting on terrorist financing in Washington DC on 29–30 October 2001, the FATF expanded its mission from fighting money laundering to curbing terrorist financing. It agreed on eight special recommendations in this regard. After that meeting, the FATF intensified its co-operation with the UN, the Egmont Group (consisting of financial intelligence units), the G20 finance ministers and central bank governors, and the international financial institutions (IFIs). In February 2002, it held a plenary meeting in Hong Kong that concentrated on countering the financing of terrorism.

Even if Italy did not get to host an extraordinary G8 summit on how best to combat terrorism, it managed to instigate a gradual process of making the G8 a political actor in the fight against terrorism. The G8 foreign ministers agreed under the Italian presidency that heinous terrorist attacks required a collective response and the G8 members adopted a 25-point action plan to combat terrorism. In June 2002, G8 foreign ministers (2002b), in issuing their recommendations on counterterrorism, called upon states to 'ensure, in conformity with international law and, in particular, the 1951 Convention Relating to the Status of Refugees and its 1967 Protocol, that refugee status is not abused by the perpetrators, organizers or facilitators of terrorist acts'. When the foreign ministers reported on their progress in June 2002 very little of note had been achieved (G8 Foreign Ministers 2002a).

Inclusive Globalisation

In November 2001, Nicholas Bayne (2001) called attention to the G7/8's long history in dealing with terrorism, highlighting the fact that an expert group on terrorism had been set up in 1986. He also pointed out that the last time terrorism was dealt with at the summit level was in Lyon, France, in 1996 following a terrorist attack on U.S. service personnel in Saudi Arabia. After the Lyon Summit, terrorism had been a regular concern for G8 foreign ministers, but it had not been discussed at the top table.

Bayne did not regret the G8's dismissal from the political frontline in the fight against terrorism. Instead, he called attention to the importance of freezing and confiscating terrorist assets. According to Bayne, the FATF had not accomplished much in more than a decade of existence. In 2000–01, it had identified a list of 'non-cooperating jurisdictions' that were open to money launderers, and it had published recommendations that Western financial institutions should follow in dealing with these countries. Unfortunately, these suggestions were not followed. The banking community was not committed to them and doubted their potential effectiveness. Bayne stressed that many of the things that governments are now doing should have been done years ago.

The biggest contribution that the G8 can make in the fight against terrorism is to make globalisation more inclusive, to, in Bayne's words, 'bring more of the benefits of globalisation to poor countries'. There is now 'a greater incentive and a greater prospect of moving towards goals already established: bridging the digital divide, through the DOT Force [Digital Opportunity Task Force] established at Okinawa; attacking infectious diseases through the Global AIDS and Health Fund agreed at Genoa; bringing about the revival of Africa, through the Action Plan promised at Genoa and to be completed at Kananaskis'. Bayne thus presented a traditional view of the G8 as a group with a main focus on the field of economics and for which security activities are of secondary importance.

Despite U.S. reluctance to make the G8 the focal point of the war on terror, Washington welcomed and encouraged Canadian plans to make terrorism one of the key items on the agenda of the 2002 Kananaskis Summit. Consequently, fighting terrorism became one of the Summit's three priorities, together with strengthening global economic growth and building a new partnership for African development. Terrorism was discussed at Kananaskis, but once again the agenda was overtaken by an acute international crisis. This time the Israel-Palestine conflict and presumed U.S. plans to remove Iraqi president Saddam Hussein from power dominated the discussions. The most important development was Russia's full integration into G8 proceedings.

Previously, as noted earlier, Russia had been excluded from the economic deliberations that had taken place within the old G7 structure. Now this 'upstairs downstairs' arrangement came to a clearly enunciated end at the behest of the Bush administration. No one had any doubt why this happened: the G8 was once again used, as it had been in the context of NATO enlargement, to reward Russia for co-operating with Washington and its Western allies.

At Evian, counterterrorism was awarded a central place in the summit agenda. The leaders took an approach that had two dimensions. First, the leaders concentrated on the need to build stronger international political will in order to improve counterterrorism co-operation. Second, they endorsed practical steps to be taken in order to create better capacity for action. The approach was rooted in the work of the UNSC's Counter-Terrorism Committee.

The G8 Action Plan to Combat Terrorism

The G8 Action Plan to Combat Terrorism concentrated on capacity building, assistance, and co-operation with existing institutions. First, the leaders concentrated on measures aimed at denying terrorists the means to commit terrorist acts (for example, to prevent the financing of terrorism and denial of false documents and weapons), depriving terrorists of a safe haven and ensuring they are prosecuted or extradited, and overcoming vulnerability to terrorism (for example, to enhance domestic security measures and capability for crisis management and consequence management). Second, the G8 leaders noted that their countries may receive trainees, dispatch specialists, and provide equipment as requested by recipient countries. Third, the leaders endorsed the work of the Counter-Terrorism Committee and promised to ensure it is sufficiently staffed. They encouraged UN member states to enact the relevant UNSC resolutions. They also lent support to steps by the G7 finance ministers to co-ordinate counterterrorism financing measures and to work with the FATF and the IFIs to address terrorist financing, capacity building, and other counterterrorism objectives in their assessment and assistance initiatives.

In order to achieve these ends, the G8 leaders decided to create a Counter-Terrorism Action Group (CTAG). Membership was by invitation only: mainly donor countries would be invited to join the group. A representative of the Counter-Terrorism Committee would be invited to all CTAG meetings, and representatives from relevant UN bodies, IFIs, and other regional and functional organisations would be invited to relevant meetings only. CTAG members would provide funding, expertise, or training facilities. Each member would focus on areas and countries where it has expertise.

The CTAG is very action-oriented. It reviews requests for capacity-building assistance, exchanges information on the needs of assessment missions carried out by CTAG members, facilitates joint initiatives, and shares best practices and lessons learned. An important part of the group's work is to encourage regional and functional organisations such as the World Customs Organization, the International Civil Aviation Organization (ICAO), and the International Maritime Organization (IMO) to put pressure on their member states to implement relevant UNSC resolutions. The CTAG also urges countries that are not party to all international counterterrorism conventions and protocols to become parties and to accelerate domestic implementation of required measures.

Arms Control: The Emphasis on Nonproliferation

The G8's Global Partnership against the Spread of Weapons and Materials of Mass Destruction is a leading case of the U.S. advancing its own interests through the G8. It is also an excellent case of fruitful co-operation between the hegemon and second-tier powers on an issue of highest international importance. Some experts have criticised the Global Partnership for being much talk and little action (Allison 2004). Nevertheless, the initiative remains an impressive programme that could hardly have been launched by any other international organisation.

The Global Partnership was announced at the G8 Kananaskis Summit in June 2002. The leaders pledged US$20 billion over the next ten years to support efforts, initially in Russia and expanded in 2004 to include Ukraine, to address nonproliferation, disarmament, counterterrorism, and nuclear safety issues. The aim was to 'prevent terrorists, or those that harbour them, from acquiring or developing nuclear, chemical, radiological and biological weapons; missiles; and related materials, equipment and technology' (G8 2002b). The partnership was aimed at Russia because of the surplus of old Soviet-era weapons and materials of mass destruction. Tens of thousands of Russian nuclear warheads and hundreds of tonnes of nuclear weapons–usable materials were dispersed at inadequately secured sites. Furthermore, Russia inherited more than 40 000 tonnes of chemical weapons from the Soviet Union as well as its sizeable biological weapons programme.

The partnership has been important in shaping U.S. attitude toward the G8. A group first seen as having only limited value in the fight against terrorism (albeit in a vitally important area of curbing the finances of terrorism) was now recognised as being an important tool in combating WMD terrorism. The partnership was also important in showing the value of G8 multilateralism; because of the old nuclear rivalry, it would have been difficult for the Russians to accept a helping hand from the United States alone in dismantling old WMD stockpiles.

The Global Partnership has also been important in showing that other G8 members can successfully bring new issues to the G8 agenda even when they deal with vital American interests. The idea of strengthening G8 activities in arms control was first discussed between Canada and Russia. The funding requirements of the partnership programme, however, are large. It is therefore unlikely that any other international organisation could have mobilised in such a short time a project with colossal funding requirements. It should be noted that the Global Partnership has been opened to non-G8 countries, and Finland, Sweden, Norway, the Netherlands, Switzerland, and Poland have so far joined.

In the lead-up to the Sea Island Summit, Sam Nunn and Michele Flournoy (2004) suggested that its success should be measured in large part by whether the G8 leaders take concrete and urgent steps to reduce the risk of catastrophic terrorism. Indeed, they maintained that 'over time, and without our decisive intervention, al Qaida could become the world's 10th nuclear power'. Measured against this yardstick, Sea Island was not a total success. Graham Allison (2004) pointed out after the Summit that the Global Partnership was lagging behind its own time-table: 'at the current rate, the global partnership will not secure Russia's loose nukes until 2017'.

Neither was there much progress made with regard to the Iranian and North Korean nuclear programmes. The only concrete action to come out of the Sea Island Summit was a statement of concern about the spread of nuclear weapons. The leaders repeated their commitment to the six-party talks that aim to persuade North Korea to dismantle its nuclear programme. On Iran, the leaders urged Tehran to co-operate with the International Atomic Energy Agency (IAEA), saying that despite some progress, Iran is still dragging its feet on full disclosure.

The North Korean issue produced friction between the U.S. and China. During the Sea Island Summit, John Bolton, the U.S. Undersecretary of State for Arms Control and International Security, told the press that Washington had provided Beijing with clear evidence of North Korea's nuclear activities for the past year and a half (Mitton 2004). 'We've given them very substantial evidence. But they've apparently still taken the position that they don't know whether North Korea has a uranium-enrichment programme', he said. Bolton went on to suggest that 'North Korea wants to drive a wedge between the United States and Japan'. This was manifested by the fact that the North Korean government had indicated to Japan's prime minister Junichiro Koizumi that it was ready for a compromise while it was entirely unyielding in its dealings with the U.S. government.

North Korea showed its true colours by issuing a strongly worded response. The government accused the G8 leaders of conspiring to turn North Korea into 'another Iraq', and said that gives it a 'strong catalyst' to strengthen its nuclear weapons development ('N. Korea Threatens to Strengthen Nuke Development after G8 Statement' 2004).

Airline Security

Airline security is another case of the G8 advancing American — and, at the same time, wider global — interests. The so-called 'Action Program' set out in Sea Island's Secure and Facilitated International Travel Initiative (SAFTI) to improve global airline security includes 28 wide-ranging measures to improve international airline security in the face of increased terrorist threats (G8 2004b). The action points contain suggestions pertaining to passenger screening, travel documents, and intelligence sharing. The only arms control measure is the joint commitment of the leaders to accelerate efforts to destroy excess and obsolete man-portable air defence systems

(MANPADS). In recent years, terrorists have used these weapons, both successfully and unsuccessfully, against both military and civilian aircraft.

Both SAFTI and the Global Partnership were launched at G8 summits. As such, they represent the contribution of the leaders themselves — rather than their foreign ministers or groups of experts — to arms control. In the history of the G7/8, leaders have contributed to arms control, first, by giving impetus to important arms control negotiation (in much the same way the leaders have repeatedly given momentum to world trade negotiations). Second, they have taken up 'new security issues', such as airplane hijacking in the early 1980s, and by doing so have lifted them to a more significant place in the global arms control agenda.

The Comprehensive Test Ban Treaty and the Anti-Ballistic Missile Treaty

There are also cases of recent arms control issues where G8 member states have not seen eye to eye. The CTBT and the ABM Treaty have created considerable friction between the U.S. and the other G8 members. However, the friction has not been manifested at the summit. On these issues, the G8 members have followed the old rule of not appearing to disagree in public. At the time of the 2001 Genoa Summit, missile defence was a hot topic, but it was not discussed as part of the official agenda, nor was it part of the official agenda of the foreign ministers meeting in Rome immediately before the leaders met. It was, therefore, quite unexpected that this issue stole the limelight on the last day of the Summit. Bush and Putin agreed to start new talks based on linking U.S. plans for a missile defence shield with reductions in nuclear stockpiles. The heads of the other G8 members declined to comment substantively on these bilateral talks.

The incident showed that as far as the ABM Treaty was concerned the U.S. administration did not see any need for the added legitimacy that a concerted approach would have brought (which is the first condition for the concert model to work). A bilateral agreement on this issue was enough. The U.S. did not want to discuss the issue with other member states, so there was no possibility for the second-tier powers to gain influence over the matter. Thus, the second condition of the functioning of the concert model did not become an issue. Since the U.S. was intent on circumventing — or, indeed, declaring obsolete — an existing arms control regime, the question of whether the issue should be taken to another multilateral forum did not arise.

Conflict Prevention

Since the Kosovo War, the G8 has paid increasing attention to the issue of conflict prevention. Conflict prevention is an abstract concept with no universally definition, nor is its relationship with arms control absolutely clear. The Carnegie Commission on the Prevention of Deadly Conflict has sought to clarify the concept by dividing it into operational (or short-term) and structural (or long-term) conflict prevention. The G8 has been engaged in both. A good example of structural conflict prevention is the

New Partnership for Africa's Development (NEPAD). The first of NEPAD's five major issue areas was peace and security (Fowler 2004). An example of operational conflict prevention is the pressure that the G8 leaders put on Moscow to withdraw Russian troops from the Baltic states. Their orderly withdrawal was an important element in achieving a peaceful transition to Baltic independence. The G8 is well placed to make a difference with regard to both short- and long-term conflict prevention, provided that the members agree. Sea Island's Broader Middle East and North Africa (BMENA) Initiative is an attempt to use the G8 as a vehicle for structural, long-term conflict prevention. It remains unclear what the commitment of the G8 member states to this initiative will be.

The term 'preventive action' is normally used to refer to political action, but in some cases it has been extended to include preventive military action. If the term is used liberally to include preventive military action, the situation changes dramatically: conflict prevention becomes a highly sensitive, flammable issue. Several experts, among them Charles Grant (2003) and the aforementioned Task Force on Atlantic Relations, have encouraged the EU and the U.S. to discuss the principle of pre-emptive warfare. Given that all members of the G8 (as well as the wider world community) have a stake in the matter, the G8 ought to take up the issue. The clarification of the principles of the use of military force would contribute both to arms control and to conflict prevention.

Regional Security: The Broader Middle East, North Africa, and Peace Support

It is customary for G8 summits to issue statements of concern on several regional conflicts that are going on at the time of the summit. It is much rarer for the summits to agree on a proper follow-up. The Sea Island Summit launched two initiatives designed to improve long-term stability in the Middle East and North Africa. Both initiatives had a clear follow-up plan.

The Broader Middle East and North Africa Initiative

The BMENA Initiative was the centrepiece of the Sea Island Summit. It aimed to improve security, stability, and prosperity in the region — yet it did not mention arms control, peacekeeping, or other traditional issues of regional security (G8 2004c). Instead, it concentrated on providing the conditions for long-term stability in the region. It featured initiatives designed to promote democratic institutions, provide microfinance loans to businesses, train teachers to combat illiteracy, train women entrepreneurs, and invest US$100 million to finance small and medium-sized enterprises (SMEs).

The ultimate success or failure of the initiative will become clear only in years to come. For the purposes of this chapter, however, it is significant for two reasons. First, it is another example of the United States changing its attitude toward the usefulness of the G8. When the U.S. assumed the chair of the G8 for 2004, the Bush administration entertained the idea of not hosting a G8 summit at all (Davies 2004). The idea would have been to give member states a chance to reflect on the usefulness of the G8 summitry. This view was given up as U.S. officials began to recognise the potential of the G8 as an instrument for U.S. interests. Finally, Washington decided to use the G8 summit to create momentum for its drive for democracy in the Middle East. This was, after all, a unique opportunity for the U.S. government.

Second, the BMENA Initiative is also a clear case of other G8 countries being able to influence U.S. policies. The G8 members had serious reservations concerning the first version of the initiative, originally known as the Greater Middle East Initiative (GMEI). The Sea Island Summit was initially set to consider U.S. proposals on reforming the region from Mauritania to Afghanistan, possibly including former Soviet republics in Central Asia and the Transcaucasus. Later, after objections from Europe, including Russia, these vast geographical areas were narrowed down to some extent (Belenkaya 2004). There was also a change in the tone of the initiative. The early version was criticised for not sufficiently involving the regional actors. The final version emphasised partnership and established the Forum for the Future, which would bring together local governmental and nongovernmental actors to discuss the future of their own region. The Japanese were also able to influence the wording of the statement. Aides accompanying Junichiro Koizumi to Sea Island said Japan had exchanged views with Arab countries long before the Summit and asked the United States and other G8 members to give due consideration to those countries. As a result of those exchanges, the statement included the phrase of respect for the 'uniqueness' and 'diversity' of the region, as proposed by Japan (Igarashi 2004). According to Russian press reports, Vladimir Putin was also satisfied with his influence with regard to the wording of the BMENA Initiative. As one journalist put it, 'in most cases the point at issue for Moscow was principles, not vital interests, which is why it often found itself in the role of a mediator, rather than a debater, helping the sides to reach a compromise' (Filippov 2004).

By the time of the Sea Island Summit, the initiative had been amended to the extent that the G8 was able to establish the '"Partnership for Progress and a Common Future" with the Broader Middle East and North Africa to support efforts to advance freedom, democracy, and prosperity in the region' (White House 2004).

The BMENA Initiative is an ambitious and extensive programme that will have a significant impact on the stability and security of the region, but it is a political programme — not a security-policy initiative. The other initiative launched at the Sea Island Summit, the peace support initiative, is a more traditional security initiative.

The Peace Support Initiative

At the Sea Island Summit, the G8 leaders also launched the Action Plan for Expanding Global Capability for Peace Support Operations (G8 2004a). The number of peace support operations throughout the world has continued to grow, while the capacity to undertake such operations has not been increased. The situation is especially critical in Africa, where more comprehensive measures for ensuring peace are needed.

Sea Island's peace support action plan was a follow-up to two earlier summits. At Kananaskis in 2002, the leaders resolved in the Africa Action Plan to provide 'technical and financial assistance so that, by 2010, African countries and regional and sub-regional organizations are able to engage more effectively to prevent and resolve violent conflict on the continent, and undertake peace support operations in accordance with the United Nations Charter' (G8 2002a). At Evian in 2003, they followed up with the Joint Africa/G8 Plan to Enhance African Capabilities to Undertake Peace Support Operations as an annex to the implementation report submitted by the African personal representatives (APRs) to the leaders (G8 2003). In that plan, they committed to work with African partners, step by step, to develop key building blocks that will help to channel existing resources more effectively in support of the longer-term African vision for its peace and security architecture.

At Sea Island, the G8 leaders emphasised collaboration with the UN: 'All peace support operations and other related activities undertaken by G8 members under this initiative would be in accordance with the UN charter' (G8 2004a). Furthermore, they noted, since most of the peace support operations around the world, particularly those in Africa, operate under the aegis of the UN and with a Security Council mandate, that 'all actions undertaken by the G8 to expand global capability for peace support operations should be implemented in close cooperation with the UN, in accordance with its technical standards, and take into account the recommendations of the Brahimi Report [a UN report on peacekeeping operations]. In Africa, these actions should also be implemented in close cooperation with the African Union and sub-regional organizations, in line with the African ownership principle.' The plan also included training for gendarmes, or 'heavy police', to control crowds, prisons, and borders.

The Action Plan contained the following commitments:

- to train and, where appropriate, equip a total of approximately 75 000 troops worldwide by 2010;
- to co-ordinate with African partners, the UN, the EU, and others to maximise individual efforts to enhance African peace support operations capabilities and their related activities;
- to build peace support operations capabilities in other regions by 2010, the idea being that many of the trained peace support units could be deployed to Africa, as well as to crises in their own regions;
- to work with interested parties, before the 2005 Gleneagles Summit, to develop appropriate arrangements that will help provide countries with transportation to deploy to peace support operations and logistics support to sustain units in the field; and
- to increase their contribution to the training of gendarme-like forces by continuing to support existing centres dedicated to that purpose, notably those in France and Italy and those in Africa, and by supporting new initiatives in that respect.

The Action Plan did not invite traditional peacekeepers, such as Sweden and Finland, to participate in the training of African peacekeepers. Nor did it rule such co-operation out. Were such countries to show an interest in contributing to the training of African peacekeepers, their offer would likely not be turned down.

According to the critics, the Action Plan was yet another case of the G8 providing words, not action. One nongovernmental group, Africa Action, declared it a travesty to talk about developing capabilities for peace support when an immediate military intervention was called for to stop an unfolding genocide in Darfur. The group's executive director, Salih Booker, stated, 'instead of talking out of their hats about training 50,000 peacekeepers, the G8 leaders must act NOW to put boots on the ground in Sudan to halt genocide, as is required by international convention' (Africa Action 2004). Another observer pointed out that 'neither budget arrears nor additional U.S. support for the UN were mentioned when the White House announced "new" support from the group of G8 rich countries for African peace efforts this week' (Minter 2004).

The critics were correct in the details, but they missed the larger picture. One of the reasons why there was no willingness to intervene in Sudan was the lack of peace support troops. Without such troops, a military intervention could easily turned into an unending occupation — a prospect that was all the more uninviting because, at the time, the unrest in Iraq was still escalating. If the Action Plan were to live up to its commitments, it would provide a significant boost to stability in Africa.

The G8 as Global Security Actor

What kind of a role should the G8 aim for as an actor in global peace and security? Most experts agree that the G8 is not and should not become a conflict manager or conflict preventer in itself. It can contribute best by acting as a leader for other organisations in setting the agenda for the broader international community. That is why the French, as Robert Fowler (2004, 40) points out, 'have long held that this summit vehicle is not a *directoire politique*, but rather a very effective *instance d'impulsion*, something more than an agent of influence whereby its agreements on the vital issues of the moment have enormous impact on world management'. As such the G8 is a meta-institution: an institution that transcends and directs the work of other international organisations, mobilises political will, and makes funds available.

Global Alliance for Security?

Is this enough? Should the G8 aim to have a more robust role? Should it transform itself into a new entity, a global alliance for security, as suggested by three distinguished strategic thinkers — Graham Allison, Karl Kaiser, and Sergei Karaganov (2001)? According to their proposals such an alliance should start with the G8 membership and its modes of operation, but should make a special effort to include China. In due course, other responsible countries should be included, provided that they share the same objectives and are prepared to contribute significantly to their achievement. The mission should be 'to prevent and fight terrorism, the proliferation of weapons of mass destruction, and the infrastructure of international criminal activities and drug traffic that feed terrorist networks. It should also address the causes of terrorism in failed or failing political regimes and societies.'

The joint proposal of the three strategic thinkers has distinct merits: at a time when the reform of the UNSC continues to be a distant dream, it is useful to think of other approaches. It is also correct to point out that an alliance of this sort would not be credible without involving China. However, the proposal has one weakness. Turning an informal concert into a formal alliance would remove the positive aspects of an informal concert without necessarily adding value in any meaningful way.

Writing about concerts and condominiums, Hedley Bull (1995) noted: 'The great powers cannot formalise and make explicit the full extent of their special position. International society is based on the rejection of a hierarchical ordering of states in favour of equality in the sense of the like application of basic rights and duties of sovereignty to like entities.' So far, G8 leaders have declined calls for a secretariat to be established. They have also refused to adapt a charter and set clear rules. They ought to reject such demands in future as well. Indeed, the challenge for the G8 is not how to have more meetings and a more developed structure, but how to concentrate on key issues on the global security agenda. Unless this challenge is confronted, the G8 will not be able to develop a more robust role in global security.

Another question related to the security role of the G8 has to do with new members. The theory of concerts states that in order to qualify as a concert, a system of governance must include every power that can destroy the existing international system by changing its policies (Jervis 1986). The G7 did not include Russia and, therefore, did not fulfil this criterion. After the admission of Russia, the G8 assumed the role of a global concert. The question is whether membership should be widened to include China and possibly even India.

China and India

At Sea Island, extending the membership to include China and India was discussed — at least during press conferences. German chancellor Gerhard Schroeder said China would be a good candidate for inclusion if the G8 decides to accept a ninth member ('Schroeder Backs China' 2004). 'I believe that this is very, very obvious from both the political and economic aspect,' he said at the end of the Summit. The issue should be discussed 'in the next years', and he added that no other country had affected the world's economy 'in such an unbelievably dramatic and dynamic way'.

Italy's Prime Minister, Silvio Berlusconi, went further, saying the leaders were considering inviting China and India into the G8 fold. 'It doesn't make much sense for us to talk about the economy of the future without two countries that are protagonists on the world stage,' he said (Teather 2004). Berlusconi said the leaders had discussed the strength and rapid expansion of the Chinese economy, and the fact that it was not constrained by the same labour laws as the West. 'But we said we shouldn't be afraid of China, because it is a huge consumer market, and the idea was put forward to call China and India to join the G8, making it the G9 or G10.'

Tony Blair, the British Prime Minister, said there was 'certainly a case for including countries like China and India' (Teather 2004). He said that the debate was ongoing about the format of the G8. 'We have already begun the process of outreach and I'm sure that will continue,' he stated. Canada's Prime Minister, Paul Martin, floated the idea of a G20 leaders summit (L20), in addition to the annual G8 meeting. Japan's prime minister Junichiro Koizumi refused to comment on whether the two countries should be admitted ('Koizumi Flies Asian Flag' 2004). John Bolton said that people were always speculating about whether China should be invited to join the group, but that 'we didn't see it as being appropriate this year' (Mitton 2004).

It is noteworthy that none of the leaders mentioned security issues when discussing the prospect of China's or India's membership. Yet it is quite clear that admitting two countries with very strong regional security profiles would have a significant impact on the security role of the G8. It would decrease the cohesion of the group but make it an even more powerful actor if unanimity were reached. From the point of view of creating a genuine global concert, Chinese membership would bring clear advantages.

The friction between Beijing and Washington over North Korea's nuclear programme gives some indication of the possible difficulties that Chinese membership could bring to the group. Zhou Wenzhong, China's Deputy Foreign Minister, issued a statement that coincided with the Sea Island Summit expressing doubts about U.S. claims that North Korea has been making nuclear weapons with enriched uranium (Mitton 2004). While the Chinese statement clearly irritated the Americans, its impact should not be exaggerated. After all, Zhou's statement did not materially differ from the doubts expressed by three existing G8 members concerning WMD in the lead-up to the Iraq war. The Chinese may simply have wanted to express pique at being excluded from the G8 summit.

Regardless of the membership issue, the G8 will not be able to play a successful role in international peace and security without increasing its legitimacy in the eyes of non-members. One way of achieving greater legitimacy might be occasionally to use the L20 as a forum for discussing security policy.

Conclusion

The G8's future security role will depend on the willingness of its members, particularly the U.S., to use the group as an instrument of policy co-ordination and crisis management. Two core question remains: Why would the U.S. want to engage the G8 in the joint management of international security? Why would other G8 member states want this to happen?

For the United States, two reasons support the use of the G8 as an instrument for the advancement of U.S. interests in arms control, counterterrorism, and regional security. First, the U.S. would increase the legitimacy of its actions by consulting other great powers in an orderly multilateral fashion. Second, it would be able to strengthen cohesion between the West and Russia in relation to matters of global security. The risks involved would be limited. The G8 does not have a habit of publicly criticising or contradicting its members. Thus, even if the other member states did not agree with U.S. policies, they would be unlikely to use the G8 as a forum for concerted criticism. For the U.S., torn between a desire for greater international legitimacy and a fear of the constraints associated with international institutions, the G8 offers a neat compromise that could be called 'multilateralism light'. If hegemony is 'imperialism with good manners', as Georg Schwarzenberger (1959) has argued, the G8 would be an ideal place for the U.S. to show its command of proper etiquette.

For the other G8 members, the reason for using the G8 as a forum for joint management of international security is clear: the G8 offers a way to engage the U.S. in a constructive debate that has and can lead to significant changes in U.S. policies. It is worth remembering that a concert can provide a forum for policy co-ordination, but it can also make an important contribution to restraining its members' behaviour.

Notes

1. For a discussion of the G8 as a concert of great powers, see Chapter One in Penttilä (2003).
2. In a more recent article, Wallace (2001) notes that 'the United States cannot continue to call on its allies to share the burdens unless it is prepared to share its decision-making as well.'
3. The creeping institutionalisation of the summitry has been captured by a former sherpa: 'We were originally all mavericks, but over the years the mavericks have lost the battles with the regular bureaucracy' (Putnam and Bayne 1987, 55).
4. On European attitudes toward the U.S., see Pew Research Center for the People and the Press (2004).

References

Africa Action (2004). 'Africa Action Dismisses "Misdirected" G8 Announcements on Africa'. 10 June. <www.africaaction.org/newsroom/release.php?op=read&documentid=563&type=2> (November 2004).

Allison, Graham (2004). 'Loose Nukes: The Eight Spoke Loudly, and Did Little'. *International Herald Tribune*, 12 June.

Allison, Graham, Karl Kaiser, and Sergei Karaganov (2001). 'The World Needs a Global Alliance for Security'. *International Herald Tribune*, 21 November.

Bayne, Nicholas (2001). 'The G8's Role in the Fight against Terrorism'. Remarks to the G8 Research Group, Toronto, 8 November. <www.g8.utoronto.ca/speakers/baynenov2001.html> (November 2004).

Bayne, Nicholas (2004). 'Concentrating the Mind: Decision Making in the G7/8 System'. In J. J. Kirton and R. Stefanova, eds., *The G8, The United Nations, and Conflict Prevention*, pp. 21–38. Ashgate, Aldershot.

Belenkaya, Marianna (2004). 'G8 Rules Out Solving Middle East Problems'. *RIA Novosti*, 10 June.

Bull, Hedley (1995). *The Anarchical Society: A Study of Order in World Politics*. Columbia University Press, New York.

Davies, Glyn (2004). Interview with author. Washington DC, 1 June.

Deans, Bob (2004). 'G8 Members Snub U.S. Appeal for Iraq Troops'. *Altanta Journal-Constitution*, 14 May.

Filippov, Yuri (2004). 'G8 and Vladimir Putin's Personal Result'. *RIA Novosti*, 10 June.

Fitchett, Joseph (2001). 'NATO Unity, but What Next? Allies Unsure of What a Counterterrorism Offensive Might Require'. *International Herald Tribune*, 14 September.

Fowler, Robert (2004). 'The Intricacies of Summit Preparation and Consensus Building'. In J. J. Kirton and R. Stefanova, eds., *The G8, The United Nations, and Conflict Prevention*, pp. 39–42. Ashgate, Aldershot.

G7 Finance Ministers (2001). 'Action Plan to Combat the Financing of Terrorism'. <www.g8.utoronto.ca/finance/fm100601.htm#action> (November 2004).

G8 (2002a). 'G8's Africa Action Plan'. <www.g8.utoronto.ca/summit/2002kananaskis/africaplan.html> (November 2004).

G8 (2002b). 'Statement by the Leaders: The G8 Global Partnership against the Spread of Weapons and Materials of Mass Destruction'. <www.g8.utoronto.ca/summit/2002kananaskis/arms.html> (November 2004).

G8 (2003). 'Implementation Report by Africa Personal Representatives to Leaders on the G8 Africa Action Plan'. Evian, 1 June. <www.g8.utoronto.ca/summit/2003evian/apr030601.html> (November 2004).

G8 (2004a). 'G8 Action Plan: Expanding Global Capability for Peace Support Operations'. Sea Island, 10 June. <www.g8.utoronto.ca/summit/2004seaisland/peace.html> (November 2004).

G8 (2004b). 'G8 Secure and Facilitated International Travel Initiative'. Sea Island, 9 June. <www.g8.utoronto.ca/summit/2004seaisland/travel.html> (November 2004).

G8 (2004c). 'Partnership for Progress and a Common Future with the Region of the Broader Middle East and North Africa'. Sea Island, 9 June. <www.g8.utoronto.ca/summit/2004seaisland/partnership.html> (November 2004).

G8 Foreign Ministers (2002a). 'G8 Foreign Ministers' Progress Report on the Fight against Terrorism'. Whistler, BC, 12 June. <www.g8.utoronto.ca/foreign/fm130602b.htm> (November 2004).

G8 Foreign Ministers (2002b). 'G8 Recommendations on Counter-Terrorism'. Whistler, BC, 13 June. <www.g8.utoronto.ca/foreign/fm130602f.htm> (November 2004).

Grant, Charles (2003). 'Transatlantic Rift: How to Bring the Two Sides Together'. July. Centre for European Reform, London.

Igarashi, Aya (2004). 'Japan Makes G8 Presence Felt'. *Yomiuri Shimbun*, 10 June.

Jervis, Robert (1986). 'From Balance to Concert: A Study of International Security Cooperation'. In K. A. Oye, ed., *Cooperation under Anarchy*. Princeton University Press, Princeton.

Kirton, John J. (2000). 'United States Foreign Policy and the G8 Summit'. Lecture given at the Faculty of Law, Chuo University, Tokyo, 6 July. <www.g8.utoronto.ca/g7/scholar/kirton20004> (November 2004).

Kissinger, Henry, Lawrence H. Summers, and Charles Kupchan (2004). 'Renewing the Atlantic Partnership'. Council on Foreign Relations, Washington DC. <www.cfr.org/publication.php?id=6871> (November 2004).

'Koizumi Flies Asian Flag'. (2004). *Taipei Times*, 12 June.
Minter, Walter (2004). 'USA/Africa: Peacekeeping Repackaged'. *AfricaFocus Bulletin*, 10 June. <www.africafocus.org/docs04/us0406a.php> (November 2004).
Mitton, Roger (2004). 'China Odd One Out in WMD Issue'. *Straits Times Interactive*, 10 June.
'N. Korea Threatens to Strengthen Nuke Development after G8 Statement'. (2004). *Associated Press*, 13 June.
Nunn, Sam and Michele Flournoy (2004). 'G8 Leaders Need to Move against Terrorism'. *Newsday*, 9 June.
Penttilä, Risto E.J. (2003). *The Role of the G8 in International Peace and Security*. Oxford University Press, Oxford.
Pew Research Center for the People and the Press (2004). 'A Year after Iraq War: Mistrust of America in Europe Ever Higher, Muslim Anger Persists'. <people-press.org/reports/display.php3?ReportID=206> (November 2004).
Putnam, Robert and Nicholas Bayne (1987). *Hanging Together: Co-operation and Conflict in the Seven-Power Summit*. 2nd ed. Sage Publications, London.
Raum, Tom (2004). 'Bush Says He Doesn't Expect New NATO Troops in Iraq'. *Associated Press*, 10 June.
'Schroeder Backs China'. (2004). *Straits Times*, 11 June.
Schwarzenberger, Georg (1959). *Hegemonial Intervention: Yearbook of World Affairs*. Stevens & Son, London.
Schwegmann, Christoph (2001). 'Modern Concert Diplomacy: The Contact Group and the G7/8 in Crisis Management'. In J. J. Kirton, J. P. Daniels and A. Freytag, eds., *Guiding Global Order: G8 Governance in the Twenty-First Century*. Ashgate, Aldershot.
Talbott, Strobe (2002). *The Russia Hand: A Memoir of Presidential Diplomacy*. Random House, New York.
Teather, David (2004). 'China and India Groomed for Membership'. *The Guardian*, 11 June.
Wallace, William (1984). 'Political Issues at the Summits: A New Concert of Powers?' In C. Merlini, ed., *Economic Summits and Western Decisionmaking*. St. Martin's Press, London.
Wallace, William (2001). 'Europe, the Necessary Partner'. *Foreign Affairs* vol. 80, no. 3, pp. 16–35.
White House (2004). 'Fact Sheet: Broader Middle East and North Africa Initiative'. Sea Island, 9 June. <www.g8.utoronto.ca/summit/2004seaisland/fact_mena.html> (November 2004)

Chapter 7

Economic Growth and National Security

David B. Audretsch, Richard M. Stazinski, and T. Taylor Aldridge[1]

Economists have long held that the unfettered mobility of factors of production across national borders is conducive to long-run economic growth.[2] The major impact of transnational labour mobility was to increase the supply of labour and, ultimately, restore the labour market to equilibrium levels of desired wages. Although some G8 countries were more hospitable to foreign labour, the impact was generally thought to be similar throughout the G8.

In the post–Berlin Wall era, however, the comparative advantage of the G8 countries evolved from being based on the factors of capital and labour to that of knowledge. Along with this shift came the recognition that knowledge capital was also important for economic growth (Lucas 1993; Romer 1986). The emerging role of knowledge workers as the crucial factor generating economic growth resulted in a chasm between Europe and North America. The economic value of knowledge and human capital is conditional upon complementary knowledge and human capital at a specific geographic location (Audretsch and Feldman 1996; Audretsch and Stephan 1996), and a recognition of this value accentuated the contribution of transborder knowledge-worker mobility to economic growth. While the North American countries attempted to bias immigration toward knowledge workers, Europe maintained the more traditional approach toward the inward migration of foreign workers. For example, an article in *The Economist* observed that 'sending foreigners home after paying to educate them is not the only contradiction in Germany's immigration rules' ('Brains Not Welcome Here: The Difficulty of Changing a Policy that Drives Talent Away' 2004).

As the gap in economic growth between Europe and North America increased during the 1990s, public policy in Europe began to link the higher levels of economic performance in North America to immigration policies with a greater focus on facilitating access to knowledge workers. The growing acknowledgement that knowledge workers were essential for a knowledge-based economy has led to a number of reforms in Europe that facilitate the entry and integration of foreigners into Europe. For example, in the late 1990s the German government introduced a green card for information technology workers that targeted the immigration of high-technology workers. As *The Economist* pointed out, 'things started to change in the late 1990s. The new coalition of Social Democrats and Greens changed the citizenship law, making it easier for immigrants and their children to become German. And it dawned on the country that, in the internet era, it was losing the 'battle for the best brains' ('Brains Not Welcome Here' 2004).

The events of 11 September 2001 changed the growing consensus among the G8 that mobility of knowledge workers across national boundaries was essential to generate economic growth. Instead, priority for homeland security pre-empted the principle of unfettered mobility of such workers. For example, another article in *The Economist* reported that 'the number of scientists and engineers going to America to study and work is dropping precipitously. An important reason is the length of time it now takes to get a visa. This is both deterring would-be visitors from coming, and hindering some of those who try. Not only may this lead to a decline in America's scientific strengths, it is also an underserved obstacle for many students ... The current mess could prove costly to America' ('Short-Sighted: Visas and Science' 2004).

There is thus an opportunity cost of attaining homeland security: the foregone knowledge workers that would have added to the stock of knowledge capital results in lower levels of entrepreneurship, innovation, and, eventually, economic growth. The purpose of this chapter is to make explicit the policy tradeoff between economic growth and homeland security. In the second section of this chapter, the traditional role contributed by immigration is contrasted to the role emerging in the knowledge-based economies of the G8 countries. The cross-border mobility of knowledge workers is found to be important not only for increasing the stock of knowledge, but also for the magnitude of knowledge spillovers through entrepreneurial activity. The third section depicts the tradeoff between homeland security and economic growth. Finally, a summary and conclusions are provided in the last section. In particular, only by working together with a common goal can the G8 mitigate the tradeoff that has emerged between homeland security and economic growth.

Transborder Labour Mobility and Homeland Security

The traditional labour market view of immigration is that it equilibrates labour markets at targeted wage levels. While some G8 countries experienced higher levels of immigration, the impact was of a similar qualitative nature, if not a quantitative one. High immigration countries, such as the United States, received a greater injection of the factor of labour.

As growth rates diverged in gross domestic product (GDP) per capita in the 1990s (see Figure 7-1), the qualitative as well as the quantitative contribution of transnational labour mobility became increasingly clear. Along with globalisation has come a shift in the comparative advantage of G8 countries toward knowledge. This has altered the economic impact of transnational border mobility of workers. Rather than merely affect the labour market by the supply effect, the stock of knowledge in the economy is increased. The spillover of knowledge implies that the impact of knowledge workers on economic growth is convex and associated with increasing returns (Romer 1986; Lucas 1993). In the United States, policy responded to the new role for immigration as knowledge workers by enacting the *Immigration Act of 1990*, which defined and divided high-skilled immigrants into work visa categories.

One prime example of the need for a more educated workforce is in the information technology industry. The U.S. Department of Labor expects this to remain the fastest-growing industry for some time and predicts that the three fastest-growing occupations will be information technology occupations until 2012 (Horrigan 2004).

The *Workforce Improvement and Protection Act of 1998* raised the cap on the number of employment visas issued to highly skilled foreign professionals hired by American businesses (see Figure 7-2). High-tech businesses and research universities need this program to recruit foreign talent, especially when an insufficient number of highly skilled Americans are available to fill current job openings. One recent report states that the computer industry has 578 000 unfilled jobs, while American universities produce only 130 000 computer science graduates a year ('Prospects for 2003 College Graduates: Your Life' 2003). In order to compete globally, American businesses and universities need the ability to hire foreign talent freely to fill some of these positions.

The impact of knowledge worker immigration on economic growth has not gone unnoticed ('How Immigrants Keep the Hive Humming' 2002). Alan Greenspan, Chair of the U.S. Federal Reserve, has observed that 'under the conditions that we now confront, we should be carefully focused on the contribution which skilled people from abroad can contribute to this country' (Jachimowicz and Meyers 2002). The divergence in growth rates between Europe and North America in the 1990s has also

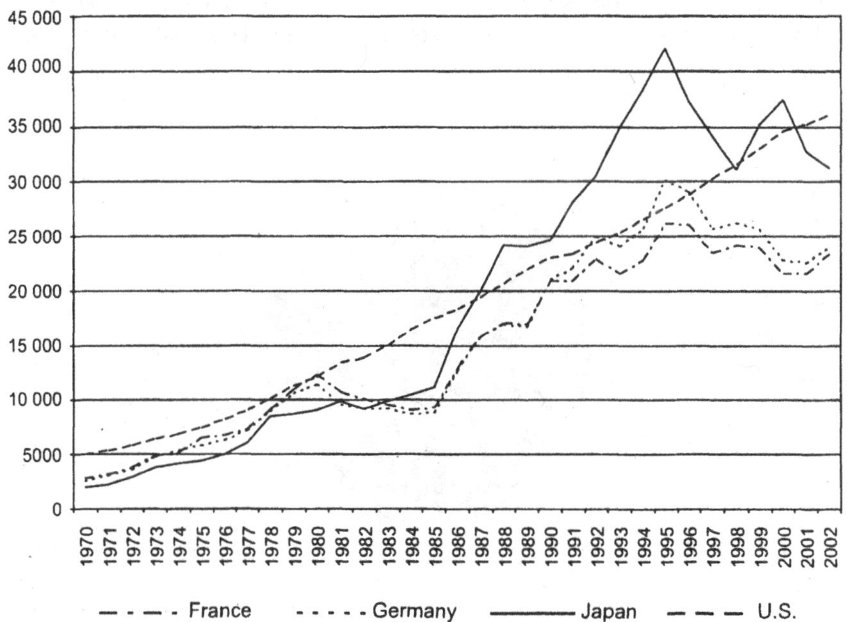

Figure 7-1 Per Capita Gross Domestic Product, 1970–2002

not escaped the attention of European policy makers. While it had always been recognised that the U.S. was a 'melting pot', the contribution from foreign-born knowledge workers in generating economic growth became increasingly apparent (see Figure 7-3.) For example, in Germany the traditional post-war view was that being German was based on blood links. As *The Economist* observed, 'for older folk, at least, being German is a question of blood links, which makes integration of non-Germans harder. Yet in reality, Germany needs more, not less, immigration ... This is one of the less open countries in an increasingly global marketplace. The world's best brains will surely take note — and go elsewhere.' Joschka Fischer, Germany's foreign minister, observed that 'other countries would slip a passport to such talented people' ('Brains Not Welcome Here' 2004).

Diversity, Entrepreneurship, and Growth

The insights of the great classical economists such as Adam Smith focussed on the allocation and distribution mechanisms of the economy, as well as the roles of capital, labour, and land, while paying only nominal attention to knowledge as an economic phenomenon. Writing in the post-war era, Robert Solow (1956) followed in this classical tradition. He based his model of economic growth on the neoclassical production function with its key factors of production — capital and labour. Solow, of course, did recognise that knowledge contributed to economic growth, but in terms of his formal model, it was considered to be an unexplained residual, which 'falls like

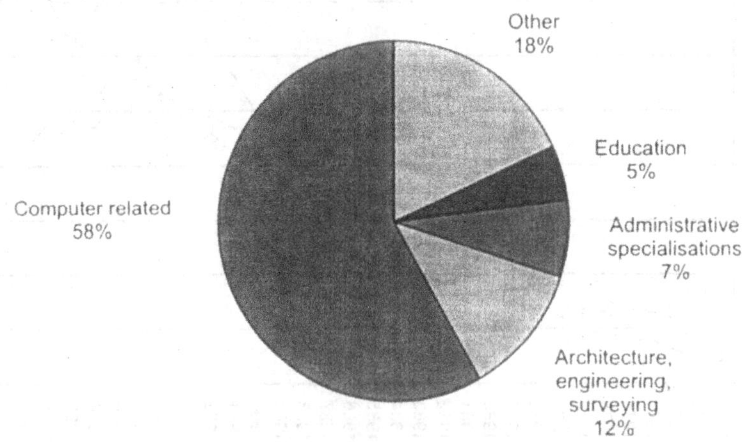

Figure 7-2 Breakdown of U.S. Workers in Specialty Occupations, 2001

manna from heaven'. A generation of economists subsequently relied upon the model of the production function as a basis for explaining the determinants of economic growth.

The focus on labour and capital as the primary factors of production, and the general exclusion or trivialisation of the role of knowledge, was not limited only to the sphere of macroeconomics. The most compelling theories of international trade were based on factors of capital and labour (and sometimes land). For example, the fundamental theorem for international trade, the Heckscher-Ohlin theory, later extended to the Heckscher-Samuelson-Ohlin model, concentrated on the factors of land, labour, and capital. According to this theory, the proportion of productive factors determines the trade structure. If there exists an abundance of physical capital relative to labour, a country will tend toward the export of capital-intensive goods; an abundance of labour relative to physical capital leads to the export of labour-intensive goods.

In fact, what became known as the Leontief Paradox was based on the statistical evidence refuting, or at least not consistent with, the Heckscher-Samuelson-Ohlin model. In particular, the Leontief Paradox pointed out that the actual patterns of U.S. trade did not correspond to the predictions of the model (Bowen, Leamer, and Sveikauskas 1988). According to systematic empirical evidence, however, the U.S. exports labour-intensive goods and imports capital-intensive goods, which suggested that the comparative advantage for post-war U.S. was based on unskilled labour rather than on capital.

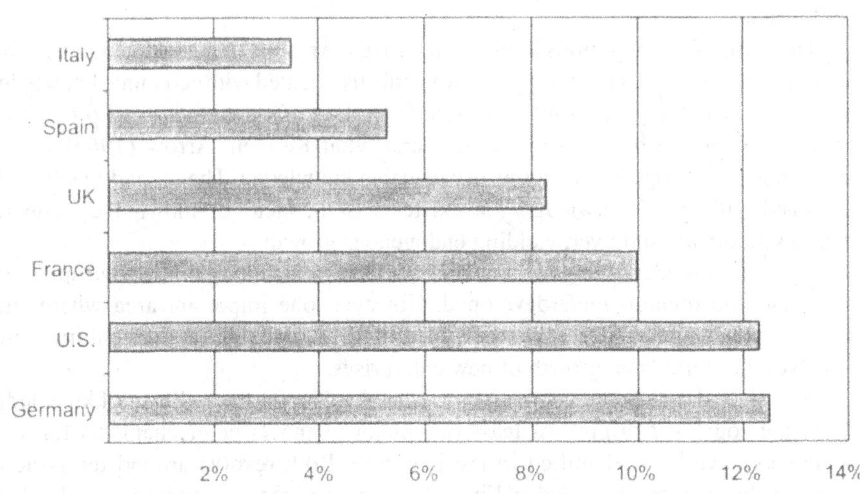

Source: Dumont and Lemaître 2004.

Figure 7-3 Foreign-Born U.S. Population as Percentage of Total, 2001

As economists struggled to resolve the Leontief Paradox, they began shifting the perspective of the model from an exclusive focus on the factors of inputs of capital and labour to probing inclusion of various aspects of knowledge. Early extensions included human capital, skilled labour, and technology. The neo-technology theories focussed on the role of research and development (R&D) and the creation of new economic knowledge in shaping the comparative advantage and flows of foreign direct investment (FDI). R&D expenditures have been thought to reflect a temporary comparative advantage resulting from products and production techniques that have not yet been adapted by foreign competitors (Gruber, Mehta, and Vernon 1967). Thus, industries with a relatively high R&D component are considered conducive to the comparative advantage of firms from the most developed countries.

The human skills hypothesis extended the Heckscher-Samuelson-Ohlin theory by including human capital as a third factor (Keesing 1966, 1967). In the presence of a relative abundance of a labour force with a high level of human capital, countries were found to export human-capital–intensive goods. Similarly, the abundance of skilled labour tended to promote the export of skill-intensive goods.

The introduction of knowledge into macroeconomic growth models was formalised by Paul Romer and Robert Lucas. Romer's (1986) critique of the Solow approach was not with the basic model of the neoclassical production function, but rather with what he perceived to be omitted from that model — knowledge. Romer, as well as Lucas (1988) and others, argued that knowledge was an important factor of production, along with the traditional factors of labour and capital, and that it was particularly important because it was endogenously determined as a result of externalities and spillovers.

There are two assumptions implicit that drive the results of the endogenous growth models. The first is that knowledge is automatically equated with economic knowledge. In fact, knowledge is inherently different from the traditional factors of production, resulting in a gap between knowledge and what Kenneth Arrow (1962) termed economic knowledge, or economically valuable knowledge. The second involves the assumed spillover of knowledge. The existence of the factor of knowledge is equated with its automatic spillover, yielding endogenous growth.

The literature identifying mechanisms actually transmitting knowledge spillovers is sparse and remains underdeveloped. However, one important area where such transmission mechanisms have been identified involves entrepreneurship, which involves the startup and growth of new enterprises.

Why should entrepreneurship serve as a mechanism for the spillover of knowledge from the source of origin? At least two major channels or mechanisms for such spillovers have been identified in the literature. Both revolve around the issue of appropriability of new knowledge. Firms develop the capacity to adapt new technology and ideas developed in other firms and are therefore able to appropriate some of the returns accruing to investments in new knowledge made externally (Cohen and Levinthal 1989). This view of spillovers is consistent with the traditional model of the knowledge production function, where the firm exists exogenously and then undertakes (knowledge) investments to generate innovative output.

By contrast, a proposed shift moves the unit of observation away from exogenously assumed firms to individuals, such as scientists, engineers, or other knowledge workers — agents with endowments of new economic knowledge (Audretsch 1995). When the lens moves from the firm to the individual as the relevant unit of observation, the appropriability issue remains, but the question becomes one of how economic agents with a given endowment of new knowledge can appropriate the returns from that knowledge. If the scientist or engineer can pursue the new idea within the organisational structure of the firm developing the knowledge, and appropriate roughly the expected value of that knowledge, that worker has no reason to leave the firm. If, however, the scientist or engineer places a greater value on his or her ideas than does the decision-making bureaucracy of the incumbent firm, the individual may choose to start a new firm to appropriate the value of that knowledge. Small enterprises can compensate for their lack of R&D through spillovers and spin-offs. Typically, an employee from an established large corporation — often a scientist or engineer working in a research laboratory — will have an idea for an invention and ultimately for an innovation. Accompanying this potential innovation is an expected net return from the new product. The inventor would expect to be compensated accordingly. If the company has a different, presumably lower, valuation of the potential innovation, it may decide not to pursue its development, or it may decide that the innovation merits a lower level of compensation than that expected by the employee.

In either case, the employee will weigh the alternative of starting his or her own firm. If the gap in the expected return accruing from the potential innovation between the inventor and the corporate decision maker is sufficiently large, and if the cost of starting a new firm is sufficiently low, the employee may decide to establish a new enterprise. Since the knowledge was generated in the large corporation, the new start-up is considered to be a spin-off from the existing firm. Such start-ups typically do not have direct access to a large R&D laboratory. Rather, these small firms succeed in exploiting the knowledge and experience acquired from the R&D laboratories with their previous employers.

University research laboratories provide a source of innovation-generating knowledge that is available to private enterprises for commercial exploitation. Indeed, the knowledge created in university laboratories spills over to contribute to the generation of commercial innovations by private enterprises (Jaffe 1989; Audretsch and Feldman 1996).

In the metaphor provided by Albert Hirschman (1980), if voice proves to be ineffective within an incumbent organisation, and loyalty is sufficiently weak, a knowledge worker may choose to exit the firm or university where the knowledge was created in order to form a new company. In this spillover channel, the knowledge production function is actually reversed. The knowledge is exogenous and embodied in a worker. The firm is created endogenously in the worker's effort to appropriate the value of his or her knowledge through innovative activity. Thus, entrepreneurship serves as the mechanism by which knowledge spills over from the source to create a new firm where that knowledge is commercialised.

A second way that entrepreneurship capital exerts a positive influence on economic output is through increased competition by the increased number of enterprises. Competition has been argued to be more conducive to knowledge externalities than is local monopoly (Jacobs 1969; Porter 1990). It should be emphasised that in this context, local competition does not mean competition within product markets, as has traditionally been envisioned within the industrial organisation literature. Rather, the competition for the new ideas is embodied in economic agents. Not only do an increased number of firms provide greater competition for new ideas, but also, in addition, greater competition across firms facilitates the entry of a new firm specialising in some particular new product niche. This is because the necessary complementary inputs and services are likely to be available from small specialist niche firms, but not necessarily from large, vertically integrated producers. Empirical evidence supports the hypothesis that an increase in competition, as measured by the number of enterprises in a city, increases the growth performance of that city (Feldman and Audretsch 1999; Glaeser et al. 1992).

A third way that entrepreneurship capital generates economic output is by providing diversity among the firms. Entrepreneurship capital generate, a greater number of enterprises, and it also increases the variety of enterprises in the location. A key assumption made in the population ecology literature is that each new organisation represents a unique approach (Hannan and Freeman 1989). A series of theoretical arguments has suggested that the degree of diversity in a location, as opposed to homogeneity, will influence the growth potential.

The theoretical basis linking diversity to economic performance is provided by Jane Jacobs (1969), who has argued that the most important sources of knowledge spillovers are external to the industry in which the firm operates and that cities are the source of considerable innovation because the diversity of these knowledge sources is greatest there. According to Jacobs, it is the exchange of complementary knowledge across diverse firms and economic agents that yields a greater return on new economic knowledge. Her theory emphasises that the variety of industries within a geographic region promotes knowledge externalities and ultimately innovative activity and economic growth.

The first important test linking diversity to economic performance, measured in terms of employment growth, was by Edward Glaeser, Hedi Kallal, José Scheinkman, and Andrei Shleifer (1992), who employed a data set on the growth of large industries in 170 cities between 1956 and 1987 in order to identify the relative importance of the degree of regional specialisation, diversity, and local competition in influencing industry growth rates. The authors found evidence that diversity promotes growth in cities.

Maryann Feldman and David Audretsch (1999) identified the extent to which diversity influences innovative output. They linked the innovative output of product categories within a specific city to the extent to which the economic activity of that city is concentrated in that industry or, conversely, diversified in terms of complementary industries sharing a common science base. Entrepreneurship capital can therefore contribute to output and growth by serving as a conduit for knowledge spillovers, increased competition, and diversity. At the heart of the evolutionary theory proposed by Richard Nelson and Sidney Winter (1974) is the selection mechanism in the economy across diverse alternatives. It is the existence of alternative and competing ways of doing things, ideas, and proposed solutions — that is, diversity — that confronts economic agents and institutions with a choice. In a most general consideration, diversity represents both the simultaneous existence of different possible actions and a differential in the valuation of potential actions by economic decision makers. The selection mechanism in the economic process serves to choose some of the proposed actions while others will be rejected.

If each economic agent were identical, such divergences in beliefs would not arise. The greater the degree of heterogeneity among agents, the greater would be the tendency for beliefs in evaluating uncertain information to converge. But individuals are not homogeneous. Rather, agents have varied personal characteristics and different experiences that shape the lens through which each evaluates where to get new information and how to assess it. That is, reasonable people confronted by the same information may evaluate it very differently, not just because they have different abilities, but because each has a different set of life experiences that shapes the decision-making process. Perhaps this helps to explain why IBM, for all its collective knowledge, not to mention resources, was proven wrong about its early rejections of the minicomputer. Steve Jobs, a college dropout, was able to see something that the decision-making hierarchy at IBM did not. Jobs had emerged from the milieu of computer 'hackers' and 'freaks' in northern California, which provided him with experience and knowledge that must have seemed invisible to the IBM decision makers, who generally populated upper middle class East Coast residential areas such as White Plains.

Thus, the phenomenon of entrepreneurship — the establishment of a new enterprise — represents not only uncertainty under imperfect information, but also the existence of diversity among the underlying population of economic agents. Diversity in the population of economic agents may ultimately lead to diversity in the types of firms populating the enterprise structure. To some extent, these diverse firms represent experiments based on differing visions about the product and how to produce it.

Diversity, however, may be the source of the increasing turbulence that is also apparently experienced in at least the United States, if not in all the member countries of the Organisation for Economic Co-operation and Development (OECD). Markets are characterised by a high degree of churning, with a high degree of entry of new enterprises and a relatively low survival rate of those startups, and only a few growing to displace the incumbent giants (Audretsch 1995). Is this market turbulence desirable or undesirable? The notion that a turbulent market is more conducive to economic growth than a stable market dates back at least to 1920, when Alfred Marshall (1920) described the dynamic process of markets where one can observe 'the young trees of the forest as they struggle upwards through the benumbing shade of their older rivals'. Building on Marshall's analogy, Charles Brown, James Hamilton, and James Medoff (1990) point out that 'the health of a forest fluctuates from year to year, depending upon rainfall, temperature, etc. and their effect on the rates of birth, death, growth, and decline. In the long run, the forest will get larger or smaller and more or less dense depending upon how these rates react to the ecological environment, the richness of the soil, disease, management practices, and so forth. And, over extended periods, a forest may [will] need new varieties of trees or new strains of existing vegetation in order to adapt to changing circumstances.' Even before Marshall, however, Joseph Schumpeter (1911) argued that a process of creative destruction takes place, where new firms with entrepreneurial spirit displace the tired old incumbents, leading to higher economic growth.

Thus, a divergence in beliefs across economic agents about potential innovations leads to a plethora of experiments and triggers the subsequent market selection process. Ultimately, it is through this selection process that industries evolve by incorporating those new ideas of economic agents that survive, either within the incumbent organisations or through the alternative — by starting new firms. This again evokes the metaphor provided by Hirschman (1980): if voice proves to be ineffective within incumbent organisations, and loyalty weakens, economic agents will resort to exit, in the form of taking their ideas elsewhere.

Several studies have suggested that the degree of diversity versus homogeneity may account for differences in rates of growth and technological change. On the one hand, specialisation of industry activities is associated with lower transactions costs and therefore greater (static) efficiency. On the other hand, a diversity of activities is argued to facilitate the exchange of new ideas and, therefore, greater innovative activity and (dynamic) efficiency.

One view, which has been attributed to the Marshall-Arrow-Romer externality, suggests that homogeneity facilitates knowledge spillovers across firms because all workers are engaged in identical activity (Glaeser et al. 1992). By contrast, it can be said that diversity facilitates knowledge spillovers (Jacobs 1969). The exchange of complementary knowledge among diverse firms and economic agents yields a greater return on new economic knowledge (Jacobs 1969; Porter 1990). Indeed, Jacobs (1969) emphasises that diversity among economic agents and firms promotes knowledge externalities and, ultimately, innovative activity and economic growth.[3]

Recent studies have provided evidence testing for the impact of diversity versus specialisation on the performance of regions, measured in terms of growth (Glaeser et al. 1992) and in terms of innovative activity (Feldman and Audretsch 1999). These studies provide systematic empirical support for the thesis that diversity is more conducive than specialisation to knowledge spillovers and innovative activity and subsequent growth.

Davud Audretsch and Max Keilbach (2004) have identified a positive impact of entrepreneurship capital on economic growth for German regions during the 1990s. In particular, their econometric results show that, if the stocks of physical and knowledge capital are held constant, a greater amount of entrepreneurship capital results in greater economic growth in German regions.

The Security-Growth Tradeoff

The events of 11 September 2001 triggered an unprecedented mandate for homeland security. There a direct cost of undertaking this security, as well as an indirect cost of mitigating the inward flow of scientists, engineers, and other knowledge workers; these costs will ultimately generate less economic growth. As *The Economist* reports,

> The State Department and the Department of Homeland Security, which are jointly responsible for visas, are struggling to respond to the concerns of scientists but they are woefully ill-equipped — files are exchanged twice weekly with the Federal Bureau of Investigation (FBI) on computer disks, while the FBI takes up to three days to reply that a person has not appeared on its database. Furthermore, the State Department keeps inadequate data about visa delays and applications. This is inexcusable. All manner of businesses use software today to segment and understand their customers' behaviour. The government's failure to use the same technology is leading to both inefficiency and a decrease in security ('Short-Sighted' 2004).

Figure 7-4 depicts the fundamental short-run tradeoff between homeland security and economic growth. Raising the costs of transnational mobility of knowledge workers as a result of increased homeland security leads to an inverse relationship, at least in the

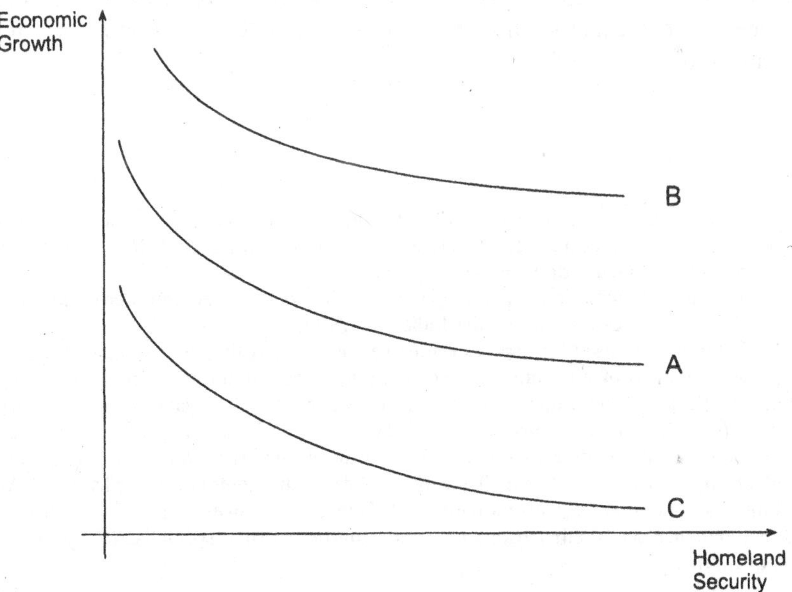

Figure 7-4 Tradeoff between Homeland Security and Economic Growth

short term. A reduced terrorist threat will shift the tradeoff from curve A to curve B, indicating that at each level of homeland security, additional growth can be attained. By contrast, an increased terrorist threat will shift the tradeoff from curve A to curve C, indicating that at each level of homeland security, less growth will be attained. A more efficient homeland security administration will also shift the curve from A to B, while a less efficient homeland security administration will shift the curve from A to C.

Conclusion

Globalisation triggered a new role for transborder labour mobility. Although immigration has always had an impact, the emergence of knowledge capital as a driving force for economic growth meant that highly skilled knowledge workers make a crucial contribution to economic growth. Not only can such knowledge workers contribute to the knowledge stock of an economy, but they are also an important source for entrepreneurial activity, which can provide a key mechanism for the spillover of knowledge. The empirical evidence suggests that, even in the European context, entrepreneurship is positively associated with economic growth.

However, the demand for homeland security has impeded the transborder flows of knowledge workers, resulting in a tradeoff between homeland security, on the one hand, and economic growth on the other hand. Homeland security may have not only a direct cost, but also an indirect cost, in terms of lower rates of economic growth. By working toward a common goal, the G8 can address this tradeoff, enabling the attainment of homeland security at the lowest possible cost in terms of foregone economic growth.

Notes

1. The authors are grateful to Bruce Jaffee and the participants of the project on 'Security, Prosperity, and Freedom: Why America Needs the G8' for their helpful comments and suggestions on an early draft of this chapter.
2. See, for example, documents submitted to the hearing of the Subcommittee on Immigration and Claims of the Committee on the Judiciary (1999).
3. The first important test of the specialisation versus diversity theories to date focussed not on the gains in terms of innovative activity, but rather gains in terms of employment growth. Glaeser, Kallal, Scheinkman, and Shleifer (1992) employed a data set on the growth of large industries in 170 cities between 1956 and 1987 in order to identify the relative importance of the degree of regional specialisation, diversity, and local competition in influencing industry growth rates. They found evidence that contradicted the Marshall-Arrow-Romer model but was consistent with Jacobs's theories. However, their study provided no direct evidence on whether diversity is more important than specialisation in generating innovation.

References

Arrow, Kenneth J. (1962). 'Economic Welfare and the Allocation of Resources for Invention'. In R. R. Nelson, ed., *The Rate and Direction of Inventive Activity*, pp. 609–626. Princeton University Press, Princeton, NJ.

Audretsch, David B. (1995). *Innovation and Industry Evolution*. MIT Press, Cambridge.

Audretsch, David B. and Maryann P. Feldman (1996). 'R&D Spillovers and the Geography of Innovation and Production'. *American Economic Review* vol. 86, no. 3, pp. 630–640.

Audretsch, David B. and Max Keilbach (2004). 'Entrepreneurship Capital: Determinants and Impact'. Max Planck Institute for Research into Economic Systems. Jena. <econpapers.hhs.se/paper/esiegpdis/2004-37.htm> (November 2004).

Audretsch, David B. and Paula E. Stephan (1996). 'Company-Scientist Locational Links: The Case of Biotechnology'. *American Economic Review* vol. 86, no. 3, pp. 641–652.

Bowen, Harry P., Edward E. Leamer, and Leo Sveikauskas (1988). 'Multicountry, Multifactor Rests of the Factor Abundance Theory'. *American Economic Review* vol. 78, no. 791–809.

'Brains Not Welcome Here: The Difficulty of Changing a Policy that Drives Talent Away' (2004). *Economist*, 1 May, p. 30.

Brown, Charles, James Hamilton, and James Medoff (1990). *Employers Large and Small*. Harvard University Press, Cambridge, MA.

Cohen, Wesley M. and D. Levinthal (1989). 'Innovation and Learning: The Two Faces of R&D'. *Economic Journal* vol. 99, no. 3, pp. 569–596.

Dumont, Jean-Christophe and Georges Lemaître (2004). 'Counting Immigrants and Expatriates in OECD Countries: A New Perspective'. Organisation for Economic Co-operation and Development, Paris. <www.oecd.org/dataoecd/27/5/33868740.pdf> (November 2004).

Feldman, Maryann P. and David B. Audretsch (1999). 'Innovation in Cities: Science-Based Diversity, Specialization, and Localized Competition'. *European Economic Review* vol. 43, pp. 409–429.

Glaeser, Edward L., Hedi D. Kallal, José A. Scheinkman, et al. (1992). 'Growth of Cities'. *Journal of Political Economy* vol. 1000, pp. 1126–1152.

Gruber, William, Dileep Mehta, and Raymond Vernon (1967). 'The R&D Factor in International Trade and Investment in the United States'. *Journal of Political Economy* vol. 75, pp. 20–37.

Hannan, Michael T. and John Freeman (1989). *Organizational Ecology*. Harvard University Press, Cambridge, MA.

Hirschman, Albert O. (1980). *Exit, Voice, and Loyalty*. Harvard University Press, Cambridge, MA.

Horrigan, Michael W. (2004). 'Employment Projections to 2012: Concepts and Context'. *Monthly Labor Review* vol. 127, no. 2.

'How Immigrants Keep the Hive Humming' (2002). *Business Week*, 24 April.

Jachimowicz, Maia and Deborah W. Meyers (2002). 'Temporary High-Skilled Migration'. Migration Information Source. <www.migrationinformation.org/USfocus/display.cfm?id=69> (November 2004).

Jacobs, Jane (1969). *The Economy of Cities*. Random House, New York.

Jaffe, Adam B. (1989). 'Real Effects of Academic Research'. *American Economic Review* vol. 79, no. 5, pp. 957–970.

Keesing, Donald B. (1966). 'Labor Skills and Comparative Advantage'. *American Economic Review* vol. 56, pp. 249–258.

Keesing, Donald B. (1967). 'The Impact of Research and Development on United States Trade'. *Journal of Political Economy* vol. 75, pp. 38–48.

Lucas, Robert E. (1988). 'On the Mechanics of Economic Development'. *Journal of Monetary Economics* vol. 22, pp. 3–39.

Lucas, Robert E. (1993). 'Making a Miracle'. *Econometrica* vol. 61, pp. 251–272.

Marshall, Alfred (1920). *Principles of Economics*. 8th ed. Macmillan, London.

Nelson, Richard R. and Sidney G. Winter (1974). 'Neoclassical vs. Evolutionary Theories of Economic Growth: Critique and Prospectus'. *Economic Journal* vol. 84 (December), pp. 886–905.

Porter, Michael E. (1990). *The Competitive Advantage of Nations*. Free Press, New York.

'Prospects for 2003 College Graduates: Your Life' (2003). *USA Today (Magazine)*, May 2003. <www.findarticles.com/p/articles/mi_m1272/is_2696_131/ai_101497527> (November 2004).

Romer, Paul M. (1986). 'Increasing Returns and Long-Run Growth'. *Journal of Political Economy* vol. 94, no. 5, pp. 1002–1037.

Schumpeter, Joseph A. (1911). *Theorie der wirtschaftlichen Entwicklung: Eine Untersuchung über Unternehmergewinn, Kapital, Kredit, Zins und den Konjunkturzyklus*. Duncker und Humbolt, Berlin.

'Short-Sighted: Visas and Science' (2004). *Economist*, 8 May, p. 13.

Solow, Robert M. (1956). 'A Contribution to the Theory of Economic Growth'. *Quarterly Journal of Economics* vol. 70, pp. 65–94.

Subcommittee on Immigration and Claims of the Committee on the Judiciary (1999). 'Immigration and America's Workforce for the 21st Century'. Hearing before the House of Representatives, 21 April 1998. <commdocs.house.gov/committees/judiciary/hju58001.000/hju58001_0f.htm> (November 2004).

Chapter 8

Borders and International Terrorism

Michele Fratianni and Heejoon Kang[1]

The tragic events of 11 September 2001 were not the first act of international terrorism on U.S. soil. Just eight years earlier, a 680-kilogram bomb blew a crater in New York's World Trade Center, killing six people, injuring approximately 1000, and causing property damage worth US$500 million (Hirschkorn 2003). If one considers the period between 1968 and 2003, the number of terrorist attacks in the world averaged in excess of 400 a year, with a peak of 665 in 1988 and a low point of 125 in 1968; there were 355 such attacks in 2001 (see Figure 8-1). The U.S. has been the preferred target of international terrorists for quite some time. Figure 8-2 shows the number of attacks against the United States, both at home and abroad, as a fraction of total attacks. The average between 1968 and 2003 is 0.4, with a peak of 0.72 in 1971 and a low point of 0.2 in 1993; the ratio was 0.62 in 2001. Terrorists, as opposed to criminals, kill and destroy indiscriminately to achieve political goals and to advertise their agenda. The larger the number of casualties — defined as the sum of killed plus wounded individuals — the larger the propaganda value of the attacks. Between 1968 and 1973, the number of casualties per attack averaged 1.2; from 1974 to 1993, the average more than doubled with respect to the previous period; and from 1994 to 2003 the average tripled, again with respect to the early period (see Figure 8-3). This evidence is consistent with the general principle that, over time, the public falls into assuefaction and that terrorists resort to more spectacular attacks to draw attention to their causes.

What was new with 11 September is that terrorists signalled unequivocally their determination and organisational skill to use weapons of mass destruction (WMD) to achieve their objectives; the public quickly understood the huge discrete jump in terrorist risk. The 2001 event was also distinctive in that Islamic fundamentalist terrorists targeted the leader of the club of industrial and capitalist democracies.[2] The reaction of the U.S. government was first to close the borders, then to tighten security at airports and on airplanes, then to create the new Department of Homeland Security with a large budget, and, finally, to declare a 'war on terror'. After an initial phase of international co-operation in the war in Afghanistan, the Bush administration adopted a unilateralist approach to the war on terror, culminating with the doctrine of pre-emptive strikes and the U.S. invasion of Iraq with the 'coalition of the willing'. In sum, the United States has been willing, so far, to bear large costs to suppress international terrorism.

In the preceding chapter, David Audretsch, Richard Stazinski, and Taylor Aldridge deal with the tradeoff between economic growth and homeland security. This chapter,

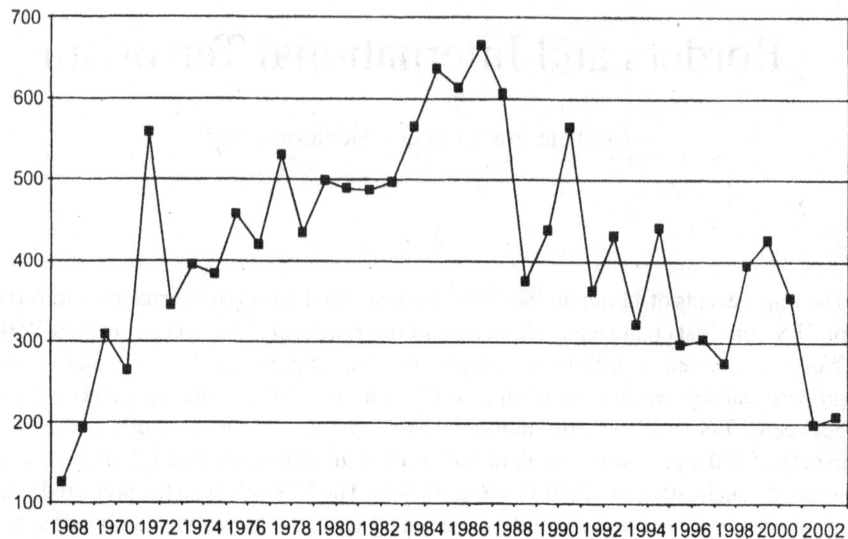

Sources: Sandler 2003, Table 1; United States Department of State 2003, 2004.

Figure 8-1 Number of Terrorist Attacks, 1968–2003

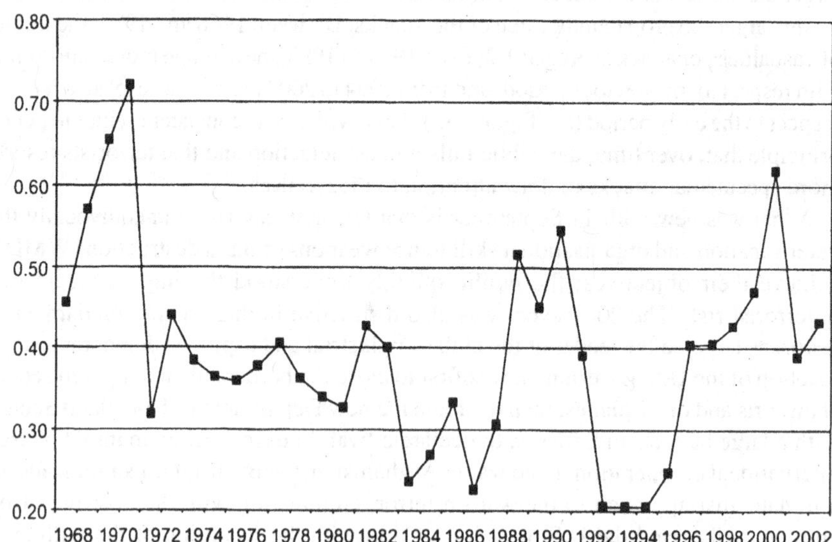

Sources: Sandler 2003, Table 1; United States Department of State 2003, 2004.

Figure 8-2 Ratio of Attacks against the United States to Total Attacks

however, analyses a different aspect of the policy of border hardening: the impact it may have on cross-country flows of human capital and goods. This analysis is based on the assumption of a positive association between counterterrorism and efforts to make national borders less permeable. Less permeable borders will slow down not only migration of bad human capital and harmful goods, but also migration of good human capital and trade flows. The prediction results from the impossibility of raising costs only on undesirable transactions.

The chapter proceeds as follows. At the moment, the U.S. is the primary counterterrorist force and has hardened its borders. Over time, other industrial economies will develop incentives to stop free riding on U.S. actions and adopt similar border security. The multilateral approach to counterterrorism, while appearing a co-operative solution, will in fact emerge because 'private' costs of international terrorism will shift progressively from the United States to the other members of the club. One aspect of counterterrorism concerns the rise in the so-called home bias of intra-national trade. Measured domestic gross domestic product (GDP) may not necessarily decline, but welfare may diminish as a result of resources being redeployed to lower value use. The search for minimising the cost of hardened borders may lead regional trade agreements to experiment with common security perimeters; this, in turn, will lead to a deeper regional trade bias.

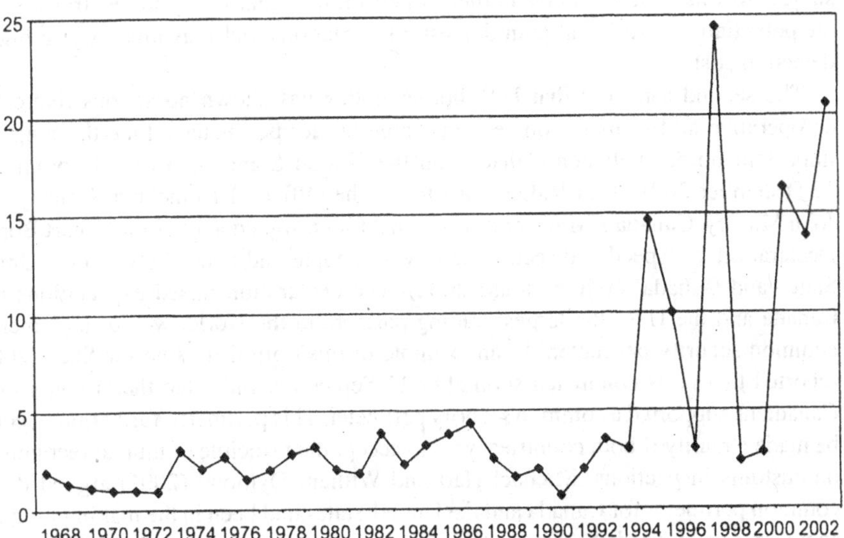

Sources: Sandler 2003, Table 1; United States Department of State 2003, 2004.

Figure 8-3 Casualties per Attack

The Hardening of the U.S. Border

Immediately following the 11 September attacks, the U.S. government virtually shut down the border — air, sea, and land. The White House (2002) issued a press release that aimed at making the border much less permeable for 'terrorists, weapons of mass destruction, illegal migrants, contraband, and other unlawful commodities'. The same press release stated the twin objectives of the new border policy:

- First, America's air, land, and sea borders must provide a strong defense for the American people against all external threats, most importantly international terrorists but also drugs, foreign disease, and other dangerous items.
- Second, America's border must be highly efficient, posing little or no obstacle to legitimate trade and travel.

Two aspects of the statement need to be underscored. The first is that there is no explicit recognition that a more secure border implies a less open border or of the difficult tradeoff between the two objectives. Yet, this exchange is inherent in the nature of terrorism: lethal transactions are imbedded into apparently legitimate transactions. To detect the potentially harmful transactions, flows of people and goods must be subject to costly inspection and monitoring. This translates into a transaction cost and, ultimately, into a reduction in total factor productivity. While all transactions are subject to this cost, a tighter border policy implies that cross-border transactions are potentially more lethal than domestic transactions and thus must bear a higher detection cost.[3]

The second aspect is that U.S. border policy has shown no serious interest in co-operative arrangements on securing large border perimeters. Take the long and important border between Canada and the United States as a case in point. On 12 December 2001, Tom Ridge, Director of the Office of Homeland Security, and John Manley, Canada's Minister of Foreign Affairs, signed a 30-point 'Smart Border Declaration' to 'speed and secure the flow of people and goods between the United States and Canada' (White House 2002). The declaration raised expectations that Canada and the U.S., the largest trading partners in the world, would implement a common security perimeter. As an example of this optimism, Andrew Shea (2001) reported that polls conducted soon after 11 September indicated that a majority of Canadians supported a common security perimeter. This perimeter, furthermore, could be made a reality if both countries were to accept the principle of mutual recognition on customs inspections. Michael Hart and William Dymond (2001) argued that a common perimeter for Canada and the United States had been in the making for quite some time, and cited the North American Air Defense Command (NORAD), the Autopact, and the North American Free Trade Agreement (NAFTA) as precursors of the common perimeter.[4] But the reality is that the U.S. government has very little interest in a policy of mutual recognition. Differences in preferences and power are too wide to build on a common security perimeter that is not a mere extension of the U.S. border system (Golob 2002). On 23 January 2003, Manley acknowledged that

> whether we want it or not, and I think probably we don't, the U.S. would not be interested in that kind of measure [that is, a common North America perimeter] ... I don't think they are any way near to eliminating or reducing borders (Fife and Dawson 2003).

Evidence bearing on the impact of a hardened U.S. border on cross-border transactions comes from the much higher cost of obtaining visas for the United States. According to the *Financial Times*, 'nearly three-quarters of [surveyed] companies had experienced unexpected delays or arbitrary denials of business visa applications, while 60 per cent said the delays had hurt their companies through increased costs or lost sales' (Alden 2004a). Furthermore, the U.S. border has been hardened relative to other national or regional borders. Consider, for example, the recent efforts by a group of U.S. universities to push the Department of Homeland Security to review border procedures. According to a survey conducted by the Council of Graduate Schools, foreign applications to U.S. colleges and universities fell 32 percent during the last reporting period over the previous one; for Chinese graduate applications, the drop was 76 percent (Grimes 2004). In contrast, foreign applications have been rising in Australia, Canada, and the United Kingdom. U.S. secretary of state Colin Powell, remarking on the difficulty of organising international scientific exchanges and conferences in the U.S. because of the new restrictions, said: 'This hurts us. It is not serving our interests. And so we really do have to work on it' (Alden 2004b).

In sum, the mostly qualitative evidence on border security can be summarised as follows. The U.S. has responded to 11 September by launching a war on terror that is based on the principle of pre-emptive strikes abroad and secure borders at home. This is, on the whole, a unilateralist policy: the co-operation of other nations is welcome but, if not forthcoming, the Bush administration will continue its policy without it. The tradeoff of a more secure border is a less open border, with adverse consequences on international trade and flows of human capital. The rest of this chapter will analyse, in a strategic context, how the U.S. border policy will affect other national borders and then provide some suggestive evidence of the likely effects of border hardening on international trade.

Counterterrorism, Unilateralism, and Co-operation

If counterterrorism were a classic public good — that is, non-excludable and non-rivalrous — the equilibrium outcome would be output underprovision or outright zero output. But, as noted, the U.S. has such high private benefits from counterterrorism that, for a broad range of cost estimates, it is willing to undertake unilateral actions, including pre-emptive strikes against sovereign states. Furthermore, U.S.

counterterrorism generates large external benefits to the rest of the industrial and capitalist club. It follows that this is an ideal scenario for other club members — the Western industrial democracies — to free ride on U.S. actions, or, if not free riding, pay riding (Lee 1988). Under pay riding, club members undertake some co-operation with the United States but, at the same time, give something of value to terrorists. A classic example of pay riding is Saudi Arabia, an ally of the U.S. but the home of radical Wahabism. A second example is Spain, which pulled its troops from Iraq after the catastrophic terrorist attack of 11 March 2004 in Madrid. Honduras and the Dominican Republic have also pulled their troop contingents from Iraq, following Spain. Poland, Thailand, Kazakhstan, and the Philippines have indicated that they may revisit their troop commitments. Free riding and pay riding have similar outcomes in that they generate equilibrium solutions that deviate from the optimal co-operative solution. They leave the U.S. in the asymmetric position of bearing the largest cost of terrorism and enforcing almost unilaterally the hardening of the border. This can be referred to as a unilateralist solution to the war on terror and border security.

Over time, the unilateralist solution is likely to turn into a multilateral one, for two reasons. The first is that the United States will exert pressure on members of the club to tighten up their border security, stop free or pay riding, and absorb a larger share of the war on terror. So far, the most visible manifestation of collective action on the part of the industrial-capitalist club is in sharing security intelligence; for the rest, club members still behave as independent sovereign nations. The second reason is that terrorists will readjust their strategy after the hardening of the U.S. border and will substitute softer targets and countries with less secure borders for harder targets and countries with more secure borders (Sandler, Tschirhart, and Cauley 1983). Walter Enders and Todd Sandler (2003, 14) summarise the evidence on this substitution effect. For example, 'metal detectors were estimated to reduce skyjackings and threats and hoaxes by 13 and 9.5 incidents per quarter, respectively. However, the number of other hostage-taking incidents and assassinations rose by almost 10 incidents per quarter'. Also, the fortification of U.S. embassies has reduced attacks against them but has brought an increase in political assassinations (15). Following 11 September and the hardening of the U.S. border, terrorists have hit Indonesia, the Philippines, Saudi Arabia, Spain, and Turkey. A shift in favour of softer targets has apparently already occurred.

The effect of these two forces will raise the marginal private benefits of counterterrorism for the other members of the club. The incentives for free riding and pay riding will diminish, borders will be hardened, and counterterrorist activity will rise. It will appear as if club members had co-ordinated their strategies. But, in fact, the outcome is one of strategically interacting independent border policies. In the long run, club members will enjoy comparable levels of border security, although they will fall short of applying mutual recognition of visa and customs inspection.[5] This can be called a multilateral scenario.

A more secure border implies a less permeable border. From a strictly economic viewpoint, borders raise trading costs, a collection of transaction costs, and regime costs, such as transport, administration, differences in legal systems and practices, languages, networks, competitive policies, and monetary regimes. Trading costs can be considered the melting part of an iceberg during its travels in warm weather or, alternatively, as a wedge between the price paid by consumers in the importing country and the exporter's net supply price (as in Anderson and van Wincoop 2003). Either way, the border represents a discrete jump in trading costs. The hardening of the border either makes the iceberg melt faster or raises the price wedge. The effects of a harder border will be a mixture of the substitution of home transactions for cross-border transactions and 'trade diversion'.

For example, if the world consisted only of Canada, Mexico, and the U.S., and the U.S. hardened its border against Mexico, and that higher bilateral border barrier raised Mexican import price from the United States, then U.S. exporters would substitute the home market for the Mexican market. By contrast, if there is substitutability between Canadian and U.S. exports, then U.S. exports to Mexico would be partly replaced by Canadian exports. Similar considerations would hold for Mexican exporters to the United States. The harder bilateral border would generate a mixture of substitution of home transactions for cross-border transactions and trade diversion from country pairs with harder borders to country pairs with softer borders. This is essentially the implication of gravity model described by James Anderson and Eric van Wincoop (2003), which responds not only to bilateral trading costs, but also to multilateral resistance factors that depend on all bilateral trading costs. In sum, a hardening of the border will reduce and redirect cross-border trade unless policy-driven liberalisation compensates for the higher trading costs.

One way to compensate for the adverse economic effect of a more secure border is to create a security perimeter that encompasses countries with similar preferences and standards for the fight on terrorism. A larger security perimeter would achieve economies of scale so long as the cost of security is proportional to the length of the perimeter and the benefits from trade are proportional to the size of the area defined by such a perimeter.[6] In addition to obvious economies of scale, the larger perimeter would reduce much of the trading costs associated with borders. Custom unions would be best suited for such perimeters because they already share a common commercial policy. To make it work, participating countries would have to accept each other's standards; trust is essential. The EU has advanced the farthest in this respect.[7] The hardening of borders would speed up regional security perimeters and attempt to capture within the region some of the trade that is being lost between regions. Regional trade bias would be accentuated.

The Impact of Counterterrorism on Trade

This section analyses the likely impact of counterterrorist policies on international trade, proceeding as follows. First, the literature is followed to proxy the unobserved trading costs with distance. If t_{ij} equals trading costs between country i and country j and d_{ij} equals the greater circle distance between country i and country j, then t_{ij} equals d_{ij}. The so-called border effect can thus be ignored at first. The estimate of α in a gravity model, in log linear form, is the elasticity of real bilateral trade flows with respect to trading cost. The impact of counterterrorism on trade works through distance: bilateral distances are stretched out by the policy to secure safe transactions. The second approach is to estimate α for different groups of countries based on the conjecture that trading costs are not homogeneous. Trading costs can be expected to be higher among developing countries than among industrial countries and among countries with conflicting cultures than among countries with similar cultures. If so, counterterrorism will have differentiated effects.

In the final approach t_{ij} equals $(br_{ij})d_{ij}$, where br_{ij} is unity when there are no borders — that is, trade occurs between two regions located in the same country, otherwise, it is one plus the tariff equivalent bilateral border (Anderson and van Wincoop 2003, equation 18). Using provincial, state, and state-provincial data for 1988, John McCallum (1995) estimated that trade among Canadian provinces, according to a gravity model, is 22 times the trade between U.S. states and Canadian provinces. This finding has been considered extremely large by the literature. Anderson and van Wincoop criticise McCallum's study for omitting the above-mentioned multilateral resistance factors and for ignoring the relative economic size of countries. Since the smaller the country, the larger the fraction of its output exposed to trading costs, border barriers have asymmetric effects: a small country such as Canada faces a much thicker border than a large country such as the United States. The analysis that follows uses Anderson and van Wincoop's empirical findings to draw inferences on the impact of hardened borders on trade flows.

Homogeneous Distance

The gravity model has had considerable success in explaining bilateral trade flows in terms of income, population, distance as a proxy of trading costs, and country characteristics. A stylised representation of this model is given by (1):

$$\begin{aligned} \ln(x_{ijt}) = {} & \alpha_0 + \alpha_1 \ln(y_i y_j)_t + \alpha_2 \ln(I_i I_j)_t + \alpha \ln(d_{ij}) + \\ & + \alpha_3 RTA_{ijt} + \alpha_4 MU_{ijt} + \alpha_5 FEAT_{ijt} + u_{ijt}, \end{aligned} \tag{1}$$

where x_{ijt} equals real bilateral trade between country i and country j at time t, y equals real gross domestic product (the counterpart of Newton's masses), I equals per capita real GDP, d equals distance, RTA equals trade between partners that belong to the same regional trade agreement, MU equals trade between country pairs that share the same currency, FEAT equals a vector of dummy variables that capture idiosyncratic country characteristics (that is, its features), and u_{ijt} is an independent and identically distributed error term. The number of dummy variables in FEAT can be very large and includes year dummy variables and time-invariant factors such as common language, common coloniser, and shared land border. RTA and MU are highlighted because there is a sizeable and growing literature on the trade bias created by regional trade agreements and currency unions (for leading examples, see Frankel 1997; Rose 2000).

Table 8-1 shows estimates of (1) using bilateral real trade flows from 1970 to 1999, at five-year intervals.[8] The dependent variable is a simple average of four bilateral flows: exports from i to j, imports of i from j and corresponding flows for the other trading partner. Some changes were made here to the data with respect to the definition of MU, regional, interregional, and individual RTA dummy variables (see Appendix 8-1). The regional dummy is equal to one when both countries belong to the same RTA; otherwise it is zero. Regionalism is defined in terms of eleven separate RTAs. The interregional dummy is equal to one when the two trading partners belong to different RTAs; otherwise it is zero.

Estimates from pooled analysis in Table 8-1 are broadly consistent with those obtained elsewhere in the literature. Trade flows respond positively to real income and negatively to population. The large and controversial positive trade bias due to monetary union is smaller than the positive bias due to regional trade agreements. The larger regional trade biases occur in Latin America, the South Pacific, and the members of the Association of Southeast Asian Nations (ASEAN). In the European Community/European Union, the bias is negative. The positive coefficient of the interregional dummy does not suggest that regionalism has created statistically significant trade-diverting effects. Altogether, the adopted specification controls for a variety of effects.

The estimate of β, which is of direct interest to this analysis, is –1.17 with an extremely low standard error of 0.014; thus, it is significantly different from –1. An increase in distance of 1 percent lowers real bilateral trade flows by 1.17 percent. If counterterrorist policies are interpreted as an increase in trading costs and an increase in trading costs as a lengthening of distance, then border security will have an economically significant adverse impact on cross-border trade. An important question is whether distance will rise uniformly for close and distant countries. For example, will exporters to the United States incur once-for-all costs to set up pre-clearing procedures at their points of shipping, or will they also incur additional costs that are proportional to distance (for example, a counterterrorist freight surcharge based on mileage)? If fixed costs were to prevail over variable costs, then the increase in distance would be proportionately much larger for close than distant countries.[9]

Heterogeneous Distance

Equation (1) assumes that trading costs were homogeneous across countries. Michele Fratianni and Heejoon Kang (2004) have tested whether homogeneity for different groups of countries can be rejected. They produced two such tests: one for member countries of the Organisation for Economic Co-operation and Development (OECD) versus non-member countries, and the other for Christian versus Islamic countries. For the first of the two tests, they divided the sample into three categories: pairs in which both countries

Table 8-1 Estimates from Gravity Model

Dependent variable is the log of real bilateral trade flows.

Variables	With RTA Effects	With Separate RTAs
Intercept	−29.28[c] (0.214)	−30.0[c] (0.218)
Log of real GDP	0.88[c] (0.004)	0.89[c] (0.004)
Log of real GDP per capita	0.42[c] (0.007)	0.43[c] (0.007)
Log of distance	−1.17[c] (0.014)	−1.17[c] (0.014)
Regional dummy	1.16[c] (0.074)	
Interregional dummy	0.35[c] (0.036)	0.30[c] (0.036)
Common currency dummy	0.80[c] (0.085)	0.92[c] (0.085)
Common land border dummy	0.43[c] (0.066)	0.48[c] (0.067)
Common colonizer before 1945 dummy	0.62[c] (0.038)	0.60[c] (0.038)
Common country dummy	1.18[a] (0.662)	1.16[a] (0.659)
Colonial relationship dummy	1.58[c] (0.077)	1.58[c] (0.077)
Common language dummy	0.35[c] (0.027)	0.32[c] (0.027)
1975, 1980, 1985, 1990, 1995, and 1999 year dummies	Estimated but not reported here	Estimated but not reported here
ASEAN dummy		1.75[c] (0.222)
Andean dummy		0.72[a] (0.380)
CARICOM dummy		2.0[c] (0.131)
CACM dummy		2.03[c] (0.257)
European Community/EU dummy		−0.62[c] (0.125)
MERCOSUR dummy		0.94 (0.600)
NAFTA dummy		0.13 (0.784)
SPARTECA dummy		3.10[c] (0.208)
USIS dummy		1.35 (1.036)
PATCRA dummy		−0.67 (0.943)
ANZCERTA dummy		−0.92 (1.056)
Number of observations	43 746	43 746
R^2	0.64	0.64

Notes: 1. The dependent variable is the average of four-way trade flows between country i and j in 1995 U.S. dollars. 2. Numbers in parentheses are standard errors: a. indicates statistical significance at the 10 percent level; b. at the 5 percent level; c. at the 1 percent level. 3. ANZCERTA = Australia-New Zealand Closer Economic Relations Trade Agreement; ASEAN = Association of Southeast Asian Nations; CACM = Central American Common Market; CARICOM = Caribbean Community and Common Market; MERCOSUR = Common Market of the South; NAFTA = North American Free Trade Agreement; PATCRA = Australia and Papua New Guinea; SPARTECA = South Pacific Regional Trade and Economic Co-operation Agreement; USIS = United States and Israel. 4. Estimates were obtained from OLS on pooled data. See Appendix 8-1 for a description of dataset.

are OECD countries, pairs in which one country is an OECD country and the other is not, and pairs in which neither is an OECD member. The estimated βs range from –0.73, when both in the pair are OECD countries, to –1.29, when neither is a member. The null hypothesis of distance homogeneity is rejected. The result accords with the expectation that trading costs are larger for developing countries than for industrial countries. Under a scenario where the absolute values of βs were positively correlated with security risks — a plausible situation since security is costly in both capital and organisational skills, for which developing countries are at a comparative disadvantage — the burden of counterterrorist measures would fall disproportionately on poorer and more open countries.

The greatest threat to industrial democracies comes from Islamic fundamentalism. Because Islamic fundamentalism is more likely to breed in Islamic countries than in non-Islamic countries, Fratianni and Kang also tested the distance homogeneity assumption with respect to religion. Defining a country as Islamic or Christian if more than 50 percent of its population is Muslim and Christian, respectively, they divided the sample into four different categories: pairs in which both countries are Islamic, pairs in which both countries are Christian, pairs in which one country is Christian and the other is Islamic, and pairs in which neither country is Christian or Islamic. Here as well, the null hypothesis of distance homogeneity was rejected at the level of 1 percent. The lowest βs, in absolute value, occurred when both countries in the pair are either Islamic or neither; the highest occurred when one of the countries in the pair is Christian and the other Islamic. Under the plausible scenario that Christian countries will apply tougher security measures on imports from Islamic countries than on non-Islamic countries, the burden of counterterrorist measures is likely to fall disproportionately on Islamic countries.

Border Effect

While there is agreement that a border represents a discontinuity in trading costs, the open question remains about the size of this discontinuity. Anderson and van Wincoop (2003) have offered the most convincing analysis on this issue. Two of their results are particularly important. The first, as already mentioned, is that the impact of the border is bigger for small countries than for large countries. The small country has a high exposure to cross-border trade, whereas the large country has a high exposure to inside-the-border trade. When Anderson and van Wincoop re-estimate McCallum's equation both from the viewpoint of Canada and the United States, the ratio of intra-national trade to cross-border trade for Canada is approximately ten times that of the United States; in other words, relative bilateral border barriers are proportional to the relative economic sizes of the trading countries.[10] The second is that an increase in border barriers reduces cross-border trade between large countries more than between small countries. In the Anderson and van Wincoop model, cross-border trade declines when bilateral border barriers rise relative to the multilateral resistance factors of the two trading countries (Anderson and van Wincoop 2003, equation 13). The rise in border barriers has a small impact on the multilateral resistance factor of the large country and a large impact on that of the small country (first result). It follows that, under a uniform increase in border barriers, cross-border trade falls more for large than small countries (Anderson and van Wincoop 2003, equation 15 and Table 4).

Implications for Border Policy

Let us consider the implications for counterterrorism, starting with the first scenario of unilateral hardening of the U.S. border. By assumption, only bilateral border barriers between the United States and all its trading partners rise. Reductions in cross-border transactions will be highest for large country pairs such as the U.S.-EU, U.S.-Japan, and U.S.-China. The rise in border barriers will cause a substitution of home trade for cross-border trade, and this will be highest for small economies. Another adjustment resulting from the hardening of the borders comes from the substitution of trade between country pairs with lower trading costs for country pairs with higher trading costs. International trade would be diverted toward lower-barrier countries and would further penalise trade with the United States.

In the second scenario, the multilateral, other industrial economies eventually respond to the terrorist challenge and harden their borders. If one assumes that border hardening is high for the G7 — which in 1999 accounted for approximately 50 percent of total real U.S. trade flows — and low for every one else. Trade diversion to country pairs with lower trading costs would be diluted relative to the unilateralist scenario; substitution of intra-national trade for cross-border trade would rise, again relative to the unilateralist scenario. Of course, there is no way to rank these outcomes in a welfare sense, in the absence of information on the preferences of policy makers about the tradeoff between more open and less secure borders.

Common Security Perimeters and Regional Trade Bias

Unilateralism provides the benefit of aligning policies to domestic preferences but ignores the costs due to feedback effects and negative externalities. Countries and regions that are adversely affected by tighter border security would be looking for ways to reduce its cost. Seen from the perspective of the gravity model, international trade suffers from several biases, one of which is regionalisation (see Table 8-1). U.S. unilateralism on the war on terror and border security may actually accelerate the process of regional deepening through the launch of common security perimeters. Regional trade agreements with homogeneous countries and preferences would be the fastest in implementing such a perimeter — the EU being the obvious candidate. Customs unions would face lower co-ordinating costs than free trade associations. On the whole, U.S. unilateralism would accentuate the regional trade bias.

Conclusion

The savage attacks on the United States of 11 September 2001 fundamentally altered the attitude and policy of the leader of the industrial democracies with respect to international terrorism. Unilateralism has characterised the initial phase of this policy. It is a very costly policy in terms of resources devoted to secure the national border and military expenditures to fight terrorism abroad and to pre-empt attacks of so-called rogue states. It is also likely to be costly in terms of reduced transnational flows of trade, physical capital, and human capital — the focus of this chapter. Unilateralism cannot last: in addition to it not being in the interest of the United States, the search for softer targets on the part of terrorists will ultimately yield a multilateral solution to terrorism, at least within the confines of the large industrial democracies. Unlike a pure public good, counterterrorism generates large private benefits and mitigates free riding.

In this chapter, border security has been interpreted as an increase in trading costs. In the first exercise, these unobserved increases were proxied with a longer distance. Since there is no metric to transform border security into distance, the predictions here were more qualitative than quantitative. The impact of distance on cross-border trade is not homogeneous across different groups: it is higher among developing countries than among industrial countries and higher when Islamic countries trade with Christian countries than when either Islamic or non-Islamic countries trade among themselves. One implication of these findings is that the actions to secure borders by industrial democracies will have differentiated effects across countries and will affect those societies most adversely that already have animosity and resentment against the West. The third and final exercise considered the impact of higher border security on the so-called border effect and cross-border trade. In the context of the work by Anderson and van Wincoop, it can be inferred that safer borders by the industrial democracies will disproportionately thicken the economic borders of small and open economies, leading to a larger home bias of intra-national trade. It will also divert cross-border trade toward countries with smaller border restrictions. In an attempt to minimise the cost of hardened borders, some regional trade agreements may experiment with common security perimeters. This will lead to a deeper regional trade bias.

This chapter ends with two caveats. The first is that the underlying premise here is that terrorism is imbedded more in cross-border transactions than in intra-national transactions. So far, this premise is justified by actual policy that behaves as if the premise were true. The alternative hypothesis is that terrorism is just as probable in domestic transactions as it is in cross-border transactions; in that case, the focus of the research should be on total factor productivity. Recent work suggests that terrorism affects economic growth negatively, but much less than internal conflict or wars (Blomberg, Hess, and Orphanides 2004). The second caveat is that counterterrorist measures are likely to have differentiated effects on countries and industries. The findings in this chapter showed that distance affects different groups of countries differently. The natural extension is to study distance and border asymmetries with respect to different industries.

Notes

1. The authors thank George von Furstenberg for detailed comments on a previous draft of this chapter and Anand Jha for research assistance.
2. There is a growing literature on the causes of Islamic fundamentalism, which are not critical for the analysis presented in this chapter. Whatever the causes, Islamic fundamentalism considers the industrial democracies a legitimate target of indiscriminate violence.
3. This is not to say that cross-border transactions are, on average, more lethal than domestic transactions. The policy assumes that they are.
4. Hart and Dymond (2001) fail to note that NAFTA is not a customs union and, hence, has no common commercial policy.
5. In fact, some evidence is emerging that matters are already moving in this direction. For example, the *New York Times* reports that the European Union's counterterrorist co-ordinator has been trying to reassure the U.S. government that the EU will harden its counterterrorist practices (Smith 2004).
6. For example, the elasticity of the area of the circle with respect to the radius is twice as large as the elasticity of the circumference with respect to the radius.
7. In addition to accepting each other's passports, the member countries of the EU pledged to develop a common policy on asylum and migration by 2004 (see EU 2001).
8. Because of data limitation, the last year here is 1999, which represents a four-year interval relative to 1995. The dataset and data description are taken from Andrew Rose (2003).
9. The authors thanks George von Furstenberg for raising this point.
10. According to the last column of Table 1 in Anderson and van Wincoop (2003), the ratio of the two borders is actually 8.77.

References

Alden, Edward (2004a). 'Visa Delays Cost Corporate America "More than Dollars 30bn" over Two Years'. *Financial Times*, 2 June, p. 1.

Alden, Edward (2004b). 'Washington Launches Border Control Review'. *Financial Times*, 23 April, p. 2.

Anderson, James E. and Eric van Wincoop (2003). 'Gravity with Gravitas: A Solution to the Border Puzzle'. *American Economic Review* vol. 93, no. 1, pp. 170–193.

Blomberg, S. Brock, Gregory D. Hess, and Athanasios Orphanides (2004). 'The Macroeconomic Consequences of Terrorism'. *Journal of Monetary Economics* vol. 51, no. 5, pp. 1007–1032.

Enders, Walter and Todd Sandler (2003). 'What Do We Know about the Substitution Effect in Transnational Terrorism?' In A. Silke and G. Ilardi, eds., *Researching Terrorism: Trends, Achievements, Failures*. Frank Cass, Ilford.

European Union (2001). 'Coordination of the Community Immigration Policy'. <www.europa.eu.int/scadplus/leg/en/lvb/l33155.htm> (November 2004).

Fife, Robert and Anne Dawson (2003). 'Border Stays: Manley'. *National Post*, 23 January, p. A04.

Frankel, Jeffrey A. (1997). *Regional Trading Blocs in the World Economic System*. Institute for International Economics, Washington DC.

Fratianni, Michele and Heejoon Kang (2004). 'Heterogeneous Distance-Elasticities in Trade Gravity Models'. Kelley School of Business, Indiana University. Unpublished.

Golob, Stephanie R. (2002). 'North America Beyond NAFTA? Sovereignty, Identity, and Security in Canada-U.S. Relations'. *Canadian-American Public Policy* vol. 52 (December), pp. 1–44.

Grimes, Christopher (2004). 'Universities Hit by "Unwelcoming" Visa Rules'. *Financial Times*, 29 April, p. 1.

Hart, Michael and William Dymond (2001). 'Common Border, Shared Destinies: Canada, the United States, and Deepening Integration'. Centre for Trade Policy and Law. Ottawa. <www.carleton.ca/ctpl/borders/hartdymondweb.htm> (November 2004).

Hirschkorn, Phil (2003). 'New York Remembers 1993 WTC Victims'. CNN, 26 February. <edition.cnn.com/2003/US/Northeast/02/26/wtc.bombing> (November 2004).

Lee, Dwight R. (1988). 'Free Riding and Paid Riding in the Fight against Terrorism'. *American Economic Review* vol. 78, no. 2, pp. 22–26.

McCallum, John (1995). 'National Borders Matter: Canada-U.S. Regional Trade Patterns'. *American Economic Review* vol. 85, no. 3, pp. 615–623.

Rose, Andrew K. (2000). 'One Money, One Market: The Effects of Common Currency on Trade'. *Economic Policy* vol. 30 (April), pp. 9–45.

Rose, Andrew K. (2003). 'Which International Institutions Promote International Trade?' Data set. <faculty.haas.berkeley.edu/arose/RecRes.htm#Software> (November 2004).

Sandler, Todd (2003). 'Collective Action and Transnational Terrorism'. *World Economy* vol. 26, pp. 779–802.

Sandler, Todd, John T. Tschirhart, and John Cauley (1983). 'A Theoretical Analysis of Transnational Terrorism'. *American Political Science Review* vol. 77, pp. 36–77.

Shea, Andrew (2001). 'Border Choices: Balancing the Need for Security and Trade'. Conference Board of Canada, October. <www.conferenceboard.ca/documents.asp?rnext=61> (November 2004).

Smith, Craig S. (2004). 'Europe's Chief on Terrorism to Reassure U.S. on Efforts'. *New York Times*, 10 May, p. 6.

United States Department of State (2003). 'Patterns of Global Terrorism 2003'. <www.state.gov/s/ct/rls/pgtrpt/2003/> (November 2004).

United States Department of State (2004). 'Patterns of Global Terrorism: The Year in Review (Revised)'. 22 June. <www.state.gov/s/ct/rls/pgtrpt/2003/33771.htm> (November 2004).

White House (2002). 'Securing America's Borders Fact Sheet: Border Security'. 25 January. <www.whitehouse.gov/news/releases/2002/01/20020125.html> (November 2004).

Appendix 8-1
The Data

The dataset used in this study was compiled by Andrew Rose (2003), but modified or expanded with respect to the definition of currency unions (CU), regional, interregional, individual regional trade agreements (RTAs), OECD/non-OECD countries, and Islamic countries.

CU countries include, for different years, those in the following areas:

- the U.S. dollar (United States, Dominican Republic, Guatemala, Panama, Bahamas, Bermuda, and Liberia),
- the East Caribbean dollar (Antigua and Barbuda, Dominica, Grenada, St. Vincent and the Grenadines, St. Kitts and Nevis, and St. Lucia),
- the pound (United Kingdom, Guyana, Ireland, Malta, Cyprus, Oman, Gambia, Malawi, Mauritius, Seychelles, Trinidad and Tobago, Kenya, Tanzania, Uganda, Somalia, Malaysia, and Singapore),
- the Central African franc (Central African Republic, Cameroon, Chad, Republic of Congo, Equatorial Guinea, Gabon, Benin, Burkina Faso, Ivory Coast, Mali, Niger, Senegal, and Togo),
- the franc (France, Comoros, Madagascar, and Mauritania),
- Australian dollar (Australia, Kiribati, Solomon Islands, and Tonga),
- the rihal (Quatar and United Arab Emirates),
- the Indian rupee (India and Bhutan),
- the Portuguese escudo (Portugal, Angola, Cape Verde, Guinea-Bissau, and Mozambique),
- the euro (Austria, Belgium, Finland, France, Germany, Ireland, Italy, Luxembourg, the Netherlands, Spain, and Portugal),
- the rand (South Africa, Botswana, Lesotho, Namibia, and Swaziland), and
- the Pakistani rupee (Pakistan and Burma).

Regionalism is defined in terms of eleven RTAs:

- Andean (Bolivia, Colombia, Ecuador, Peru, and Venezuela),
- ASEAN (the Philippines, Indonesia, Malaysia, Singapore, Thailand, Vietnam, Laos, Burma, and Cambodia),
- CARICOM (Antigua and Barbuda, Bahamas, Barbados, Belize, Dominica, Grenada, Guyana, Haiti, Jamaica, St. Kitts and Nevis, St. Lucia, St. Vincent and the Grenadines, Suriname, and Trinidad and Tobago),
- CACM (Costa Rica, El Salvador, Guatemala, Honduras, and Nicaragua),
- NAFTA (Canada, the United States, and Mexico),
- MERCOSUR (Argentina, Brazil, Paraguay, and Uruguay),
- USIS (the United States and Israel),

- PATCRA (Australia and Papua New Guinea),
- ANZCERTA (Australia and New Zealand),
- SPARTECA (Australia, New Zealand, Fiji, Kiribati, Papua New Guinea, Solomon Islands, Tonga, Vanuatu, and Samoa), and
- European Community/EU (Belgium, France, Germany, Italy, Luxembourg, the Netherlands, Denmark, Ireland, United Kingdom, Greece, Portugal, Spain, Austria, Finland, and Sweden).

The interregional dummy is equal to one when the countries in the pair belong to different RTAs; otherwise it is zero.

Real GDP and real GDP per capita are measured in 1995 U.S. dollars; distance is the greater circle distance between two countries in miles; the common land border is equal to one when both countries share a common land border; the common coloniser before 1945 dummy is equal to one when both countries had a common coloniser before 1945; the common country dummy is equal to one when both countries or entities belong to the same nation; the colonial relationship dummy is equal to one if either country ever colonis ed the other; and the common language dummy is equal to one when both countries share a common language.

Chapter 9

The G8 and the Governance of Cyberspace

Jeffrey A. Hart

The representatives of the countries that comprise the G7/8 began to address the problems of co-ordinating policies regarding the governance of cyberspace in the early 1990s. Initially, they dealt with governance issues including, among others, the establishment of norms, principles, and rules regarding the interconnection of computer networks via networks of networks such as the internet, rights of access to those networks, pricing of access, monitoring of network-mediated economic transactions, intellectual property protection, taxation of goods and services delivered though the networks, privacy, security, and a variety of other matters thought to affect the confidence of users. Toward the end of the decade, the G8 turned to a new issue: reversing the tendencies toward an increasing 'global digital divide' between rich and poor countries. After 11 September 2001, the G8 turned its attention to a variety of cyberspace security issues and began to link its digital divide discussions to broader questions related to North-South relations, focussing particularly on the Middle East and the rest of the Islamic world.

One of the key questions addressed in this chapter is why the G8 turned from the previous set of cyberspace governance issues in 1999 to a consideration of how to bridge the digital divide. This chapter posits that the main reason was the G8's need to respond to the criticisms by antiglobalisation forces that G8 governance was undemocratic and therefore contributed to increased global inequality. For this reason, one important way to evaluate the success of the G8 in this area was in terms of its ability to provide a counterargument to the claims of the antiglobalisation movement. More important, however, was the attempt by the G8 to transcend its inherently intergovernmental character by including representatives from civil society in its deliberations on the global digital divide. The Digital Opportunity Task Force (Dot Force) invented a method called the 'multistakeholder approach' to do this. Many of the participants in the Dot Force considered this invention to be a success, but only time will tell whether the approach will spread to other issues under the G8's purview.

The shift of attention after 11 September toward security concerns temporarily diverted the G8's attention away from North-South issues and toward preventing cyberattacks and cyberterrorism mainly in the North. Although these may at first sight appear to be traditional national security concerns, the heavy reliance on the private sector to build and maintain computer and telecommunications networks made the multistakeholder approach innovated by the Dot Force of continuing relevance to G8 deliberations. In addition, the problem of winning the hearts and minds of those who could potentially be recruited to terrorist causes would require an eventual return to issues connected with North-South inequalities such as the global digital divide.

Historical Context

Although originating in the late 1960s in research begun under the auspices of the United States Department of Defense Advanced Research Projects Agency (ARPA), the internet emerged in the 1990s as the most important network of networks with the capability, in principle, to interconnect every computer (large or small) on the planet. While the ARPANET was built in the 1970s to interconnect military contractors with one another, it was succeeded first by the NSFNET (National Science Foundation Network), which expanded interconnection to university scientists and engineers, and then by the internet. Commercial interconnection to the internet began in the late 1980s, and soon many businesses had shifted at least some of their activities to cyberspace (Hart, Bar, and Reed 1992).

By the early 1990s, the U.S. government began to ask the rest of the world to adopt policies that it believed would be conducive to the spread of internet-based commercial activity. This was the Global Information Infrastructure (GII) initiative of the Clinton administration.

One particularly important aspect of the GII initiative was the push for policies of minimal restrictions on e-commerce in order to encourage the shift of economic transactions to the internet. According to 'The Framework for Global Electronic Commerce', there was a danger of killing off the goose that lays the golden eggs:

> Commerce on the Internet could total tens of billions of dollars by the turn of the century. For this potential to be realized fully, governments must adopt a non-regulatory, market-oriented approach to electronic commerce, one that facilitates the emergence of a transparent and predictable legal environment to support global business and commerce. Official decision makers must respect the unique nature of the medium and recognize that widespread competition and increased consumer choice should be the defining features of the new digital marketplace (White House 1997).[1]

The Clinton administration called on the World Trade Organization (WTO) to declare the internet a tax-free environment and to request the development of a uniform commercial code for electronic commerce. The U.S. asked that there be a WTO effort to make national intellectual property regimes more consistent and enforceable. A series of reports was issued to provide background information for these and other related policy proposals over the next three years (Smith et al. 2001, 12). The U.S.

government was largely successful in these policy initiatives, although not without generating considerable controversy.

The Clinton administration also called for a meeting of the information ministers of the G7 to be held on 25–26 February 1995 in Brussels. The main topic of discussion was the means by which to 'encourage and promote the innovation and development of new technologies, including, in particular, the implementation of open, competitive, and world-wide information infrastructures' (Information Society Website 1995). The conference concluded with the identification of a set of pilot projects that would benefit from international co-operation. These projects were adopted formally and funded by the G7 at the next year's summit.

At around the same time, in 1995, a joint symposium of the Asia-Pacific Economic Cooperation (APEC) countries and the Organisation for Economic Co-operation and Development (OECD) met in Vancouver to address 'Building the Foundation for the 21st Century'. The APEC-OECD symposium laid the framework for a market-led policy for infrastructure and service development. The OECD followed up in Turku, Finland, in 1997 with a joint government and business conference on the theme of 'Dismantling the Barriers to Global Electronic Commerce'. In 1998, the OECD held a ministerial conference in Ottawa on 'A Borderless World: Realising the Potential of Electronic Commerce' (OECD 1998). It was at this conference that the members of the OECD agreed to the Ottawa Taxation Framework Conditions (see below). APEC also held follow-up meetings that focussed on using the internet and information technologies to solve problems of economic development. These meetings probably influenced later discussions on bridging the digital divide among the G8 (Beaird 2003).

The World Bank formed the Global Information Infrastructure Commission (GIIC) in February 1995. Its first full meeting took place in Washington in July 1995, and it has met annually since then. The GIIC was designed to facilitate co-operation between governments and the private sector in order 'to foster private sector leadership and private-public sector cooperation in the development of information networks and services to advance global economic growth, education and quality of life' (GIIC 1995).

Internet Governance Issues at the Organisation for Economic Co-operation and Development

The OECD began to take up issues connected with the internet and electronic commerce in the late 1990s. One major effort was connected with the Ottawa Taxation Framework Conditions of 1998. That agreement set out a variety of principles to be followed by OECD governments regarding the taxation of the emerging sector. One principle stated that taxation should be neutral with respect to conventional and electronic forms of commerce. The other general principles to be followed involved neutrality, efficiency, simplicity, effectiveness, fairness, and flexibility. Follow-up work on the framework was delegated to the OECD's Committee on Fiscal Affairs (OECD 2003a, 11–12).

Within the OECD, there has been substantial debate about direct taxes, such as sales taxes. A large issue of contention is determining taxation rights. Under the OECD Model Tax Convention, such taxes require the concept of a 'permanent establishment', a 'fixed place of business through which the business of an enterprise is wholly or partly carried on' (OECD 2000). Preliminary discussions determined that a website is not such a permanent establishment, nor is the internet service provider that hosts the website. Discussion of this issue continues in the OECD.

At the 1998 Ottawa meeting, the OECD ministers reaffirmed 'their commitment to the protection of privacy on global networks in order to ensure the respect of important rights, build confidence in global networks, and to prevent unnecessary restrictions on transborder flows of personal data' (OECD 2003b, 12). They agreed to take the necessary steps to extend the existing OECD Privacy Guidelines (published in 1980) to global networks. Progress in achieving this goal was discussed at the Paris Forum in 1999 and the Emerging Market Economies Forum in Dubai in 2001.

The OECD's Committee for Information, Computer, and Communications Policy and that committee's Working Party on Information Security and Privacy were given the task of formulating an action plan for online privacy protection. They focussed on the following subtasks:

- Encouraging the adoption of privacy policies.
- Encouraging online notification of privacy policies to users.
- Ensuring that enforcement and redress measures are available in cases of non-compliance.
- Promoting user education and awareness about online privacy and the means at their disposal for protecting privacy.
- Encouraging the use of privacy-enhancing technologies.
- Encouraging the use and development of contractual solutions for online transborder data flows (OECD 2003b, 13).

Part of what was going on here was an adjustment of earlier policies regarding transborder flows of personal data. In the 1980s and 1990s, European governments had moved in the direction of stronger guarantees for privacy of online personal data than existed in the United States. Accordingly, they placed rather strict limits on transborder flows of personal data. However, the rapid rise of internet data traffic and e-commerce resulted in a reconsideration of those earlier decisions. European authorities did not want the EU to be excluded from the benefits of e-commerce because of overly restrictive privacy guarantees. In addition, the U.S. government and many U.S.-based multinational corporations (MNCs) strongly urged a relaxation in European privacy guarantees in order to maximise the potential benefits to all of moving to web-based commerce. Therefore, in pursuit of greater international harmonisation of privacy policies within the OECD, there was considerable support for greater transparency of national privacy rules and practices.

It quickly became apparent to participants in these discussions that governments depended on private firms to implement and enforce privacy guarantees, since most OECD countries had to some extent privatised the ownership of data conduits and personal data storage systems. Accordingly, private firms were invited to participate in OECD policy discussions. As in other areas of global governance, other private sector groups and organisations asserted their rights to participate in discussions on privacy. For example, Marc Rotenberg (2003) of the Electronic Privacy Information Center (EPIC) presented a plan for integrating civil society organisations into OECD discussions on online privacy matters at the Global Forum on Information Systems and Network Security held in Oslo, Norway, in October 2003. Rotenberg stressed the importance of going beyond government and private business participation in such discussions because of the need to foster consumer trust in global networks in order to realise their potential benefits.

A lot of the activity in this area and in the related areas of authentication (electronic signatures) and cybersecurity has related to raising consciousness. A survey of EU businesses done for the European Commission, for example, revealed that 75 percent of companies had no cybersecurity strategy whatsoever. Spending in this area was very low and most companies had understaffed information technology security offices (Skantze 2003). Similarly, many governments were struggling to deal effectively with problems of consumer confidence posed by viruses, worms, and spam, often with inadequate resources. It is not surprising, therefore, that international discussions such as those in the OECD would focus on information sharing and the pooling of costs in dealing with these increasingly global problems.

The Global Digital Divide

In 2000, the U.S. Commerce Department's National Telecommunication and Information Administration ([NTIA] 2000) issued a report entitled 'Falling Through the Net: Toward Digital Inclusion'. This was the first major U.S. governmental effort to study and document inequalities in access to and use of the internet across social groups. The report showed a trend of increasing usage, but also an increasing gap in usage between urban and rural, minority and non-minority groups, and high and low socioeconomic status households. For some variables, such as gender and income, the gap was decreasing. But the key finding was that 'noticeable divides still exist between those with different levels of income and education, different racial and ethnic groups, old and young, single and dual-parent families, and those with and without disabilities'.

The NTIA report focussed mainly on the U.S., but it did not take long for similar studies to appear that highlighted international aspects of the digital divide. For example, the World Economic Forum (2003) launched its Global Digital Divide Initiative in 2000 'to develop public-private partnerships that would help bridge the gap between those who have ICT [information and communication technology] access, skills and resources and those who do not'. The International Labour Organization ([ILO] 2001) released a study in 2001 arguing that lack of access to ICT on the part of workers in the developing world denied them access to jobs in the technology sector. The report noted that access to ICTs without appropriate education and training would not be a sufficient response to the growing North-South digital divide. Similar studies were done by the World Bank and special agencies of the United Nations.

The Okinawa Charter

At the Okinawa Summit on 22 July 2000, the G8 adopted the Okinawa Charter on Global Information Society. A draft for this document had been prepared for pre-Summit discussions with representatives from developing countries at a meeting in Tokyo just before the Summit under the sponsorship of Japanese prime minister Yoshiro Mori. The Japanese government wanted the G8 to go beyond the scheduled discussions of debt relief at Okinawa, partly as a response to the demonstrations against the G8 and the WTO that had taken place in Seattle in 1999 (Chandler 2000).

The Okinawa Charter started by stating that ICT is 'fast becoming a vital engine for the world economy' (G8 2000). It argued that ICT has the potential to transform economies and societies because of its 'power to help individuals and societies use knowledge and ideas'. The Okinawa Charter put forward a principle of inclusion in which 'everyone, everywhere should be enabled to participate in and no one should be excluded from the benefits of the global information society'. It stressed the importance of governmental leadership in creating an 'appropriate policy and regulatory environment' that included fostering competition and innovation in an overall environment of economic and financial stability. It called for 'collaboration to optimise global networks, fight abuses that undermine the integrity of the network, bridge the digital divide, invest in people, and promote global access and participation'. The last paragraph of the first section of the charter reiterated the G8's commitment to bridging the global digital divide.

The second section of the Okinawa Charter focussed on the need to create the right policy and regulatory environment for ICT to have a positive impact. The private sector 'plays a leading role' but 'it is up to governments to create a predictable, transparent, and non-discriminatory policy and regulatory environment'. The document went on to stress the importance of enforcing intellectual property rights and liberalising international flows, especially e-commerce. It urged taxation policies consistent with those pursued by the OECD, 'continuing the practice of not imposing customs duties on electronic transmissions', and the adoption of interoperable, market-driven standards. Like the OECD efforts mentioned above, the Okinawa Charter identified privacy protection, electronic authentication, and security as important for future discussion.

The remainder of the document reaffirmed the commitment of the G8 to bridging the global digital divide and suggested ways of working with other international organisations and private sector groups to achieve this goal. In the final pages, the Okinawa Charter announced the decision of the G8 to establish the Dot Force to respond to the needs of the developing countries. The Okinawa Charter became the foundational document for a G8 effort that was to begin in 2000 and end in 2003 with the creation of a number of pilot programmes, reports, and policy dialogues meant to advance the state of art in applying ICT to development concerns.

The Dot Force

After the Okinawa Summit, 43 teams from organisations representing governments, the private sector, nonprofit organisations, and international organisations were assembled to 'identify ways in which the digital revolution can benefit all the world's people, especially the poorest and most marginalized groups' (Dot Force 2001). The first meeting of the Dot Force was held in Tokyo on 27–28 November 2000, chaired by Japanese deputy foreign minister Yoshiji Nogami. A schedule was established for the preparation of a report prior to the next summit in Genoa. The report, to be finished by May 2001, would be drafted with the help of the World Bank and the United Nations Development Programme (UNDP). It would deal with the issues discussed in the Okinawa Charter and would be 'action-oriented' (Dot Force 2000).

The report that resulted, 'Digital Opportunities for All: Meeting the Challenge', concluded that 'when wisely applied, ICT offer enormous opportunities to narrow social and economic inequalities and support sustainable local wealth creation, and thus help to achieve the broader development goals that the international community has set' (Dot Force 2001). It proposed four areas for action:

- fostering policy, regulatory, and network readiness;
- improving connectivity, increasing access, and lowering costs;
- building human capacity; and
- encouraging participation in global e-commerce and other e-networks.

The members of the Dot Force went so far as to assert that 'basic right of access to knowledge and information is a prerequisite for modern human development'. The enthusiasm for using ICT as the primary vehicle to facilitate access was palpable in the report's verbiage.

The report went on to discuss and summarise the UN Millennium Declaration and the related Millennium Development Goals (MDGs), which include, among other items, reducing the number of people living in extreme poverty by half between 1990 and 2015. It stressed the potential utility of using ICT to reduce global inequality but also the need to put 'in place the appropriate infrastructure', which 'is a multi-sectoral and multi-stakeholder task'. The report referred to the need for governments to work together with nonprofit organisations, private firms, and international organisations. The report claimed that the Dot Force was the first G8 initiative to take this idea seriously. This emphasis on multistakeholder participation was no doubt partly a response to the criticisms of the civil society organisations about their lack of access to decision making in the G8, the WTO, and the World Bank/International Monetary Fund (IMF) systems.

The report did not ignore the difficulties of the tasks it recommended the G8 to undertake. It included discussions of the problem of general skepticism about the potential role of ICT in development, opposition to using ICT to enhance transparency and thereby reduce corruption, and the possibility of negative reactions to the effects of ICT diffusion on employment patterns. It called for fresh thinking on these matters and for a search for best practices on a global basis. The report concluded with nine 'action points' that formed the proposed Genoa Plan of Action. The plan was fully endorsed by G8 leaders at the Genoa Summit in July 2001.

The G8 was led by Italy in 2001 and Canada in 2002. The governments of the two countries were given the responsibility to facilitate the work of the Dot Force after the Genoa Summit. The Dot Force implementation teams proposed a number of new projects in the areas of national e-strategies, access and connectivity, human capacity building, entrepreneurship, ICT for health, local content and applications, and global policy participation.

These projects and the subprojects associated with them would continue beyond the lifespan of the Dot Force itself, mainly via a hand-off to working groups of the UN's newly created ICT Task Force.

In June 2002, the Dot Force published its final document, entitled 'Report Card: Digital Opportunities for All', in time for discussion at the G8 Kananaskis Summit. This report asserted that the 'multi-stakeholder approach of the DOT Force now serves as the model for other global "ICT for development" initiatives that follow in its footsteps' (Dot Force 2002a, 2). With the conclusion of the Kananaskis Summit, the Dot Force officially ceased operations.

Evaluating the Effectiveness of the Dot Force

The Dot Force was certainly effective in terms of the metrics devised by John Kirton (2004) to evaluate the overall effectiveness of other G8. The task force generated lots of paper, there were many attendees of meetings, and there were several substantial financial commitments on the part of the G8. But its main accomplishment seems to have been experimenting successfully with a different way of operating. Unlike previous G8 initiatives, the Dot Force consciously employed a multistakeholder approach, in which government officials worked together with representatives of private firms, nonprofit organisations, and international organisations to write reports and propose new projects to be funded by a combination of governmental, intergovernmental, and private sources. The fact that the OECD appears to be adopting such an approach in dealing with e-commerce issues is not a coincidence.

It is probably still too soon to evaluate the effectiveness of the Dot Force projects, but they at least had the appearance of originality and careful thought that is not always characteristic of development projects. Another hopeful sign was the tempering of the ambitions of a few overly enthusiastic advocates of ICT and the replacement of unrealistic notions with more realistic ones. A particularly poignant example of this is the network of public internet access points (ADEN, or Appui au désenclavement numérique) sponsored by the French government. ADEN would create shared access points to the internet in Africa in public locations and with local community associations as partners. To deal with the many interruptions in power and telephone services and the high cost of connectivity in Africa, these access points would employ a technology using short bursts of interconnection for storage of information most likely to be needed at the access point.

Similarly, a passage from the part of the report card summarising the work of the human capacity team shows how their collective thinking about how to apply e-learning technologies in the developing world influenced (mostly for the good) the technological enthusiasts among them:

> The team realizes the need for a more adjusted and differentiated view of the potential associated with the implementation of ICTs in low-income countries. It is also aware of excluding vast majorities from this potential. Meeting these particular needs should enable a more fruitful discussion with critics who perceive the issue — in light of the often overwhelming problems of hunger, water scarcity, and physical threat — as a diversion from basic development needs. It should also, and more importantly, foster sustainable, bottom-up developments and applications that take advantage of basic and enhanced ICTs to improve the living conditions of all citizens (Dot Force 2002b, 4).

The entrepreneurship team was different from the others in asking for US$32 million from the G8 governments to create the Dot Force Entrepreneurial Network (DFEN). The DFEN would focus on financially supporting small and medium-sized enterprises engaged in ICT activities in the developing world. The DFEN was renamed Enablis in 2002 after it received CA$10 million (about US$6.6 million) in funding from the Canadian government. It is sponsored in addition by three private firms that were involved in the entrepreneurship task force of the Dot Force: Accenture, Hewlett-Packard, and Telesystem. Enablis set up a regional office in South Africa in 2004, and plans to extend its reach into the rest of Africa and other regions in the developing world (Enablis 2004).

The Shift to Cybersecurity Issues

Immediately after the attacks on the World Trade Center and the Pentagon on 11 September 2001, the G8 leaders shifted their attention away from issues such as those discussed in the Dot Force toward cyberspace issues related to security ('cybersecurity' for short). The G8 had begun already to consider these issues prior to 11 September, having created the Senior Experts Group on Transnational Organized Crime (later renamed the Lyon Group) in 1995 at the Halifax Summit. The experts group presented its first report at the G8 Summit in Lyon, which included recommendations for reviewing 'their laws in order to ensure that abuses of modern technology that are deserving of criminal sanctions are criminalized and that problems with respect to jurisdiction, enforcement powers, investigation, training, crime prevention and international cooperation in respect of such abuses are effectively addressed' (P8 Senior Experts Group 1996, 4). They were given an open-ended mandate to implement the proposed recommendations. Since then, the Lyon Group has developed into a permanent, multidisciplinary body helping to provide information for meetings of the G8 justice and interior ministers.

In October 1999, the G8 justice and interior ministers authorised a Lyon Group meeting on Confidence and Security in Cyberspace to be held in Paris in May 2000. There was a follow-up meeting in Berlin in October of that year. A third conference was held in Tokyo in May 2001. The agenda of the Tokyo meeting including the issues of data retention, data preservation, threat assessment and prevention, protection of electronic commerce, and user authentication and training. After 11 September, the Lyon Group was given the initiative to devise methods for detecting and intercepting international transfers of funds for the purpose of supporting terrorism. Its purview also included consideration of methods to detect and prevent money laundering, an issue that became particularly relevant after information about funding of al Qaeda operations was made public (G8 Lyon Group 2002; Miyake 2001). The Lyon Group also pushed successfully for the adoption of the UN Convention against Transnational Organized Crime on 15 November 2000 (UN General Assembly 2000, Annex I).

At the G8 Summit in Paris in 1989, the Financial Action Task Force (FATF) was set up to co-ordinate G8 policies with regard to international money laundering. The FATF came to have 33 members by 2003, most of them members of the OECD but also including some Latin American countries, the Gulf Cooperation Council, and the EU.[2] In 1996, the FATF issued the Forty Recommendations on money laundering that was modified and expanded after 11 September 2001 under the leadership of the G8, to include eight recommendations on the financing of terrorism (FATF 2003b).

While the FATF recommendations included policies directed at electronic funds transfers, the main concern in the area of terrorist finance was informal money/value transfer networks such as the hawala system used in Islamic banking, where international payments are made via linked money swaps that defy international monitoring.[3] Nevertheless, since June 2000 the FATF has maintained a list of Non-

Cooperative Countries or Territories (NCCTs) that includes large countries such as Nigeria and small island republics such as Nauru that are notorious not just for money laundering but also for serving as shelters for all kinds of illicit internet and email scam operations (see Chapter 12).

The governments of Western Europe, North America, and Japan adopted a variety of policies to respond to a heightened level of threat after 11 September, some of which would directly influence the G8's future deliberations on cyberspace governance. In June 2001, the European Commission (2001) issued a document entitled 'Communication on Network and Information Security', which outlined an approach to security on computer networks that included policies to deal with cyberattacks, identity thefts, attacks on infrastructures, and other types of cybercrime. The document stressed the importance of raising consciousness about these matters and of establishing computer emergency response teams (CERTs) in member states. It highlighted the importance of standards for electronic signatures (authentication), encryption, and interoperability, and called for greater international co-operation in this area.

In 2002, the European Union adopted its e-Europe 2002 Action Plan, which included a number of proposals for policies for maintaining cybersecurity. The EU subsequently issued the Electronic Signatures Directive and launched the European Electronic Signature Standardization Initiative to help companies implement the directive. The EU endorsed the Council of Europe's 1990 Convention on Cybercrime and proposed its own Framework Decision on Child Pornography, which included provisions to prevent the exchange of child pornography over the internet. The European Commission established a European network of hotlines under the Safer Internet Action Plan to ease the reporting of illegal internet content, including child pornography. In February 2003, the European Commission proposed the establishment of the Network and Information Security Agency. This agency would co-ordinate and assist the CERTs of EU member states and help to raise awareness of the dangers of cybercrime and the need to adopt appropriate countermeasures.

The U.S. government established the Department of Homeland Security after 11 September, which included among its many new sub-agencies the National Cyber Security Division. In September 2003, a former vice-president of Symantec Corporation became the director of this division. At about the same time, Homeland Security secretary Tom Ridge announced the creation of a U.S. CERT in co-operation with Carnegie-Mellon University (Ferrell 2003). In Japan, an Information Technology Security Office was established in the Cabinet Secretariat to develop countermeasures against cyberattacks and to protect e-government operations. The office was given the lead in co-ordinating the government's various cybersecurity efforts. In a joint statement, the governments of the two countries announced that they were considering becoming parties to the Council of Europe's Convention on Cybercrime (U.S. Embassy in Tokyo 2003).

To summarise, the most important activities of the G8 during this period were those undertaken within the Lyon Group and the FATF. But the broader array of cybersecurity issues — which included, among others, laws, technologies, and technical standards to prevent cyberattacks, infrastructure attacks, identity thefts, and the exchange of child pornography — would clearly be on the G8's agenda in the future.

Conclusion

In conclusion, the Dot Force, the FATF, and the Lyon Group demonstrated the potential effectiveness of the G8, especially relative to other international regimes, in creating solutions to collective action problems in cyberspace. The main problem that the Dot Force solved was providing an answer to antiglobalisation critics of the tendency of intergovernmental organisations such as the G8 to exclude participants from civil society — that is, private firms, nongovernmental organisations (NGOs), and other social groups. As to how the various Dot Force projects would do in bridging the digital divide, only time would tell. Nevertheless, the new collaborative approach embodied in the multistakeholder model was bound to be more successful than the purely intergovernmental approach because it permitted the G8 to tap directly some of the best ideas of participants in civil society with greater knowledge than the government officials that normally participated in G8 deliberations.

Similarly, the Lyon Group provided an excellent foundation upon which to build a credible G8 response to 11 September. The participation of private sector interests in the Lyon Group was partly responsible for its success, even when the main work was done by law enforcement agencies of G8 governments. Even in primarily security-related areas of the G8's work, it has become necessary for the intergovernmental essence of the G8 to be modified so that the resources of members of civil society can be added to those of G8 governments to solve important collective action problems.[4]

It should be noted, however, that the only reason the G8 was able to pursue these experiments with multistakeholder participation in discussing governance issues was its original stress on 'heads only' or at least 'heads primarily' in G8 meetings. That is, since the G8 had started with the idea that a periodic assembling of heads of state without too much representation of cabinet or sub-cabinet level officialdom was the best way to resolve the most important issues, there was always some flexibility to invite nongovernmental parties to participate in G8 discussions. More formally organised intergovernmental organisations are generally less able to do this.

There is always a danger of overstating the benefits of incorporating civil society actors in international governance because, at least in some cases, civil society may not be well represented in the entities claiming to do so. Because of their superior financial resources, private firms (and particularly large private MNCs) may be able to plead for special treatment in ways that are contrary to the public interest. They may 'capture' the public or quasi-public governance institutions to the detriment of other members of civil society. The same can occur for transnational environmental groups, labour organisations, or international financial institutions (IFIs). Thus, one must be skeptical about general claims about the superiority of the multistakeholder approach to international governance. Nevertheless, in areas, such as internet governance, where private actors are needed both to provide accurate informational inputs to form and implement new norms, rules, and procedures, a properly configured multistakeholder approach is both necessary and desirable.

Notes

1. The document bears the names of both President William Clinton and Vice-President Albert Gore.
2. For a list of members, see FATF (2004).
3. See, for example, FATF (2003a). Such informal money swaps do not require computers or telecommunications technology and can be arranged via telephone or fax.
4. Nicholas Bayne has argued in this volume and elsewhere that the 'heads only' aspect of the G8 permits it to have the flexibility to do this whenever the heads of state so desire.

References

Beaird, Richard (2003). 'Opening Remarks'. OECD-APEC Forum: Policy Frameworks for the Digital Economy, 14–17 January. Honolulu. <www.oecd.org/dataoecd/19/56/2492657.pdf> (November 2004).

Chandler, Clay (2000). 'In Tokyo, Rich Pay Heed to the Poor as G8 Summit Opens'. *Washington Post*, 21 July, p. A19.

Digital Opportunity Task Force (2000). 'First Meeting of the G8 Digital Opportunity Task Force'. 30 November. <www.g8.utoronto.ca/dot_force/summary-nov-00.html> (November 2004).

Digital Opportunity Task Force (2001). 'Digital Opportunities for All: Meeting the Challenge. Report of the Digital Opportunity Task Force (DOT Force) Including a Proposal for a Genoa Plan of Action'. <www.g8.utoronto.ca/summit/2001genoa/dotforce1.html> (November 2004).

Digital Opportunity Task Force (2002a). 'Report Card: Digital Opportunities for All'. <www.g8.utoronto.ca/summit/2002kananaskis/dotforce_reportcard.pdf> (November 2004).

Digital Opportunity Task Force (2002b). 'Team Report: Human Capacity and Knowledge'. Ottawa, June.

Enablis (2004). 'Enablis in Brief'. <www.enablis.org> (November 2004).

European Commission (2001). 'Network and Information Security: Proposal for a European Approach'. Communication from the Commission to the Council, the European Parliament, the European Economic and Social Committee, and the Committee of the Regions. <europa.eu.int/information_society/eeurope/2002/news_library/pdf_files/netsec_en.pdf> (November 2004).

Ferrell, Keith (2003). 'Homeland Security Getting Its House in Order'. *Security Pipeline*, 17 September. <www.securitypipeline.com/news/showArticle.jhtml?articleId=14800063> (November 2004).

Financial Action Task Force (2003a). 'Combating the Abuse of Alternative Remittance Systems: International Best Practices'. 20 June. Paris. <www.fatf-gafi.org/pdf/SR6-BPP_en.pdf> (November 2004).

Financial Action Task Force (2003b). 'The Forty Recommendations'. Organisation for Economic Co-operation and Development, Paris. <www1.oecd.org/fatf/40Recs_en.htm> (November 2004).

Financial Action Task Force (2004). 'Members and Observers'. <www.fatf-gafi.org/Members_en.htm> (November 2004).

G8 (2000). 'Okinawa Charter on Global Information Society'. Okinawa, 22 July. <www.g8.utoronto.ca/summit/2000okinawa/gis.htm> (November 2004).

G8 Lyon Group (2002). 'The G8 Lyon Group'. <www.auswaertiges-amt.de/www/en/aussenpolitik/vn/lyon_group_html> (November 2004).

Global Information Infrastructure Commission (1995). 'GII Commission Inaugural Meeting'. World Bank, 11–12 July. Washington DC. <www.giic.org/events/ann1.asp> (November 2004).

Hart, Michael, François Bar, and Robert Reed (1992). 'The Building of the Internet: Implications for the Future of Broadband Networks'. *Telecommunications Policy* vol. 16 (November), no. 666–689.

Information Society Website (1995). 'G7 Information Society Conference'. 25–26 February. Brussels. <europa.eu.int/ISPO/intcoop/g8/i_g8conference.html> (November 2004).

International Labour Organization (2001). 'World Employment Report 2001: Life at Work in the Information Economy'. Geneva. <www.ilo.org/public/english/support/publ/wer/index2.htm> (November 2004).

Kirton, John J. (2004). 'Explaining G8 Effectiveness: A Concert of Vulnerable Equals in a Globalizing World'. Paper prepared for the International Studies Association conference. Montreal, 17–20 March. <www.g8.utoronto.ca/scholar/kirton2004/kirton_isa_040304.pdf> (November 2004).

Miyake, Kuriko (2001). 'G8 Concludes Tokyo High-Tech Crime Meeting'. CNN, 21 May. <archives.cnn.com/2001/TECH/internet/05/31/g8.cyber.crime.idg> (November 2004).

National Telecommunication and Information Administration (2000). 'Falling Through the Net: Toward Digital Inclusion'. United States Department of Commerce. <www.ntia.doc.gov/ntiahome/fttn00/contents00.html> (November 2004).

Organisation for Economic Co-operation and Development (1998). 'A Borderless World: Realising the Potential of Global Electronic Commerce'. Organisation for Economic Co-operation and Development, Paris.

Organisation for Economic Co-operation and Development (2000). 'E-Commerce: Implementing the Ottawa Taxation Framework Conditions'. Report to Ministers, C/MIN (2000)9. <www1.oecd.org/subject/mcm/2000/e_comm_ott.pdf> (November 2004).

Organisation for Economic Co-operation and Development (2003a). 'Implementation of the Ottawa Taxation Framework Conditions: The 2003 Report'. Paris. <www.oecd.org/dataoecd/45/19/20499630.pdf> (November 2004).

Organisation for Economic Co-operation and Development (2003b). 'Privacy Online: OECD Guidance on Policy and Practice'. Paris. <www1.oecd.org/publications/e-book/9303051E.PDF> (November 2004).

P8 Senior Experts Group (1996). '40 Recommendations to Combat Transnational Organized Crime'. April, Paris. <www.auswaertiges-amt.de/www/de/ infoservice/download/pdf/vn/g8_recommandations.pdf> (November 2004).

Rotenberg, Marc (2003). 'Global Forum on Information Systems and Networks Security: The Role of Civil Society'. Oslo, 13–14 October. <www.oecd.org/dataoecd/25/19/17842138.pdf> (November 2004).

Skantze, Pernilla (2003). 'European Cyber Security'. OECD Global Forum on Information Systems and Network Security: Towards a Global Culture of Security. <www.oecd.org/dataoecd/53/43/17979495.pdf> (November 2004).

Smith, Marcia S., John D. Moteff, Lennard G. Kruger, et al. (2001). 'Internet: An Overview of Key Technology Policy Issues Affecting Its Use and Growth'. 31 January. CRS Report for Congress. <www.4uth.gov.ua/usa/english/tech/reports/98-67.pdf> (November 2004).

United Nations General Assembly (2000). 'Crime Prevention and Criminal Justice: Report of the Ad Hoc Committee on the Elaboration of a Convention against Transnational Organized Crime'. A/55/383. 2 November.

United States Embassy in Tokyo (2003). 'U.S.-Japan Joint Statement on Cyber Security'. 9 September. <japan.usembassy.gov/e/p/tp-20030909d2.html> (November 2004).

White House (1997). 'A Framework for Global Electronic Commerce'. 1 July. <www.technology.gov/digeconomy/framewrk.htm> (November 2004).

World Economic Forum (2003). 'Global Digital Divide Initiative'. <annualmeeting.weforum.org/site/homepublic.nsf/Content/Global+Digital+Divide+Initiative.html> (January 2003).

Chapter 10

U.S. Energy Security and Regional Business

Alan M. Rugman[1]

In spring 2003, the war in Iraq illustrated the military power of the hegemony of the United States, and the inability of the G8 and the United Nations to reach a consensus on the matter. The G8 fractured, with only the United Kingdom supporting the United States in Iraq to any significant military extent. Italy was a strong ally and Japan offered some qualified support. In contrast, France and Germany were strongly opposed to the U.S. action, while Canada did not offer its usual support for U.S. foreign policy. Russia was also opposed to the U.S.-led war in Iraq, so the G8 was divided, with four members being strongly opposed and the other four in support of the military option to varying degrees.

Since the initial Iraq war concluded in April 2003, these divisions have remained, with France, Germany, and Russia unable to reach an agreement with the United States over the restructuring of Iraq, and with the United Nations also still out of the picture. Paul Martin, the new Canadian Prime Minister, elected in June 2004, signalled somewhat closer ties to the United States, but no with military support forthcoming. Other countries involved in the 'coalition of the willing' have been withdrawing, principally Spain in April 2004. Does the fissure over Iraq spell the end of the G8? In this chapter, this issue is examined from an economic viewpoint with particular emphasis on U.S. energy security and the nature of regional business activity.

The result of the breakdown of the traditional G8 spirit of co-operation and mutual support on security issues and terrorism (due to the Iraq war) will likely be to reinforce regional economic integration policies at the expense of multilateral institutions, such as the United Nations and the World Trade Organization (WTO). The United States already exports 37 percent of its goods and services to Mexico and Canada, its partners in the North American Free Trade Agreement (NAFTA), and its trade with Canada alone exceeds U.S. exports to all 15 member states of the European Union. In terms of energy, the United States already obtains the vast majority of its oil and gas from the Americas, and this regional self-sufficiency is likely to increase as security concerns remain.

The Logic of North American Energy Self-Sufficiency

The main theme of this chapter is that the United States has no long-term economic interest in the Middle East. It has very little trade or foreign direct investment (FDI) in the region, and it does not need to import oil. Indeed, in 2002, the entire Persian Gulf area supplied less than 12 percent of the oil consumed in the United States (largely because nearly 60 percent of its oil is supplied regionally, either within the United States or by Canada and Mexico). In terms of other energy sources, the United States is already self-sufficient. Net imports of electricity are insignificant at 0.62 percent. Net imports of natural gas are 95 percent from its NAFTA partners. Coal supplies are entirely internal.

The economic logic of energy security implies that the United States can be fully self-sufficient in energy production and consumption, provided it increases its trade in oil with its primary NAFTA partner, Canada. With much needed new (but costly) investments in the Athabaska Tar Sands in Alberta, Canada could entirely replace the Persian Gulf as a supplier of oil for the United States. This could be achieved within a few years. There are unlimited supplies of oil from Alberta's Tar Sands, provided the technology to process the shale is developed and installed. In all other areas of energy production and consumption, the United States is already self-sufficient, or virtually so with its NAFTA partners. In this regard, energy is no different from other sectors — both manufacturing and services, all of which operate on a regional basis, rather than globally (Rugman 2000).

The political logic of energy security should build on this underlying economic logic of regional economic activity. The United States has no long-run strategic political interest in the Middle East. It is not in Iraq for the oil. If any countries need oil from Iraq and the rest of the Persian Gulf, they are Japan and members of the EU. These are the countries that need to be concerned on economic grounds with Middle East politics and oil supplies. The United States needs to focus on NAFTA and the realities of regional business integration.

Only in the short term does the Persian Gulf matter to the United States in economic terms. This is because the members of the Organization of Petroleum Exporting Countries (OPEC), mainly concentrated in the Middle East, can effectively control the world supply of oil and thereby the world price of oil. This matters to U.S. consumers, as much as to other consumers. However, by developing self-sufficiency in energy production and consumption in North America, the United States could largely insulate itself from the world oil price, especially in terms of consumption. Ultimately, the manufacturing productivity of other countries could be helped by a permanent fall in the world price of oil if the United States is locked into investments to help develop more expensive Alberta oil production. But the short-run price and production effects need to be distinguished from the long-run North American self-sufficiency in consumption that is possible, albeit at a higher price than the predicted long-term oil prices.

Obviously, the mechanics of developing a policy of energy self-sufficiency are more complicated than can be sketched out here. In order to encourage private oil companies to invest in costly North American oil production, it would be necessary for NAFTA governments to agree to a common North American energy policy. This would lock in private oil companies with long-term contracts and would prevent them from selling oil in the world market. A regional NAFTA-based oil market would replace the world oil market, and it would require effective government regulations to be sustainable. This may not be popular with intellectual advocates of free trade, but one can observe a lack of free trade in many sectors now operating within regional blocks of which agriculture is the prime example, being massively subsidised by the U.S., EU, and Japanese governments.

American Oil Supply Is Regional

The importance of NAFTA, and a potential Free Trade Agreement of the Americas (FTAA), is relevant to the United States in terms of energy security. In contrast, in strictly economic terms Iraq and the rest of the Middle East are of minimal importance to the United States. Although the United States has free trade agreements with Israel and Jordan, total trade to these areas is less than 1 percent of its trade. In contrast, the United States has 37 percent of its trade with its NAFTA partners.

In terms of consumption of oil, the United States has 58.7 percent of all its oil produced within NAFTA. It produces 41.1 percent of its own consumption internally and imports another 17.7 percent from its two NAFTA partners. Another 8.3 percent comes from Venezuela and Colombia, so 67 percent of all U.S. oil consumption is from the Americas. The United States does not need oil from Iraq. Indeed, it only consumed 11.5 percent of all its oil from all the states in the Persian Gulf, namely Iran, Iraq, Kuwait, Qatar, Saudi Arabia, and the United Arab Emirates. Even though this area has large oil reserves, there are similarly large oil reserves in Canada (in the Athabaska Tar Sands), so this U.S. position of relative oil security is not likely to be threatened for many years (see Table 10-1).

In terms of oil imported by the United States (and given that it produces 41.1 percent of its consumption itself), the Persian Gulf supplies 19.8 percent of all U.S. imports. Yet this figure is lower than the NAFTA partners of the United States, as Canada alone supplies 17.1 percent and Mexico 13.5 percent of all U.S. oil imports (a total of 30.6 percent from these two NAFTA neighbours). In addition, Venezuela supplies 12.2 percent and Colombia 2.3 percent, so more than 45 percent of all U.S. oil imports are from the Americas (see Table 10-2).

Electricity In one area of energy supply the United States is completely self-sufficient. This is in electricity, where less than 1 percent of consumption is imported. There is a high degree of interdependence with Canada, especially in the U.S. Northwest and

Midwest, as was experienced in the energy blackout of August 2003. However, the blackout was apparently due more to inadequate maintenance and control systems than to a basic lack of power supplies. Quebec's James Bay and other parts of Canada's hydroelectric systems are now integral parts of a North American electricity grid, and it is important to ensure continued co-operation in the management of bilateral electricity supplies.

Nuclear Power Due to environmental concerns, the United States has not increased its development of nuclear power stations (unlike France, which depends on nuclear power for much of its energy supply). The United States relies on nuclear power for about 8 percent of its power. If necessary, this source of energy could be increased, and the risks of Middle East oil imports may, in the future, change the calculus of relative energy costs more in favour of nuclear power. For the purposes of this chapter, however, this possibility is ignored and only current sources of energy supply are considered.

Table 10-1 U.S. Consumption of Petroleum, by Country of Origin, 2002[a]

	2002[b]	Percentage of Total
United States[c]	8075	41.1
Canada	1939	9.9
Mexico	1532	7.8
NAFTA	11 546	58.7
Venezuela	1383	7.0
Colombia	256	1.3
Persian Gulf Nations[d]	2254	11.5
Others	4217	21.5
U.S. Consumption	19 656	100.0

Notes:

The country of origin for refined petroleum products may not be the country of origin for the crude oil from which the refined products were produced. Totals may not equal the sum of components due to rounding.

a. Thousand barrels per day.

b. Preliminary data.

c. Consists of Production less Exports less Stock Change plus Crude Oil Losses and Unaccounted-for.

d. Bahrain, Iran, Iraq, Kuwait, Qatar, Saudi Arabia, and United Arab Emirates.

Source: Energy Information Administration 2003.

Alternative Power Again, it is possible for the United States to invest in an increase in energy conservation and the development of alternative power sources, such as solar energy. These trends could be extended to the development of alternatively fuelled automobiles, which would be an important step forward in reducing oil imports, as gasoline refining is a major use of imported oil. However, these developments are also likely to be long term, and so they are also put on hold in this chapter.

The Business Reality of the Triad

The importance of economic-based regionalisation and the triad, and the lack of globalisation, is now being reflected in political alignments. Following the definitive change to U.S. political attitudes toward national security after the 11 September 2001 terrorist attacks, a new world political system is emerging. This is based on the triad reality of regionalisation.

Table 10-2 U.S. Petroleum Imports, 2001[a]

	2002[b]	Percentage of Total 2002
Canada	1939	17.1
Mexico	1532	13.5
NAFTA	3471	30.6
Norway	379	3.3
United Kingdom	477	4.2
Venezuela	1383	12.2
Colombia	256	2.3
Non-Persian Gulf Nations[c]	9104	80.2
Persian Gulf Nations[c]	2254	19.8
Total Imports	11 358	100.0

Notes:

The country of origin for refined petroleum products may not be the country of origin for the crude oil from which the refined products were produced. Totals may not equal the sum of components due to rounding.

a. Thousand barrels per day.

b. Preliminary data.

c. Bahrain, Iran, Iraq, Kuwait, Qatar, Saudi Arabia, and United Arab Emirates.

Source: Energy Information Administration 2003.

The United States already has economic security on a regional basis. This was affirmed by the NAFTA agreement of 1994 (Rugman 1994). Now Canada and Mexico supply energy and other natural resources to the United States in exchange for the enhanced business access to the world's single largest and richest market. NAFTA does not provide the depth of economic integration of the EU, and it has none of its political and currency integration. Yet it ties together these three economies in a gigantic and highly successful free trade area to the mutual economic benefit of all three partners.

So successful is NAFTA that it is in the process of being expanded to the FTAA in 2005. This will lock all 34 countries of the Americas into an extension of NAFTA. The U.S. economy will serve as the regional regime for growth and renewed prosperity for Latin America and the Caribbean, just as NAFTA has done for Mexico.

The economic data on NAFTA show ever increasing interdependence in trade and FDI. Table 10-3 shows that intra-regional trade has increased from 33.6 percent to 56 percent between 1997 and 2002. Today the United States has 22.6 percent of its exports going to Canada and 14.1 percent to Mexico, for a total of 36.7 percent. In 2002, it had only 21.3 percent going to all 15 states that were then members of the EU. The United States is a regional player in terms of trade. In addition, at firm level, the 169 U.S. firms in the list of the world's 500 largest firms have an average of 77.3 percent of all their sales within NAFTA (Rugman 1994). Of course, Canada and Mexico pull more than pulling their weight on intra-regional trade. Canada has 87 percent of its exports to the United States; Mexico has 88.7 percent.

Table 10-3 also demonstrates that Europe and Asia are also highly regionalised. Intra-regional trade in the EU is over 60 percent. In Asia, even without a formal trade agreement across the region, the intra-regional trade is 50 percent in 2002, up from 35 percent in 1980. The table also shows a very recent reduction in Asia's intra-regional trade, largely due to Chinese extra-regional exports. Regionalism is the dominant economic force. As a direct corollary to this trend, there is even less trade between the triad blocks. Elsewhere, it has been shown that the blocks are closing and becoming

Table 10-3 Intra-regional Trade in the Triad, 1980–2002

	Intra-regional Exports (%)		
Year	EU	NAFTA	Asia
2002	61.0	56.0	50.0
2000	62.1	55.7	55.7
1997	60.6	49.1	53.1
1980	52.1	33.6	35.3

Source: International Monetary Fund 1980–2002.

more inward looking and less global (Rugman 2000, 2004). This economic reality is now being reflected in politics.

In this analysis of the G8's lack of consensus for both the Iraq war of 2003 and the subsequent rebuilding of Iraq, the transatlantic political relationships now reflect the broken economic one. Only the United Kingdom actually has any significant economic interest in North America. This is now through FDI (not trade, in which the majority of UK trade is with its EU partners). As shown earlier, the UK has about 40 percent of its outward stock of FDI in North America, giving a strong business linkage (Rugman and Kudina 2002). This is matched by a similar large inward stock. In contrast, Germany and France have most of their FDI within the EU, not across the Atlantic.

The EU now represents, as a block, an economic alternative to North America. The 119 large European-based multinational corporations (MNCs) have an average of 62.8 percent of their sales within Europe (Rugman 2004). European business does not really need America, just as America does not need Europe. There is no global business, only regional business.

All of this economic analysis also works for Asia. This region is becoming more interdependent, and it has almost identical intra-regional growth in trade to match its triad partners. Again, most of the sales of Asian-based MNCs are within the region (see Table 10-2). This trend is increasing. The 75 large Asian MNCs have an average of 74.3 percent of their sales within Asia (Rugman 2004).

The world picture is one of expanding regionalism. The EU admitted ten new members on 1 May 2004. NAFTA will extend from three nations to 34 in the FTAA by 2005. Asia, China, Japan, and South Korea will develop stronger ties with the countries in the Association of Southeast Asian Nations (ASEAN). Any business within the triad must become affiliated to a triad region in order to grow and succeed.

The Empirical Reality of Regional — Not Global — Activity

Today, much economic activity (both in manufacturing and services) is bound by location, taking place in clusters in the principal regions of the broad 'triad' of the EU, North America, and Asia. The choice of entry mode and location are complementary strategic management decisions of profound importance to multinational enterprises.

A key theoretical insight from several scholars reveals that in most regional clusters of value-added activities in the triad, the MNCs are embedded as leading participants (Dunning 2001; Enright 2000; Rugman and Verbeke 2004). The most lucid and extreme articulation of this viewpoint states that MNCs act as 'flagship firms' to lead, direct, co-ordinate, and manage strategically the value-added activities of partner firms in a business network, including key suppliers, key customers, and the non-business infrastructure (Rugman and D'Cruz 2000). While flagships can be considered leaders only of vertical clusters, as in autos (Dunning 2001), there can also be horizontal clusters, as in textiles, financial services, and so on (Rugman and D'Cruz 2000).

The average intra-regional sales of the world's 500 largest MNCs is 71.9 percent (Rugman and Verbeke 2004). Of the 380 firms studied, more than 80 percent (320) derive most of their sales in their home region of the triad. This relative sales dominance in a specific regional market, rather than a very wide and evenly distributed spread of sales, reflects five underlying issues critical to the MNCs' functioning. First, it demonstrates the fallacy of so-called 'global' products. If most MNCs' sales are unevenly distributed across the globe, and mainly concentrated in just one geographic market, this means that products are not really global in the sense of being equally attractive to consumers all around the world.

Second, the lack of global market success reflects the limits to the non-location–bound nature of the MNCs' knowledge base — its firm-specific advantages (FSAs). Firms may have sophisticated and proprietary technological knowledge, brand names, and so on, but there appear to be severe limits to the joint international transferability of this knowledge and its acceptance by customers across regions, irrespective of whether such knowledge is embodied in final products and then exported, transferred as an intermediate product through licensing, or used in foreign affiliates through FDI.

Third, the perceived lack of market performance across regions also points to a relative inability to access and deploy the required location-bound FSAs, which would lead to benefits of regional and national responsiveness.

Fourth, if the MNC's market position is very different in the various regions of the world, this indicates the need for very different competitive strategies: a leadership role in one market requires very different patterns of decisions and actions than the role of a (perhaps ambitious) junior player in another market. This should obviously be reflected in the deployment of specific combinations of non-location–bound and location-bound FSAs in each region. Unfortunately, in spite of much 'think global, act local' rhetoric in both the academic and popular business press, there appears to be little empirical evidence that this approach has permitted host-region market penetration levels similar to the ones obtained in the home region.

Fifth, the four elements above have important implications for MNC governance. It might be incorrect to attribute the present relative lack of overseas market success of many firms to an inappropriate governance structure. The presence of multiple environmental circumstances may also be critical here (powerful foreign rivals in other triad regions, government shelter of domestic industries, buyer preferences for local products, cultural and administrative differences as compared to the home region, and so forth). However, the need for regional strategies does suggest the parallel introduction of a regional component in the MNCs' governance structure to deal appropriately with the distinctive characteristics of each leg of the triad, and with the regions outside of it, much in line with the prescriptions set out by Kenichi Ohmae (1985). This perspective is developed further on.

This need for distinct regional strategies is an important observation as many well-known strategy and international business scholars keep developing normative models that advocate simple globalisation strategies as a set of purposive decisions and actions instrumental to a broad and deep penetration of foreign markets, that is, extreme geographical fragmentation of sales. Authors who have recently argued in favour of a global strategy and ignore the realities of regionalisation include Vijay Govindarajan and Anil K. Gupta (2001), Jean-Pierre Jeannet (2000), and George Yip (2002). Regionalisation should be viewed as an expression of semi-globalisation (Ghemawat 2003). It implies that international markets are characterised neither by extreme geographical distribution of sales nor by complete integration. Incomplete integration means that location specificity — in this case regional specificity — matters. Only in the context of incomplete integration is there scope for international MNC strategies that are conceptually distinct from conventional domestic strategies.

The Meaning of Regional Strategies

The majority of the world's 500 largest companies are MNCs; they produce or distribute products or services across national borders. Yet very few MNCs are 'global' firms, with the ability to sell the same products and services around the world. The challenge of selling standardised products and services across borders, as originally advocated by Theodore Levitt (1983), has been dealt with appropriately in most of the mainstream literature on international business. It is now widely recognised that benefits of integration resulting from global-scale economies can only be reaped if accompanied by strategies of national responsiveness, guided by both external pressures for local adaptation and internal pressures for requisite variation. What is unfortunately not correctly understood is that, irrespective of MNCs' efforts to augment their alleged non-location–bound FSAs with a location-bound component, no balanced geographical dispersion of sales is achieved in most cases. Instead, the data indicate that most MNCs are regionally based in their home-triad market, of either North America, the EU, or Asia (principally Japan). An apparent paradox is that a very large MNC in terms of overall foreign sales volume can have a concentration of its international activities in its home-triad region and lack a truly global dimension. It could be argued that there is more to globalisation than sales dispersion; for example, foreign assets and foreign employment have sometimes been used together with foreign sales to compose a 'transnationality index'. However, it should be recognised that only sales dispersion constitutes a true performance measure at the output level.

If MNCs have exhausted their growth potential in the home-triad region and then decide to venture into other regions, they may face a liability of regional foreignness, including several additional risks that were absent in the host region and may be of an economic, cultural, administrative, or geographic nature, in accordance with the recent observation that distance still matters (Ghemawat 2001). Given the size of each triad region, most of the advantages of standardisation can often be achieved within the home-triad region, and this process is enhanced if governments in this region pursue policies that promote internal coherence through social, cultural, and political harmonisation (as in the EU) or even merely through economic integration (as in NAFTA and Asia).

A related point is that inter-block business is likely to be restricted relative to intra-regional sales by government imposed barriers to entry. For example, the EU and the United States are likely to fight trade wars and respond to domestic business lobbies seeking shelter in the form of subsidies or protection. Cultural and political differences among members of a single-triad region may remain, but these will mostly be less significant than across triad regions (Rugman 2000). The end result is the persistence of MNCs that will continue to earn 80 percent or more of their income in their home-triad region. There will only be a limited number of purely global MNCs in the top 500.

In a study of 380 firms, data for 365 firms were available that permitted a further decomposition of their foreign sales (Rugman and Verbeke 2004). It should be noted that many of the remaining 135 of the world's 500 largest companies actually operate solely in their home region, with no sales elsewhere, and for others there are insufficient data. As reported above, of the 365 with data, the vast majority (320) are based in their home region, having few sales in the triad's other two regions. A limited set is 'bi-regional' (25 firms), defined as having at least 20 percent of sales in two legs of the triad, or 'host-region based' (11 firms), defined as having more than 50 percent of sales in a foreign region. Only nine MNCs are truly global, with at least 20 percent of their sales in all three regions of the triad (see Table 10-4).

The definitions adopted in this study follow.

Home-Region Oriented In the study, 320 firms have at least 50 percent of sales in their home region of the triad. The threshold of 50 percent was chosen because it was assumed that a region that represents more than 50 percent of total sales would

Table 10-4 Classification of the Top 500 Multinational Corporations

Type of MNC	Number of MNCs	% of 500	% of 380	Weighted Average % Intra-regional Sales
Home-region oriented	320	64.0	84.2	80.3
Global	9	1.8	2.4	38.3
Bi-regional	25	5.0	6.6	42.0
Host-region oriented	11	2.2	2.9	30.9
Insufficient data	15	3.0	3.9	40.9
No data	120	24.0		NA
Total	500	100.0	100.0	71.9

Source: Rugman and Verbeke 2004.

systematically both shape and constrain most important decisions and actions taken by the MNC. It also implies a concentration of its 'consumer-end' FSAs in that region. The concept of customer-end FSA is explained below.

Bi-regional As mentioned, 25 MNCs are bi-regional, defined as firms with at least 20 percent of their sales in each of two regions, but less than 50 percent in any one region. This set includes 25 firms with sales ranging between 20 percent and 50 percent in the home region and 20 percent or over in a second region. The threshold of 20 percent was chosen because having two regional markets each representing at least one fifth of a '$10+ billion' firm's sales was assumed to reflect impressive market success resulting from extensive customer-end FSAs in those two markets. The question could then be raised whether a particular absolute volume of sales, regardless of the 20 percent threshold percentage, would make a firm bi-regional. In the framework used in the study, an absolute sales volume is, in itself, insufficient. The status of a region was viewed from a micro-level, corporate-strategy perspective; here, this status depends fully on the relative sales achieved vis-à-vis market performance in other regions.

Host-Region Oriented Eleven firms have more than 50 percent of their sales in a triad market other than the home region.

Global Only nine of the MNCs included are global, defined as having sales of 20 percent or more in each of the three regions of the triad but less than 50 percent in any one region of the triad. The 20 percent figure is less than the one third required for an equal triad distribution, and so is biased downward in favour of finding global MNCs. Conceptually, it implies the successful deployment of customer-end FSAs in three distinct markets. The North American and European region of the broad triad are approximately equal in size, as measured by gross domestic product (GDP). Asia is smaller than either as measured by GDP, but is nearly equal in terms of purchasing power parity (PPP). In other words, weighing the broad triad by GDP or PPP will not increase the number of firms that qualify as global.

Within each of the groups above, the home-triad region sales weighted averages are as follows:

a. Home-region oriented (320 firms): 80.3 percent
b. Bi-regional (25 firms): 42 percent
c. Host-region oriented (11 firms): 30.9 percent
d. Global (9 firms): 38.3 percent

In Table 10-5, these firm-level data are applied in a G8 context. As can be seen from the last column, all of the G8 member countries are home to the world's 500 largest firms that have the vast majority of the sales in their home region. The 169 U.S. firms and the 16 Canadian firms average 77.2 percent of their sales in North America. The five Italian firms average 83.4 percent in Europe, while the large German, French, and British firms average 68.1 percent, 64.8 percent, and 64.5 percent respectively. The 66 large firms for Japan average 74.7 percent in the Asian region.

These data reinforce the basic economic point on the strength of intra-regional business activity. These large firms are often flagship firms at the hubs of clusters of other suppliers and key distributors; they represent the geographic locus of regional business activity (Rugman and D'Cruz 2000). No data can be found to support growing inter-block trade. A U.S. energy policy that is regional would be consistent with these basic economic data.

Conclusion

According to John Kirton (2004), the Sea Island Summit of 2004 continued a successful history of co-operation in global energy issues. Specifically, the G8 leaders welcomed OPEC's pledge to increase oil production and agreed to explore mechanisms to conserve energy and seek alternatives to oil. However, these words of energy co-operation do not address the basic underlying issue of increasing U.S. isolationism and self-appointed military leadership exhibited over the Iraq war begun in 2002. This process, confirmed by the re-election of President George Bush in November 2004, is highly likely to lead to increased momentum toward U.S. oil self-sufficiency and less reliance for U.S. security on its G8 partners.

The political events of the Iraq war and its aftermath simply reflect the economic reality of the triad. The United States, as a superpower, does not need military, political, or economic support from the leading countries in Europe or Asia, even from its G8

Table 10-5 Regional Sales of Large Firms in the G8 Countries

Country	Number of Firms	Average Revenues (US$bn)	Average Intra-regional Sales (%)
United States	169	30.3	77.3
Canada	16	13.5	74.1
NAFTA	185	28.8	77.2
Italy	5	38.7	83.4
Germany	29	37.3	68.1
France	27	27.2	64.8
Britain	27	25.3	64.5
Japan	66	28.9	74.7

Note: Adapted from the database used in Rugman and Verbeke (2004). There are no Russian firms in the global 500 from which these data are constructed.

partners. It does not even need it from its NAFTA partners. What is the role of G8 members such as France, Germany, Italy, the UK, Russia, and Japan after the Iraq war? The relationship between the United States and the UK is strong, and it provides the UK with independent leverage across the enlarged EU and all of Europe. France has largely destroyed its ability to influence U.S. policy. It now ranks below Russia as a political U.S. ally. Germany ranks below Italy.

The United States is unlikely to look to the G8 for any military or political alliance in the near future. It does not need the G8 as much as the G8 needs the United States. The G8 was not rebuilt in 2004 as the United States hosted the summit based on the themes of security, prosperity, and freedom. The meeting was polite but largely irrelevant to the United States. In the long run, it is likely that the G8 will continue its slide into irrelevancy in the face of increasing regionalisation pressures. Prosperity is already regional, and this chapter shows that the United States can achieve energy self-sufficiency on a regional, rather than on a global basis.

Note

1. The author thanks Cecilia Brain for the development of the tables and the underlying firm-level data base used in this chapter.

References

Dunning, John H. (2001). *Global Capitalism at Bay?* Routledge, London.

Energy Information Administration (2003). 'Annual Energy Review 2002'. October. United States Department of Energy, Washington DC. <tonto.eia.doe.gov/FTPROOT/multifuel/038402.pdf> (November 2004).

Enright, Michael J. (2000). 'The Globalization of Competition and the Localization of Competitive Advantage: Policies Towards Regional Clustering'. In N. Hood and S. Young, eds., *The Globalization of Economic Activity and Economic Development*, pp. 330–331. Macmillan, Basingstoke.

Ghemawat, Pankaj (2001). 'Distance Still Matters: The Hard Reality of Global Expansion'. *Harvard Business Review* vol. 79, no. 8, pp. 137–147.

Ghemawat, Pankaj (2003). 'Semi-globalization and International Business Strategy'. *Journal of International Business Studies* vol. 34, no. 2, pp. 138–152.

Govindarajan, Vivay and Anil K. Gupta (2001). *The Quest for Global Dominance*. Jossey-Bass/Wiley, San Francisco.

International Monetary Fund (annual). *Direction of Trade Statistics Yearbook*. International Monetary Fund, Washington DC.

Jeannet, Jean-Pierre (2000). *Managing with a Global Mindset*. Pearson Educational, London.

Kirton, John J. (2004). 'The G8 and Energy'. Unpublished manuscript.

Levitt, Theodore (1983). 'The Globalization of Markets'. *Harvard Business Review* May-June, pp. 92–102.

Ohmae, Kenichi (1985). *Triad Power: The Coming Shape of Global Competition*. The Free Press, New York.

Rugman, Alan M. (1994). *Foreign Investment and NAFTA*. University of South Carolina Press, Columbia, SC.

Rugman, Alan M. (2000). *The End of Globalization*. Random House, London.

Rugman, Alan M. (2004). *The Regional Multinationals*. Cambridge University Press, Cambridge.

Rugman, Alan M. and Joseph R. D'Cruz (2000). *Multinationals as Flagship Firms: Regional Business Networks*. Oxford University Press, Oxford.

Rugman, Alan M. and Alina Kudina (2002). 'Britain, Europe, and North America'. In M. Fratianni, P. Savona and J. J. Kirton, eds., *Governing Global Finance: New Challenges, G7 and IMF Contributions*, pp. 185–196. Ashgate, Aldershot.

Rugman, Alan M. and Alain Verbeke (2004). 'A Perspective on Regional and Global Strategies of Multinational Enterprises'. *Journal of International Business Studies* vol. 35, no. 1, pp. 3–18.

Yip, George (2002). *Total Global Strategy II*. Prentice-Hall, Upper Saddle River, NJ.

PART III:
FINANCE AND SECURITY

Chapter 11

Combating Black Money: International Co-operation and the G8

Donato Masciandaro[1]

In the aftermath of 11 September 2001, there has been growing attention paid to the role of Non-Cooperative Countries and Territories (NCCTs) in money laundering and terrorist financing.[2] NCCTs do not meet the criteria consistent with the Forty Recommendations of the Financial Action Task Force on Money Laundering ([FATF] 2003).[3] Policy makers concentrate their attention on the possibility that NCCTs might facilitate the task of terrorists as well as criminal organisations (such money is referred to as black money, as it is not reported to government). Since 1989, the G7/8 countries have expressed the general commitment to define a strategy to combat black money (see Table 11-1); in October 2001, the G7 finance ministers explicitly stressed the urgency to develop a process to identify jurisdictions that facilitate black money and to recommend actions to achieve co-operation from such countries.

Two interacting principles commonly feature in the debate on the relationship between money laundering and NCCTs: money laundering is facilitated by lax financial regulation (see Appendix 11-2), and countries adopting lax financial regulation do not co-operate in the international effort to combat money laundering (Camdessus 1998; Holder 2003). These two principles characterised the mandate of the FATF for preventing money laundering. On the one hand, to address the problems associated with money-laundering risks, legal standards for rules and regulations must be developed. The FATF standards (the Forty Recommendations) became the benchmark for measuring the degree of laxity of financial regulation in every country setting. On the other hand, to monitor the compliance of countries with international standards, the FATF uses a list of specific criteria — consistent with the standards — to determine the NCCT jurisdictions.[4]

The FATF produces periodic reports on the NCCTs, commonly described as black lists. Between June 2000 and February 2004, nine NCCT lists were published; to date, the FATF has monitored a total of 45 countries, selected for potential weakness in regulations. Of a worldwide dataset on the main 130 countries, these 45 countries represent 8 percent of total gross domestic product (GDP) of the world, 15 percent of the total population, and 25 percent of foreign bank deposits. Obviously, these figures understate the overall relevance of the problem, given the relationships between the non-cooperative attitude, on the one hand, and the global economic and social costs due to the growth of the money-laundering risks, on the other.[5]

Table 11-1 G7/8 Terrorism Financing and Money Laundering

1978 Bonn Statement on Air Hijacking: Terrorism enters in G7 agenda.

1981 Ottawa Summit: G7 issues a statement on terrorism.

1984 London Declaration on International Terrorism: The international character of the terrorist threat is recognised.

1986 Tokyo Summit: The first network of experts on international terrorism is established.

1989 Paris Summit: G7 recognises the need for a task force to fight money laundering; Financial Action Task Force on Money Laundering is created.

1990 Houston Summit: G7 members commit to full implementation all of the FATF's Forty Recommendations.

1995 Ministerial Declaration on Counter Terrorism, Ottawa: Guidelines to fight terrorism, including 'depriving terrorists of funds', are issued.

1996 Ministerial Conference on Terrorism, Paris: Agreement on 25 measures includes those specifically defined to prevent terrorist fundraising (goals 19, 20, and 21).

1997 Counterterrorism Directory of Skills and Competencies is created.

1998 G8 Justice and Interior Ministers Virtual Meeting on Organized Crime and Terrorism: Ministerial underlines international co-operation in fighting money laundering and terrorist funding. France proposes a United Nations convention on terrorist financing.

1999 Moscow Conference: G8 supports the negotiations on the draft international convention against financing of terrorism.

2000 Okinawa Summit: Action against Abuse of the Global Financing System (first report) defines a comprehensive strategy against money laundering, tax havens, and offshore financial centres; G7 declares it is prepared to implement countermeasures against 15 non-cooperative countries identified by the FATF; G7 welcomes the creation of Financial Intelligence Units (FIUs).

2001 Fighting the Abuse of the Global Financial System (second report), Rome: G7 monitors the FATF's work.

2001 G8 statements (after 11 September): G8 declares the need for a comprehensive, international strategy against terrorism and highlights the main role of specific financial measures; plans to implement UN sanctions to block terrorist assets. FATF's mandate to combat terrorist financing is expanded; FATF issues Special Recommendations to fight terrorism financing and defines its Action Plan. G7 issues Action Plan to Combat the Financing of Terrorism and implements UN Security Council Resolutions 1333 and 1373; all states are called on to freeze terrorist funds and financial assets. International Monetary and Financial Committee of the International Monetary Fund issues communiqué setting out specific measures against terrorist financing.

2002 Progress Report on Combating the Financing of Terrorism, Ottawa: Implementation of the strategy against terrorist financing is monitored. Many countries set up FIUs. G8 foreign ministers issue Progress Report on the Fight against Terrorism and G8 Recommendations on Counter-Terrorism, revising the 25 measures adopted in Paris in 1996. G7 issues 'Combating the Financing of Terrorism: First Year Report', monitoring the implementation of the G7 Action Plan.

2003 Evian Summit: 'Building International Political Will and Capacity to Combat Terrorism: A G8 Action Plan' underscores the support for the UN's Counter Terrorism Committee, the FATF, and fulfilment of UNSCR 1373; Counter-Terrorism Action Group (CTAG) created.

2004 Washington: Joint Statement on Combating Terrorist Financing released.

Therefore, the blacklist instrument represents the cornerstone of the international effort to reduce the risks that single countries or territories became havens for money-laundering activities. But is this institutional device effective?

It has been argued that the overall result of the blacklisting mechanism is positive, since transparency regarding which countries do not comply has important effects in the financial markets, increasing the market pressures on the NCCTs.[6] But why is it, then, that various jurisdictions — notwithstanding the blacklist threat — delay or fail to change their rules, confirming their non-cooperative attitude, in what could be termed the 'reluctant friend effect'? Furthermore, it is true that most jurisdictions placed on the black list have enacted regulatory measures in an effort to be removed from it. But is regulatory reform sufficient to prove that a country has really changed its non-cooperative attitude — that is, the 'false friend effect'?

Perhaps the key problem is that such discussions often assumes that some countries offer financial services to terrorism and organised crime by adopting lax financial regulations. In other words, lax financial regulation is treated as an independent variable. Therefore, any regulatory reform consistent with international standards is sufficient to prove that the country is attempting to co-operate, while why specific countries continue in their non-cooperative attitude, notwithstanding the blacklist stigma, cannot be explained.

This chapter takes a different perspective. It develops the assumption that lax financial regulation may be a strategic dependent variable for national lawmakers seeking to maximise the net benefits produced by any public policy choice. Therefore, given the structural features and endowments of their own countries, lawmakers may it find profitable to adopt regulations that attract capital of illicit origin (money-laundering services) or destination (terrorism finance services), therefore choosing to be an NCCT.

From a methodological point of view, this chapter follows the classic intuitions of the new political economy, basing its work on three hypotheses: 1) the definition of regulatory policy is not independent, as in the conventional economics, but endogenous; 2) policy is not determined by maximising a social welfare function but by taking into account the political cost-benefit payoff; and 3) lawmaker maximisation is constrained and influenced by the structural framework, economic as well as institutional.[7] This

Table 11-2 Binary Laxity Index Determinants (130 countries and territories)

Dependent Variable	Binary Laxity Index	
Land use	0.0079108[a]	(0.003060)
GDP per capita	–0.0000723[a]	(0.0000190)
Foreign deposits per capita	3.18E–06[a]	(1.36E–06)
Terrorism and organised crime	–0.5737521[a]	(0.2436112)

Notes: Standard errors are in parentheses. Superscript asterisks indicate statistical significance at 0.01 (a), 0.02 (b), 0.05 (c), 0.10 (d).

analysis is indebted to a strand of literature, usually associated with the 'law and economics' movement, that is strictly — though indirectly — related to the subject matter, namely the literature on the competition in regulation. More specifically, this chapter takes the approach developed by authors who have tackled the issue in the 'transaction cost economics' tradition, and applies it in a novel area.[8]

The chapter proceeds as follows. The second section uses a simple model to describe, through the lawmaker payoff maximisation, the relationships between specific country features and endowments, on the one hand, and lax financial regulations, on the other hand. Given that in the real world relatively lax regulation means a non-cooperative attitude in the international fight against money laundering, the third section includes an empirical test of the above theoretical relationship in the case of the NCCTs. The policy consequences on the pros and cons of international blacklisting procedures are discussed in the concluding section.

Country Endowments, Lawmakers, and Lax Financial Regulation: A Simple Model

To design the key elements of this approach, a very simple model is used, in order to present the economic intuitions in a compact and causal framework.[9] The goal is to discuss the possible relationships between specific country features, lawmaker payoff maximisation, and lax financial regulation against money laundering, highlighting the key variables of the problem.

For this analysis, it is assumed that a lawmaker is aware that a potential demand for money laundering exists on the part of one or more criminal or terrorist organisations, for a total amount equal to W.[10] The international market for money laundering in this analysis is driven by demand, as it is likely to be in the real world. Therefore, every potential lax regulation jurisdiction is a relatively 'small country'.

The lawmaker can decide to launder an amount of money Y, $0 < Y < W$. For the sake of simplicity in this model, the decision on the optimal level of money-laundering services is equivalent to the choice of the optimal degree of laxity in financial regulation. If the payoff function of the lawmaker is called U, it is obvious that the expected payoff from unlaundered liquidity is zero, whatever the amount:

$$U(W - Y) = 0 \tag{1}$$

Money laundering has a positive expected value for the lawmaker, if his or her country derives benefits from offering financial services. In particular, the lower the national income and the higher the proportion of that income that depends on the financial industry, the greater will be the propensity to offer money-laundering services, all other things being equal. In general, those expected benefits are defined as laxity national benefits.

To be more precise, laundered money provides B expected profit to the lawmaker:

$$B = mY \tag{2}$$

where $m > 0$ is the expected net rate of return on money-laundering services.

The inflow of black and grey foreign capital produces national revenues, increasing the activity of the financial industry and then throughout the traditional macroeconomic multiplier effects.[11] On the contrary, the implementation of a severe regulation against money laundering generates high compliance costs (Masciandaro 1999).

If the decision to launder were cost free, then $Y = W$. But other elements intervene.

First of all, lawmakers may face international reputation costs. To be more attractive to criminal or terrorist organisations, a country must make legislative and regulatory choices that increase its credibility as a lax financial regulation jurisdiction (Masciandaro and Portolano 2003). Second, the activity of money laundering implies the strengthening of organised crime and terrorism.

Within this framework, expected crime costs are not separated from expected terrorism costs. From the theoretical standpoint, it is preferable to stress the different sensitivities of the lawmaker to expected international costs and expected national costs, based on a clearly different political cost-benefits analysis. Furthermore, for each country, it should not be difficult to introduce a specific parameter in expression (3) for each expected national cost factor. The chosen cost specification, C, consists of two parts. The first is reputational cost, captured by parameter $c > 0$. The second is the cost against crime or terrorism that rises as the amount of laundered money increases, captured by γ^2. On the assumption that, all other things being equal, for political-electoral reasons the lawmaker is more sensitive to the crime or terrorism costs — which can weigh directly on the country's citizens — than to the international reputation costs — which probably have a less perceptible or direct effect on the citizen-voters. Thus:

$$C = cY + \gamma^2 Y \tag{3}$$

Finally, a lax financial regulation jurisdiction must be considered a source of economic, political, and social risk for the international community and prompts possible sanctions and punitive countermeasures. If S denotes the monetary value of sanctions and p the associated probability of discovering money laundering, then S must at least equal Y.[12] In reality, the damage from a sanction is a multiple, because of the value of collateral damages related to the sanction:

$$S = tY^2 \tag{4}$$

where t denotes the degree of international political enforcement.

The lawmaker, modelled as a risk-neutral agent, is thus faced with the problem of deciding on the optimal level of laxity. The lawmaker's expected payoff E can now be better specified as:

$$E(U) = [(1 - p)(B - C) - p(C + S)] \tag{5}$$

But since we have defined $B = m\,Y$ and $C = c\,Y + \gamma^2 Y$, then (5) becomes:

$$E(U) = (1 - p)\{mY - cY - \gamma^2 Y\} - p(cY + \gamma^2 Y + tY^2) \tag{6}$$

and the optimal level of laxity is:

$$Y^* = \frac{m(1 - p) - c - \gamma^2}{2\,pt} \tag{7}$$

For $Y^* > 0$, $m(1 - p) - c - \gamma^2 > 0$, the expected benefit from money laundering must exceed the cost of loss of reputation and the cost of fighting crime and terrorism. It is easy to check that Y^* rises as m rises and falls as c, γ, and p rise.

An Empirical Investigation of Lax Financial Regulation and Non-Cooperative Countries

In this section, the implications of the simple model developed above will be tested. In the real world, the international community considers countries with lax financial regulation to be potential NCCTs in the fight against money laundering. If NCCTs are assumed to share common structural features, then the econometric techniques described below can be applied.

In particular, given a constant international environment, an NCCT has:

- scant physical resources to spend in international trade, which gives an incentive for lax financial regulation;
- the potential for developing financial services and can gain from lax financial regulation; and
- social characteristics that shield it to some extent from the risks of terrorism or organised crime, and thus reduce the expected cost of lax financial regulation.

Since 22 June 2000, the FATF has published a periodic report on the NCCTs. The report lays down 25 criteria plus eight recent Special Recommendations on Terrorist Financing that, if violated, identify the national rules that in each country are detrimental to international co-operation in the fight against money laundering. Between June 2000 and February 2004, 45 countries were monitored, and nine black lists were published, indicating the jurisdictions that fail to conform to the criteria.

A probit analysis can be made using a worldwide data set on the main 130 countries.[13] The dependent variable is a binary probit variable equal to one for the 45 potential NCCTs and zero otherwise.

The best estimated equation is as follows (Masciandaro 2005a; 2005b; Masciandaro and Portolano 2004):

$$(BinaryLI)_t = \beta_1 + \beta_2 (A1)_t + \beta_2 (C1) + \beta_4 (E1) + e_t \quad (7)$$

with $t = 1 \ldots N$ (7)

where: $A1$ = land use; $B1$ = GDP per capita; $C1$ = foreign deposits per capita; and $E1$ = terrorism and organised crime index.[14]

The results of Table 11-2 confirm that the probability of being an NCCT depends on specific country endowments. The probability that a country is an NCCT tends to be higher the lower the level of economic development measured by per capita GDP and degree of land exploitation; the higher the flow of foreign deposits, the lower the extent of terrorism and organised crime. Given the limitations of this dataset, it was not possible to test for the role of international reputation sensitivity.

However, one can go a step further by hypothesising different levels of non-cooperation: the first level being non-cooperation for countries just monitored by the FATF, the second being non-cooperation for countries that have appeared on the black list at least once, and the third being non-cooperation for countries that permanently stay in the black list.[15] These rankings, which are shown in Table 11-3, can be used as an ordered probit variable (complying countries are set equal to zero). The estimates of the ordered probit are shown in Table 11-4.

The regressions confirm the robustness of the two channels of national laxity benefits, while the proxy of the terrorism and organised crime risks has the right sign but is not statistically significant. If the organised crime dummy is split from the terrorism dummy, the former is statistically significant and the latter is not.

It should be noted that non-cooperation is not associated with tax competition. There is a theoretical presumption that international tax evasion and money laundering through offshore financial centres should overlap (Yaniv 1994, 1999; Alworth and Masciandaro 2004). However, this is not necessarily the case.

Offshore financial centres are possibly more prone to regulatory laxity than non-offshore centres (see Table 11-5). The dependent variable acquires a value of unity when a country is listed as an offshore centre by the Organisation for Economic Co-operation and Development (OECD); otherwise it is zero (Alworth and Masciandaro 2004).

With the exception of the crime and terrorism index, none of the variables has any explanatory power. This seems to suggest that the underlying economic characteristics of offshore centres and NCCTs tend to differ. In general, the hypothesis that the causes

Table 11-3 Ordered Laxity Index

	Countries	Ordered Laxity Index
1	Antigua	1
2	Bahamas	2
3	Barbuda	1
4	Belize	1
5	Bermuda	1
6	British Virgin Islands	1
7	Cayman Islands	2
8	Cook Islands	3
9	Cyprus	1
10	Czech Republic	1
11	Dominica	1
12	Egypt	2
13	Gibraltar	1
14	Grenada	2
15	Guatemala	3
16	Guernsey	1
17	Hungary	2
18	Indonesia	3
19	Isle of Man	1
20	Israel	2
21	Jersey	1
22	Lebanon	2
23	Liechtenstein	2
24	Malta	1
25	Marshall Islands	2
26	Mauritius	1
27	Monaco	1
28	Myanmar	3
29	Nauru	3
30	Nigeria	3
31	Niue	2
32	Panama	2
33	Philippines	3
34	Poland	1
35	Russia	2
36	Samoa	1
37	Seychelles	1
38	Slovak Republic	1
39	St. Kitts and Nevis	2
40	St. Lucia	1
41	St. Vincent	2
42	Turks and Caicos	1
43	Ukraine	2
44	Uruguay	1
45	Vanuatu	1

of lax financial regulation decisions and offshore activities are exactly the same can be rejected.

Therefore, non-cooperation seems to depend on key structural features of the country. Now, what are the consequences of this analysis on the debate over the effectiveness of blacklisting procedures?

Conclusion: Is Blacklisting Effective?

This chapter has discussed and empirically tested the relationships among specific country features, lawmaker choices regarding lax financial regulation, and national non-cooperative attitudes with respect to the international effort to combat money laundering. The results suggest two main prescriptions for designing international policies aimed at reducing the global risks of terrorism and organised crime. These

Table 11-4 Ordered Laxity Index Determinants (130 countries and territories)

Dependent Variable	Ordered Laxity Index			
Land use	0.0135717[a]	(0.0049385)	0.0144398[a]	(0.0049597)
GDP per capita	–0.0000523[a]	(0.0000155)	–0.0000527[a]	(0.0000161)
Foreign deposits per capita	8.86E–08[b]	(3.98E–08)	9.04E–08[b]	(4.05E–08)
Terrorism and organised crime	–0.3313072	(0.2245221)		
Organised crime			–0.4018445[d]	(0.2414516)
Terrorism			0.0099674	(0.0293882)

Notes: Standard errors are in parentheses. Superscript asterisks indicate statistical significance at 0.01 (a), 0.02 (b), 0.05 (c), 0.10 (d).

Table 11-5 Comparison of Binary Offshore Index and Binary Laxity Determinants (130 countries and territories)

Dependent Variable	Binary Laxity Index		Binary Offshore Index	
Land use	0.007[b]	(0.003)	–0.002	(0.005)
GDP per capita	–7.07E-05[a]	(1.92E–05)	–2.04E-07	(2.60E–07)
Foreign bank deposits per capita	3.18E–06[a]	(1.36E–06)	1.71E–06	(1.33E–08)
Terrorism organised crime	–0.508[b]	(0.224)	–1.888[a]	(0.448)

Notes: Standard errors are in parentheses. Superscript asterisks indicate statistical significance at 0.01 (a), 0.02 (b), 0.05 (c), 0.10 (d).

prescriptions can help to identify a possible role for the G8 countries in combating black money.

First of all, a pure and just formal 'name and shame' approach may, in fact, prove counterproductive. Given that the international community is capable of effectively singling out NCCTs that are indeed involved in black money schemes, a cautious approach is still deemed necessary. When the international community points a finger at a given country as a leading supplier of money-laundering financial services, it may also be identifying — to the benefit of the country itself — that the country is indeed specialised in that business. The signalling effect embedded in the name-and-shame approach should not be underestimated. The main difficulty for a country with genuinely lax financial regulations is solving the commitment problem credibly. Thus, it is a good choice for such a country to have the international community — not exactly its closest friends — solve that problem through a public statement declaring a non-cooperative attitude (that is, the reluctant friend effect).

Listing should also be regarded as a sort of third-party bonding, which is likely to generate two interacting effects. It is capable of cementing the commitment by the country with lax financial regulations. And listing increases the reputation of the transaction-specific nature of investments. Inclusion in a black list increases the value of the sunk investment. In terms of the analysis presented in this chapter, blacklisting raises the expected benefits rather than improves international political enforcement. Furthermore, a blacklisted country will find it even more difficult to switch course and decide to exit the market, thus being encouraged to compete more aggressively in that market.

Second, given the empirical evidence, there remains the possibility that there are countries with lax regulations not currently under observation by the FATF. This is true, perhaps, because they are highly effective in bringing their formal rules in line with international precepts, while in fact they remain lax. By the same token, by modifying the formal rules NCCTs may not shake off their acquired reputation for laxity (that is, the false friend effect). The name-and-shame approach may not be effective on its own. Countries can be blacklisted, but only if blacklisting goes hand in hand with other measures.

Appropriate countermeasures that increase the actual level of international political enforcement or the level of international reputation costs should be grounded on the premise that in today's global context even the most efficient country with lax regulations will still need to be integrated into the world financial markets. Thus no matter how many layers of transactions cover the targeted offence, terrorism or criminal organisations will still need to place that money within the lawful financial sector. This step is necessary, at a minimum, to exploit the capital in lawful uses, once it has been laundered. Money laundering is by definition instrumental for a later use.

In this regard, there is one fundamental feature of the initiative taken by the FATF that appears to be pivotal for its success: the FATF has not limited its initiative merely to recognising 'non-cooperative countries and territories'. FATF member states have also applied Recommendation 21 to the countries included in the list (FATF 2000b;

2003).[16] Recommendation 21 requires a higher degree of scrutiny by financial intermediaries in evaluating the suspect nature of transactions with counter parties, including legal persons, based in a country listed as non-cooperative. As a result of the FATF initiative, many countries included in the list have already taken initiatives aimed at overcoming the serious deficiencies observed by the FATF (2000a).

These initiatives need to be evaluated over the long term because some of the enacted laws, for example, will require secondary regulations to become effective, or, more generally, the initiatives taken at the legislative level will need to be followed by concrete actions. It can be argued, however, that the threat of being crowded out by the international community has played a key role in spurring the adoption of the above-mentioned initiatives. Nonetheless, it may be necessary to go beyond that. The international community could do well to consider the possibility of introducing effective punitive measures, such as a financial quarantine for every country that does not adhere to the internationally set standards.[17] The G8 members could play the role in promoting a complete strategy to combat black money focussed on the financial quarantine threat; such a threat could be the effective stick to combine with the appropriate carrots in defining a new name-and-shame approach.

Finally, the above conclusions imply a constant effort on the part of international organisations, particularly the FATF, to update the criteria and monitor the noncompliant countries.

Notes

1. The author wishes to thank all the participants in the research project on 'Security, Prosperity, and Freedom: Why America Needs the G8', in particular John Kirton, Bernard May, and Alan Rugman. The author is also indebted to Michele Fratianni and George von Furstenberg for useful suggestions.
2. Money laundering is defined as the processing of criminal proceeds to disguise their illegal origin in order to legitimise the gains of crime, while terrorist finance can be characterised as the direct or indirect provision of funds — illegal or legal — with the intention that they should be used in terrorist acts (Norgren 2004). But the techniques are quite similar, or at least overlapping. On similarities and differences between money laundering and terrorism finance (or money dirtying), see Appendix 11-1 and Chapter 12; see also Barry Rider (2003) and Donato Masciandaro (2004). On the key role of the U.S. legislation in promoting the international financial war against terrorism, see Miriam Wasserman (2002), Ray Banoun, Derrick Cephas, and Lawrence Fruchtman (2002), Ethan Preston (2003), and Carol Van Cleef (2003); see also Kevin Davis (2003).
3. The FATF is an intergovernmental organisation that promotes policies at both national and international levels to combat money laundering. It was established at the G7 Summit held in Paris in 1989. Initially, it was composed of the G7 member states, the European Commission, and eight other countries, but it now has a membership of 29 jurisdictions, with the European Commission and the Gulf Cooperation Council as international member organisations. The 29 member jurisdictions are Argentina, Australia, Austria, Belgium, Brazil, Canada, Denmark, Finland, France, Germany, Greece, Hong Kong, Iceland, Ireland, Italy, Japan, Luxembourg, Mexico, the Netherlands, New Zealand, Norway, Portugal, Singapore,

Spain, Sweden, Switzerland, Turkey, the United Kingdom, and the United States. The FATF has a small secretariat housed in the headquarters of the Organisation for Economic Co-operation and Development (OECD) in Paris, but it is a separate international body and not part of the OECD. See also Kern Alexander (2001).

4. On the differences and similarities between NCCT jurisdictions and offshore financial centres, see Daniel Mitchell (2002) and Julian Alworth and Donato Masciandaro (2004); on the offshore centres issues, see also Luca Errico and Alberto Musalem (1999), Mark Hampton and John Christensen (2002), and Donato Masciandaro (2004).
5. On the qualitative and quantitative aspects of money laundering, see Vito Tanzi (2000, 186–200).
6. See Claes Norgren (2004). An economic analysis of the FATF's effects is performed by Jackie Johnson and Y. C. Desmond Lim (2002). On the first different country reactions to the blacklisting process, see Jackie Johnson (2001b; 2001a).
7. For the new political economy, see Allan Drazen (2000) and Torsten Persson and Guido Tabellini (2000).
8. See Roberta Romano (1985; 1993; 1999).
9. For an in-depth analysis of the model, see Masciandaro (2005a; 2005b).
10. For a general microeconomic analysis of money-laundering demand, see Masciandaro (1998; 1999). For the peculiar relationship between money-laundering demand and tax evasion, see Gideon Yaniv (1994; 1999); see also Peter Alldridge (2001).
11. For a macroeconomic analysis of the interrelationships between money laundering, the banking industry, legal sectors, and illegal economic sectors, see Masciandaro (2000). For the peculiar vulnerability of securities markets, see Dayanath Jayasuriya (2003).
12. For sanctions and enforcements, see Gary Becker (1968).
13. Given that there are 267 countries in the world (180 members of the United Nations), the 130 countries in this sample represent 98 percent of the world's GDP and 90 percent of the world's population.
14. 'Land use' contains the percentage shares of total land area for five different types of land use: arable land, cultivated for crops that are replanted after each harvest, such as wheat, maize, and rice; permanent crops, land cultivated for crops that are not replanted after each harvest, such as citrus, coffee, and rubber; permanent pastures, used permanently for herbaceous forage crops; forests and woodland, land under dense or open stands of trees; other — any type of land not mentioned above specifically, such as urban areas. 'GDP per capita' shows GDP on a purchasing power parity basis divided by population (for 2001). 'Foreign deposits per capita' is derived from reports as such or calculated by subtracting separately reported data on positions other than deposits from total external assets and liabilities. The only exception is the Netherlands Antilles, which does not provide this information separately (for 2001). The deposit data are then divided by the population (for 2001). With regard to the 'terrorism and organised crime index', the size of the drug market dimension is evidently an indirect and imperfect indicator. At the same time, the drug market provides organised crime its massive resources. During the 1970s the drug trade became far too profitable and easy for even traditional and 'conservative' organised crime organisations to ignore. Furthermore, even terrorist groups entered the market and, by so doing, became virtually indistinguishable from 'ordinary' organised crime. The index was created by summing two separate variables for each country: 'Organised Crime Dummy = 1' if there is drug production or drug markets in the country — otherwise it is 0; 'Normalised terrorism indicator = average number of terrorist episodes in the country (1968–1991) / max average number of terrorist episodes in a country (1968–1991); the terrorism indicator therefore ranges from 0 to 1. Consequently, the index here ranges from 0 to 2. (Sources: Central Intelligence Agency 2004; Bank for International Settlements 2002; Rider 2002, 27; Chirico 2001; Blomberg, Hess, and Weerapana 2002; ITERATE dataset).

15. As of February 2005, the list of NCCTs is Myanmar, Nauru, and Nigeria.
16. In addition, in June 2001 the FATF agreed to stricter countermeasures for reluctant NCCTs (see Norgren 2004).
17. On the possible features of such a financial quarantine, see Tanzi (2000).

References

Alexander, Kern (2001). 'The International Anti-Money Laundering Regime: The Role of the Financial Action Task Force'. *Journal of Money Laundering Control* vol. 4, no. 3, pp. 231–248.

Alldridge, Peter (2001). 'Are Tax Evasion Offences Predicate Offences for Money Laundering Offences?' *Journal of Money Laundering Control* vol. 4, no. 4, pp. 350–359.

Alworth, Julian and Donato Masciandaro (2004). 'Public Policy: Offshore Centres and Tax Competition — The Harmful Problem'. In D. Masciandaro, ed., *Global Financial Crime: Terrorism, Money Laundering, and Offshore Centres*, pp. 181–217. Ashgate, Aldershot.

Bank for International Settlements (2002). 'BIS Quarterly Review – June 2002 — Statistical Annex'. <www.bis.org/publ/qtrpdf/r_qa0206.pdf> (November 2004).

Banoun, Ray, Derrick Cephas, and Lawrence Fruchtman (2002). 'U.S. Patriot Act and Other Recent Money Laundering Developments Have Broad Impact on Financial Institutions'. *Journal of Taxation of Financial Institutions* vol. 15, no. 4.

Becker, Gary (1968). 'Crime and Punishment: An Economic Approach'. *Journal of Political Economy* vol. 2, pp. 169–217.

Blomberg, S. Brock, Gregory D. Hess, and Akila Weerapana (2002). 'Terrorism from Within: An Economic Model of Terrorism'. <econpapers.hhs.se/paper/clmclmeco/2002-14.htm> (November 2004).

Camdessus, Michel (1998). 'Money Laundering: The Importance of International Countermeasures'. Address to the Plenary Meeting of the Financial Action Task Force on Money Laundering, Paris, 10 February. <www.imf.org/external/np/speeches/1998/021098.htm> (November 2004).

Central Intelligence Agency (2004). 'Notes and Definitions'. World Factbook. <www.cia.gov/cia/publications/factbook/docs/notesanddefs.html> (November 2004).

Chirico, Francesco (2001). 'Leaders, Elezioni, Governi e Sistemi Politici: Stati Sovrani e Territori — Democracy Index (al 31/12/200)'. <www.geocities.com/CapitolHill/Lobby/3535/country/list-di.htm> (November 2004).

Davis, Kevin E. (2003). 'Legislating against the Financing of Terrorism: Pitfalls and Prospects'. *Journal of Financial Crime* vol. 10, no. 3, pp. 269–274.

Drazen, Allan (2000). *Political Economy in Macroeconomics*. Princeton University Press, Princeton.

Errico, Luca and Alberto Musalem (1999). 'Offshore Banking: An Analysis of Micro- and Macro-Prudential Issues'. International Monetary Fund Working Paper No. 99/5. Washington DC. <www.imf.org/external/pubs/ft/wp/1999/wp9905.pdf> (November 2004).

Financial Action Task Force (2000a). 'Progress Report on Non-Cooperative Countries and Territories'. 5 October. Paris. <www1.oecd.org/fatf/pdf/PR-20001005_en.pdf> (November 2004).

Financial Action Task Force (2000b). 'Review to Identify Non-Cooperative Countries or Territories: Increasing the Worldwide Effectiveness of Anti-Money Laundering Measures'. First Review to Identify Non-Cooperative Countries or Territories, 22 June. Paris. <www1.oecd.org/fatf/pdf/NCCT2000_en.pdf> (November 2004).

Financial Action Task Force (2003). 'The Forty Recommendations'. Organisation for Economic Co-operation and Development, Paris. <www1.oecd.org/fatf/40Recs_en.htm> (November 2004).

Hampton, Mark P. and John Christensen (2002). 'Offshore Pariahs? Small Island Economies, Tax Havens, and the Re-configuration of Global Finance'. *World Development* vol. 30, no. 9, pp. 1657–1673.

Holder, William E. (2003). 'The International Monetary Fund's Involvement in Combating Money Laundering and the Financing of Terrorism'. *Journal of Money Laundering Control* vol. 6, no. 4, pp. 383–387.

Jayasuriya, Dayanath (2003). 'Money Laundering and Terrorism Financing: The Role of Capital Market Regulators'. *Journal of Financial Crime* vol. 10, no. 1, pp. 30–36.

Johnson, Jackie (2001a). 'Blacklisting: Initial Reactions, Responses, and Repercussions'. *Journal of Money Laundering Control* vol. 6, no. 3, pp. 211–225.

Johnson, Jackie (2001b). 'In Pursuit of Dirty Money: Identifying Weaknesses in the Global Financial System'. *Journal of Money Laundering Control* vol. 6, no. 1, pp. 122–132.

Johnson, Jackie and Y. C. Desmond Lim (2002). 'Money Laundering: Has the Financial Action Task Force Made a Difference?' *Journal of Financial Crime* vol. 10, no. 1, pp. 7–22.

Masciandaro, Donato (1998). 'Money Laundering Regulation: The Micro Economics'. *Journal of Money Laundering Control* vol. 2, no. 1, pp. 49–58.

Masciandaro, Donato (1999). 'Money Laundering: The Economics of Regulation'. *European Journal of Law and Economics* vol. 3 (May), pp. 245–240.

Masciandaro, Donato (2000). 'The Illegal Sector, Money Laundering, and Legal Economy: A Macroeconomic Analysis'. *Journal of Financial Crime* vol. 2, pp. 103–112.

Masciandaro, Donato, ed. (2004). *Global Financial Crime: Terrorism, Money Laundering, and Offshore Centres*. Ashgate, Aldershot.

Masciandaro, Donato (2005a). 'Could Sticks Become Carrots? Money Laundering, International Black Lists, and Offshore Centres'. *Finance India*.

Masciandaro, Donato (2005b), 'False and Reluctant Friends? National Regulation, International Compliance, and Non-Cooperative Countries', *European Journal of Law and Economics*, forthcoming.

Masciandaro, Donato and Allessandro Portolano (2003). 'It Takes Two to Tango: International Financial Regulation and Offshore Centres'. *Journal of Money Laundering Control* vol. 6, no. 4, pp. 311–331.

Masciandaro, Donato and Allessandro Portolano (2004). 'Financial Policies: Offshore Centres and Competition in Regulation — The Laxity Problem'. In D. Masciandaro, ed., *Global Financial Crime: Terrorism, Money Laundering, and Offshore Centres*, pp. 125–179. Ashgate, Aldershot.

Mitchell, Daniel J. (2002). 'U.S. Government Agencies Confirm that Low-Tax Jurisdictions Are Not Money Laundering Havens'. *Journal of Financial Crime* vol. 11, no. 2, pp. 127–133.

Norgren, Claes (2004). 'The Control of Risk Associated with Crime, Terror, and Subversion'. *Journal of Money Laundering Control* vol. 7, no. 3, pp. 201–206.

Persson, Torsten and Guido Tabellini (2000). *Political Economics: Explaining Economic Policy*. MIT University Press, Cambridge MA.

Preston, Ethan M. (2003). 'The U.S. Patriot Act: New Adventures in American Extraterritoriality'. *Journal of Financial Crime* vol. 10, no. 1, pp. 104–116.

Rider, Barry A. K. (2002). 'Weapons of War: The Use of Anti-Money Laundering Laws against Terrorist and Criminal Enterprises'. *International Journal of Banking Regulation* vol. 4, no. 1, pp. 13–31.

Rider, Barry A. K. (2003). 'Financial Regulation and Supervision after 11th September, 2001'. *Journal of Financial Crime* vol. 10, no. 4, pp. 336–358.

Romano, Roberta (1985). 'Law as a Product: Some Pieces of the Incorporation Puzzle'. *Journal of Law, Economics, and Organisation* vol. 1, no. 2, pp. 225–283.

Romano, Roberta (1993). *The Genius of American Corporate Law*. AEI Press, Washington DC.

Romano, Roberta (1999). 'Corporate Law and Corporate Governance'. In G. Carroll and D. J. Teece, eds., *Firms, Markets, and Hierarchies: The Transaction Cost Economics Perspective*. Oxford University Press, New York.

Tanzi, Vito (2000). *Policies, Institutions, and the Dark Side of Economics*. Edward Elgar, Cheltenham.

Van Cleef, Carol (2003). 'U.S. Patriot Act: Statutory Analysis and Regulatory Implementation'. *Journal of Financial Crime* vol. 11, no. 1, pp. 73–101.

Wasserman, Miriam (2002). 'Dirty Money'. *Regional Review* Q1. <www.bos.frb.org/economic/nerr/rr2002/q1/dirty.htm> (November 2004).

Yaniv, Gideon (1994). 'Taxation and Dirty Money Laundering'. *Public Finances/Public Finance* vol. 49 (Suppl), pp. 40–51.

Yaniv, Gideon (1999). 'Tax Evasion, Risky Laundering, and Optimal Deterrence Policy'. *International Tax and Public Finance* vol. 6, no. 1, pp. 27–38.

Appendix 11-1
Key Concepts in Money Laundering and Terrorist Financing, Formal and Informal Finance

Since 11 September 2001, the financial systems, overt and covert, have come increasingly into the sights of the state agencies appointed to combat terrorism. In that context, the need to increase the fight against the laundering of illicit capital was included in their agendas.

In terms of economic analysis, the financing of terrorism (money dirtying) is a phenomenon conceptually different from the recycling of capital (money laundering). To understand the similarities and differences, therefore, it is necessary to review briefly the economic peculiarities of money laundering. In recent years, particular emphasis has been placed on the study of this phenomenon because of its central theoretical and practical role in the development of any crime that generates revenues.

In fact, the conduct of any illegal activity may be subject to a special category of transaction costs, linked to the fact that the use of the relative revenues increases the probability of discovery of the crime and therefore incrimination.

Those transaction costs can be minimised through an effective laundering action, a means of concealment that separates financial flows from their origin, an activity whose specific economic function is to transform potential wealth into effective purchasing power.

In this sense, money laundering performs an illegal monetary function, responding to the demand for 'black finance' services expressed by individuals or groups that have committed income-producing crimes.

The financing of terrorism resembles money laundering in some respects and differs from in others. The objective of the activity is to channel funds of any origin to individuals or groups to enable acts of terrorism and, therefore, crimes. Again, in this case, a party with such an objective must contend with potential transaction costs, since the financial flows may increase the probability that the crime of terrorism will be discovered, thus leading to incrimination. Therefore, an effective money-dirtying action, an activity of concealment designed to separate financial flows from their destination, can minimise the transaction costs. Thus, money dirtying can also perform an illegal monetary function, responding to the demand for covertness expressed by individuals or groups proposing to commit crimes of terrorism.

The phenomena of money laundering and money dirtying may coexist, of course, when terrorism is financed by funds originating from criminal activities. A typical example is the financing of terrorism with the proceeds from the production and marketing of narcotics. In those specific situations, at least on the logical level, the importance of the transaction costs is doubled, since the need to lower the probability of incrimination concerns both the crimes that generated the financial flows and the crimes for which they are intended. As a result, the value of a concealment operation is even more significant.

But who satisfies the demand for concealment, whether its purpose is money laundering or financing terrorism?

Drawing upon the literature on information asymmetries, it is easy to demonstrate that banking and financial intermediaries can perform an important function in the concealment activity, whether the underlying motive is money laundering or financing terrorism.

By reducing the overall transaction costs for the other economic agents, financial intermediaries improve the consumers' capacity to decide how to allocate their purchasing power in terms of consumption, savings, and investment. Thus, intermediaries ultimately animate an industry in which the services offered and sold are intrinsically intangible, with an information content that is high but not uniformly distributed among all the market participants. The diverse characteristics of the operators are thus known to, and co-ordinated by, the financial firms through the supply and sale of their services, and the individual intermediaries seek to maximise their profit precisely through the management and enhancement of their information assets, in a sector where information is not uniformly distributed. Therefore, financial firms are ultimately characterised as having information assets greater than, different from, and more specialised than all the others. As a result, the financial industry acquires a reputation for two crucial attributes with regard to the purpose of concealment: a greater-than-normal degree of 'opacity' (information asymmetry), because the exchanges and flows of purchasing power are filtered, co-ordinated, and administered by specialised operators, and the privileged position of those intermediaries.

It should be stressed, however, that the connotation of incomplete, asymmetrical distribution of information between the parties stipulating the various forms of contract or agreement is accentuated in the provision of financial services but is not the exclusive prerogative of those markets. It manifests itself, for example, when the characteristics of the provision of professional services are examined. In any case, the quantitative and qualitative centrality of the financial industry within the overall economic system clearly evidences information asymmetry and centrality of the specialised operators.

Within the financial sector, a particular role is played by banks, intermediaries distinguished by the simultaneous offering of deposit contracts, fungible for payment and monetary requirements, and credit contracts, generally not transformable *prima facie* into market-negotiable assets. Banks thus emerge as a special intermediary, because both their deposit and loan contracts provide them with significant economies of scale and diversification in the management of information. In markets that are opaque by definition, banks therefore become a depositary of confidential information on both the beneficiaries of loans and on the users of payment services, or whatever services they provide.

The management of the payment system also puts banks in a crucial position regarding the purpose of concealment. The more a payment system minimises the costs paid by operators to transform their potential options for allocating purchasing power into actual options, the more efficient it becomes. But, if this is true, that system can be a potentially optimal, efficient vehicle for transforming the potential purchasing power of illicit revenues into actual purchasing power and therefore for performing money-laundering functions effectively. At the same time, through the payment system, the provision of funds to terrorist organisations can be concealed.

In other words, the management of the payment system has a positive value for legal economic agents, since it facilitates their resource allocation decisions. At the same time, it may be crucial for illegal parties, which are seeking not only to reduce transaction costs but especially to minimise the risks of discovery — and therefore the costs of sanctions and punishment — associated with both money-laundering and terrorism-financing activities.

Banking and financial intermediaries are therefore at the centre of attention of both criminal and terrorist organisations and the law enforcement authorities. For criminal parties, the presence of intermediaries that are co-operative (contaminating intermediaries) or inefficient in protecting their integrity (unknowing intermediaries) increases the possibility of using the payment or lending systems, or financial services system in general, for their concealment objectives. At the same time, for the inquiring and investigative authorities, the information assets in the possession of those companies can serve an essential reporting function in identifying and verifying the presence of criminal or terrorist organisations or individuals.

An examination of the role of the unknowing intermediaries, to which the authorities assign the task of reporting suspicious financial movements, will cast light on the similarities and differences between money laundering and money dirtying.

With respect to any financial transaction, money laundering is a transaction that not only performs an economic function of its own but also, if its purpose is to launder funds, performs an additional irregular function. The hypothesis is that precisely because the transaction in question is responding to an uncommon (and illegal) purpose, it will possess irregular features that distinguish it from normal, physiological characteristics.

What will the sources of the irregularity be? The irregularity could arise from at least one of the base elements of the definition of money laundering, in which an economic agent institutes procedures to transform a given amount of potential purchasing power into actual purchasing power. The irregularity could therefore refer to at least one of the three elements: the party, the procedures, and the amount of a given banking or financial contract.

Money-laundering techniques now pose greater difficulties of identification and monitoring, precisely because they have made concealment and the separation of the three components of a laundering operation increasingly effective. A first important point is therefore the growing difficulty of recognising money-laundering irregularities. A second is the fact that a banking or financial transaction may embody irregular elements without this signifying that it derives from a laundering attempt: irregularity can therefore be considered a necessary but insufficient condition for identifying money-laundering activity.

These reflections on the logical and operational difficulties related to the hypothesis of irregularity are strengthened when this postulate becomes the cornerstone on which the obligations of intermediaries to collaborate in the war on the financing of terrorism are based. It is wholly evident, in fact, that the existence or detectability of irregular elements can become even more problematic when the sources of the financial flows to be concealed are totally licit activities conducted by individuals or organisations equally overt and legal.

In summing up this analysis of the relationship between the laundering of capital and financing terrorism, the operational techniques, and therefore the channels of dissemination, the two phenomena might seem at least in part coincident. It is important, however, for the partial coincidence of money dirtying and money laundering to remain a working hypothesis rather than a theorem, so that it is possible to attempt the construction of a system of rules that can combine the effective enforcement of laws with the efficiency of the banking and financial markets.

And it is precisely from the standpoint of possible channels for financing terrorism that the theme of informal finance emerges, although it is not a new concept.

The focus on the relationship between informal banking and financial systems, on the one hand, and the potential risks of money laundering and terrorism financing, on the other, is quite recent, and the few studies on the subject are exclusively descriptive in nature. From the standpoint of economic analysis, the description of those systems leads us to conclude that those informal networks, beyond the obvious historical, geographical, and technical-operational differences, seem to be distinguished by the following: informality and trust on an ethical basis.

Informal finance systems, in fact, develop without the stable or long-lasting support of a system of formal laws, administrative rules, and relative documentary, paper-based records, as is characteristic of formal finance systems, bank based and otherwise. What fuels and catalyses these systems is trust founded in ethics: in individual communities, strongly identified on the ethnic level, financial transactions are carried out that create *de facto* debtor-creditor relations of variable duration on the basis of a common fiduciary heritage. In informal systems, the reliability of these relations cannot be based, by definition, on the threat of legal sanctions, but rests instead on the advisability of avoiding the social and moral sanctions that strike members of the community who fail to fulfil their obligations, with highly concrete effects associated with exclusion and isolation.

The systems of informal finance thus seem to be heavily used by migrants belonging to the ethnic communities from which these systems originated. This observation is obviously not based on robust statistical series, given the covert nature of the phenomenon, but on a growing volume of specific case studies and on specific sample surveys.

The combination of high fiduciary content and ethnic affinity makes those informal, naive channels — consisting of networks among friends and relatives of the same ethnic group or by more complex structures of informal finance — particularly attractive. The use of ethnic-national networks is strictly tied to the strength of relationships of trust among immigrant compatriots.

Informal finance is characterised by great simplicity and rapidity of procedures, operational flexibility, and a capacity to adjust to the needs of the migrants. Informal finance also displays maximum capacity in integrating the economic element into the social context and in linking organisational decisions to cultural influences and traditions. The operations of informal financial institutions are based on trust and on gradually established schemes and procedures and customary rules. The functioning of informal finance mechanisms is normally ensured by 'social control', that is, the censure of improper conduct exercised by the community through the marginalisation of migrants who fail to adhere to the rules (typically ethical or religious rules linked to the cultural background). It is not rash to maintain, in fact, that the mechanism for enforcing the relations created within informal networks is repeated within the local immigrant communities, which are particularly sensitive to cultural identity and relative 'marginalisation risk'.

The assurance of confidentiality and the minimal request of information are known to be crucial aspects of the banking and financial industry, and become even more so where some specific customer characteristics are present. Such characteristics include illegal immigrants; legal immigrants but with little clarity or legality regarding their social security, employment, and residential positions; legal immigrants with a preference for informal channels for regulatory reasons (fiscal aspects, rules on currency flows, and so on) in the country of origin; and legal immigrants who, for psychological motives, dictated by the social context of the host country, desire minimal visibility and do not appreciate any type of control or disclosure of personal information.

The relationship between informal finance and migrants, in essence, reveals yet another example of the now-classic lesson of recent economic analysis: exchanges occur only where information and sufficient trust exist. In effect, the capacity of the informal systems to succeed where the formal systems tend to fail has been explored by economic analysis, particularly regarding credit mechanisms.

Under certain conditions, therefore, the informal systems are more efficient than the formal systems. Unexplored, however, is the relationship between covertness and integrity, in terms of the risk that these channels may satisfy the demand for illegal financial services and particularly serve for purposes of money laundering and financing terrorism.

Based on the considerations advanced earlier regarding the characteristics that make a system attractive to those individuals or organisations wishing to conceal the origin or destination of given monetary flows, it seems evident that informal finance may appear particularly effective with respect to these purposes.

Both money laundering and money dirtying are based on a need for concealment. Informality, other conditions being equal, reduces the traceability of both the origin and destination of the financial flows. While the sharing of common fiduciary assets also imposes confidentiality, or better secrecy, the impermeability of informal systems to the acquisition of information by outsiders is greatly reduced, especially if the outsiders are authorities, and all the more if they are representatives of foreign countries. Therefore, at least at the level of deductive reasoning, the riskiness of informal finance systems, in terms of their use by criminal or terrorist organisations, seems greater than that attributable to overt finance, banking, and non-banking.

Appendix 11-2
Key Concepts in Lax Financial Regulation

The relationship between money laundering and national financial regulation is a key issue in the international debate. To discuss this issue from an economic point of view, it can be useful to treat the regulation of money laundering as a product, with a demand-and-supply schedule. But whose demand schedule is driving the system?

For the purposes of this analysis, it assumed that the lawmaker in a given country has not yet decided the direction to impose on its financial regulation, with specific regard to money laundering. The lawmaker may thus decide to implement regulations that create serious obstacles to money laundering, and thus to terrorism and organised crime, or he or she may decide — at the other extreme — to make the opposite choice, devising lax regulations that facilitate money laundering.

Money laundering generates costs as well as benefits for the parties involved. The costs for society depend on the fact that more predicate offences will be committed by terrorist or criminal organisations if money laundering is possible, and on the possible negative impact that money laundering will have on the economic system.

The benefits of money laundering accrue, first of all, to terrorist and criminal organisations, which can employ the proceeds of crime and avoid the threat of prosecution for predicate offences (money laundering in the strict sense), or which can use legal capital to finance illegal activities (money dirtying). The similarities and differences between money laundering and money dirtying were discussed in Appendix 11-1.

On the other side of the transaction, money laundering offers the host country the possibility to earn a commission in exchange for its services — what can be called the expected national benefits due to lax financial regulation.

Therefore, four different categories of actors potentially interested in regulation can be identified: the lawmakers; terrorist and criminal organisations, deriving utility from the possibility of laundering money; those who bear the costs of money laundering; and the financial community and, in general, the citizens who receive benefits from the inflow of foreign black and grey capital.

In terms of this last category, it seems difficult to predict which side the financial community will take. In general, the utility function of financial intermediaries does not appear to be affected by whether profits stem from legal or illegal financial activities (*pecunia non olet*). The intermediaries simply maximise the expected revenues and, given the asymmetric information issues, are not able to distinguish clearly the customers' nature, legal or illegal.

The interests of terrorist and criminal organisations and those who bear the costs of money laundering are obviously incompatible, as the gains of the former depend on the losses of the latter; the lawmaker appears to be caught in the middle, having to decide which demand schedule to follow.

Note that this analysis does not assume that the terrorist and criminal organisations, and those who bear the money-laundering costs are necessarily based outside the country in which the lawmaker is based. This is, in fact, the consequence of this line of argument. As with all policy issues, as long as the costs and benefits of a decision fall within the boundaries of the area of influence of the lawmaker, an efficient decision can be expected. Lawmakers in countries where crime or terrorism is persistent will tend to bear at least some of the costs associated with a decision to favour money laundering.

Countries where organised crime or terrorism is pervasive might appear to play a minor role in the offer of black or grey financial services at the international level, because they are sensitive to terrorism- and crime-related national costs. This might be so because the widespread presence of organised crime or terrorism in the country increases, for the lawmaker, the costs of regulations that favour money laundering.

The public will bear the costs of the decision and will hold the lawmaker responsible. Entering the international market for money-laundering services has a greater potential for countries that are immune from terrorist or criminal activities. By definition, such countries would almost be able to externalise the costs associated with the increase of predicate offences. A negative correlation between crime rate or terrorist episodes in the country and the role played in the offering of money-laundering services appears likely.

As a result of this process, some countries that do not bear the costs associated with money laundering become predisposed to adopting lax regulations that facilitate money laundering. The other side of the coin is that both criminal and terrorist organisations and those who bear the costs stemming from money laundering will tend to be situated in countries other than the one where the regulations are adopted.

Thus attention here has been limited to lawmakers based in countries different from those in which the other actors potentially interested in the regulations are based. From this starting point, the confrontation between those who benefit from money laundering and those who suffer from it is almost a win-win game for criminal and terrorist organisations.

Organised crime and terrorism enjoy huge asymmetrical organisational advantages over those who bear the costs of money laundering. A small, powerful group opposes a large, dispersed group, thus making the outcome predictable.

To be sure, money-laundering regulation could be opposed — and indeed is opposed — by political authorities that represent the public interest. The dispersion of the costs, however, makes money laundering an issue with low salience for the public, and consequently quite low on the political agenda. The individual on the street simply does not feel the bite of money laundering, and political actors will act accordingly.

Chapter 12

Terrorist Finance: Within the Grip of the G8?

George M. von Furstenberg[1]

This chapter concentrates on private terrorist funding, defined as funding that operates without the complicity, encouragement, or knowing toleration of any government. Such private funding thus is distinguished from official funding, which is defined as the government-sponsored, but normally covert, financing of terrorists or their organisations and conduits.

Official terrorist finance may pass through the formal financial sector or it may be drawn from secret (not publicly accountable) government funds that are transferred by such means as couriers or the diplomatic pouch. Such financing, if found out, may be discouraged directly by sanctions imposed on the country whose government engages in it. Whether private terrorist finance is amenable to pressure on governments at all, at least indirectly — for instance, by countries all over the world being induced to increase their surveillance over all financial transactions, including those occurring in the hitherto undocumented informal sector — is the principal subject of this chapter.

Specific Features of Private Terrorist Financing

Private terrorist financing makes use of multipurpose undocumented payment and settlement systems operating out of sight of regulatory and tax authorities in the vast majority of the world's countries, including all G8 countries. Each operation tends to function individually on a small scale outside formal networks or business combinations, often as an adjunct to other local economic activities. Each may offer only a single payment link from point to point. Yet, taken together, these operations and their trusted correspondents often have both nationwide and international reach through a crisscross of payment and settlement loops. Officially, these are called alternative money/value transfer (MVT) systems; hawala is only one of several names by which this alternative payment and settlement scheme is known (for a list of regional and ethnic synonyms, as well as functional synonyms such as underground or parallel banking, see Financial Action Task Force [FATF] 2004, 42).

These schemes, while generally not designed by terrorists or for them, remain open for their use with comparative safety and at low cost. On account of the anonymity traditionally supplied to customers, the system's operators may or may not be aware of their involvement in terrorist financing when there are financial transactions linked to terrorism. If operators are aware of a terrorist connection, they may not want to reveal that knowledge even to their counterparties, let alone to third parties, through imposing special handling charges.

Thus, the private terrorist finance addressed in this chapter needs to be distinguished from official, or officially condoned, terrorist finance or subversion, such as the government of Afghanistan's support for Osama bin Laden under the regime from 1996 to 2001, Iran's continuing support for Hezbollah (the 'Party of God' founded in 1982), or Anglo-American or U.S. government support for the elimination of an elected or 'popular' regime by force, for instance, in Iran in 1953 and in Chile in 1973.[2] Official terrorist finance is not the subject here, since it is unlikely to be inhibited by the inability to fund operations given that the government has its own financial conduits and means of conveyance.

Unlike private terrorist funding that is not condoned by governments but not readily interdicted, when practiced by non-G8 countries without a veto-wielding protector on the United Nations Security Council (UNSC), such official funding may, in principle, be subjected to international sanctions that could be effective in changing an offending government's foreign policy. Terrorist organisations that have branched out into organised social service, such as Hezbollah in Lebanon, defend their hold on tangible assets and facilities not with legal titles and proceedings but with political pressure and the threat of armed resistance to seizure. International pressure on governments that play host, voluntary or coerced, to terrorist organisations operating in the open may cause these governments to shut those organisations down or to force them underground. As long as these organisations use their funds to run quasi-public institutions, they are not representative of the intentionally fragmented private terrorist finance addressed here. That type of financing carefully camouflages its sources and uses at all stages.

From Anti-Money Laundering Recommendations to Special Recommendations to Combat Terrorist Financing

In 1989, at the Paris Summit, the leaders of the G7 nations and the president of the European Commission established the Financial Action Task Force on Money Laundering (FATF) to spearhead an international campaign against criminal money laundering. Established as an independent international body with a secretariat housed at the Organisation for Economic Co-operation and Development (OECD) in Paris, the FATF now has 31 member countries including the European countries, the five largest countries of the western hemisphere, Japan, Australia, and New Zealand.[3] In 1990, it drew up the Forty Recommendations 'to combat the misuse of the financial systems by persons laundering drug money', which were first revised in 1996 and more recently in 2003 (FATF 2003, 3). In October 2001, the FATF expanded its mandate to deal with the issue of the financing of terrorism, and created eight Special Recommendations on Terrorist Financing (FATF 2004, 92; 2001).

Because of this seeming integration of anti–money-laundering and anti–terrorist-financing strictures, it is common to find money laundering and terrorist financing treated in official documents as twins rather than distant cousins. Hence it may be useful to stress some of the essential distinctions. These bear on the relative effectiveness of using the same set of tools on rather different problems.

Political Differences

In some isolated cases, micro-states or countries at low levels of development that are in turmoil may institute a money-laundering haven. This may involve capturing state regulatory and control systems, or could cause the weakening, chronic underdevelopment, or disregard of such systems.[4] After the terrorist attacks of 11 September 2001 and the expulsion of the Taliban regime, private terrorist financing is far less likely than money laundering to continue to look to organs of state for protection.

Only terrorists' means, but not their motivation and ends, are primarily pecuniary. By contrast, self-enrichment is the most prominent goal of those who supply and demand money-laundering services. The covert physical and human 'assets' acquired by terrorists are very different from the tradable capital assets sought by money launderers.

Economic Differences

Hence terrorists want to turn illegally collected funds, whether donated, extorted, or skimmed off the drug trade or other activity, into goods, services, and local network construction and maintenance. Terrorists also accept goods and services in kind and are quite willing to use non-monetary media as a means of transaction. By contrast, money launderers primarily seek to convert ill-gotten funds to legitimate investment assets and to stores of value with property rights that are secure.

Terrorists thus transact internationally primarily on current account, while money launderers transact on capital account, with the former having none and the latter having some of their transactions recorded.

The bulk of money laundering is a wholesale business benefiting criminal cliques of the super-rich. Terrorist financing is more likely to resemble a series of retail operations with a variety of clients from across the economic spectrum. Unlike with money laundering, resources for terrorist activities are laundered — if at all — before, as opposed to after, the crime. Hence 'the anti-money laundering enforcement pillar serves at best on the margin as a deterrent to terrorism, perhaps by making potential terrorists recognize the difficulty in acquiring funds' (Reuter and Truman 2004, 140).

Placement, Organisation, and Transaction Differences

Money laundering moves through more centralised financial channels than private terrorist finance. Compared with money-laundering transactions, the scale of individual terrorist financings tends to be small. Entry into unlicensed MVT operations is easy for those with established relations of trust, and fixed costs are low.

Terrorist funds end up in goods and services frequently procured or delivered in insecure developing countries. These are not countries that could supply the kind of secure investment opportunities and titles attractive to successful money launderers.

Money laundering is institutionalised to a much greater extent than private terrorist finance. The latter avoids all institutional identification or formality. Given that MVT services are available almost everywhere, terrorists can bypass the formal financial sector in many instances at low cost and without incurring the 'protection tax' or rake-off characteristic of money-laundering operations.[5]

Almost all the eight special recommendations adopted in the wake of 11 September recognise that terrorists' payments and settlements utilise different connections and channels than does money on the way to the laundry. Admittedly, the second recommendation argues for prosecuting terrorist financing 'as money laundering predicate offences' (FATF 2003, 1), but economising on legislation does not mean that the financial technology and endpoints of the two types of offences are the same. Counterterrorist financing measures deal with 'all forms of money/value transfer systems, [but] particularly those traditionally operating outside the conventional financial sector and not currently subject to the [40 regular] FATF Recommendations' (FATF 2004, 41). The 'term "money/value transfer service" refers to a financial service that accepts cash, cheques, other monetary instruments or other stores of value in one location and pays a corresponding sum in cash or other form to a beneficiary in another location by means of a communication, message, transfer or through a clearing network to which the money/value transfer service belongs. Transactions performed by such services involve one or more intermediaries and a third party final payment' (42). In fact, due both to the cumulation and to the netting of settlement obligations, any settlement across borders, when it occurs, may bear no discernible relation to the amount or timing of any of the underlying individual transactions, which may include transactions for terrorists. This netting and commingling of funds make it very difficult in interception operations to link sources to terrorist uses of funds.

The People's Global Money/Value Transfer Service

If one considers the transaction uses rather than store of value function of money, MVT services are a form of popular finance, transferring people's money over distances small and large. There are millions of people who lack access to their domestic, and hence potentially global, banking system — indeed, hundreds of millions — in many countries of the world. Those who want to send them money or need to have other financial dealings with them use hawala, or whatever the preferred local name for the informal financial networks that connect people. At least until 2000, the market share of 'chop shop' or 'fei-chien' ('flying money') parallel banking in the People's Republic of China (PRC), for instance, was still higher than that of licensed banks for personal and small-business financial transactions. And 80 percent of Pakistani financial dealings with abroad, such as remittances from the United Kingdom to Pakistan, are handled by the hawala system (Findeisen 2000, 2127).

Even in countries that have liberalised financial systems, such as Japan and Korea, parallel banking services — almost all of them perfectly legal — are more than holding their own (Findeisen 2000, 2127). Among the reasons are the low cost, promptness, and high reliability of 'parallel' payment services, with charges equalling 0.5 to 1.0 percent of the amounts transferred. This is appreciably less than is charged for retail cross-border transfers by Japanese commercial banks and much less than the 9 percent charged by Moneygram and Western Union for wire transfers, for instance, from the United States to Mexico (Findeisen 2000, 2129, 2132). Indeed, this ubiquity and the very large number of independently organized, low-cost hawala service loops make them impervious, or at least highly resistant, to replacement by the formal sector and its requirements to 'know your customer' and monitor and report suspicious transactions. In view of the efficiencies and cost savings associated with popular finance, the assertion by Jochen Sanio, president of the FATF, that 'it is only the terrorist, the money launderer and the people behind them who profit from opaque financial structures and who gain from lax regulation in this field' is far too strong (FATF 2004, 5).[6]

A Record of Achievement?

As shown in Box 12-1, the financial transfers in hawala are based on a small network of personal relationships. A shared ethnic and religious identity or membership in a common clan serves as the foundation of trust. There are no written records that could be used to construct a paper trail. Because hawala fulfills many legitimate purposes for underserved communities, including immigrant communities, there is no point in trying to outlaw or uproot it. Although some countries have tried that route, the FATF does not advocate criminalising hawala *per se*. Instead, the special recommendations propose that countries 'license or register all operators of money transmission services, formal or informal, and subject them to the FATF Recommendations that apply to banks and other financial institutions, with appropriate penalties for illegal operators' (FATF 2004, 12). Of course, the facilitators of hawala know their customers well, but their customers do not want that knowledge — or knowledge of their financial affairs, suspicious or otherwise — to be shared with outsiders. To them, the licensing or registration to be required by all countries according to the special recommendations is just another way of trying to put them out of business.

A Brief Document Study for Germany

Germany is one of the few countries that has long done what the special recommendations first proposed in October 2001. For this reason, it is useful to reflect briefly on the German experience to gauge the likely success of the recommendations in curbing private terrorist financing.

To provide a minimum of institutional background requires a reference to two federal supervisory agencies that deal with banking and credit and with financial services as a whole, respectively. They are the Bundesanstalt für Finanzdienstleistungen (BaFin) and the Bundesaufsichtsamt für Kreditwesen (BaKred). BaKred became part of BaFin, as did two other supervisory agencies dealing with insurance and securities, when the latter was formed in April 2002. Since 1 January 1998, BaKred shares responsibility for supervising financial services and implementing laws and regulations against money laundering.

When a number of financial services, including money transfer services, were subjected to an authorisation or licensing requirement at the start of 1998, enterprises that had previously engaged in such activities legally — that is, without needing to meet a licensing requirement — were given until 1 April 1998 to seek a licence without having to discontinue their business while their application was pending. Any request for licences first sought or granted thereafter could apply only to new establishments. Since the end of this brief transition period, any business engaged in finance transfer in Germany for a specified length of time for commercial purposes required a licence from BaFin (Findeisen 2000, 2131).

By 2000, only 51 MVT suppliers in all of Germany had applied to obtain permission to engage in their business, and most of these were traditional, documented suppliers,

Box 12-1 Hawala: A Hypothetical Example

A mosque in Cologne accepts a charitable contribution, some of which it intends to divert to terrorist causes. Its imam hires a licensed ethnic-Turkish contractor in Cologne to do some repair work on the mosque, which the contractor over-invoices by prior arrangement. The contractor then calls his 'uncle' in Istanbul or otherwise sends word to pay an amount equal to the over-invoicing in euros, dollars, or Turkish liras in cash to a designated party. That party in turn is instructed to arrange for cash payment to an arms dealer through a set of sanitising intermediaries. The arms dealer then delivers the required ordnance, hand-held missile, or other materiel to the terrorist, again through a buffer of intermediaries, perhaps for anonymous pickup.

Up to this point, the only time the official banking system may have been involved is in the local payment of the contractor's invoice for repair services by the imam in Cologne. However, there is still an open claim of the so-called uncle in Istanbul on his nephew in Cologne, which the latter settles in cash, carried legally on his person, on his next visit to Turkey.

such as wire transfer services. In other cases, official permission may have been sought to provide cover for an unlicensed MVT activity continued alongside. Enforcement actions against such operations appear to have been extremely rare except in cases where customers were defrauded or there was a suspicion of terrorist financing. Such a suspicion may have been triggered initially not by purely financial intelligence but by other types of surveillance and investigative work or by referrals from abroad.

Among all the BaFin's press releases from 1998 through May 2004, only two refer to shutting down illegal money transfer schemes in their titles announcing an enforcement action. One such action, dated 16 July 2002, closed down Dahabshiil Transfer Services Limited, a business operating out of Somalia, for engaging in unauthorised money transfers amounting to around one half million euros from the time it was registered as a society (e.V.) on 14 January 2002 *('Seit seiner Eintragung am 14. Januar 2002 hat der Verein Gelder in Höhe von rund einer halben Million Euro transferiert')* (BaFin 2002). Then on 15 September 2003, MoneyNett, an operation with branches in several German cities, was ordered to stop its money transfer business, which had allegedly transferred €277 000 mostly to Nigeria (*'wurden in diesem Jahr nachweislich bereits Gelder i.H.v. ? 277.000,- ins Ausland transferiert'*) (BaFin 2003a).

Checking further in BaFin's 2003 Annual Report, a total of 201 new administrative actions (*'neue Verfahren'*) were started on account of the unauthorised provision of financial and exchange services (BaFin 2003b, 73). Infractions include failure to obtain permission for deposit taking, brokerage or investing for clients, money and asset management, exchange and money transfer, and unauthorised operation of any other financial service requiring a licence. In 14 of these cases there was an actual on-the-spot investigation, and in 17 cases a cease-and-desist order was issued in conjunction with referral to the government prosecutor. Such a referral may lead to formal charges and successful prosecution in a few cases, hardly any of which principally involve MVT.

This record for Germany since 1998 gives the impression that there is a very high cost with a small yield of enforcement actions. In view of the low degree of institutionalisation and correspondingly low costs of entry in the MVT business, it is easy to build and rebuild the many little loops and channels that together form a vast popular finance sector. Hence, there may be no lasting systemic effect from individual prosecutions, even if they succeed in shutting down a particular operation. BaKred may be quite right to focus on those operations that are tipped off as having terrorists among their clients. Inevitably and almost irrespective of any laxity in enforcement, MVT operations all over the world will continue — no matter what the effort to shut them down. They thus remain accessible to all, including terrorists. This means that terrorists and their organisations must be taken on one by one, painstakingly, and from one lead, suspicious activity report, or criminal investigation to another in a protracted struggle, without expecting any help from financial dragnets on the MVT sector or from self-incriminating transparency requirements, which that sector will reject and elude.

Conclusion

What are the lessons for the FATF's special recommendations of October 2001 and their touting at every G8 summit and finance ministers meeting since? The fragmented private terrorist financing chiefly relied on by the independently acting terrorists loosely referred to as al Qaeda since 2002 is largely invisible and beyond the reach and current control of national governments.[7] Penalising governments that do not condone terrorist financing but are unable to police it effectively is neither helpful nor justifiable. This is all the more true since highly advanced countries, such as the UK with regard to its large Pakistani population or Germany in relation to its Turkish population, are included in the group unable to interdict terrorist financing emanating from their jurisdictions.

Terrorist financing does not necessarily require the transfer of any of the funds raised within the official and documented financial sector or even passing through it. Indeed, terrorist financing may not require any transactional interface with the official financial sector at all. Hence reforms of that sector need not affect it. Consequently, the FATF's special recommendations and the interpretative notes that accompany most of them are laced with cautions not to rely solely on big sticks, lest they force hawala to become even more secretive. They speak of being sensitive to maintaining proportionality between means and ends while counselling the use of carrots, incentives, inducements, and outreach activities; they call for not being overzealous in penalties and enforcement, or for not imposing or expecting too much. A brave argument is put forward that getting a licence and registering can be advantageous for the business of the MVT operations themselves. But the tone is tentative, suggesting that the appeal to self-interest — that transparency is good for business — is unlikely to be believed or acted upon by those operations.

Although the FATF also advocates specific investigative strategies and enforcement measures, it shows prudent concern about the effect of driving hawala deeper underground rather than making it more transparent and open to monitoring (FATF 2004, 48, 51). Indeed, the higher the monitoring and reporting requirements in the formal financial sector, the more popular and cost effective hawala may become, given its low overhead.

Given the intractability and immeasurability of the problem of terrorist finance and the complete lack either of quantitative criteria for success or of even a narrative record of achievement in countries that have tried to license hawala and make it more transparent, the trumpeting of G8 successes in the fight against terrorist finance should have been muffled at the 2004 Sea Island Summit and at the meeting of G7 finance ministers earlier. Promulgating and then stroking the FATF's special recommendations from summit to summit does not leave them any less unfulfilled. Whatever the effectiveness against money laundering of blacklisting or imposing sanctions on small offending countries, such measures cannot be applied well against elusive and potentially ubiquitous terrorist financing that is not sponsored or condoned by governments. Moreover, MVT facilities provide a popular form of finance used by hundreds of millions of people the world over who cannot get affordable financial services otherwise — or, indeed, any service at all.

Under these conditions it is futile to try to irradiate, and thus to destroy, an entire parallel MVT system in the hope of thwarting the terrorists who may use it as well. While this chapter offers no recommendations for what would work against terrorist finance without external intelligence, it may be useful to discourage false hope and hype nonetheless.

Notes

1. This chapter was written while the author was a visiting researcher at the Deutsche Bundesbank in the first half of 2004 and subsequently revised, but responsibility for the views expressed is solely his own.
2. The popular support and elective legitimacy of Iran's Dr. Mohammad Mossadegh may be a matter of degree and hence of some dispute, but there is no doubt about the freedom and normality of Salvador Allende's election in Chile. In both instances, the actual and intended outcome of U.S. intervention was not democracy but anticommunist autocracy.
3. With regard to the last two members of FATF listed here, it is somewhat discouraging to note that two of the seven entities on the FATF's February 2004 list of Non-cooperative Countries and Territories (NCCTs) identified Australia (Nauru) or New Zealand (Cook Islands) as responsible for their defence and external affairs. Australia and New Zealand were either unable or unwilling to bring influence to bear on their charges in the South Pacific. Russia, another current FATF member, was on the NCCT blacklist until 2002, and it may still generate a large demand for capital flight and money-laundering services.
4. Most money laundering by value may well occur in or with the countries most advanced in international finance. In May 2004, Riggs National Bank of Washington DC, proud occupants of many of Washington's historic buildings — including one on 15th and Pennsylvania Avenue NW, one block from the White House — was fined US$25 million and put on special forms of financial supervision for having laundered massive plunder for Saudi and West African officials under the nose of U.S. regulatory agencies for years. The Senate Banking Committee and Timothy O'Brien (2004) provide preliminary reports. Earlier, in the summer of 1999, individuals at the Bank of New York, but not the bank itself (Reuter and Truman 2004, 134), were found to be involved in money laundering US$7 billion for a Russian customer through setting up fake transactions with a nonexistent Russian bank. Money-laundering charges have also been levelled at officers of U.S. non-financial corporations such as Enron (42). Indeed, Peter Reuter and Edwin Truman (180) note that 'a case can be made that money laundering is substantial in the United States and should receive special attention as part of the global AML [Anti-Money Laundering] Regime'.
5. Alexander Hofmann (2004) describes how the money-laundering tariff is collected in the tiny South Pacific island of Nauru, a broad-based money laundering centre, as follows: 'Allegedly US$70 billion from shady sources flowed through the accounts of 400 banks registered in Nauru. All of them had the same address, a government post office box' (translated by author). This centralised 'tax' office through which all transfers passed would then take its cut and use the same banking connections to launder the proceeds. These proceeds are, of course, not treated as part of public revenue or used for the benefit of Nauru but for the benefit of its corrupt operators. These tend to rotate out eventually with their laundered funds, leaving the remaining population in chronic poverty. Thus the United States

Central Intelligence Agency (CIA) estimates Nauru's annual per capita income to be only about US$5000 on a purchasing power parity basis, the same as for other South Pacific island states, few of which specialise in money laundering (CIA 2004).

6. In the preceding chapter, Donato Masciandaro takes a much more balanced view, noting that informal finance can be economically efficient for certain communities and attractive also to individuals without criminal intent.
7. The term 'al Qaeda' is a designation by the U.S. Federal Bureau of Investigation based on a longer Arabic phrase meaning base of operations or method, according to Jason Burke (2004).

References

Bundesanstalt für Finanzdienstleistungsaufsicht (2002). 'Die Bundesanstalt für Finanzdienstleistungsaufsicht untersagt der Dahabshiil das Finanztransfergeschäft'. 19 July. Frankfurt. <www.bafin.de 'Presse & Publikationen: Pressemitteilungen 2002' (Mai - Dezember 2002)"> (November 2004).

Bundesanstalt für Finanzdienstleistungsaufsicht (2003a). 'BaFin untersagt Zweigstellen von MoneyNett@Nationalbank das Finanztransfergeschäft'. 18 September. Frankfurt. <www.bafin.de 'Presse & Publikationen: Pressemitteilungen 2003'> (November 2004).

Bundesanstalt für Finanzdienstleistungsaufsicht (2003b). 'Jahresbericht 2003'. Frankfurt. <www.bafin.de 'Presse & Publikationen: Publikationen: Jahresberichte'> (November 2004).

Burke, Jason (2004). 'Think Again: Al Qaeda'. *Foreign Policy* May/June. <www.foreignpolicy.com/story/cms.php?story_id=02536> (November 2004).

Central Intelligence Agency (2004). 'Nauru: Economy'. World Factbook. <www.cia.gov/cia/publications/factbook> (November 2004).

Financial Action Task Force (2001). 'Special Recommendations on Terrorist Financing'. Organisation for Economic Co-operation and Development, Paris. <www1.oecd.org/fatf/pdf/SRecTF_en.pdf> (November 2004).

Financial Action Task Force (2003). 'The Forty Recommendations'. Organisation for Economic Co-operation and Development, Paris. <www1.oecd.org/fatf/40Recs_en.htm> (November 2004).

Financial Action Task Force (2004). 'The Financial War on Terrorism: A Guide by the Financial Action Task Force'. Organisation for Economic Co-operation and Development, Paris.

Findeisen, Michael (2000). '"Underground Banking" in Deutschland: Schnittstellen zwischen illegalen "Remittance Services" i.S.v. Paragraph 1, Abs. 1a Nr. 6 KWG und dem legalen Bankgeschäft (Underground Banking in Germany: The Intersection between Illegal Remittance Services in the Sense of Paragraph ... and Legitimate Banking Activities)'. *Wertpapier-Mitteilung*, no. 43, pp. 2125–2133.

Hofmann, Alexander (2004). 'Pazifikinsel Nauru: Paradies vor der Pleite'. *Frankfurter Allgemeiner Zeitung*, 22 April.

O'Brien, Timothy (2004). 'Senators Raise Doubts about Banks' Antiterror Measures'. *New York Times*, 4 June, p. C3.

Reuter, Peter and Edwin M. Truman (2004). *Chasing Dirty Money: The Fight against Money Laundering*. Institute for International Economics, Washington DC.

PART IV:
THE G8 AND INTERNATIONAL TRADE POLICY

Chapter 13

Summitry and Trade: What Sea Island Could Do for Doha

Sylvia Ostry

In 1975, the G7 was the first institution established after the creation of the post-war architecture, and it was not an initiative of the leading power or hegemon, the United States. Indeed, it was a response to the erosion of American power due to the reconstruction and rapid growth of Europe and Japan in the 1950s and '60s. That erosion of American power had created a vacuum in global co-operation and represented a serious threat to global security. The threat became clearer as the Bretton Woods system collapsed in 1971 and a new 'non-system' of floating exchange rates emerged in 1973. Finally, the first oil crisis with the Organization of Petroleum Exporting Countries (OPEC) of 1973 triggered action. Valéry Giscard d'Estaing of France and Helmut Schmidt of Germany created the economic summit. It was held at Rambouillet in France and included the U.S., France, the United Kingdom, Japan, and Italy. Canada was included the following year. Both Giscard and Schmidt were former finance ministers. They intended the summit meetings to be small, informal, and secret. The objectives were limited, confined to international economic issues, especially financial stability and trade. The objective was to establish basic norms and principles for policy co-operation.

In this chapter the role of the summit in trade policy will be reviewed briefly, in the context of the Tokyo and Uruguay rounds of the General Agreement on Tariffs and Trade (GATT). But before any discussion of the Doha Development Agenda, it is essential to describe the evolution or transformation of summitry — and, of course, of the global system. It is a long, long way from Rambouillet to Sea Island.

Summitry and Trade: The Tokyo and Uruguay Rounds

There seems to be general agreement that the G7 summits — from 1975 to 1978 — were successful in bolstering the GATT during the Tokyo Round. From 1976, the ministerial meetings of the Organisation for Economic Co-operation and Development (OECD) were held before the summit and this facilitated a co-ordination of agendas.

There was concern about rising protectionism, termed the 'new protectionism', consisting of border non-tariff measures such as voluntary export restraints and domestic non-tariff measures such as subsidies. The Tokyo Round was launched in September 1973, but was dragging on because of disagreements both within and between the European Commission and the U.S. essentially over the impact of structural change stemming from the oil shock and the rise of the so-called 'Asian Tigers', as well as agriculture.

From its inception, the G7 played a role in encouraging the negotiations and setting deadlines. But it was not possible to mask the disagreements completely. Indeed, the communiqué issued at the London Summit in 1977 included not only a reference to the 'new impetus to the Tokyo Round' but also the unprecedented statement that the Tokyo Round 'should not remove the right of individual countries under existing international agreements to avoid significant market disruption' (Cohn 2002, 96).[1]

But, as is often the case with summits, people matter. Summits are episodic in nature, this can produce good or bad — and largely unexpected — results. U.S. president Jimmy Carter, who attended the London Summit, had appointed Robert Strauss as U.S. Trade Representative (USTR). Strauss seized the initiative to prod the round, and negotiations among the U.S., the European Community, Japan, and Canada were concluded just before the Bonn Summit in July 1978. But given the rise of the so-called New International Economic Order (NIEO) — a short-lived consequence of the OPEC crisis — it was important to placate the developing countries, and the concept of special and differential treatment was included in the GATT. So the round was completed in 1979 and hailed by the G7 leaders at the Tokyo Summit that year as 'an important achievement'.

It is very difficult to evaluate the role of the G7 in the Tokyo Round. Strauss, a most energetic and skilled trade diplomat, was certainly assisted by Carter's initiative and the pressure exerted by his allies among his fellow heads of state and government. However, for the Americans, the Tokyo Round was less than satisfactory. The wide transatlantic differences over agriculture and domestic subsidies, as well as lack of transparency in procedures concerning standards or government procurement, fed a growing view that the American system was more open and competitive and therefore more fair. The weak GATT dispute settlement mechanism was another source of complaint. The Tokyo Round use of codes that excluded developing countries led to serious fragmentation of an already weak legal structure. One could argue, indeed, that a major result of the Tokyo Round was the addition to the declining credibility of the multilateral system in the U.S.

Of course, the outcome of the Tokyo Round had nothing to do with summitry. But this comparison does illustrate an important point. The original summiteers were very concerned with substance, especially with respect to the international financial system. Their common background as former finance ministers was the reason both for the origin of the institution and its mode of operation. But it would be impossible for the G7 summit as an institution to deal with the complexities of other policy issues. So the role of the summit in trade (or energy or whatever) has to be procedural. And in that context one would judge the completion of the Tokyo Round as 'an important achievement' — when one considers the alternative.

Disappointment with the Tokyo Round led the U.S. to try to launch a new round almost as soon as the ink was dry. At the 1981 GATT ministerial, the new USTR, William Brock, asked the OECD to launch a programme of research on agriculture and on new issues such as trade in services and trade-related investment measures. At the 1981 Ottawa Summit, a GATT ministerial was endorsed and was convened in 1982. The timing could not have been worse. The world was in a serious recession. A serious debt crisis had emerged in Latin America. The old GATT club no longer existed, and countries in the South were firmly opposed to another negotiation. Fortunately, the GATT as an institution survived. Furthermore, an offspring of the Ottawa Summit was the Quadrilateral Trade Ministers, or Quad, which played an important role in efforts to launch the Uruguay Round.

Subsequent summits in Williamsburg (1983) and London (1984) were unable to paper over the growing transatlantic differences, especially over agriculture. But there were other serious problems of global imbalance arising from U.S. fiscal policy and a rising dollar feeding protectionist fury in Congress. So Brock considered a new round crucial, and the 1985 Bonn Summit was the proposed venue. Moreover, the major U.S. trade advisory committees had made clear in a report to the USTR that they would support a GATT round only if the 'new issues' of services, intellectual property, and investment were included and if action was taken to lower the dollar. On 22 September 1985, the Plaza Accord launched the new policy on the dollar. And the USTR initiated a new multitrack policy: multilateral (the GATT), bilateral (the Canada-U.S. Free Trade Agreement), and, if necessary, unilateral under the so-called Section 301 of the *Trade Act of 1974*. The Bonn Summit of 1985 failed to launch the round: indeed France's François Mitterrand briefly walked out in opposition. Finally, at Tokyo in May 1986, the G7 leaders declared themselves in support of a GATT round that would include the new issues and agriculture. The Uruguay Round subsequently began in September 1986 at Punta del Este. Summitry probably helped nudge along the tortuous launching process. But the most important outcome of the Tokyo Summit was the creation of a new forum, the G7 finance ministers, which began the process of shifting summitry from the original focus on international economic policies.

The main role of summitry in the launch of the Uruguay Round was as a focal point for co-ordinating among different institutions, the OECD, the Quad — amplified by the inclusion of some Southern countries — and the GATT. The OECD's research on agriculture and services was crucial in facilitating discussions in the GATT, since it had very meagre research capability. Canada played an active role in this co-ordination, and, indeed, the creation of the World Trade Organization (WTO) was a Canadian initiative.

The launch of the Uruguay Round took almost as long as the entire Tokyo Round negotiations. The role of summitry was constrained not only by the transatlantic disagreement on agriculture, but also because for the first time in the history of the GATT several Southern countries were active participants. In particular, a group of developing countries, tagged the G10 hardliners and led by Brazil and India, was bitterly opposed to the new issues, and helped with the European foot-dragging. Other Southern countries joined the Australian-led Cairns Group to support liberalisation in agriculture. Summitry did not weigh heavily in their policy-making process.

If the word 'tortuous' was not too strong for the launch, it could also describe the negotiations. The Uruguay Round almost collapsed at a mid-term ministerial in Montreal in 1988. It was supposed to conclude by the 1990 Brussels ministerial. But it dragged on until December 1993 — the final agreement was signed in April 1994 at Marrakesh. The transatlantic divide over agriculture was the core of the problem. By the onset of the 1990s, the G10 coalition had disappeared, decimated by the debt crisis and the role of the International Monetary Fund (IMF) and the World Bank. So the main players were the EC and the U.S., yet the role of summitry in promoting the agreement was negligible. While communiqués included support for trade liberalisation at summit after summit, nothing was able to overcome French opposition to reform of the Common Agricultural Policy. Indeed, despite the summit declaration at London that the round be completed before the end of 1991, the 1992 Munich Summit provided the weakest declaration of all: 'we expect that an agreement can be reached before the end of 1992'. This reflected a bow to France from its German partner. Finally, the Blair House Accord of November 1992 settled the agriculture agreement between the U.S. and the EC, and the round was completed in Geneva at the end of 1993.

Even on procedural grounds, the role of summitry in both the launch and completion of the Uruguay Round was less effective than was the case in the Tokyo Round, although it should be noted that the summit co-ordinating role with respect to the Quad was important. Just before the Tokyo Summit in 1993, the Quad reached an agreement on market access under pressure of a deadline posed by the leaders. To placate developing countries, the Quad made some concessions in the GATT.

It is pertinent to ask why the role of summitry in trade policy had weakened in the late 1980s and 1990s. A full exploration of this important question is beyond the scope of this chapter, but it is useful to suggest some likely reasons. First, not only were the issues in the Uruguay Round far more complex than any previous negotiation, but what could be called 'mission creep' had taken over G7 summitry. During the 1980s, there was a major move from the economic to the political. But much more was added. Communiqués grew longer and annexes were added. The main players in the policy domain for which the summit had been created were no longer the summiteers but the finance ministers and central bank governors. While efforts were made to contain the expansion of agendas and paper output, these attempts were not very successful. Even today, there has been an enormous expansion of ministerial meetings that have added more paper. Perhaps to add to the gravitas of the institutional commitment and the credibility of the piles of paper, the summiteers are inclined to include specific goals. When these are not met or are not likely to be met, this mode of operations has led to an increasingly sceptical view of the institution in the media and among some academics and nongovernmental organisations (NGOs) (Ostry 2002).

So, given the growing number of issues now included in the G7/8 summit agenda, trade can hardly claim pride of place. But there is another reason why the impact of summitry has weakened. As noted, the old GATT magic is gone and the role of Southern countries has become more significant. The transatlantic duo agreement was certainly necessary to complete the Uruguay Round but not sufficient without involving other players who are not involved in summitry, the Quad, or the OECD. The role of Southern countries in trade negotiations cannot be dealt with in a perfunctory fashion. One of the major results of the Uruguay Round — albeit an unintended consequence — was the creation of a serious North-South divide. The grand bargain that concluded the negotiations — the North would open their markets to Southern agriculture and labour-intense products, in particular textiles and clothing, in exchange for the South's acceptance of the new issues and, virtually as a last-minute piece of the deal, the creation of a new institution, the WTO, with the strongest dispute settlement mechanism in the history of international law and next to no executive or legislative authority (apart from negotiations) — turned out to be a bum deal.

The Northern market opening in agriculture and textiles and clothing was far less than expected. The new issues require major institutional upgrading and change in the infrastructure of most Southern countries. These changes take time and cost money. Implementation thus involves considerable investment with uncertain medium-term result. The Uruguay Round thus generated a North-South divide and the WTO became a magnet for dissent by the increasingly activated NGOs.

While the South is hardly homogenous, there is a broad consensus that the Uruguay Round was asymmetrical and the WTO system must be rebalanced. The debacle at Seattle in 1999 ended with a walkout of almost all the developing countries. It is more than symbolic that the outcome of the Doha ministerial in 2001 was termed a 'development agenda' and not a round. The main objective of the Doha meeting was to avoid another Seattle. The declaration repeatedly refers to technical assistance and capacity building. Pushed by the successful NGO campaign about HIV/AIDS in Africa, the Americans even seemed willing to antagonise the big pharmaceutical companies. Doha was thus unique in its focus on the South and development. Of course, there were other issues, such as agriculture and the so-called 'Singapore issues' of competition, investment, government procurement, and trade facilitation. But the Doha declaration was a masterpiece of creative ambiguity. The devil remained in the details of the negotiations — and the devil ensured that deadlines were missed. And at the Cancun mid-term ministerial in September 2003, the meeting broke up with no agreement on agriculture or the Singapore issues, the core items of North-South conflict.

The role of G7/8 summitry in either the Doha launch or negotiations was minimal, consisting of some promises concerning the poorest countries, which were largely irrelevant to the negotiations. Nor was there any direct link between the proposals made at the 2002 Kananaskis Summit on Africa and the Doha Development Agenda. Of course, there were more commitments and goals. As one expert has remarked, if people could eat international resolutions and summit agreements, Africans would be among the best-fed people in the world (International Food Policy Research Institute 2004). One ought not to forget World Bank president Robert MacNamara's pledge in 1973 to eradicate poverty by 2000.

Conclusion: The 20-20 Solution

At Cancun, as at Montreal in 1988, the meeting broke up over agriculture. And at Montreal it was a group of developing countries, led by Brazil, that announced to the European Community and American negotiators that if there was no agriculture, there was no agreement on anything. But that is where the replay ends. At Cancun, two new coalitions were formed. The so-called G20 of developing countries, led by Brazil and India as well as China (the Big Three) and including South Africa and a number of Latin American countries, has not collapsed under American pressure and is still playing a significant role in the negotiations.[2] The other coalition, the G90, includes the poorest developing countries, mainly from Africa. After failing to convince the U.S. to eliminate cotton subsidies and the EC to remove the Singapore issues, the G90 terminated the negotiations. But this group, too, is still involved in the negotiations and, as was clearly evident at Cancun, is assisted by a number of NGOs providing ongoing information as well as research and policy analysis. The WTO negotiations for the framework agreement concluded in Geneva on July 31 included a new coalition, the Five Interested Parties (FIPs) of the U.S, the EU, Brazil, India, and Australia (of the Cairns Group). Thus, at Cancun there appeared to be an axial shift in the political economy of trade policy-making. The Big Two — the European Commission and the United States — cannot produce another Blair House if the Big Three do not agree. And the G90 cannot make the Doha Development Agenda, but it can break the process, in what is now referred to as the New Geography.

The central concern is how to achieve not simply a re-launch of Doha — desirable as that would undoubtedly be — but a discussion of the range of fundamental issues concerning the trading system. The list is long — trade and growth, trade, poverty, inequality, trade and environment, capacity building and development, WTO institutional reform, international coherence, and so on and so forth. But there is very meagre research capability at the WTO, and another Uruguay Round of unintended consequences is not at all needed.

The G8 summit is an inappropriate forum for trade policy in today's world. There has been a plethora of proposals to expand the membership. But the most popular candidate is the G20 of finance ministers and central bank governors, which was chaired for its first two years by Canada's previous finance minister Paul Martin before being chaired by India, Mexico, Germany, and China. This is not to say that the G20 ought to replace the G8. That is a matter for another time. A joint meeting of the finance ministers' G20 and the WTO's G20 trade ministers (there is some overlap, and members of the G90 should be included), with a mandate to launch a discussion of the trading system that includes a new round but goes well beyond that to deal with systemic issues would be a good idea. This 20-20 project would have to be provided with research capabilities, which should consist of knowledge networks involving researchers from a range of institutions, academics, NGOs, and so on. The details could be worked out later. The objectives of this project would be to acknowledge that the trade issue is no longer just about trade but has been transformed into a far more complex policy template and the institutional architecture — perhaps including the G8 summit — needs repair and reform. A new 20-20 vision?

Notes

1. For analysis of summitry and trade, there are a number of sources. See, for example, Nicholas Bayne (2001, 171–187), Nicholas Bayne and Stephen Woolcock (2003), Michael Artis and Sylvia Ostry (1986), and Sylvia Ostry (1991, 2002).
2. This G20 is not to be confused with the G20 finance ministers and central bank governors, which have been meeting annually since 1999. In addition to the G8 members, the G8-related G20 includes Argentina, Australia, Brazil, China, India, Mexico, Saudi Arabia, South Africa, South Korea, and Turkey, as well as representation from the European Union, and the International Monetary Fund and World Bank (G8 Research Group 2004). The G20 of developing countries includes Argentina, Bolivia, Brazil, Chile, China, Cuba, Egypt, Guatemala, India, Indonesia, Mexico, Nigeria, Pakistan, Paraguay, the Philippines, South Africa, Tanzania, Thailand, Venezuela, and Zimbabwe (G20 2004).

References

Artis, Michael and Sylvia Ostry (1986). 'International Economic Policy Coordination'. Chatham House Paper 30, Royal Institute of International Affairs. London.

Bayne, Nicholas (2001). 'The G7 and Multilateral Trade Liberalisation: Past Performance, Future Challenges'. In J. J. Kirton and G. M. von Furstenberg, eds., *New Directions in Global Economic Governance: Managing Globalisation in the Twenty-First Century*, pp. 23–38. Ashgate, Aldershot.

Bayne, Nicholas and Stephen Woolcock (2003). *The New Economic Diplomacy: Decision-Making and Negotiation in International Economic Relations*. Ashgate, Aldershot.

Cohn, Theodore H. (2002). *Governing Global Trade: International Institutions in Conflict and Convergence*. Ashgate, Aldershot.

G8 Research Group (2004). 'What Is the G20?' <www.g8.utoronto.ca/g20/g20whatisit.html> (2004 November).

G20 (2004). 'G20 Members'. <www.g-20.mre.gov.br/members.asp> (November 2004).

International Food Policy Research Institute (2004). 'Funding Africa's Farmers'. *IFPRI Forum*, March, pp. 1, 10–12. <www.ifpri.org/pubs/newsletters/ifpriforum/if200403.htm> (November 2004).
Ostry, Sylvia (1991). 'Canada, Europe, and Economic Summits'. In C. H. W. Remie and J.-M. Lacroix, eds., *Canada on the Threshold of the 21st Century: European Reflections upon the Future of Canada*. John Benjamin Publishing Company, Amsterdam.
Ostry, Sylvia (2002). 'Globalization and the G8: Could Kananaskis Set a New Direction?' O. D. Skelton Memorial Lecture, Queen's University and the Department of Foreign Affairs and International Trade.

Chapter 14

Effective or Defective? The G8 and Multilateral Trade Negotiations

Heidi K. Ullrich[1]

The G7/8 have consistently supported the role of the General Agreement on Tariffs and Trade (GATT) and, since 1995, its successor, the World Trade Organization (WTO), in working to achieve greater openness in international trade, monitoring trade agreements, and as a forum for trade negotiations.[2] From the time of the first economic summit in Rambouillet, France, in 1975, the leaders of the most industrialised countries have voiced their support for a more liberal international trading system. In words that still echo 30 years after they were first written in the 1975 Rambouillet Declaration, the G7 stated:

> we must seek to restore growth in the volume of world trade. Growth and price stability will be fostered by maintenance of an open trading system. In a period where pressures are developing for a return to protectionism, it is essential ... to avoid resorting to measures by which they could try to solve their problems at the expense of others, with damaging consequences in the economic, social and political fields (G7 1975).

The impact of the summits on multilateral negotiations has been the source of special negotiating terminology, including the 'Rambouillet effect', which describes the G7/8's ability to bring about incremental progress in international negotiations by having the leaders make vital political decisions (Bayne 2000, 21).

However, this effect has often been lacking at critical times during multilateral trade negotiations. The G7/8 has received criticism due to its lack of consistent positive impact on multilateral trade negotiations. This is particularly due to the lack of political leadership and the apparent inability or unwillingness of the leaders to implement their communiqué pledges fully once they have returned home. Summit communiqués called for the completion of the Tokyo Round every year from 1975 through 1978, urged progress in the Uruguay Round from 1990 through 1993, and have expressed various levels of support for the current Doha Development Agenda. The stalemates during the Tokyo and Uruguay rounds occurred due to bilateral issues between Europe and the United States. In the Doha Development Agenda, the stalemate that existed through to the end of July 2004 was due primarily to divisions between developed and developing countries, stemming in part from the 'bum deal' they received in the Uruguay Round, as Sylvia Ostry describes in Chapter 13. Given these deep divides, the G7/8 perhaps should not be faulted for its lack of consistent success in providing effective political leadership within the negotiations, but rather commended for its continued determination in bringing about an eventual agreement. In fact, Nicholas Bayne has observed that:

> The summits do not achieve results by flashes of prescient, inspirational decision-making, sparked by the personal chemistry between leaders. There are a few examples of this, but they are very rare. Nor do they often achieve, at the first attempt, a definitive settlement of issues which can then be handed on to other institutions. Nearly always their achievement comes from dogged persistence, a sort of 'worrying away' at the issues until they have reached a solution (Bayne 1999, 25).

Effective summits for the promotion of international trade liberalisation, specifically the support of multilateral trade negotiations, have been characterised primarily by several factors: an agreed-upon agenda prior to the start of the summit, which often requires the issue having been discussed at a previous summit, at the earlier ministerial council meeting of the Organisation for Economic Co-operation and Development (OECD), among small, informal groups such as the Quadrilateral Trade Ministers (Quad), or the more recent Five Interested Parties (FIPs)[3]; public political pressure; the existence of a viable negotiating framework; and the personal commitment of the leaders.

Although the G8 has the potential to provide effective leadership to the international trading system, specifically in multilateral trade negotiations, this chapter argues that all too often the G7/8 has failed to provide consistent and effective leadership. To explore the role that the G7/8 has played in providing impetus to the multilateral trading system, this chapter examines the leadership provided by the G7/8 summits during the Uruguay Round and the current Doha Development Agenda. The first section defines the factors necessary for an effective G7/8 summit and offers a summary of the effectiveness of selected G7/8 summits. The second section evaluates the performance of the G7 during the Uruguay Round. The third section analyses the G7/8 during the current Doha Development Agenda negotiations.[4] The concluding section offers recommendations for the 2005 Gleneagles Summit.

The Varying Effectiveness of Summits

This section reviews the factors that may create both effective and ineffective G7/8 summits in the area of trade. Effective summits may be defined as those that result in strong statements on trade that include political leadership, detailed language suggesting the way forward, and the personal commitment of the leaders. Effective G7/8 summits serve several purposes: to call for new trade rounds, to shape the negotiating agenda, to break impasses through increasing political pressure on individual member governments to offer concessions, and to function as useful deadlines for negotiators. Examples are drawn from the G7 summits that dealt with the Uruguay Round as well as the G8 summits that took place immediately prior to and during the Doha Development Agenda negotiations. The summits covered are listed below (note that – symbol indicates a G7/8 summit that had little or negative impact on multilateral trade negotiations, while a + symbol indicates an effective summit resulting in a positive impact).

- Uruguay Round
  1985 Bonn — Members divided on new round (–)
  1986 Tokyo — Political impetus for new round (+)
  1990 Houston — Political re-commitment (+)
  1993 Tokyo — Market access breakthrough due to political pressure (+)
- Doha Development Agenda
  1998 Birmingham — Focus on the anniversary of GATT, not on a new round (–)
  1999 Cologne — Members divided on a new round (–)
  2000 Okinawa — Lack of political leadership and personal commitment (–)
  2001 Genoa — Pledges of personal commitment, need for transparency, and incorporation of developing country concerns (+)
  2002 Kananaskis — Brief re-statement of need to resist protectionism; no new initiative (–)
  2003 Evian — Lack of personal commitment and political leadership (–)
  2004 Sea Island — Calls to move core issues of Doha Development Agenda forward, taking into consideration needs of developing countries; political call for G8 trade ministers as well as other WTO members to agree to a negotiating framework by July 2004; no long-term commitments on trade (+)

G7 Performance during the Uruguay Round

Since the 1980s, G7 summits have been used as platforms by individual G7 leaders in calling for new multilateral trade talks. At the 1985 Bonn Summit, U.S. president Ronald Reagan recommended an early start to a new trade round. However, the leaders were divided, with France's president François Mitterrand refusing to accept a start date of early 1986. Thus, the communiqué read '*most of us* think [that the starting date of a new round] should be in 1986' (G7 1985, emphasis added). The U.S., especially Congress, felt rebuffed and initiated protectionist legislation such as the Export Enhancement Program. However, the Bonn Summit was exceptional for its lack of cohesiveness and it was one of only two economic summits considered by Robert Putnam and Nicholas Bayne (1987) to have 'exacerbated international tensions'.

In contrast to the weak and divisive position G7 leaders took in Bonn, the 1986 Tokyo Summit gave political impetus to the Uruguay Round by issuing a strong and cohesive statement in support of a new round. In fact, the leaders went so far as to suggest which issues should be included in the negotiations by stating: 'The new round should, *inter alia*, address the issues of trade in services and trade related aspects of intellectual property rights and foreign direct investment' (G7 1986). An additional paragraph was dedicated to the contentious issue of agriculture. The Tokyo Summit was effective in that the leaders agreed on a common and detailed statement on the Uruguay Round. They also provided useful political pressure and pledged to stay involved in the GATT process to ensure the round was successfully launched by September 1986.

As host of the 1990 Houston Summit, the U.S. was eager to make progress on the Uruguay Round negotiations, especially the difficult agricultural discussions. So critical was the successful outcome of the agricultural negotiations to the heads of state and the representatives of the European Community (EC) that the 'dominated proceedings ahead of aid to the Soviet Union; the issue of reform of the Common Agricultural Policy (CAP) forced itself above the end-game to the Cold War' (Kay 1998, 64).[5]

The Houston communiqué sent a clear and firm message to the negotiators that the political leaders had placed the conclusion of the Uruguay Round at the top of their agenda. They pledged to 'take the difficult political decisions' as well as to 'maintain a high level of personal involvement' (G7 1990). The immediate impact of the Houston Summit on agriculture was minimal due to the EC's back-pedalling on its pledges.[6] However, the long-term impact was more significant as it provided many summit innovations. It was the first time that the leaders had provided negotiators with detailed advice on moving the trade negotiations forward. A critical factor that qualifies the Houston Summit as being effective with regard to trade was that for the first time the leaders pledged to become personally involved in the negotiations. This has proven to be a key element in the G7/8 leaders having a positive impact on negotiations both at and between summits.

The expiration of U.S. fast-track authority on 15 December 1993 provided a critical deadline for the Uruguay Round. Therefore, immense political pressure was placed not only on Japan, the host of the 1993 Tokyo Summit, but also the other members of the Quad. It was reported that in the run up to the Tokyo Summit, the Quad trade ministers 'zig-zagged across the world — from Toronto to Paris to Tokyo, back to Toronto and to Tokyo … in an attempt to hammer out agreement' (Torday 1993).

After marathon talks and a surprise concession from Japan on whiskey and brandy, a significant breakthrough was achieved by the Quad on 7 July in the form of a substantial market access package. The next day the G7 was able to announce the deal at the Summit. A press report stated:

> In what could well end up as the biggest surprise and most important accomplishment of the G7 summit meeting, trade representatives of the world's major economies appear to have succeeded in what some had thought impossible. On [7 July] they gave a new lease on life

to moribund world trade negotiations and a boost to the idea of free trade at a time when the concept is under attack by word and deed (Pollack 1993).

Following the summit, the other GATT contracting parties discussed the Quad's agreement in Geneva. At the same time, the U.S. and the EC held several months of intense bilateral negotiations, primarily over agriculture, but also financial and audiovisual services. On 6 December 1993, the U.S. and the EC announced that they had reached an agreement on the 'clarifications' in the 1992 Blair House Accord on agriculture as demanded by France. Japan also agreed to allow foreign rice to be imported. On 14 December, it was reported that the gavel had 'fallen on most of the Uruguay Round agreement' (Dodwell 1993). The Quad/G7 initiative had helped pave the way for the successful conclusion of the Uruguay Round.

G7/8 Performance during the Doha Development Agenda

The summits leading up to the planned launch of the Doha Development Agenda negotiations showed a surprising lack of effective leadership among the G7/8. Critically, their failure to offer solid proposals on contentious issues such as trade and the environment and trade and labour rights contributed to the difficult and frustrating discussions among WTO ambassadors in Geneva in the last few months before the 1999 ministerial in Seattle that was meant to launch a new round of trade talks.

The 1998 Birmingham Summit took place one week prior to the 1998 WTO ministerial held in Geneva marking the 50th anniversary of the establishment of the GATT. Thus, the Birmingham communiqué focussed on a general reaffirmation of the merits of continued liberalisation. As they had done in Lyon in 1986 and in Denver in 1997, the leaders again called for greater participation by developing countries within the multilateral trading system. However, no new initiative was proposed. Notably, the G8 did not address the need for new trade negotiations.

In 1999 at Cologne, the G7/8 leaders failed to reach a consensus on the agenda of the planned new Millennium Round. This was a significant failure as it gave their trade ministers no shared political direction in the critical period before the Seattle ministerial. The main points on the agenda were the pursuit of an ambitious new trade round, ways to involve developing countries more widely in the negotiations, increased input by civil society, the incorporation of environmental and labour concerns in future trade negotiations, and biotechnology. However, the U.S. and the EU failed to come to an agreement on various elements of the proposed round. While the EU insisted on having an ambitious comprehensive round, the U.S. favoured a more limited agenda. There was also disagreement on the extent that trade-related environmental and labour issues should be discussed.

In the end, the Cologne communiqué pleased no one by calling weakly for 'a new round of broad-based and ambitious negotiations with the aim of achieving substantial and manageable results' (G8 1999). More critically, compared to the 1996 Lyon Summit — which offered considerable detail for the upcoming WTO ministerial in Singapore — at Cologne the leaders offered little in the way of specific suggestions for Seattle.

Following the failure of the 1999 Seattle ministerial to launch a new round of multilateral trade negotiations and the weak trade statements coming out of the G7/8 summits in previous years, the 2000 G8 Summit in Okinawa was critical for the issue of trade. In particular, strong political leadership regarding the launch of the Doha Development Agenda was needed.

Although there was no meeting of the Quad immediately prior to the Summit, trade was high on the agenda at the EU-Japan Summit on 19 July 2000. Japanese prime minister Yoshiro Mori and EU leaders, including French president Jacques Chirac, who held the six-month rotating European Council presidency, and Commission president Romano Prodi, stressed their commitment to launch the next round 'during the course of this year' and that it:

> should be designed as a single undertaking and, beyond the negotiations in the built-in agenda on agriculture and services, be comprehensive in that it should reflect the varied interests and priorities of all WTO members in a balanced way' (Daily Yomiuri 2000).

At a press conference in Tokyo on the same day, Charlene Barshefsky (2000), the U.S. Trade Representative (USTR), stated the U.S. position:

> Consensus for a new round should be sought and achieved at the earliest possible opportunity including this year. Every country has politics. Every country has elections. The United States is concerned that a vacuum not develop, and that the process of trade liberalization move forward. But key to the launch of the new round will be the substance. And when that substance will be achieved whether this year or next, a new round will be able to be launched.

Barshefsky's statement hinted that, while the U.S. strongly supported a new round, it would hesitate to support a launch fully before the agenda was clarified. Therefore, the Okinawa Summit began without a clear consensus, at least among three members of the Quad.

During discussions on the second day of the Summit, G7 participants at one point reportedly expressed their strong support of launching a new round by the end of 2000.[7] However, the leaders agreed that it be left to the sherpas to prepare the final communiqué language. The sherpas subsequently watered down the document's wording.

Similar to Cologne's, the Okinawa communiqué resulted in a relatively weak statement due to a lack of both consensus and political leadership. In words identical to those issued after the EU-Japan Summit, it stated that the leaders pledged to 'intensify our close and fruitful cooperation in order *to try together* with other WTO members to launch such a round during the course of this year (G8 2000; EU-Japan Summit 2000, emphasis added).

However, while the G7's call for a new round was disappointing, the Okinawa Summit did include other current issues relating to the multilateral trading system. The leaders addressed the 'legitimate concerns' of the WTO's developing country members to be incorporated better into the multilateral system. Additionally, the G7/8 recognised the need for communicating with their citizens on the issue of trade. They stressed the importance 'to establish a constructive dialogue on the benefits and challenges of trade liberalization' (G8 2000).

In Genoa at the 2001 Summit, the communiqué was stronger than in previous years on the issue of trade, but there were still critical omissions that served to undermine its overall impact on the multilateral trading system. Regarding a new round, the G7 leaders issued a statement on the first day of the Summit in which they agreed to 'engage personally and jointly' in launching an ambitious new round at the WTO ministerial meeting scheduled to take place in Doha later in the year (G7 2000). In addition to calling for a balanced agenda, the leaders also stated the need for increased WTO transparency and interaction with civil society as well as more effective dispute settlement procedures. The G7 addressed the need for the new trade talks to involve developing countries more, including increased market access to developed countries, capacity building, and technical assistance. Nonetheless, many of the more contentious issue areas such as agriculture or the new issues were not addressed. However, the personal and political engagement of the G7 leaders was evident in Doha in November 2001, where the Doha Development Agenda was successfully launched, albeit with last-minute compromises in language that left many somewhat unsure of what exactly had been agreed.

The 2002 Kananaskis Summit, rather than producing the regular communiqué, resulted in a brief chair's summary with trade mentioned only in passing. The statement was extraordinarily concise as well as weak in announcing that the leaders had 'agreed to resist protectionist pressures and stressed [their] commitment to work with developing countries to ensure the successful conclusion of the Doha Development Agenda by January 1, 2005' (G8 2002).

Given that the 2003 Evian Summit took place only four months prior to the WTO Cancun ministerial, it was of utmost importance that the G8 show solidarity and accountable political leadership in acting to ensure that the Doha negotiations were put back on track. Leading up to the Summit, there were indications that Evian had the potential to be strong on trade. Four factors generally lead to effective summits for promoting trade liberalisation, and specifically for supporting multilateral trade negotiations: an agenda agreed upon before the start of the summit, public political pressure, the existence of a viable negotiating framework, and the personal commitment of the leaders themselves. Two of these characteristics were in evidence; however, two key elements were not.

An Agreed Agenda Prior to the Start of the Summit

An agreed summit agenda often requires the issues having been discussed at a previous ministers' meeting or at earlier senior-level meetings such as the OECD ministerial immediately prior to the summit. As chair at Evian, Chirac placed trade and the strengthening of the global economy high on the Summit agenda. At their April 2003 meeting, the G7 finance ministers and central bank governors stated that they:

> underscore the importance to global growth and poverty reduction of successful trade liberalization through the timely implementation of the Doha Development Agenda, notably in financial services (G7 Finance Ministers 2003).

Additionally, Luzius Wasescha, chair of the OECD Trade Committee, highlighted the need for responsibility and co-operation among OECD members at the OECD ministerial in late April:

> This year's Trade Message to the OECD Ministerial Council Meeting is being delivered at a time of general uncertainty about prospects for the world economy and, more broadly, about the international environment for peace and security. In such a context, it is the special responsibility of OECD Members to show leadership and to act decisively to ensure the successful conclusion of the Doha Development Agenda (DDA) and thereby help underpin international co-operation, stability and economic integration (Wasescha 2003).

Public Political Pressure

The heads of the WTO, the International Monetary Fund (IMF), and the World Bank, who met with the leaders at Evian, issued a joint statement in May 2003 directed at the G8 urging political leadership:

> By pulling together in a multilateral context the G8 will help to maintain the momentum of structural economic reform over the longer term in developed and developing countries alike (WTO 2003).

In addition, interest groups and civil society groups were vocal in emphasising the need for a successful conclusion of the Doha Development Agenda and the necessity of G8 leadership. Representatives of the International Chamber of Commerce (ICC) presented Chirac with a statement to the G8. This statement was shortly followed by a letter signed by the directors of the Canadian Council of Chief Executives, Japan's Nippon Keidanren, the European Round Table of Industrialists, the European Employers Confederation, the U.S. Business Round Table, and the ICC, calling on the G7/8 to make a 'strong commitment' to the Doha negotiations (Betts 2003).

The Existence of a Viable Negotiating Framework

The Doha declaration provides the framework for the Doha Development Agenda negotiations and establishes a series of deadlines for several of the issues being discussed. However, many of the key deadlines were missed prior to the WTO ministerial in Cancun in September 2003. This resulted in the Cancun ministerial agenda being dangerously overloaded, making the established negotiating framework less viable. The main issues that needed to be agreed at Cancun included agriculture, services, and the contentious new Singapore issues of competition policy, investment, transparency in government procurement and trade facilitation.

Personal Commitment of the Leaders

Despite the support of several G8 members for further liberalisation within the framework of the Doha Development Round, recent summits — including Evian — failed to show significant personal commitment and engagement by the leaders. Such political support is a critical element as it directly affects the work of their respective trade ministers. Given that the G8 leaders were to meet with several leaders of key developing states immediately prior to the Evian Summit, a joint statement of personal commitment from both developed and developing leaders would have provided a show of solidarity as well as a much-needed political boost to the Doha negotiations.

However, at Evian the G8 managed only to produce a general statement on trade that failed to offer the leadership, political will, or personal commitment necessary to place the Doha negotiations back on track before the Cancun ministerial. Rather than offering progress on such critical issues such as agricultural export subsidies, domestic support, and market access, the G8 merely agreed to:

> promote the multilateral system by providing leadership in the ongoing negotiations so that improved access to markets for all WTO members is realized, particularly for the poorest, to ensure their integration into the multilateral system, and their development more broadly. We are therefore committed to delivering on schedule, by the end of 2004, the goals set out in the Doha Development Agenda, and to ensuring that the Cancun Ministerial Conference in September takes all the necessary decisions to help reach that goal (G8 2003).

The Evian Summit was a lost opportunity for the G8's leadership in trade as well as for the multilateral trading system. The stalemate that occurred within the Doha Development Agenda following the failure at Cancun resulted in a statement by EU trade commissioner Pascal Lamy that the negotiations were 'in need of intensive care' (Jonquières 2003).

The Sea Island Summit

The original negotiating schedule of the Doha Development Agenda set the beginning of 2005 as the deadline for the negotiations. Thus, the Sea Island Summit, held 8–10 June 2004, was to be the final meeting of the G8 leaders during this round of multilateral trade negotiations. Crucially, the Summit was held less than two months prior to a 31 July deadline for WTO members that required agreement on a negotiating framework package. Thus, Sea Island was critical in terms of showing whether the G8 was effective or defective in providing leadership in the area of multilateral trade negotiations. Prior to the Sea Island Summit, three out of the four factors that generally lead to effective summits existed.

An Agreed Agenda Prior to the Start of the Summit

On the previously agreed-upon agenda, the U.S. hosts recognised the crucial opportunity that the Sea Island Summit represented for the Doha Development Agenda. First, prosperity was one of three themes of the summit.[8] This indicated that the health of the world economy and trading system would be placed at the top of the agenda. Additionally, the importance of the economy in the 2004 U.S. presidential campaign ensured that President George Bush would work hard to forge a consensus among the other leaders of the G8 to enable a strong statement on the moving the Doha negotiations forward.

Public Political Pressure

In the weeks leading up to the Sea Island Summit, international organisations voiced strong political pressure for the G8 to show leadership in trade and development issues. In March, United Nations Secretary General Kofi Annan met with the G8 Contact Group on Food Security in Africa. He urged the developed countries of the G8 to reduce agricultural subsidies and encouraged G8 involvement in the New Partnership for Africa's Development (NEPAD) (Annan 2003).

At the conclusion of the OECD Ministerial Council, held 13–14 May, the Chair's Summary stated:

> Ministers were determined to reach basic agreements on frameworks for key issues of the Doha Agenda by July of this year. They shared the view that these agreements need to build on the lessons of the Fifth WTO Ministerial Conference in Cancun and on the work performed and the contributions made since then. They noted that momentum has been building, and that they should take advantage of the window of opportunity that has now opened … Ministers agreed that all participants must now translate political will into concrete and decisive actions that give impetus to the technical work in Geneva until July, and which move forward the Doha Development Agenda, to the benefit of citizens worldwide (OECD 2004).

The Existence of a Viable Negotiating Framework

Unlike the series of missed negotiating deadlines and lack of political will on the part of key G8 members prior to the 2003 Evian Summit, the U.S. and the EU made significant efforts to move the Doha negotiations forward prior to the Sea Island Summit. In an attempt to break the stalemate in the Doha negotiations following the Cancun ministerial, USTR Robert Zoellick sent a letter to the other members of the WTO in January 2004 suggesting that frameworks for negotiations in the stalled trade round be agreed by mid year. He stated that 'the Doha negotiations will require a commitment to work toward effective and productive compromises by all WTO Members, and the United States recognizes its responsibility to help push towards our mutual success' (USTR 2004). A month later, Zoellick embarked on a whirlwind visit to key capital cities in both developed and developing countries to seek a way forward.

Additionally, less than a month prior to the Sea Island Summit, the EU's Pascal Lamy and agriculture commissioner Franz Fischler issued a joint letter to the other members of the WTO that showed new flexibility on agriculture and the contentious new issues as well as offering least developed countries greater market access to developed country markets. The commissioners urged other countries with high agricultural subsidies to 'show ambition and courage' (European Commission 2004).

There was also evidence of increasing discussion between developed and developing WTO members, including Brazil, China, and India, on the most contentious issues, including a mini-ministerial on the sidelines of the OECD's mid-May ministerial and informal discussions between various coalitions including the U.S., the EU, the Cairns Group, and the WTO's G20 consisting of developing countries.

Personal Commitment of the Leaders

Despite strong signals from the G8 on the necessity to reach a framework agreement within the WTO in order to break the stalemate in the Doha Development Agenda, none either engaged personally or offered a personal commitment to ensure that the stalled negotiations were put back on track.

Nonetheless, with three of the four factors present, the Sea Island Summit produced a relatively strong, albeit short-term, statement on trade that acknowledged the window of opportunity that existed to reinvigorate the Doha Development Agenda for ensuring that the July framework agreement package be met on time. The G8 leaders stated in part:

> Our most pressing task is to focus on the core issues in the negotiations, which are drivers of economic development and growth: substantially reducing trade-distorting agricultural subsidies and barriers to access to markets; opening markets more widely to trade in goods; expanding opportunities for trade in services; overhauling and improving customs rules and other relevant procedures to facilitate trade; and advancing the development of all countries, especially the poorest, within the WTO system. A consensus appears to be emerging on a way forward for

> these issues. We must ensure that we maintain a high and consistent level of ambition in all areas, while bearing in mind all members' sensitivities ... We are determined to seize this moment of strategic economic opportunity. Therefore, we direct our ministers and call on all WTO members to finalize the frameworks by July to put the WTO negotiations back on track so that we can expeditiously complete the Doha Development Agenda (G8 2004).

The G8 leaders specifically highlighted the need for progress in agriculture, cotton, and trade facilitation. The Sea Island statement on trade shows that the G8 has the ability to show effective political leadership in multilateral trade negotiations when its commitments are implemented by the G8 trade ministers and supported by similar commitments among the wider WTO membership.

As the members of the WTO entered the final phase of negotiations prior to the 31 July deadline, Director General Supachai Panitchpakdi (2004) acknowledged the political leadership that existed: 'The political guidance and direction which we need to be able to move ahead is there. The onus is now fairly and squarely on negotiators in Geneva to do the deals that our political leaders clearly want us to achieve.'

Following two weeks of talks described as 'an arduous process of discussions and negotiations' including a final meeting lasting nearly 24 hours, WTO member negotiators agreed on a package of negotiating frameworks in the areas of agriculture, non-agricultural market access, development issues, trade facilitation, and services (WTO 2004). The negotiating package established the guidelines for the completion of the Doha Development Agenda and set the date of the next WTO ministerial for December 2005. Hailing the 'truly historic' accomplishment, Supachai acknowledged the 'political courage, commitment and sheer hard work' of WTO governments (WTO 2004).

Despite the relative strength of the Sea Island trade statement and its contribution to bringing about the WTO July framework package, the document had two key weaknesses. First, the statement was relatively short-sighted given that no commitments past the 31 July deadline were made. Second, the G8 did not invite the participation of developing countries, international organisations such as the WTO, the IMF, or the World Bank, or representatives of civil society.

As the world trading system becomes increasingly politicised with a greater direct impact on developing countries and citizens, the G8 must adapt to the new, more inclusive, multilateral trading system. Within the Doha Development Agenda negotiations, developed and developing countries are increasingly recognising that they may often gain through forming alliances that bridge the traditional North/South or developed/developing country distinctions. This relatively new development, first seen with the establishment of the Cairns Group during the Uruguay Round and more recently with the FIPs, points to the need of the G8 leaders to reach out to the heads of states of key developing countries and work with them to provide the necessary political leadership and 20-20 vision within multilateral trade negotiations (see Chapter 13).

Conclusion and Recommendations for the 2005 Gleneagles Summit

This chapter has argued that the G8 has not been consistent in showing effective political leadership in the area of multilateral trade, specifically during multilateral trade negotiations. Through examining the history of G7/8 summits during the Uruguay Round and Doha Development Agenda, it may be concluded that effective summits for the promotion of trade liberalisation, specifically the support of multilateral trade negotiations, are characterised primarily by an agreed-upon agenda prior to the start of the summit, public political pressure, a viable negotiating framework, and the personal commitment of the leaders.

To increase the effectiveness of the G8's political leadership in the area of trade, the G8 must both be more consistent in providing strong commitments as well as adapt to the new realities of the multilateral trading system in which developing countries and civil society groups play a greater role.

A key challenge of the 2005 Gleneagles Summit will be for the G8 to recognise that in the new multilateral trading system developed and developing countries must work together to make progress in multilateral trade negotiations. Additionally, the G8 should acknowledge the concerns of civil society regarding the content and pace of trade liberalisation. Therefore, the G8 should establish a forum for dialogue on trade, similar to the Forum for the Future between the G8 and the countries of the broader Middle East established at Sea Island, in which the leaders of the G8 and their trade ministers would be joined by their counterparts from key developing countries. There should also be a parallel dialogue for civil society representatives from developed and developing countries. In such a way, the G8 may be able to ensure effective, rather than defective, leadership.

Notes

1. Earlier versions of this chapter were presented at the International Studies Association meeting 17–20 March 2004, and revised for the research project on 'Security, Prosperity and Freedom: Why America needs the G8'. The author wishes to thank Bernhard May, Aseem Prakash, and the anonymous reviewers for their valuable comments.
2. The G7, consisting of Canada, France, Germany, Italy, Japan, the United Kingdom, and the United States, expanded to the G8 in 1998 with the addition of Russia. Since 1977, the European Union has been a participant in the G7/8 summits, represented by the European Commission as well as the presidency.
3. The Quad was established in 1982 with the support of the G7. Although it was very active during the Uruguay Round, its activity has declined since, last meeting officially in 1999. The FIPs group consists of the U.S., EU, Australia, Brazil, and India.
4. Despite the G7's expansion to the G8 in 1998 with the addition of Russia, between 1998 and 2002 it was the G7 that discussed trade at the annual summits, since Russia was not a

member of the WTO. In 2003, with the imminent accession of Russia to the WTO, the Evian Summit was the first to discuss all topics, including trade, as the G8.

5. The European Union was known as the European Community prior to 1 November 1993, when the Treaty on European Union went into force.
6. The first Bush administration welcomed the conveniently released GATT document known as the De Zeeuw text as a basis for further discussion on agriculture. The De Zeeuw compromise was agreed by all summit participants as the 'means to intensify the negotiations' (G7 1990, para. 23). However, less than one week later, the EC's General Affairs Council declared that the De Zeeuw text was only 'one way to intensify' the agricultural negotiations ('Europe Daily Bulletin' 1990). The retreat was due to the Council feeling that the EC, which speaks for the now 25 member states of the EU on matters relating to trade, had gone past its negotiating mandate.
7. Stated by a UK spokesperson during a press briefing at the Okinawa Summit.
8. The other two themes were freedom and security.

References

Annan, Kofi (2003). 'Secretary-General's Remarks to Open the Meeting of the G8 Contact Group on Food Security in Africa'. New York, 5 March. <www.un.org/apps/sg/printsgstats.asp?nid=272> (November 2004).

Barshefsky, Charline (2000). 'Transcript: Barshefsky Says Deregulation Key to Japan's Recovery'. Transcript of press conference on 'Trade Policy in the U.S.-Japan Relationship, 1993 to 2000, Tokyo, 19 July. <japan.usembassy.gov/e/p/tp-2841.html> (November 2004).

Bayne, Nicholas (1999). 'Continuity and Leadership in an Age of Globalisation'. In M. R. Hodges, J. J. Kirton and J. P. Daniels, eds., *The G8's Role in the New Millennium*, pp. 21–44. Ashgate, Aldershot.

Bayne, Nicholas (2000). 'The G7 Summit's Contribution: Past, Present, and Prospective'. In K. Kaiser, J. J. Kirton and J. P. Daniels, eds., *Shaping a New International Financial System: Challenges of Governance in a Globalizing World*, pp. 19–35. Ashgate, Aldershot.

Betts, Paul (2003). 'Executives Urge G8 to Unite for Growth'. *Financial Times*, 21 May.

Daily Yomiuri (2000). 20 July, p. 3.

Dodwell, David (1993). 'The Gavel Falls on Most of Uruguay Round'. *Financial Times*, 14 December.

'Europe Daily Bulletin' (1990). *Agence Europe*, 18 July, p. 6.

European Commission (2004). 'WTO-DDA: EU Ready to Go the Extra Mile in Three Key Areas of the Talks'. Brussels, 10 May. <europa.eu.int/comm/trade/issues/newround/pr100504_en.htm> (November 2004).

European Union-Japan Summit (2000). 'Joint Conclusions'. 19 July. <europa.eu.int/comm/external_relations/japan/summit_7_19_2000> (November 2004).

G7 (1975). 'Declaration of Rambouillet'. 17 November. <www.g8.utoronto.ca/summit/1975rambouillet/communique.html> (November 2004).

G7 (1985). 'The Bonn Economic Declaration Towards Sustained Growth and Higher Employment'. 4 May. <www.g8.utoronto.ca/summit/1985bonn> (November 2004).

G7 (1986). 'Tokyo Economic Declaration'. 6 May. <www.g8.utoronto.ca/summit/1986tokyo> (November 2004).

G7 (1990). 'Houston Economic Declaration'. 11 July. <www.g8.utoronto.ca/summit/1990houston> (November 2004).

G7 (2000). 'G7 Statement'. 21 July. <www.g8.utoronto.ca/summit/2000okinawa/statement.htm> (November 2004).

G7 Finance Ministers (2003). 'Statement of G7 Finance Ministers and Central Bank Governors'. Washington DC, 12 April. <www.g8.utoronto.ca/finance/fm041203.htm> (November 2004).

G8 (1999). 'G8 Communiqué Köln 1999'. 20 June. <www.g8.utoronto.ca/summit/1999koln> (November 2004).

G8 (2000). 'G8 Communiqué Okinawa 2000'. <www.g8.utoronto.ca/summit/2000okinawa/finalcom.htm> (November 2004).

G8 (2002). 'The Kananaskis Summit Chair's Summary'. <www.g8.utoronto.ca/summit/2002kananaskis> (November 2004).

G8 (2003). 'Co-operative G8 Action on Trade'. Evian, 2 June. <www.g8.utoronto.ca/summit/2003evian/trade_en.html> (November 2004).

G8 (2004). 'G8 Leaders Statement on Trade'. Sea Island, 9 June. <www.g8.utoronto.ca/summit/2004seaisland/trade.html> (November 2004).

Jonquières, Guy de (2003). 'Poorer Countries Are Likely to Be the Biggest Losers from the Unexpected Breakdown in the Doha Round'. *Financial Times*, 16 September, p. 21.

Kay, Adrian (1998). *The Reform of the Common Agricultural Policy: The Case of the MacSharry Reforms*. CAB International, New York.

Organisation for Economic Co-operation and Development (2004). 'Chair's Summary'. OECD Ministerial Council Meeting, Paris, 13–14 May.

Panitchpakdi, Supachai (2004). 'Ministerial Support Must Be Translated into Geneva Progress'. Opening Remarks, Trade Negotiations Committee, 30 June. <www.wto.org/english/news_e/news04_e/tnc_30june04_e.htm> (November 2004).

Pollack, Andrew (1993). 'Summit Breathes Life into World Trade Talks'. *International Herald Tribune*, 8 July.

Putnam, Robert and Nicholas Bayne (1987). *Hanging Together: Co-operation and Conflict in the Seven-Power Summit*. 2nd ed. Sage Publications, London.

Torday, Peter (1993). 'Hurdles Stand in Way of Deal'. *Independent*, 8 July.

United States Trade Representative (2004). 'Zoellick Embarks on Global Push to Make Strong Progress on Doha Negotiations'. 8 February. <www.ustr.gov "Press Room"> (November 2004).

Wasescha, Luzius (2003). 'Trade Policy Message to Ministers from the Chairman of the Trade Committee'. Council Meeting at the Ministerial Level, Organisation for Economic Co-operation and Development, Paris, 29–30 April. <www1.oecd.org/subject/mcm/2003/mcmtrade.PDF> (November 2004).

World Trade Organization (2003). 'Joint Statement'. Supachai Panitchpakdi, Director-General of the World Trade Organization, Horst Köhler, Managing Director of the International Monetary Fund, and James Wolfensohn, President of the World Bank group, WTO General Council meeting on coherence, Geneva, 13 May. <www.wto.org/english/news_e/pres03_e/pr341_e.htm> (November 2004).

World Trade Organization (2004). 'Round-the-Clock Meetings Produce "Historic" Breakthrough'. DDA July 2004 Package, Meeting Summary 31 July. <www.wto.org/english/news_e/news04_e/dda_package_sum_31july04_e.htm> (November 2004).

CONCLUSION

Chapter 15

New Perspectives on the G8

John J. Kirton, Michele Fratianni, Alan M. Rugman, and Paolo Savona

The analyses in this book all answer some fundamental questions about the performance of the G8 from 1975 to 2004, about the future of the G8 as an institution, about its relationship with its co-founder and still most powerful member — and 2004 host — the United States, and about the new perspectives needed to understand the G8's role in the 21st century world. Together these contributions portray a G8 system of global governance that has substantial power, a strong performance, and even greater potential for America, its partners, and the global community as a whole, especially if the G8 is modernised to meet the new generation of demands. Equally importantly, they point to several conceptual innovations that together form the foundation of a new perspective with which to understand a rapidly evolving G8 and its role in this new age.

G8 Performance from 1975 to 2004

In the first instance, these chapters provide a rich set of conclusions on the key question of whether the G8 has been a success, over its 30-year history, in the troubled 21st century, and under American hosting at Sea Island in 2004. Together they provide a generally positive assessment of the G8's performance in the past.

The First Thirty Years' Legacy

In examining the past three decades of G8 summitry, John Kirton concludes that the G8 summit has shown a rising level of performance across most of the major functions it performs, as do most international institutions. Similarly, Nicholas Bayne sees a G8 that has engaged in effective collective management over these years. Most ambitiously, Risto Penttilä suggests it has served as a meta-institution, overseeing, directing, and, where necessary, reforming the complex network of other international institutions and organisations and the system of global governance as a whole.

In the traditional field of trade, Sylvia Ostry and Heidi Ullrich both argue that the G7/8 summit has made a real contribution, although inconsistent and episodic. Ostry sees a general decline from the high, if procedural, contribution of the G7 summit in the 1970s. This is due to the summit's shift to political subjects and politically oriented leaders, to the growing complexity of the trade agenda, and to the rise of consequential new country and civil society players in the trade field. In contrast, Ullrich sees a steadier performance, with the G7 still exerting its 'Rambouillet effect' and thus proving its worth in helping launch and conclude the 1993 Uruguay Round of multilateral trade negotiations.

In the new field of cyberspace, Jeffrey Hart views the G8 as effectively taking up the issue in the early 1990s and producing the principles, norms, and rules that define the regime in many aspects of the field. In the war on terror, Donato Masciandaro notes that the G7 acted decisively as early as 1978. Since 1989, through the Financial Action Task Force on Money Laundering (FATF) created at that year's summit in Paris, it has created the standards that became the benchmark in every country. The G8 has also moved to enforcement action through black lists, even though they have had an uncertain and potentially counterproductive effect. Similarly George von Furstenberg portrays the G8 as moving steadily and effectively against money laundering since 1989.

A strikingly different view comes from Alan Rugman. He alone sees the G8 as having been in decline for several years. He implies that it has been unable to resolve recurrent trade wars between the United States and the European Union, in contrast to its effective action in the distant past.

The Twenty-First Century Record

Most authors in this volume see a solid G8 performance during the 21st century. This is despite, or in some cases because of, the 11 September 2001 terrorist attacks on the U.S., the advent of an allegedly unilateralist American president, George Bush, at the Genoa Summit of 2001, and the transatlantic divisions among G8 members over the 2003 war in Iraq that bedevilled the G8 Summit at Evian in 2003.

Kirton concludes that the G8 has thrived in response to the 11 September assaults, and has survived Bush's divisive decision to go to war in Iraq backed only by Britain, Italy, and Japan within the G8. Bayne, too, concludes that the G8's collective management survived under Bush. In the trade field, Ullrich argues that the 2001 Genoa Summit helped launch the long-awaited Doha Development Agenda, even if the 2002 and 2003 G8 summits did little to move it along. In the realm of cyberspace, Hart sees the G8 from 2000 to 2002 turning to issues of cybersecurity and bridging the digital divide, and setting new principles for dealing with these issues and privacy. He also sees it pioneering a multistakeholder approach through the Digital Opportunity Task Force (Dot Force), which led to more informed governance, largely silenced the antiglobalisation critics, and was adopted by the Organisation for Economic Co-operation and Development (OECD). In the field of terrorist finance, Masciandaro portrays the G8 as swiftly adopting a bold new strategy within a month of the 11 September terrorist attacks. Von Furstenberg gives even more emphasis to the FATF's creation of eight special recommendations in October 2001 and their endorsement and strengthening ever since. But he also argues that even Britain and Germany are unable to enforce them and that blacklisting and sanctioning will not eliminate private terrorist finance. Again, it is Rugman who offers a dissenting view. He sees the G8 as having been fractured under the impact of the divisive Iraq war of 2003, in ways that have yet to be repaired.

The Sea Island Summit

Against this general backdrop of a well-performing G8, there is a widespread consensus that George Bush's 2004 Sea Island Summit was a substantial success, for its American host, for its G8 partners, and for the global community as a whole. Kirton judges Sea Island to have been a summit of substantial achievement. This is due to its work on poverty reduction in Africa, the nonproliferation of weapons of mass destruction (WMD), regional security, the world economy, and, above all, its bold vision and historic beginning to bring democracy, reform, prosperity, security, and sovereignty to Iraq and the Broader Middle East and North Africa (BMENA). The Summit issued 16 documents covering 10 separate issue areas, generated 253 commitments, specified 12 remit mandates for subsequent reports or work, mobilised an estimated US$2.77 billion in new money, created or directed 19 G8 or G8-centred institutions, and issued more than 500 instructions to a vast array of other international institutions. On virtually all these dimensions, it set historical highs. Yet whether it will go down as a summit of historical significance depends ultimately on whether America's allies can make Bush's brave beginning toward a democratic Middle East a permanent, expanding, well-financed priority at G8 summits in subsequent years.

Kirton's favourable assessment is largely shared by Bayne, who concludes that the G8's collective management gained some ground at Sea Island in 2004. Similarly, Penttilä sees Sea Island as a summit where America engaged in policy co-ordination and launched major initiatives central to U.S. foreign policy. More modestly, Bernhard May concludes that Sea Island was neither a big success nor a big failure, but was nevertheless important in continuing to bring the participants of the G8 summit together, to create confidence among them, and to work out a better understanding of what role the U.S. should play in today's globalising world.

Ullrich sees Sea Island as having issued a 'relatively strong' statement on trade, thus showing that the G8 can still exert effective political leadership in multilateral trade negotiations. Ostry seems more doubtful, declaring that a successful conclusion of the Doha negotiations cannot be done within or by the G8 alone. Hart suggests that Sea Island moved appropriately to broaden its concern with cybersecurity and extend its earlier concern with crossing the digital divide to the Middle East and the Islamic world as a whole.

Implicitly, some authors see Sea Island as well as previous summits as a disappointment, for ignoring some key subjects that should have taken up in the interests of simultaneously enhancing security and growth. David Audretsch, Richard Stazinski, and Taylor Aldridge underscore the importance of the international mobility of knowledge workers and entrepreneurial capital in the new economy of G8 countries, a subject Sea

Island addressed in only a very limited fashion through its treatment of the role of the private sector and entrepreneurship in development in the South. Similarly, the Sea Island Summit failed to focus on devising faster and more effective multilateral solutions to lower the security and trade costs highlighted by the analysis of Michele Fratianni and Heejoon Kang. However, the G8's advances on the Secure and Facilitated International Travel Initiative (SAFTI) and economic engagement with the Middle East constitute desirable steps consistent with the analysis they provide. Von Furstenberg is more directly critical, noting that the Sea Island summiteers should have been silent instead of trumpeting their current strategy to combat terrorist finance. Even the generally skeptical Rugman is willing to give Sea Island the benefit of the doubt. He judges it an open question whether G8 unity can be rebuilt after the fractures over Iraq.

The Future of G8 Summitry

Is the success of the Sea Island Summit a prelude to a high-performing future for the G8, as it addresses the key challenges of global governance in the years ahead? Most contributors see a bright future for the G8, as it takes up critical issues in ambitious fashion under British leadership at Gleneagles in July 2005, and under Russian hosting in 2006. Yet many see a strong case for reforming the summit to strengthen its future effectiveness, largely through adjusting its agenda or including more countries in its summit-level deliberations. But there are differences about whether the latter should be done through the incremental inclusion of individual emerging major powers such as China and India, or through an association with the G20 meeting in a new leaders-level (L20) form (English, Thakur, and Cooper 2005). Whichever of these two options is favoured by a particular contributor, none sees any need to adopt any of the more dramatic proposals that have recently flourished in several intellectual centres to reform or replace the G8 with a radically different membership and role (O'Neill and Hormats 2004; Kenen et al. 2004; Bergsten and Koch-Weser 2004).

Gleneagles 2005

In looking into the immediate future, Kirton predicts a very productive summit at Gleneagles in 2005, if its likely host, Tony Blair, gives a prominent place to following up in expansive fashion George Bush's Sea Island centrepiece of bringing democracy, freedom, and reform to the greater Middle East. With Bush now re-elected, and heralding his quest for freedom in the Middle East as the central theme of his foreign policy during his second term, it will be even more important for the British to find a way to adjust to the burning priority of their American ally. Moreover, while Sea Island proved that America and the G8 could absorb the emphasis the British and others wanted to place on African development, Sea Island did very little on the climate change agenda that Blair also wants to feature at Gleneagles. On this issue, Bush still stands opposed to the Kyoto Protocol that all his G8 allies have now ratified and that has thus globally come into legal force.

Russia 2006

Looking two years ahead, Bayne estimates that the present G8 focus on combining economics and politics could persist through 2005 and 2006, but will eventually run out. Britain will seek to revive the G8 economic agenda, while Russia may prefer more political subjects. Should Russia choose to emphasise energy as an issue, it could simultaneously address a potentially critical economic subject and help find a way for George Bush's America to support the global effort, beyond Kyoto, in controlling global warming and climate change. Victoria Panova sees Russia in 2006 using its first chance to host a regular G8 summit to affirm its status as a full-strength G8 member. It will thus host a familiar form of summit, with a comprehensive agenda that could include United Nations reform. Notably, none of the authors expresses much concern about Russia under Vladimir Putin acting in ways that are contrary to accepted democratic practices in other G8 countries, and that might make G8 co-operation more difficult as a result.

The Longer-Term Future

Peering further into the future, in Penttilä's view, the G8 will continue to be a meta-institution, transcending and directing other international organisations, mobilising political will, and making funds available. May argues that the G8 will become even more important in a globalising world. In contrast, Rugman suggests that in the critical field of energy and, more broadly, the G8 will fade into irrelevance in a world where regionalism, not globalisation, is by far the dominant trend. Indeed, he predicts: 'In the long run, it is likely that the G8 will continue its slide into irrelevancy in the face of increasing regionalisation pressures.'

Reform through Revised Action

Future estimates of the G8's effectiveness are often contingent on whether some specified reforms to its actions, agenda, membership, and format are carried out. The first and most modest set of reform proposals relates to the specific actions the G8 should take. Kirton suggests that more funds are needed if the bold beginning to develop the Middle East democratically is to take flight. Fratianni and Kang's analysis points to the possibility that a G8-wide free trade area or even customs union, with a common security perimeter, might be a desirable step on both counterterrorism and open trade grounds. In the field of black money, Masciandaro advises the G8 to adopt different enforcement measures, moving beyond 'naming and shaming' non-adherents through blacklisting to stronger measures such as implementing a strategy of complete financial quarantine. Von Furstenberg suggests that the G8 members should discourage hype and false hope in their existing strategy against terrorist finance, while deliberately declining to present alternative measures to get the job done.

Reform through Agenda Revision

A second set of still modest reform proposals concern the agenda the summit should set. Kirton approves the full-strength agenda that Sea Island set, while noting the need for the leaders to adopt key topics that were largely left unaddressed, such as macroeconomic management and climate change. Bayne signals a preference for a core set of ambitious agenda items that directly link politics and economics. In this spirit, Audretsch, Stazinski, and Aldridge propose that the G8 leaders explicitly address the important tradeoffs between homeland security and economic growth in a knowledge-intensive age.

Reform through Incremental Expansion

A second set of reform proposals relate to participation and membership. Most contributors see a future in which the G8 will — or should — expand to embrace other countries, in order to maintain or increase its effectiveness in a world where power is dispersing to several powers on the rise. Here the first option is incremental inclusion, with China or India as the widely acknowledged first choice. Bayne believes there are good grounds for a G9 summit, embracing China, even though there is no clear view about how this can be done. Penttilä believes that adding China and democratic India as full members would enormously increase the G8's importance and impact as a global security concert. Panova thinks Russia will invite outsiders that could include China and India, and the neighbouring Commonwealth of Independent States (CIS) as well.

Reform through G20/L20 Association

Beyond expanding membership lies the issue of the G8's relationship with other bodies, or even replacement by them, most notably a prospective L20. How the G8 would relate to a prospective L20 is a matter of some dispute. May estimates that the G8 will not expand its membership, but will instead forge greater links with the G20 and the summit-level equivalent that may emerge. Bayne feels that converting the summit from the G8 to the L20 would change the essence of the organism and judges that the current G8 heads do not wish to do so. Yet he leaves open the possibility of the G8 co-operating with a new L20 in a world where each body has a distinctive, mutually reinforcing role to play.

In the trade field, Ostry also offers a G20-based solution. In her '20-20' proposal, the G8 summit would have G20 finance ministers meet with the Cancun G20 of emerging trade powers led by China, India, Brazil, and South Africa. Together they would produce the North-South bargain needed to get the Doha Development Agenda done.

The Broader Reform Agenda

In addition to outreach to other governments and intergovernmental organisations, there is a demand for downreach to involve civil society actors directly in G8 governance. In trade, Ullrich argues that the G8 needs not only to work with leaders of other key countries, but also to involve developing countries, international organisations, and civil society. Hart similarly implies that the G8's multistakeholder model could usefully be adopted in other areas of the G8's work.

The Dynamics of G8 and American Adjustment

The G8 Adjusts to America

These estimates of the past, present, and future performance of the G8 are grounded in an underlying analysis of how much, how, and why America and its G8 partners adjust to one another within the G8 summit and system to produce effective global governance. This dynamic in turn depends on an analysis of how much, how, and why the G8 as an informal, small-membership, club-like institution exercises an autonomous effect on its members to induce collective governance.

The traditional answers have come from the first major explicit theory of G8 co-operation — the American leadership model of Robert Putnam and Nicholas Bayne (Putnam 1994; Putnam and Bayne 1987). It argues that G8 co-operation arises in those years where an always able America is willing to lead and also secures the support from a strong second for the directions it wishes the G8 to pursue. This view is supported by Kirton's evidence showing how America secured much of its brand-new Sea Island priority of bringing democratic development to the greater Middle East. It is also supported by Hart, who shows how the U.S. successfully led the G7's entry into the cyberspace issue in the early 1990s, pressed for a minimal taxation and regulation regime that would favour its own firms, pioneered the 1995 Brussels ministerial and the resulting pilot projects, and had its Commerce Department release a report in 2000 that supported the G8's turn to focus on the digital divide. Consistent with this argument is Rugman's view of an America unwilling to lead and a G8 destined for decline. In his words, the 'United States is unlikely to look to the G8 for any military or political alliance in the near future'.

America Adjusts to the G8

Yet important though American leadership, initiative, investment, and involvement are to the G8's success, other members can be equally important, beyond just one of them seconding whatever America suggests. This is the view of the concert equality model developed by Kirton (1989) on the basis of an insight by William Wallace (1984). It argues that the G8 is a modern democratic concert of equals that performs highly on its functions of deliberation, direction setting, decision making, delivery, development of global governance, and domestic political management. It does so when its member countries are more equal in capability, and when its members meet alone, address issues directly related to the shared social purpose of open democracy, and are in political control at home. In this concert of equals, any member can lead, combine with any others to form a winning coalition, and have an initially resistant America and others adjust to a G8 agreement that is adopted and implemented outside.

Kirton's analysis in this volume shows how America adjusted to its partners at Sea Island to give their priorities on Africa and elsewhere an equally central place. Hart, too, shows how G8 members had longstanding differences over taxation rights and privacy in cyberspace, and how it was Japan at its 2000 Okinawa Summit that led the G8 into its emphasis on the digital divide agenda and principles, in part by holding a meeting with developing country leaders on the eve of that summit.

To be sure, Rugman judges that the U.S. has no need to adjust to the G8, in a world where its energy supplies and firms sales come largely from the region at home. His analysis, however, could suggest that, as there are few American multinational corporations (MNCs) heavily engaged in distant regions, they may need their government, through the G8, to open liberalised trade opportunities for them abroad.

The G8 and America's Need for Each Other

Why the G8 Needs America

This debate over the processes and propellers of reciprocal adjustment within the G8 leads to the more basic questions of why the G8 needs America, why America needs the G8, and, ultimately, why the G8 works as an autonomous institution embracing all the democratic major powers in the world. As an informal institution without a formal legal charter, separate bureaucracy, budget, or building, the G8 is an institution in which all of its members are, at first glance, institutionally unbound. It lives on only by the continuing personal consent of the leaders who attend and by their calculations of what it can do for them, their countries, and the global community as a whole.

The traditional American leadership model assumed that all the G8 members needed America and its leadership as an indispensable necessary element if the G8 was to work at all (see Appendix 15-1). But in the 21st-century world, all G8 members have moved without America to bring the Kyoto Protocol into global legal force. And the U.S. seems determined to remain outside several other regimes, such as those for the International Criminal Court and against antipersonnel landmines, by which all or most of its G8 partners abide. With America absent from several consequent global regime-building achievements, it is relevant to inquire if the G8 can work without America and, if not, why not.

One clear answer as to why America's major power democratic partners need America within the G8, perhaps now more than ever, comes from Fratianni and Kang. They point to the substitution effect in which terrorists shut out of a unilaterally homeland hardened America will strike at softer targets in less hardened countries. The point is no longer a hypothetical one, now that the terrorists, on 11 March 2004, have struck the Madrid subway, in a Spain that is a member of the EU and thus the G8. As the al Qaeda network has identified all G8 members as American allies and thus targets, regardless of whether they have combat troops in Iraq, all of America's G8 partners are vulnerable if they try to ride free, pay to ride, or go it alone.

Another clear answer comes from Rugman. He points out that Europe and Japan, unlike the U.S., depend heavily on Middle Eastern oil and thus need the U.S., working through the G8 and elsewhere, to stabilise and secure the region so that low-cost oil in large volume will continue to flow from there. Consistent with this view is the evidence, noted by Kirton, of the strong desire by France, Germany, and Russia to restore G8 unity over Iraq in 2004.

Why America Needs the G8

If the G8 still needs America, how much, how, and why does America need the G8? Perhaps in some fields the answer is very little, or even not at all. Penttilä points to how Bush underused the G8 in the response to 11 September, politely declining Silvio Berlusconi's suggestion, inspired by a proposition made by Canada's Paul Martin to Jean Chrétien, that a special emergency G8 summit be held to devise and deliver a collective response (Gray 2003). Fratianni and Kang agree that America's first response to 11 September was a unilateralist 'close the borders' one. Moreover, Rugman argues that in the field of energy, where American vulnerability appears acute, the solution lies in a regional North America response rather than a G8-wide one, through a common North American energy market that develops and gives America access to Canada's Athabaska Tar Sands. In Rugman's estimation, the U.S., as a superpower 'does not need the G8 as much as the G8 needs the United States'.

Yet the classic concert equality model argued that America needed the G8 and all its members as much as the G8 needed an America able and willing to lead (see Appendix 15-1). And most analyses in this volume point to a long list of reasons why the U.S. now needs the G8 much more than ever before. Kirton suggested that the G8 is the continuing in-place 'coalition of the willing' that America can count on, available to multiply its power with that of the world's most capable countries the instant a crisis afflicts a vulnerable America in an interconnected world. The G8 and its members can also serve as America's source of new ideas, such as the role of the private sector in development, a centre of sober second thought, and a loyal opposition that can induce prudence on the part of an assumed America unbound.

Audretsch, Stazinski, and Aldridge show how the U.S. economy now needs a steady inflow of knowledge workers and entrepreneurial capital from its G8 partners and beyond, and, implicitly a G8 dialogue to discover how it can get them while still meeting its homeland security needs. Their analysis points to America's need to meet those needs by concerted G8 action at the terrorists' global source, rather than have America alone do it all at its very shores. The unattractive alternative is for America to foot the whole bill, cope less effectively with the danger already at its gates, and watch its high tech jobs get outsourced to the knowledge workers in foreign countries that America will not let in.

Fratianni and Kang, in their analysis, point to a broader set of reasons why America needs the G8 in the wake of the 11 September terrorist attacks. One reason is to share and thus reduce the heavy costs of providing border security, conducting pre-emptive military action, and closing its borders to trade, physical capital, and human capital inflows that an unilateralist America is incurring in the first instance by acting alone. Another is the way co-ordinated G8 action can produce faster, more similar, and more effective counterterrorist action than the multilateralist dynamic of interdependent strategic decision making can.

In the field of cyberspace, Hart shows how the internet, which started within America in its military institutions, soon became a global network connecting the U.S. to the world, and a network that needed global governance, if America as well as its G8 partners and its global partners were to benefit. His analysis shows that even after 11 September put cybersecurity concerns at the centre of America's attention, the U.S. lacked a unilateralist option in governing the internet.

More broadly, this volume points to broader reasons why the G8 and America need each other, now more than ever. The first is to rescue themselves and the world, from the failure or fragility of the old, heavily legalised, multilateral organisations of the Bretton Woods–United Nations system first formed in 1944–45. The democratic institutional model of G8 effectiveness, developed by Ella Kokotsis (1999) on the basis of reform proposals first advanced by John Ikenberry (1993), argued that G8 effectiveness depended on the availability of such hard law institutions, controlled by G8 members, to put G8 decisions into effect.

Yet the analyses in this volume suggest the many ways in which the old organisations are a hindrance rather than a help. Kirton suggests that the International Atomic Energy Agency (IAEA) was at best a failure and at worst a hindrance to the G8's efforts to stop WMD being acquired by a terrorist-tied Iran. Hart suggests that in governing the many new areas of cyberspace, it was the G8 that was in the vanguard in creating the new institutions, in new forms, required to address this 21st-century need. And both Masciandaro and von Furstenberg show how it was the G8 that created the effective institution needed to combat money laundering.

These analyses offer another reason why the G8 and America increasingly need each other in this new world: to construct together the new defining ideas and principles needed to govern the global community in a complex and uncertain age. The false new consensus model of G8 governance, offered by C. Fred Bergsten and Randall Henning (1996) in the field of finance, suggested that all G8 members were equally imprisoned by a shared, if false, collective belief that, in an era of market-dominant globalisation, collective action on their part was doomed to fail.

Yet the analyses in this volume point in a very different direction. Kirton and Bayne show how George Bush at Sea Island pioneered the bold idea that G8 government acting collectively could bring freedom and democracy, and thus development and peace from terrorism, to the Middle East. Hart shows how, starting at Okinawa, the G8 turned from market-responsive and favourable principles to redistributional and security-centred ones in shaping the governance of cyberspace. Ostry and Ullrich describe a similar sensitivity to redistributional and equity concerns as the G8 ties to complete the Doha Development Agenda successfully. Von Furstenberg highlights how, since 11 September, the G8 is consistently trying to control the market — for private financial transfers — at the most micro level, if with no particular success. The composite image is the G8 as an a highly informal, restricted membership, leader-delivered, club-like international institution, eagerly inventing and applying bold innovative ideas to meet the new challenges of the 21st-century world.

Evolving Perspectives and Evidence on the G8

How well do scholars and policy makers understand these evolving dynamics of adjustment within the G8 and the global governance performance which results? During the past decade, they have relied in the first instance on the traditional four models of the first generation of G8 scholarship — the American leadership, concert equality, democratic institutional, and false new consensus models discussed above and outlined in Appendix 15-1 (Kirton and Daniels 1999, 5). More recently, these first four classic models have been joined by five newcomers, outlined in Appendix 15-2, that seek more to describe and explain G8 performance more adequately in the post–Cold War, rapidly globalising age. The analyses in this volume strongly suggest that all of these newer models, along with some of the old, have much to contribute to understanding how and why the G8 summit and system work well. But most also point to the need for even newer perspectives to account for the G8's role in a rapidly changing and increasingly complex 21st-century world.

Collective Management

The first of the newer models is Bayne's collective management model (Bayne 1999, 2000, 2005). It emphasises the importance of persistent, iterative treatment by the leaders at the G8 summit of the most pressing and intractable global issues, in a world where globalisation is bringing many long domestic issues onto the international agenda, creating a dark side of crime, financial crisis, and inequality as well as opportunity, and outstripping of the existing international organisations to respond. In such a world, the effectiveness of the G8 summit flows from the ability of its undistracted leaders to focus flexibly on a few big issues, and to arrive at an accommodation between America and a now equally powerful Europe, with Japan, Canada, and potentially Russia leading in areas where their interest and capacity are particularly strong.

Consistent with this argument is Kirton's emphasis on the G8's success on its continuing Africa agenda from 2000 to 2004, and his condition that Bush's 2004 bold beginning on Middle East reform be continued at the 2005 Summit and beyond if historic success is to come. Hart, too, suggests that the G8's governance of cyberspace, from the creation of the Dot Force in 2000 to the emphasis on cybersecurity after 11 September was a shared initiative from an equally empowered Japan and EU as well as the United States. Masciandaro points to the constant effort of the G8 and the FATF to modernise, update, and monitor compliance with their money-laundering guidelines. Rugman also affirms that the foundation for collective management is present, through the presence of EU- and Japanese-based MNCs that equal the ones based in the U.S.

But summit success comes not only from persistent iteration from the leaders but also from bold innovative beginnings as on the Middle East in 2004 and Kosovo in 1999, immediate response to crises, such as the 1997–99 Asian-turned-global financial crisis and the 11 September terrorist attacks, and the work of the ever expanding array of G8 institutions at the ministerial and official levels. Rugman sees regional equality in the G8 leading to regional rather than G8-wide co-operation.

Neo-Liberal Hegemonic Consensus

The second newcomer is neo-liberal hegemonic consensus model developed by Stephen Gill (1999). As with the false new consensus model, it privileges the causal importance of the ideas that G7 ministers and leaders share (without the presence of Russia), in determining how the club acts collectively. But rather than deferring to globalised markets that G7 leaders falsely assume renders them impotent, Gill claims that the leaders and their allies in the dominant class deliberately create a form of far-reaching values that enriches them and destroys the values most other share.

This argument is consistent with Sea Island's slighting of most global environmental issues, and perhaps its predominant emphasis on the role of the private sector in development. It is also supported by the G8's early emphasis on a minimally, restrictive, no-tax, and low-regulation approach to cyberspace governance, as Hart describes.

But it is contradicted by the Sea Island Summit's central emphasis on the political values of freedom and democracy in an economically unattractive Middle East and Afghanistan, and its equal attention in the end to the democratic development of Africa as well. Moreover, as Audretsch, Stazinski, and Aldridge emphasise, 11 September brought a sudden and stark new consensus, starting in America, that national closure in the interest of homeland security trumped international openness in the interest of economic growth, at least where mobility for the knowledge works critical to the 21st-century economy was concerned. It is also contradicted by the G8's move, led by Japan and the U.S. in 2000, to emphasise using cyberspace to increase equality across the digital divide. Moreover, Rugman argues that as the U.S. has no long-term interest in the Middle East economy or energy, its war in Iraq and the Middle East initiative at Sea Island were not driven by the ideology or interests of American leaders and their ruling class.

Ginger Group

The third newcomer, introduced by Michael Hodges (1999) and developed by Andrew Baker (2000), sees the G7/8 as an effective 'ginger group'. Here, a small cohesive group of officials deliberate largely in secret, and come to consensus about the new directions that their countries and the institutions and markets that they control should take. This view is supported by the effective response in the late 1990s to global financial crisis and the work of G7 and G8 finance ministers after 11 September to curtail terrorist finance. It is also supported by the fact that the forum of the G7 finance ministers and deputies continued to work very well despite the strains over Iraq that bedevilled the work of the G8 leaders from 2003 and into 2004.

But it is contradicted by the large number of outside countries that are now involved in the work of the G7 and G8 in the finance field. Russia is becoming a regular member of the G7 finance ministers club. China has started attending G7 finance meetings, first at the deputies level and then in the autumn of 2004 for a dinner dialogue with the finance ministers as well. As Masciandaro and von Furstenberg indicate, the G8's work on money laundering and terrorist finance, through the 33-member FATF and elsewhere, has seen effective co-operation flow from a much broader group than the closed, cosy, G7 club of old. More broadly, as Kirton shows, the Sea Island Summit worked well, with the presence of a large number of leaders from both Africa and the Middle East. And within the old G7 core there is still much politically generated division on important finance issues, from debt relief for Iraq to financing for development as a whole.

Group Hegemony

The fourth newcomer is Alison Bailin's (2001; 2005) model of group hegemony. This model suggests that the G8 has acted to replace the old American hegemony with G8-wide group hegemony. The G8 thus provides effective global governance, but in a way that benefits the rich North while it keeps the poor South in an impoverished subordinate class below.

Consistent with the group hegemony model is Masciandaro's insight about how G8 action against countries with lax financial regulations largely punishes the poor, in the interest of securing and enriching the wealthy G8 and industrialised world. Von Furstenberg argues even more strongly that money/value transfer (MVT) systems are designed and operated for the poor in the global South, and that G8 action to control and curtail them thus is done largely in the interests of the North.

Yet this volume also contains much evidence that the G8 has acted deliberately and effectively to reduce rather than perpetuate the old North-South divide. Kirton underscores how the G8 from Genoa to Sea Island called attention to the African agenda, working in many ways to help the world's poorest region benefit from the globalisation that helped many countries and people elsewhere in the world. Indeed, as Kirton and Bayne suggest, at Sea Island, the G8 tried to bring this programme of democratic development from Africa to a long stagnant and conflict-ridden Middle East. Similarly, Hart details how the G8, from the Okinawa Summit onward, turned its concern with cyberspace to help the poor benefit from the digital technologies being developed and adopted in the North.

Meta-Institutionalism

The fifth newcomer is Penttilä's (2003) conception of the G8 as a meta-institution, as advanced and applied in his chapter in this book. This model builds on Michael Hodges's earlier insight that an important role of the G8 summit, after deliberation and direction setting, is to direct issues to appropriate international organisations for attention and action, and to catalyse the work that these other bodies should do (Hodges 1999). In Penttilä's more elaborate and ambitious conception, the G8 is the great global traffic cop, assigning and switching issues to the most appropriate bodies, but also directing these institutions how to deal with them, how to co-operate with other bodies in this task, and how to reform themselves to serve better.

Consistent with Penttilä's conception is Ostry's call for the G8 summit to catalyse the creation of a joint G20-G20 with a mandate to produce a research-based solution to the Doha Development Agenda impasse, and to the even larger trade challenges that lie beyond. This model is further supported by Hart's portrait of the G8 handing off the detailed work of developing its new directions for governing cyberspace and cybersecurity to various established international organisations such as the OECD and UN.

Yet Kirton shows how an America intent on suppressing the G8's lead-up ministerial meetings on the road to Sea Island ended up at the Summit giving birth to a host of new G8 institutions. Hart shows the G8's initiative in creating Dot Force, and Masciandaro and von Furstenberg detail the G7 summit decision in 1989 to create the FATF. Taken together, it appears that as the global community moves into the 21st century, the G8 is increasingly becoming the global governor of first resort. It is not merely the catalyst steering difficult issues to existing organisations. It is now the creator and developer of a new generation of global governance that includes both the innovative ideas and international institutions that the world now needs.

The Need for a New Perspective: Beyond the G8

The shortcomings in these traditional and newer models, as made apparent from the analyses and the arguments in the book, point to the need for a new perspective on the G8, and the core conceptual features of what that new perspective would contain. They highlight in particular the six interconnected central components on which this new perspective on the G8 can be built.

New Problems: The New Demand for Global Governance

This new perspective starts, as its first component, on the demand side, with the new problems, and thus new demands for global governance faced by America and its G8 partners now. The first part of the new problem, already evident in the 1990s, is the new human security challenge bred by the end of the Cold War. It consists of global citizens dying in large numbers within sovereign territorial states that G8 countries, free from the old Cold War constraints, can now save through direct, military intervention as well as many other means (Kirton and Stefanova 2004). Here the G8 has come a long way from the genocide in the Balkans and Rwanda in the early 1990s to the war to liberate Kosovo in 1999. But at Sea Island and after, it still faced the burning issue of what to do about the black, African, Muslim civilians dying in large numbers in Darfur.

The second part of the new problem is the new complexity, uncertainty, and connectedness bred by globalisation in a rapidly changing, tightly wired world. The financial crisis of 1997–99 and the other dark sides of globalisation, such as transnational crime, infectious diseases, environmental degradation, employment, and income inequality, have given rise to a world in which development is tightly connected with conflict prevention and disease control, terrorism with finance and cyberspace, and security with prosperity and freedom. The complexity and uncertainty brought by these top-of-the-agenda connections are compounded by the controversial search to identify and address the root causes that lie below. Here democracy or development, current policies or embedded values, serve as some of the grand dichotomies in this debate over what the real causes are.

The third part of the new problem is the new vulnerability. This consists of the comprehensive, interconnected physical and psychological threats from many distant locations, launched by state or non-state actors with or without intended trajectories and targets, which deeply penetrate even the most powerful polities to terrorise and kill large numbers, in ways that are ultimately uncontrollable by even the world's most capable countries acting alone at home or abroad. A few of its features were evident at the dawn of the air-atomic age, and many more arose as the era of globalisation dawned (Kirton 1993). But 11 September showed how non-state actors located anywhere — and potentially everywhere — could deliberately and successfully strike the world's most powerful country at the very core of its national political capital and national military command centre, do so with unprecedented deadliness, and, starting with anthrax, potentially use WMD that could physically destroy an entire city in a single strike.

Most contributors to this book put the new problems front and centre. Indeed, for virtually all, the long shadow of 11 September looms large indeed. It was the shock of those attacks that helped America and the G8 launch the Doha Development Agenda, to provide a badly needed psychological growth stimulus, to promise development to potentially failing states that could become terrorist havens, and to help show the world that the terrorists would not win as America and its partners retreated into a North Korean–like autarchy behind a complete homeland security, border defence, or perimeter moat. Yet, as Ostry and Ullrich highlight, even if Doha can successfully address the immediate development challenges, the new issues and the new complexity of the trade-plus system present an even wider, deeper, bigger set of issues that need to be addressed, by both the G8 and a broader group.

On a broader vista, Audetsch, Stazinski, and Aldridge highlight how post–Cold War globalisation has placed a premium on the international mobility of knowledge workers and entrepreneurs as a source of American and G8 market-churning turbulence and economic growth. They emphasise how an immigrant-welcoming America in the 1990s reaped the rewards of superior economic growth. But they also highlight how 11 September has led America to close its borders to such workers in the name of homeland security, with little concern for the economic costs.

Fratianni and Kang begin by showing how 11 September was in part the latest installment of a long pattern of terrorism in which America had consistently been target number one. But the threat acquired a new dimension due to the deadliness of the terrorist attacks of 2001, the fear that terrorists would now use WMD, and the fact that the American homeland, indeed its national security command centre in the Pentagon, was now under direct and successful attack. The events of 2001 thus fundamentally altered the attitudes and actions of American policy makers, leading in the first instance to a unilateral impulse with severe security and economic costs. Yet this analysis also shows how America now confronts a much broader set of intrusive enemies — terrorism, WMD, drugs, disease, illegal immigrants, contraband goods, and other unlawful commodities. It further suggests that America's unilateral response breeds problems, through the diversion of terrorists to softer targets, for its G8 partners, and, through trade diversion, to the poorer countries of the Middle East and Islamic world beyond.

Hart shows how globalisation, in the form of private sector–led global connectivity, has driven the G8 to develop a regime that has extended from communication, commerce, privacy, and North-South development to connect, especially after 11 September, to cybersecurity, the war on terror, and the battle for the hearts and minds of those in the Middle East and Islamic world.

Rugman acknowledges that in the short term, control of the global supply and price of oil by the Organization of Petroleum Exporting Countries (OPEC) has made the U.S. as well as its European and Japanese G8 partners sensitive and perhaps in some ways vulnerable, even if long-term solutions for America lie within its own region at home (Keohane and Nye 1977). He further notes the deep transatlantic interdependence between America and Britain in foreign direct investment (FDI), if not in traditional trade measured in the form of sales. His analysis points to the outstanding question of whether the U.S. will move to develop its admittedly high-cost regional solution to its energy security problem, and, if it does, whether it can or would abandon its European and Japanese allies still dependent on Middle East oil.

Masciandaro argues that even countries with lax financial regulations need to be integrated into the now global financial market and that a sanctionist approach by the G8 could thus effectively induce them to comply. Von Furstenberg points to the new vulnerability arising from the new 'enemy within', showing that private terrorist finance operates within all G8 countries, and that through MVT systems, has easy, low-cost global reach that is difficult to detect.

New Players: The Need for Broader Participation

The new problems demand that the old G8 involve new players, if the new problems are to be addressed effectively. Such new players go well beyond the relatively narrow array of private sector financial colleagues, the dominant class interests, and the markets that some of the existing models of G8 governance include. They also extend well beyond the individual non-G8 powers and business communities that some recommend the G8 bring in (Hodges 1999; Bayne 1999). They include, at the G8 summit itself and within the G8 system, the leaders, ministers, and officials of emerging and poor countries, of multilateral organisations, and of civil society actors across a wide multistakeholder range. They point, prospectively, to how the G8 itself might combine as an equal with other similar summit bodies such as the proposed L20. The new analytical challenge is thus to identify the creative combinations of still constricted participation in the G8 core and expanded interaction with many outsiders that most enhance G8 effectiveness and global governance as a whole.

In this volume, Kirton shows that Sea Island succeeded because of, more than despite, the presence of a large number of leaders from a diverse array of very poor countries in Africa, the Middle East, and Afghanistan — which the G8 deemed to be part of the 'greater' or 'broader' Middle East region. Ostry points to the need to work with the two new G20s. Rugman's analysis raises the important question of how individual firms actually conceive their corporate strategies and interests and thus exercise influence through many routes *vis-à-vis* the intergovernmental G8. Here the need is for a more detailed and dynamic analytical lens beyond the limited and somewhat static specifications in the current models about how the business class relates to the G8. Hart shows how the G8 has worked effectively with a host of informal summit-level institutions, such as the Asia-Pacific Economic Cooperation forum, hard law bodies such as the OECD, the World Bank, the International Labour Organization (ILO), and UN, and private sector groups such as the World Economic Forum to develop and adjust the global cyberspace regime. He traces how antiglobalisation forces protesting trade liberalisation at the Seattle ministerial meeting of the World Trade Organization (WTO) in late 1999 had the impact they desired, leading the Okinawa G8 Summit to emphasise the way cyberspace could help narrow the digital divide. The pioneering multistakeholder model proposed by the Dot Force born at that summit moved well beyond the traditional formula of Westphalian intergovernmentalism, with private sector participation in particular producing more sensitive and effective governance that G8 governments can mount on their own. Taken together, this analysis shows that actors well beyond the G8's great power governments are not only increasingly involved and influential at the global level but also work together with one another and with G8 governments to produce better global governance as a result.

New Institutions: The New Institutional Supply of G8-Centred Governance

These new players, coming together to address the new problems, require new institutions to gather them together so they can effectively do their work. The response has come through the third component of the new perspective — the new institutions of a rapidly growing G8 institutional system. There has emerged a new pyramid standing at the centre of global governance. It is composed of a G8 summit flexibly involving selected leaders of outside countries and international organisations, combined with a deep, expanding network of ministerial- and official-level bodies in the G8-centred system where outside countries, international organisations, and actors are involved as permanent equals in the ongoing governance tasks. It is no longer only that there exists — beneath the visible, once-a-year summit — a much larger, largely submerged, and often secret iceberg of a G8 system that operates all year round, on a virtually full array of global, international, and domestic issues. It also now operates largely without the ongoing direction, approval, or even the detailed knowledge of the G8 summit. It can generate initiatives from below that affect the work of those at the very top. And it reaches out in a flexible architecture to involve other countries and actors as the functional task demands. Hierarchy is being reinforced or even replaced by network as the dominant organisational principle of the G8 system as a whole.

This new pyramid has heightened the importance of the existing questions about how, horizontally, the G8 should involve which outsiders, and how, vertically, the G8 summit should relate to the growing array of G8-centred ministerial- and official-level bodies below. But it also raises a new set of integrated horizontal and vertical questions. How should the lower bodies institutionally involve an ever expanding number and type of non-G8 governments and actors as permanent equals? How can the new combinations enhance the effectiveness of the G8 system? How can the broadening from below move upward to increase the effectiveness of the G8 summit itself?

The contributors to this volume offer much evidence of this solid G8-centred pyramid, and that improved G8 and global governance is the general result. Kirton shows that even a determined Bush-led America could not seriously roll back or stop the proliferation of G8 ministerial and official bodies. Indeed, Sea Island added to the expansion to a substantial degree. Nor could Bush stop the G8's new legislative component, initiated by Canada as host of the 2002 Kananaskis Summit in the form of a meeting of the speakers of the G8's legislatures that was continued to be held annually, this time in America in September after the 2004 Sea Island Summit was held — indeed, beyond the direct reach of G8 leaders themselves. Hart shows the contribution made by the G8 justice and interior ministers in several functional and integrated fields. He and others show how the FATF, created by the G7 in 1989, has done useful, if not fully effective work, in an expanding array of fields.

These analyses also point to how this G8-centred system may continue its vibrant growth. There is no global organisation beyond the G8 dedicated to deal with homeland security, let alone its tradeoff and other relationships with knowledge and entrepreneurship-intensive economic growth. It was thus hardly surprising that the U.S. kept the G8 meeting for ministers of justice and home affairs in the lead-up to Sea Island. It is more surprising that they did not deal with how this subject related to economic growth at the Summit itself. Rugman's regionalism also may help explain why the G8 energy ministers forum has not sprung to life as vibrantly as G8 ministerial bodies in many other functional fields have. On a more restricted perspective, Rugman's emphasis on the real-world regionalism that prevails at the firm level constitutes a reminder that the EU has long been a regional intergovernmental actor and has been ever more involved G8 summit and system, and that the inclusion of some form of its equivalents in the form of the North American Free Trade Agreement (NAFTA), the Association of Southeast Asian Nations (ASEAN), or the Asia-Pacific Economic Cooperation (APEC) forum might bring even more actors, agenda items, capabilities, and distinctive assets. Yet identifying what particular combinations of problems, players, and G8-centred institutions yield the best governance results remains an outstanding analytical task.

New Principles: The New Ideational Supply of G8-Centred Governance

If new problems are to be addressed successfully by new players in new groupings, they require not just new international institutions but innovative ideas as well. The fourth component of the new perspective is thus how the G8-centred system — globally and domestically — spreads, absorbs from outside, and creatively blends into more legitimate and effective composite principles and norms distinct from those at the core of the constitutionalised charters of the Bretton Woods–UN global governance system imposed by the small select band of victor powers in 1944-45 (Ikenberry 2001).

Since its 1975 start, the G8's defining commitment to globally protecting and promoting the principles of an 'democratic society, dedicated to individual liberty and social advancement' stood in sharp contrast to the UN Charter's overriding Westphalian attachment to the absolute right of non-interference in the internal affairs of a sovereign state (G7 1975). Since then the G7/8 summit has steadily generated new principles within and across the newly linked policy domains (Kirton 2002). This evolution reached a 20th-century peak in 1999 with the G8's leadership in the war to liberate Kosovo and the launch of a conflict prevention programme (Kirton and Stefanova 2004).

The 21st century has added new dimensions to G8-led ideational innovation at many levels in new ways. New combinations of old physical phenomena have demanded new principles. Most notably, the prospective marriage of non-state terrorism and WMD has led the G8 and many other actors to how the traditional state right of self-defence should extend to conflict prevention, to pre-emptive military action, and to a responsibility to protect, and what new principles need to be constructed and legitimised to guide the global community in these security tasks.

New physical phenomena of globally transformative potential have also required new principles. As Hart's treatment of cyberspace governance highlights, new interconnections and combination of concerns about prosperity and development, security, and freedom and privacy have arisen and have required the G8 and others to generate new principles with little guidance from the past.

New shocks such as 11 September 2001 have forced the G8 to apply its own old principles to new regions in newly intrusive ways. As Kirton suggests, the Sea Island Summit saw G8 leaders focus on how the G8's defining principles of open democracy, individual liberty, and social advance were to be applied to the internal affairs of sovereign states in the Middle East, as well as Africa where the G8 had been similarly at work since 2001.

Such shocks have also forced to G8 members to rethink and reinvent their dominant concepts of causation. They have had to come to a new consensus about how freedom and democracy are the root causes of reducing terrorism and poverty, as well as stopping the interstate wars that led Immanuel Kant to provide a venerable epistemic guide. Sea Island also saw G8 states that had declared and delivered much more money for official development assistance (ODA) in 2002 turn to the role of the private sector in development — not because they lacked the ability or willingness to send official money of their own. They were losing confidence in the causal theory that claimed more money from rich governments, flowing through the heavy, hard law intergovernmental organisations designed in 1944–45 to recipient governments with varying degrees of transparency and accountability, would deliver real development in the end.

The Need for Coherence: The Summit Process as an Important Institutional Variable

When so many new problems, players, institutions, and principles converge, collide, and cluster at the G8 centre of a new global governance system, the predictable result is a new need for coherence. The 1944–45 Bretton Woods–UN system, with its League of Nations legacy and functionalist logic, was deliberately partial, fragmented, and incoherent. It relied formally on the collective power of the five 'After Victory' major powers and informally on American hegemony to provide such coherences as was needed in a slow-moving, loosely wired word. It still remains without serious, strong institutional components to deal with the now critical functions of antiterrorism, hydrocarbon, energy, and the natural environment as an ecological whole (Biermann and Bauer 2005).

In sharp contrast, the G8 offers a better combination of reliable hierarchy, flexible horizontal network, and comprehensive institutional nodes in its multilayered governance. Unlike the 1944–45 architecture, it started at the top, and continues to radiate from there, with annual meetings of national government leaders dealing with a fully flexible, comprehensive agenda. While the UN has adopted the habit of *ad hoc* issue- or theme-specific summitry, it still remains a long way off (Cooper 2004). With a common G8 core, all the G8-centred bodies in the network share a common central note to provide such overall ideational or institutional co-ordination as may be necessary. And the G8 system freely and flexible generates new institutions designed to meet new governance functions as they arise. With the regional and multilateral international governmental organisatons and civil society actors as members of these bodies, starting with the EU's inclusion at the G8 summit level in 1977, the G8 system offers a multistakeholder model more suited to the needs of an embryonic and emerging post-Westphalian age.

Yet it still faces the challenge of how to bring in the old 1944–45 galaxy as a component of the more coherent new G8-centred system. The 1995 Halifax G7 Summit's focus on reforming the Bretton Woods–UN system at the time of the latter's 50th anniversary made only the modest beginning here. It may be that the next serious step will require the talents not just of the G8 but of a broader L20 summit as well.

The Need for New Constructions

If a new generation of global governance is to be created, with such new coherence among the new principles, institutions, players, and problems on which it is based, new theories will be needed to understand and guide the work. This sixth component of new theories requires a move well beyond the realist, liberal institutionalist, and historical materialist offerings that have served so well in the past. It is not merely a matter of modernising, supplementing, or selecting out the old states and international organisations whose capabilities are no longer adequate to the new demands. Some may well have to be actively deconstructed, institutionally and ideationally, and then reconstructed as part of a new order. Unlike the big bangs of 1648, 1713, 1818, 1918, and 1945, there have been no big wars to blow away the old order as a prelude to constructing the new. The victories that the G8 has generated — in end of the Cold War in 1989, over Kosovo in 1999, and prospectively in the war against global terrorism — are not just of different scales but of different kinds. They have led many venerable major powers, or even superpowers, starting with the former Soviet Union and now Russia, to reconstruct their sense of national interest and identity. But even so, their old interests and identities are powerfully held in place by the institutions and ideas of the old heavy, hard law order, staring with the Permanent Five (P5) on the UN Security Council (UNSC) and UN Charter.

This may pose a bigger challenge than the recent constructivist theories have thus far faced. Until now the attention has been on how old countries, interacting and transacting in the face of new problems, can slowly construct new concepts of their national interest and identities, with a transformed international system and new international institutions as the result. The new challenge may be to start with the international institutions as autonomous actors competing within a system of international institutional anarchy. International institutions do not act alone, against only the resistance of their sovereign member countries, to change the dominant concepts of interests and identities that these countries have. They also act alongside and against competing international institutions actively seeking to hold old conceptions in place or bring different new ones to the fore.

The first question would be how and why which institution would best capture a particular country, and transform its conception of national interest and identity in the image the institution prefers. How and why, for example, did the G7/8 and not the P5 persuade Russia in 1999 in the defining Kosovo case, and turn the P5 from being the historic veto-laden defenders of the Slavs to an open democracy instrument ready to accept military intervention in the internal affairs of a sovereign state in order to prevent the eruption of a full-scale genocide — a physical phenomenon constructed as a global problem in 1944? At Evian in 2003 and Sea Island in 2004, did the G8 help bring together, into a new conception of interests and identity, a bloc of countries led by America, and an opposing bloc led by France and Germany, two blocs that had been so divided on the basis of traditional interests and identities by the UN, its Security Council, and the P5 at its core? Could a G8 summit, in a campaign sustained beyond Sea Island, similarly transform Middle East and African countries into peaceful, prosperous, open democracies, not just in the face of intense historical, interstate rivalries, but in the face of the UN and other international institutions that keep the old conceptions of interests and identities so much alive?

A second question would be how can the conception of interests and identities of those international institutions be altered, in their constant Darwinian competition, balancing and forming alliances with one another — before they set to work on their (often overlapping) member states. Will the G8 system transform the UN galaxy into a body committed to open democracy? Or will the UN slowly transform the G8, after the latter's victory in the long Cold War, into a collection of jealous sovereigns increasingly unwilling to interfere in the internal affairs of one another (as opposed to small outsiders such as the former Yugoslavia) to the detriment of the open democracy, individual liberty, and social advance that prevails within? The crucible for this struggle could be the expanding G8-centred global governance system, which increasingly confronts the UN system at every point, including — after Kosovo and 11 September — in the hardest security sphere that the P5, along with the 'superpowers' newly constructed in 1944, long reserved to themselves alone (Fox 1944). At the immediate epicentre could stand the G20 and a prospective, possibly adjusted L20, which brings together as equals all the P5 powers, all the G8 powers, and an equal number of systemically significant newcomer countries from all geographic regions, and most linguistic, cultural, and faith communities of both the democratic and non-democratic world.

References

Bailin, Alison (2001). 'From Traditional to Institutionalized Hegemony'. G8 Governance No. 6. <www.g8.utoronto.ca/scholar/bailin/bailin2000.pdf> (November 2004).

Bailin, Alison (2005). *From Traditional to Group Hegemony*. Ashgate, Aldershot.

Baker, Andrew (2000). 'The G7 as a Global "Ginger Group": Plurilateralism and Four-Dimensional Diplomacy'. *Global Governance: A Review of Multilateralism and International Organizations* vol. 6, no. 2, pp. 165–189.

Bayne, Nicholas (1999). 'Continuity and Leadership in an Age of Globalisation'. In M. R. Hodges, J. J. Kirton and J. P. Daniels, eds., *The G8's Role in the New Millennium*, pp. 21–44. Ashgate, Aldershot.

Bayne, Nicholas (2000). *Hanging In There: The G7 and G8 Summit in Maturity and Renewal*. Ashgate, Aldershot.

Bayne, Nicholas (2005). *Staying Together: The G8 Summit Confronts the 21st Century*. Ashgate, Aldershot.

Bergsten, C. Fred and C. Randall Henning (1996). *Global Economic Leadership and the Group of Seven*. Institute for International Economics, Washington DC.

Bergsten, C. Fred and Caio Koch-Weser (2004). 'The G2: A New Conceptual Basis and Operating Modality for Transatlantic Economic Relations'. In W. Weidenfeld, C. Koch-Weser, C. F. Bergsten, W. Stützle and H. Hamre, eds., *From Alliance to Coalitions: The Future of Transatlantic Relations*, pp. 237–249. Bertelsman Foundation, Gütersloh.

Biermann, Frank and Steffen Bauer, eds. (2005). *A World Environmental Organization: Solution or Threat for Effective International Environmental Governance*. Ashgate, Aldershot.

Cooper, Andrew Fenton (2004). *Tests of Global Governance: Canadian Diplomacy and United Nations World Conferences*. United Nations University Press, Tokyo.

English, John, Ramesh Thakur, and Andrew Fenton Cooper (2005). *A Leaders 20 Summit: Why, How, Who, and When?* United Nations University, Tokyo. Forthcoming.

Fox, William T. R. (1944). *The Super-Powers: The United States, Britain, and the Soviet Union — Their Responsibility for Peace*. Harcourt, Brace, New York.

G7 (1975). 'Declaration of Rambouillet'. 17 November. <www.g8.utoronto.ca/summit/1975rambouillet/communique.html> (November 2004).

Gill, Stephen (1999). 'Structural Changes in Multilateralism: The G7 Nexus and the Global Crisis'. In M. Schechter, ed., *Innovation in Multilateralism*. St. Martin's Press, New York.

Gray, John (2003). *Paul Martin: The Power of Ambition*. Key Porter, Toronto.

Hodges, Michael (1999). 'The G8 and the New Political Economy'. In M. R. Hodges, J. J. Kirton and J. P. Daniels, eds., *The G8's Role in the New Millennium*, pp. 69–74. Ashgate, Aldershot.

Ikenberry, John (1993). 'Salvaging the G7'. *Foreign Affairs* vol. 72 (Spring), pp. 132–139.

Ikenberry, John (2001). *After Victory: Institutions, Strategic Restraint, and the Rebuilding of Order after Major Wars*. Princeton University Press, Princeton.

Kenen, Peter B., Jeffrey R. Shafer, Nigel L. Wicks, et al. (2004). 'International Economic and Financial Cooperation: New Issues, New Actors, New Responses'. Centre for Economic and Policy Research, London. <www.cepr.org/pubs/books/cepr/booklist.asp?cvno=P171> (November 2004).

Keohane, Robert O. and Joseph S. Nye (1977). *Power and Interdependence: World Politics in Transition*. 1st ed. Little, Brown, Boston.

Kirton, John J. (1989). 'Contemporary Concert Diplomacy: The Seven-Power Summit and the Management of International Order'. Paper prepared for the annual meeting of the International Studies Association, 29 March–1 April. London. <www.g8.utoronto.ca/scholar/kirton198901> (November 2004).

Kirton, John J. (1993). 'The Seven Power Summits as a New Security Institution'. In D. Dewitt, D. Haglund and J. J. Kirton, eds., *Building a New Global Order: Emerging Trends in International Security*, pp. 335–357. Oxford University Press, Toronto.

Kirton, John J. (2002). 'Embedded Ecologism and Institutional Inequality: Linking Trade, Environment, and Social Cohesion in the G8'. In J. J. Kirton and V. W. Maclaren, eds., *Linking Trade, Environment, and Social Cohesion: NAFTA Experiences, Global Challenges*, pp. 45–72. Ashgate, Aldershot.

Kirton, John J. and Joseph P. Daniels (1999). 'The Role of the G8 in the New Millennium'. In M. Hodges, J. J. Kirton and J. P. Daniels, eds., *The G8's Role in the New Millennium*, pp. 3–17. Ashgate, Aldershot.

Kirton, John J. and Radoslava Stefanova, eds. (2004). *The G8, The United Nations, and Conflict Prevention*. Ashgate, Aldershot.

Kokotsis, Eleanore (1999). *Keeping International Commitments: Compliance, Credibility, and the G7, 1988–1995*. Garland, New York.

O'Neill, Jim and Robert Hormats (2004). 'The G8: Time for a Change'. Global Economics Paper No. 112. Goldman Sachs, New York. <www.gs.com/insight/research/reports/report15.html> (November 2004).

Penttilä, Risto E.J. (2003). *The Role of the G8 in International Peace and Security*. Oxford University Press, Oxford.

Putnam, Robert (1994). 'Western Summitry in the 1990s: American Perspectives'. *International Spectator* vol. 29, no. April-June, pp. 81–94.

Putnam, Robert and Nicholas Bayne (1984). *Hanging Together: Co-operation and Conflict in the Seven-Power Summit*. 1st ed. Harvard University Press, Cambridge MA.

Putnam, Robert and Nicholas Bayne (1987). *Hanging Together: Co-operation and Conflict in the Seven-Power Summit*. 2nd ed. Sage Publications, London.

Wallace, William (1984). 'Political Issues at the Summits: A New Concert of Powers?' In C. Merlini, ed., *Economic Summits and Western Decisionmaking*. St. Martin's Press, London.

Appendix 15-1
Classic Causal Models of G7/8 Summit and System Performance

American Leadership (Putnam and Bayne 1984, 1987)
Decisional performance, occasionally high, due to:
- the U.S. being able and willing to lead with the support of a strong second
- reigning ideas and historical lessons as interpreted by leaders
- electoral certainty
- transnational actor alliances

Concert Equality (Wallace 1984; Kirton 1989)
Comprehensive performance, high, low, then very high, due to:
- collectively predominant and internally equal capabilities
- equal vulnerability activated by shocks
- common principles of open democracy, individual liberty, and social advancement
- constricted participation
- domestic political capital and control

False New Consensus (Bergsten and Henning 1996)
Decisional performance, declining during the 1990s, due to:
- false new consensus that economic globalisation makes governments impotent
- American economic and political decline due to the end of the Cold War and poor policy
- traditional differences between the U.S. and Germany

Democratic Institutionalism (Ikenberry 1993; Kokotsis 1999)
Delivery performance, increasing into the 1990s, due to:
- effective multilateral organisations controlled by the G7
- G7 institutionalisation at the ministerial and official levels
- strong G8 bureaucratic units in domestic governments
- leaders' commitments to international co-operation, G7 institutions, individual issues
- popular support for leaders and issue

Appendix 15-2
Newer Models of G7/8 Summits and System Performance

Neo-Liberal Hegemonic Consensus (Gill 1999)
Directional and decisional performance, increasingly effective but contested, due to:
- marketisation, globalisation, and liberalisation
- global concentration of wealth and power
- adherence to a similar political outlook and congruent political/economic principles
- financial and asset (bond and currency) market interest dominance in dominant states

Collective Management (Bayne 2000, 2005)
Comprehensive (five function) performance, increasingly effective, due to:
- complexity of new and unexpected global problems
- the inadequacy of other global institutions
- globalisation constraint on independent major power action
- G8 iteration, agenda focus, leaders-only format, institutionalisation

Ginger Group (Hodges 1999; Baker 2000)
Deliberative performance, increasingly effective, due to:
- financial market globalisation
- small private club of governmental agents
- common worldview

Group Hegemony (Bailin 2001, 2005)
Decisional performance, constantly high, due to:
- concentration of power > small group size > designate K-group
- group identity > small group size > designate K-group
- economic liberalism > mutual interests > reach mutual agreements
- preparatory process > mutual interests > reach mutual agreements
- system of interaction > shadow of the future > develop trustworthy relations
- documentation > shadow of the future > develop trustworthy relations

Meta-institution (Penttilä 2003)
Decisional performance, increasingly high, due to:
- concerted power of G8 members
- failure of established international organisations

DOCUMENTARY APPENDICES

Appendix A

Chair's Summary

Sea Island, 10 June 2004

We met at Sea Island for our annual Summit to advance freedom by strengthening international cooperation to make the world both safer and better.

Leaders from Afghanistan, Algeria, Bahrain, Iraq, Jordan, Yemen, and Turkey joined us at Sea Island.

We welcomed the unanimous approval of UN Security Council Resolution 1546 on Iraq. We stand together united in our support for the Iraqi people and the fully sovereign Iraqi Interim Government as they seek to rebuild their nation.

In our discussion of the Broader Middle East and North Africa, we welcomed statements from the region on the need for reform. As the leaders of the major industrialized democracies in the world, we recognize our special responsibility to support freedom and reform, and therefore we committed to:

- Forge a historic Partnership for Progress and a Common Future with the governments and peoples of the Broader Middle East and North Africa.
- Establish together with our partners a Forum for the Future, which will root our efforts in an enduring dialogue in support of the region's reform efforts. The first meeting of the Forum will be held later this year.
- Adopt a G8 Plan of Support for Reform, which commits us to intensify and, in partnership with the region, expand our already strong individual and collective engagements, and launch new initiatives to support: democracy, literacy, entrepreneurship/vocational training, microfinance, and small business financing, among other things.

Our support for reform in the region will go hand in hand with our support for a just, comprehensive, and lasting settlement to the Arab-Israeli conflict. We called upon the Quartet to meet in the region before the end of the month to restore momentum on the Roadmap.

At Evian, we recognized the proliferation of weapons of mass destruction and their delivery systems, together with international terrorism, as the pre-eminent threat to international peace and security. Determined to prevent, contain, and roll back proliferation, we adopted a G8 Action Plan on Nonproliferation to reinforce the global nonproliferation regime. This Action Plan enhances and expands ongoing efforts, such as the Proliferation Security Initiative, which now includes all G8 members, and the

G8 Global Partnership Against the Spread of Weapons and Materials of Mass Destruction. The Action Plan addresses transfers of enrichment and reprocessing equipment and technologies, and takes steps to strengthen the International Atomic Energy Agency and to counter bioterrorism. The Action Plan calls on all states to implement the recently passed U.N. Security Council Resolution 1540, and addresses the proliferation challenges in North Korea, Iran, and Libya.

International terrorism poses a direct challenge to global security and prosperity. We agreed to enhance our counterterrorism efforts by launching the Secure and Facilitated International Travel Initiative (SAFTI) to improve the security and efficiency of air, land, and sea travel. We agreed to new measures to destroy excess stockpiles of Man-Portable Air Defense Systems (MANPADS) and to prevent their proliferation.

We welcomed the increasing strength of the global economy. We agreed it was important to take advantage of the strong global economic environment to implement further reforms to accelerate growth in our countries. We noted the recent pledge by oil producers to increase production. We recognized the need for balanced energy policies, which increase energy supplies and encourage more efficient energy use and conservation, including through new technologies.

We recognized that we face a moment of strategic economic opportunity: by combining the upturn in global growth with a worldwide reduction of barriers to trade, we can deepen, broaden, and extend this economic expansion. Therefore, we directed our ministers, and called on all WTO [World Trade Organization] members, to finalize the frameworks by July to put the WTO negotiations back on track so that we can expeditiously complete the Doha Development Agenda. We welcomed recent progress toward Russia's accession to the WTO. We also recognized the need to fight counterfeiting and piracy of intellectual property.

The challenges faced by Africa, including armed conflict, HIV/AIDS, famine, and poverty, represent a compelling call for international cooperation to support the continent's efforts to achieve lasting progress. We met with the Presidents of Algeria, Ghana, Nigeria, Senegal, South Africa, and Uganda, and we committed to:

- Launch a G8 Action Plan on Expanding Global Capability for Peace Support Operations;
- Adopt a G8 Action Plan on Applying the Power of Entrepreneurship to the Eradication of Poverty;
- Endorse and establish a Global HIV Vaccine Enterprise to accelerate HIV vaccine development. The United States will host later this year a meeting of all interested stakeholders in the Enterprise;
- Take all necessary steps to eradicate polio by 2005 and close the funding gap by our next Summit. We have already closed the funding gap for 2004;
- Launch a new initiative on Ending the Cycle of Famine in the Horn of Africa, Raising Agricultural Productivity, and Promoting Rural Development in Food Insecure Countries; and

- Reaffirm our commitment to fully implementing and financing the Heavily Indebted Poor Countries (HIPC) initiative. We issued a separate statement on HIPC.

Sustainable development requires international cooperation and action on improving our environment. We endorsed the Reduce, Reuse, and Recycle ('3 R's') Initiative.

We supported progress in the multilateral effort against corruption and welcomed the completion of Comprehensive Anti-Corruption Compacts with Georgia, Nicaragua, Nigeria, and Peru. We noted the role information technology can play in promoting transparency.

We also discussed regional challenges, including:

- Afghanistan: We agreed on the need for international support for upcoming Afghan elections and counternarcotics efforts.
- Gaza Withdrawal/Middle East Peace: We issued a separate statement on Gaza Withdrawal and the Road Ahead to Middle East Peace.
- Haiti: We discussed how to meet Haiti's urgent needs for budget support, electricity, and police, and called on all donors to do their utmost to provide support at the July donors' conference and to effect a sustainable future for this country.
- North Korea: We addressed the DPRK [Democratic People's Republic of Korea] nuclear issue in our G8 Action Plan on Nonproliferation. We support the Six-Party Talks as well as efforts by all concerned parties to achieve a comprehensive solution by diplomatic means to the DPRK nuclear issue and to other security and humanitarian issues, such as the abductions.
- Sudan: We issued a separate statement on Sudan.

We welcomed the offer of the Prime Minister of the United Kingdom to host our next Summit in 2005.

Appendix B

G7 Finance Ministers and Central Bank Governors Meeting

Boca Raton, Florida, 6–7 February 2004

Statement
7 February 2004

The global economic recovery has strengthened significantly since our meeting in Dubai and risks have diminished. Growth projections for 2004 have been revised upward to their highest in three years. Fiscal and monetary policies have helped bring about these welcome changes.

Yet much more remains to be done. The pace of growth among our economies remains uneven. In our Agenda for Growth initiative, we emphasize supply-side structural policies that increase flexibility and raise productivity growth and employment. Today we released a progress report on our Agenda for Growth. This Agenda and sound fiscal policies over the medium-term are key to addressing global current account imbalances. We outlined strategies for sustained medium-term fiscal consolidation as economies recover. International trade is vital; we call for further efforts and for countries to take the steps to resume the Doha Round, which is pivotal to global growth and the alleviation of world poverty.

We reaffirm that exchange rates should reflect economic fundamentals. Excess volatility and disorderly movements in exchange rates are undesirable for economic growth. We continue to monitor exchange markets closely and cooperate as appropriate. In this context, we emphasize that more flexibility in exchange rates is desirable for major countries or economic areas that lack such flexibility to promote smooth and widespread adjustments in the international financial system, based on market mechanisms.

To combat terrorist financing, we urge all countries to strengthen their asset freezing regimes and to combat abuse of the informal financial sector and non-profit organizations. The IMF [International Monetary Fund]/World Bank should make permanent and comprehensive their assessments of countries' efforts to combat terrorism financing.

We are committed to further enhance transparency and supervisory standards in financial markets, in particular non-compliant off-shore centers.

We have a shared interest in seeing strengthened economic growth in the greater Middle East. We had a productive meeting with our counterparts from Afghanistan and Iraq. We welcome the completion of the currency exchange in Iraq and the removal of interest rate controls, and we look forward to the approval of the new central bank law. We welcome progress on reform and reconstruction in Afghanistan and the renewed efforts to collect revenues from the provinces. We call on others to join us in reducing the debt burdens of Iraq and Afghanistan. We welcome the plans of the IMF and the World Bank to provide financial and technical assistance to Iraq and Afghanistan.

The private sector plays a critical role in fighting global poverty and creating jobs in developing countries. We encourage the MDBs [multilateral development banks] to work with governments to improve investment climates and provide more resources to support the private sector. Remittances are an important source of income for many developing economies. We aim to reduce the impediments that raise the cost of sending remittances. We reaffirm our commitment to fight global poverty and to help countries achieve the international development goals of the Millennium Declaration through our work on debt sustainability, aid effectiveness, absorption capacity, and financing facilities.

We discussed the progress in our efforts to reform the international financial system, including improved surveillance, collective action clauses, limits on exceptional access, measuring results, and the use of other mechanisms, including grants, to avoid heavy debt burdens. We also discussed how to consolidate and build upon these reforms. We welcome the improvement in financial conditions, and the higher economic growth in many emerging market countries. We welcome the efforts by creditors and issuing countries to develop a code of conduct, which will be discussed in the G20. We call on Argentina to implement policies in line with its IMF program. Argentina should engage constructively with its creditors to achieve a high participation rate in its restructuring.

Action Plan on Afghanistan
Boca Raton, Florida, 7 February 2004

We met today with the Finance Minister and Central Bank Governor of Afghanistan, and we agreed on steps to support the Afghan Government's efforts to accelerate the creation of a dynamic market economy and to secure Afghanistan's future. The G7 will continue to support the Government's development priorities in accordance with the National Development Framework. To that end, we will provide assistance that will produce visible and measurable results before June, as part of our long-term commitment to the country.

Human Capital: Afghanistan is making significant commitments to education and healthcare. The G7 will continue to support these efforts to invest in Afghanistan's most valuable assets — its children — by building schools, training teachers, and providing textbooks. The G7 will also continue to help the Government build additional health care facilities, and to support efforts to improve the status of women in Afghanistan.

Physical Capital: Improving the country's infrastructure, including its transport, electricity, and telecommunications systems, is a priority for the Afghan Government. We will help it reach its goals — such as a doubling of the percentage of paved roads in six years — by completing the Kandahar-Herat highway, and by supporting the efforts of international bodies to complete, by the end of 2004, roads they are constructing.

Private Sector Development: We will continue to support the Government's efforts to foster a climate where the private sector can flourish, including by providing assistance to the Government on trade and investment, and supporting microfinance lending. We urge bilateral and multilateral institutions to consider what support they can provide to those wanting to do business in and with Afghanistan, within their rules and Afghanistan's capacity.

Economic Governance: We will support the Government's efforts to ensure an adequate revenue base through improvements in provincial revenue collection, and to strengthen expenditure management, internal debt management systems and statistical capacity. We will provide technical assistance to support the Government's strengthening of key institutions and improvement of the civil service, and will also work with all creditors to ensure that Afghanistan's debt situation is sustainable, and with bilateral donors to provide as much assistance as possible in the form of grants.

Security and Rule of Law: The Government has noted the risks to private sector development and to the well-being of the Afghan people arising from weak security and rule of law. We will continue to support the Government in its efforts to address these problems, including through reforms to the police and legal systems; the disarmament, demobilization and reintegration of excombatants; and expanding security outside Kabul through the Provincial Reconstruction Teams. We recognize that opium production poses a major threat to security, economic growth and reconstruction in Afghanistan. We call upon the international community and the Afghan authorities to join together to eliminate opium production.

Finally, we pledge to provide support to Afghanistan over both the short and long term, and to help ensure the success of the international conference in March. We will increase our assistance, through bilateral and multilateral efforts, such as the Afghanistan Reconstruction Trust Fund.

Agenda for Growth Progress Report
Boca Raton, Florida, 7 February 2004

In September 2003, we adopted the Agenda for Growth initiative to focus our efforts on the need to undertake supply-side and structural policy changes to increase flexibility, raise productivity growth and employment, and achieve higher, sustained growth in our countries. Such reforms sometimes may entail short-term costs, but have proven critical to advancing long-term growth. We also committed to experience-sharing, to reviewing our results together, and to reporting on our progress. Our focus is on cooperation. Today, in Boca Raton, we reviewed our accomplishments thus far and outlined our future priorities. In this Progress Report, we list selected accomplishments since September 2003 — one for each country — and review upcoming reform plans.

Accomplishments since September: Germany enacted key elements of the reform Agenda 2010, including labor market measures that improve work incentives and further tax reduction. Canada completed the full implementation of its five-year, $100 billion tax reduction plan. Japan formulated a pension reform plan in December 2003 with a view to securing long-term sustainability of the pension system, and is preparing for legislation to implement the reform. France is implementing key provisions of its pension reform law that significantly improves the sustainability of its public finances. The United Kingdom announced new measures to help small business raise finance and to help promote a culture of enterprise, and to improve access to its R&D [research and development] tax credit. Tax rate cuts in the United States worked their way through the economy to promote record growth. Italy's recent labor market reforms entered fully into force in October, contributing to the further reduction in the unemployment rate.

Upcoming Reform Plans: Our governments remain committed to pursuing additional pro-growth policies. The United States plans to spur saving by creating lifetime and retirement savings accounts and reducing the structural budget deficit, and to support job creation by making health care more affordable and pressing for tort reform. In an effort to raise productivity, the United Kingdom is targeting reductions in enterprise regulatory requirements including a collaborative initiative on regulatory reform across the EU over the next two years, establishing a long-term strategy for funding innovation and scientific research, and extended skills training programs. While continuing its steady reduction in the debt-to-GDP [gross domestic product] ratio, Canada will provide municipalities with the resources they need for infrastructure investment by exempting them from the Goods and Services Tax they now pay (worth $7 billion over the next decade) and examining other fiscal mechanisms to provide further predictable funding. Italy expects to push forward with its pension and corporate tax reform, including tax exemptions on dividends and capital gains, in 2004. France plans to advance health care reforms this year, while continuing to press for fewer labor market constraints. Japan will work on further fiscal expenditure and revenue reforms, including in social security, and will continue to address financial sector reforms. Pension and tax code reform remain key priorities in Germany, combined with further improvements in the framework for innovation.

Appendix C

G7 Finance Ministers and Central Bank Governors Meeting

Washington DC, 23–24 April 2004

Joint Statement on Combating Terrorist Financing
Washington DC, 23 April 2004

The fight against terrorism is our common fight and we encourage all nations to participate fully in the international effort to choke off its financing. The recent tragedies in Madrid and Riyadh show clearly that we cannot relax our vigilance and must not slacken our resolve or our efforts to combat this scourge. As international financial leaders, we have special responsibilities for the domestic and multilateral fight against terrorist financing and for protecting the integrity of the global financial system. We have made significant progress in this struggle, but much more needs to be done.

We met here today to review progress, advance priorities, and pledge our continuing cooperation to deny terrorists access to our financial systems.[1]

We welcome the recent decisions by the IMF [International Monetary Fund] and World Bank to make comprehensive assessments of country compliance with the recognized anti-terrorist financing/anti-money laundering standard a regular part of their activities. We urge more capacity building through technical assistance to shore up identified gaps in the regimes to fight terrorism finance and money laundering. We also note with satisfaction the FATF's [Financial Action Task Force] decision to expand dialogue with non-members and its February 2004 terrorist financing conference.

We will continue our efforts to achieve the worldwide implementation of the international standards to combat terrorist financing. We will work to ensure that our asset freezing regimes are effective and requests to take asset freezing action are communicated, implemented, and enforced in our jurisdictions fully and without delay. We will support efforts to make the formal financial sector more accessible and less costly while seeking to enhance the transparency of existing informal financial systems. We will work with our charitable sectors to promote awareness of terrorist financing and to develop and implement effective measures to protect charities from potential abuse. We recognize the danger posed by terrorist financiers using cash couriers or transferring cash across borders and undertake to combat this growing threat by strengthening the control of cross-border cash movements.

We pledge our best efforts to keep terrorists from raising, holding, transferring, or using financial assets to carry out their inhumane acts. We will work quickly and decisively to implement measures that the United Nations has identified as essential to combating terrorist financing. We will work with the international financial institutions, FATF, and other multilateral bodies to implement internationally recognized standards pertaining to terrorist financing, money laundering and financial sector regulation and supervision.

Note

1. G7 Finance Ministers and Central Bank Governors met today with Ministers or Governors from China, India, Indonesia, Malaysia, Morocco, Pakistan, Philippines, Russia, Saudi Arabia, Singapore, Spain, and United Arab Emirates, the heads of the IMF and the World Bank, the European Commission, and the President of the Financial Action Task Force on Money Laundering (FATF) to intensify the fight against terrorist financing. The Ministers and Governors have met with non-G7 colleagues on this issue twice before, in Washington in April 2002 and in Dubai in September 2003, in addition to having their own regular discussions since September 2001.

Statement
Washington DC, 24 April 2004

The global economic recovery continued to strengthen and broaden since we met in February. Prospects are favorable, and although risks remain, such as energy prices, overall the balance of risks to the outlook has improved. Additional pro-growth reforms are essential to deliver stronger and more balanced global growth, boost employment, and raise incomes. As part of the Agenda for Growth, we discussed our priorities for tax and labor market reform. We reaffirmed our commitment to sound public finances and monitored implementation of strategies for sustained medium term fiscal consolidation as economies recover. Progress in these fiscal areas and in the Agenda for Growth are key to addressing current global imbalances. To deliver faster and more widespread global growth, and to fight global poverty, rapid progress on and early conclusion of the Doha Round is imperative and will require action by all parties to resolve key outstanding issues.

We reaffirm that exchange rates should reflect economic fundamentals. Excess volatility and disorderly movements in exchange rates are undesirable for economic growth. We continue to monitor exchange markets closely and cooperate as appropriate. In this context, we emphasize that more flexibility in exchange rates is desirable for major countries or economic areas that lack such flexibility to promote smooth and widespread adjustments in the international financial system, based on market mechanisms.

Economic fundamentals have improved in many emerging market countries. Yet, sustained and sound policies are essential to support lasting growth and reduce external vulnerabilities. In the case of Argentina, progress has been made, but further progress is required.

In developing countries, the private sector is key to growth and poverty reduction. Small businesses play a critical role, but unfavorable business climates are often a constraint. We call on MDBs [multilateral development banks] to accelerate the development of joint action plans with governments to improve investment climate and to scale up their support for small businesses with specific measurable results. The G7 met entrepreneurs from developing countries and reiterated support for their efforts. We urge private sector views to be consistently included in MDB assistance plans. On remittances, we will continue to work on our initiatives to reduce barriers that raise the cost of sending them and to integrate remittance services in the formal financial sector. We are committed to working with governments, the private sector, and MDBs to broaden the access for families and entrepreneurs to financial services.

Official development assistance, including more effective use of grants, will remain key. We reaffirm our commitment to fight global poverty and to help countries achieve the international development goals of the Millennium Declaration through our work on debt sustainability, aid effectiveness, absorption capacity, and financing facilities.

As part of the preparation for the Sea Island Summit and to mark the 60th anniversary of the Bretton Woods Institutions, we continued our Strategic Review of these institutions. Our focus is on giving clarity to official sector policy and objectives, increasing accountability, and country ownership. We are committed to improving the delivery and results of their programs and policies.

We met again with Ministers from key countries to strengthen the fight against terrorist financing. We call on all countries to meet their commitments to tighten asset freezing regimes, to prevent abuse of non profit organizations, and to stop cash transfers used to finance terror. We strongly welcomed the IMF/World Bank commitment to comprehensive assessments. We reaffirmed our commitment to further enhance transparency and supervisory standards in financial markets, in particular non-compliant off-shore centers.

Economic growth and job creation in the greater Middle East are a shared priority. We will meet with regional Ministers this evening to discuss their reform efforts and regional economic integration including through financial reform and private sector growth. We stand ready to assist Iraq, Afghanistan, and West Bank and Gaza in their development efforts. We reviewed progress on the Afghanistan Action Plan, including the positive results of the Berlin conference. We call on others to join us in reducing the debt burdens of Iraq and Afghanistan.

Appendix D

G7 Finance Ministers and Central Bank Governors Meeting

New York, 23 May 2004

We met to prepare for the annual economic summit of our leaders. The summit is taking place at a time when the world economy is strong. The recovery is proceeding rapidly, with global growth of around 4.25 percent in 2003–04, the best growth rate in the world economy in the last 15 years. Sound pro-growth policies in our countries have contributed to this recovery through such measures as tax reform, more flexible labor, product, and capital markets, reduced regulatory burdens, pension reforms, and strengthened financial sectors and macroeconomic policy frameworks.

There is now a strong foundation for our leaders to enhance their cooperation and to advance the Agenda for Growth initiative to bolster job creation and productivity growth. We will work to implement labor market reforms, reduce regulatory and legal burdens, support entrepreneurship and innovation, and pursue healthcare reform. We reaffirm our commitment to sound public finances.

Yet risks to the outlook remain. Lower oil prices would benefit the world economy. We welcome the recent announcements by some oil producers to increase production. We now call on all oil producers to provide adequate supplies to ensure that world oil prices return to levels consistent with lasting global economic prosperity and stability, in particular for the poorest developing countries. Progress on trade liberalization is also critical to an improving world economy. We reaffirm our commitment to rapid progress on and early conclusion of the Doha round.

Remittance flows at $100 billion per year support families and finance small businesses in developing countries, making them a key factor for growth and poverty reduction in these countries. We are engaged in overcoming institutional impediments to the transmission and receipt of remittances, improving financial education, increasing the range of services, and promoting partnerships to strengthen their development impact.

Entrepreneurship is essential for development. Financial and technical assistance are core elements of our efforts to support small business, and we have asked the MDBs [multilateral development banks] to scale up these programs. We urge MDBs to work with bilateral donors and developing countries to develop and implement action plans to remove legal and regulatory obstacles to investment.

Economic reforms are underway in the broader Middle East and North Africa. We discussed ways to support the region's initiatives to improve the investment climate, support private sector growth, and provide effective technical assistance. A policy dialogue, focused on economic and financial issues based on regional ownership, is an effective mechanism to support reform in the region. We will meet again with regional Ministers this fall.

We discussed our Strategic Review of the World Bank and IMF [International Monetary Fund] and are gratified by the positive response we have received already. The goals of the Bretton Woods institutions are to promote economic and financial stability, raise economic growth, and fight poverty. We are pleased with recent reforms, including limits on exceptional access, enhanced surveillance, streamlined conditionality, collective action clauses, grants, and measurable results management. However, given the depth of change in the world economy, the institutions must reform further if they are to achieve their goals. At the time of their 60th anniversary, we believe that these reforms should be broadened on the basis of the principles of accountability and good governance, transparency, clarity of objectives and responsibility, and effective working with markets. We will continue to engage with the institutions and their shareholders on how they should best respond to these challenges.

We reaffirmed our strong commitment to debt sustainability in the poorest countries through debt relief and grants. We are committed to the full implementation of the HIPC [heavily indebted poor countries] initiative, including the provision of topping up relief where appropriate. We will bring forward proposals to address these issues.

Appendix E

G7 Finance Ministers and Central Bank Governors Meeting

Washington DC, 1–3 October 2004

Statement
Washington DC, 1 October 2004

We thank the United States for presiding over the G7 this past year and we are gratified by the international economic cooperation that has resulted in new initiatives such as the Agenda for Growth, the Strategic Review, the Global Remittance Initiative, and new G7 outreach to both the Broader Middle East and North Africa countries and to China. We welcome the United Kingdom to the G7 presidency in 2005, and we will continue to work together on these and new initiatives.

Global economic growth is strong and the outlook for 2005 remains favorable. Inflation and inflation expectations remain low in our economies. However, this is not the time for complacency. Growth is higher in some regions than in others; imbalances persist. Oil prices remain high and are a risk. So first, we call on oil producers to provide adequate supplies to ensure that prices moderate. Second, it is important consumer nations increase energy efficiency. Third, it is important for consumers and producers that oil markets function efficiently and we encourage the IEA [International Energy Agency] to enhance its work on oil data transparency. We will return to the issue of medium term energy demand and supply at our next meeting.

We reaffirmed our commitment to sound public finances and to strategies for sustained medium term fiscal consolidation. Today we released a new report on our Agenda for Growth in which we agreed to make pro-growth structural reforms a regular part of our work to create more jobs and increase productivity. We welcome recent progress on the Doha Development Round.

We reaffirm that exchange rates should reflect economic fundamentals. Excess volatility and disorderly movements in exchange rates are undesirable for economic growth. We continue to monitor exchange markets closely and cooperate as appropriate. In this context, we emphasize that more flexibility in exchange rates is desirable for major countries or economic areas that lack such flexibility to promote smooth and widespread adjustments in the international financial system, based on market mechanisms.

We remain firmly committed to continue to cooperate in combating terrorist financing, which is essential for reducing the risks of terrorist attacks.

Emerging market economies generally face favorable financial conditions; interest rate spreads are low and volatility is down in many markets. We urge emerging market countries to take advantage of the favorable global economic conditions to lessen their vulnerability to external shocks. We urge the Argentine authorities to implement, as soon, as possible the prior actions required for the completion of the Third Review while fulfilling its current obligations fully and timely. Argentina's key challenges remain structural reforms, building a sound fiscal framework, and achieving high creditor participation in a sustainable debt restructuring. We welcome the approval by the IMF of a sound and credible program for Iraq, which is an important step toward our commitment to resolve Iraq's debt before the end of 2004. We welcome the financial assurances given by Iraq's creditors that made this IMF [International Monetary Fund] program possible.

We continue to support efforts to increase economic growth and reduce poverty in poor countries. We welcome the agreement to increase funding for the Asian Development Fund and we look forward to new replenishments of the African Development Fund and IDA [International Development Association]. We reaffirm our commitment to fight global poverty and to help countries achieve the international development goals of the Millennium Declaration through our work on debt sustainability, aid effectiveness, absorption capacity, and financing facilities. There is a need for additional financial aid grounded on the principles of good policies, debt sustainability, accounting for results, and enhancing predictability and aid effectiveness. We encourage the development banks to provide quantifiable indicators and results for all projects, and to make them publicly available. We are now committed to addressing the sustainability of debt of the poorest countries by making progress on debt relief and grant financing. We will prepare a progress report on these efforts by the end of the year.

G8/Broader Middle East and North Africa Finance Ministers' Meeting Washington DC, 1 October 2004

This morning, I hosted a meeting of finance and other economics ministers from the G8 and countries of the Broader Middle East and North Africa (BMENA). This meeting continues a dialogue pursued in September 2003 and April 2004 as well as provides an opportunity to further prepare for the first meeting of the Forum for the Future that leaders from the G8 and the region called for in Sea Island. I stressed that economic freedom can best harness the region's rich human and natural resources to meet the aspirations of its people for jobs and improving living standards. Redefining the role of the state in the economy and allowing people more freedom in their economic decisions will provide them the incentives and opportunities to improve their lives.

Ministers welcomed the strong growth in economies in the region. They agreed it was important to take advantage of the strong global economic environment to implement further reforms to accelerate growth and job creation in our countries. They also welcomed the recent pledge by oil producers to increase production as a contribution to global economic stability.

Ministers from the G8 and BMENA region committed to work together to support market-oriented economic reforms, many of which they noted are already underway. They all stressed that is vitally important that reform be home-grown and initiated within the region, with strong ownership. They also stressed the importance of peace and security for private sector investment led growth. Our support for reform in the region will go hand in hand with our support for a just, comprehensive, and lasting settlement to the Arab-Israeli conflict, based upon U.N. Resolutions 242 and 338.

Ministers highlighted the importance of developing small and medium sized businesses (SMEs) and the private sector generally through targeted policy reforms and technical assistance. In particular, the ministers welcomed the launch of the International Finance Corporation's (IFC) new facility for technical assistance to support development of small businesses and the private sector in the region, which was approved by the IFC Board on September 28. Donors have already pledged at least $32.4 million to the facility, and additional donors have indicated plans to contribute. The IFC has also devoted $20 million of its own resources.

Ministers also agreed to enhance dialogue on economic and trade issues and assess the effectiveness and levels of development assistance to countries of the region. To this end, they asked experts from participating countries and both the regionally based and other development institutions to study and develop a network of funds, taking into consideration existing regional coordination mechanisms and as proposed by G8 and regional leaders in Sea Island, to advise G8 and regional governments on economic growth and job creation and to provide a forum for improved cooperation in improving effectiveness of official financing.

One priority stressed by regional ministers was the need to strengthen human capital and the institutional capacity of governments for development and reform. They asked the Arab Monetary Fund, International Monetary Fund, Arab Fund for Economic and Social Development, Islamic Development Bank and World Bank to consult with interested countries, other official donors, and other institutions active in the region to identify and survey jointly top priorities for technical assistance, particularly monetary, fiscal and financial sector, on a country by country basis and produce a prioritized list for regional governments, G8 and official donors.

To meet the goals of sustained growth, job creation and diversification, ministers underscored the central importance of enhancing the integration of the BMENA region into the global economy. In particular, ministers:

- Supported the ongoing efforts of BMENA countries at the meeting to join the WTO [World Trade Organization].
- Agreed to discuss at future meetings how each country's ongoing reforms are strengthening its investment climate, with a view to improving certain quantitative indicators that it selects, drawing on work underway in the region.

Regional representatives stressed the need for their economies to be better integrated into the global economy, including through improved opportunities for trade both within the region and with industrial countries. Some Ministers highlighted the importance of financial services liberalization.

All the G8 and BMENA ministers looked forward to the launch of the Forum for the Future to initiate a broad dialogue among their countries. Ministers welcomed the Kingdom of Morocco's offer to host the inaugural meeting of the Forum later this year. The finance and economics ministers agreed to continue their dialogue and participate in the Forum for the Future.

Statement on the Meeting of the G7 Finance Ministers and Central Bank Governors with Chinese Counterparts
Washington DC, 1 October 2004

The G7 Finance Ministers and Central Bank Governors met informally with China's Finance Minister and Central Bank Governor. They discussed the global economic outlook, macroeconomic policies in G7 economies and the Chinese economic situation in a candid way. Among other things, they exchanged views on economic impact of oil prices, fiscal and monetary policies in G7 economies, Asian economic outlook, and exchange rate flexibility. It was agreed that this meeting was a constructive channel to share views on issues of mutual concern and to promote mutual understandings.

Appendix F

G20 Finance Ministers and Central Bank Governors Meeting

Berlin, 20–21 November 2004

1. We, the Finance Ministers and Central Bank Governors of the G20, held our sixth meeting in Berlin, Germany. Our meeting confirmed the growing sense of common purpose and shared views and responsibility which has developed within the G20 over the last years.
2. We welcomed the favourable macroeconomic environment in the world economy with high growth at low inflation rates. We expect that the macroeconomic environment will remain favourable in the next year. Many countries are implementing structural reforms to foster sustainable growth and financial stability. However, downside risks have increased due to oil price volatility, persisting external imbalances and geo-political concerns. Co-operation between oil producers and consumers to ensure adequate supply, investment to expand oil production capacity, improvements in oil market transparency, greater energy efficiency and wider use of alternative sources of energy will contribute to improving the resilience and sustainability of the international economy and to more moderate oil prices in the medium term. We also discussed the impact of current macro-economic conditions, in particular oil prices, on many of the poorest countries and the adverse effects on their development prospects. We underscored the importance of medium-term fiscal consolidation in the United States, continued structural reforms to boost growth in Europe and Japan, and, in emerging Asia, steps towards greater exchange rate flexibility, supported by continued financial sector reform, as appropriate.
3. We reaffirmed our commitments made in Morelia towards the progress of developed and developing countries on implementation of the Monterrey Consensus and the Millennium Development Goals. We welcomed recent work by the World Bank and the IMF [International Monetary Fund] on the need and mechanisms for financing for development.
4. We agreed that our goal of improving welfare and employment in our countries calls for strong and sustained growth worldwide. We therefore had a thorough exchange of views on growth-enhancing strategies. Building on our own experiences as well as on our discussions on institution-building in the financial sector, on regional cooperation and integration and on demographic challenges,

we today reached an accord on a number of common principles for domestic policies which would help to foster sustained economic growth if implemented consistently and with due regard to country-specific circumstances. We will translate this G20 Accord into concrete action through measures such as found in the attached G20 Reform Agenda, and we will regularly review the progress towards implementation. We are agreed that such policy reforms need to be supported by a robust and effective international financial and trade architecture that delivers fair access to markets. In this respect, we are committed to a quick resolution and effective implementation of the Doha Round.

5. Based on an exchange of experience over the past two years, we emphasised that strong domestic financial sectors are essential in supporting economic growth and reducing external vulnerabilities.

We agreed that high priority should be given to establishing stable and efficient institutions. Progress in institution building is also important for a well-sequenced liberalisation of the capital account. Emphasis must be given to implementing the relevant internationally recognised standards and codes. We highlighted the crucial role of financial sector supervision, which should pay due regard to efficiency, operational independence and accountability of the agencies involved. We welcomed the efforts of the World Bank to develop principles and guidelines for effective insolvency and creditor rights systems and we commend efforts to develop a unified international standard in this area, in collaboration with UNCITRAL, that takes into account different legal traditions.

We identified stable and efficient payment systems as pivotal for the financial infrastructure and emphasised the role of central banks as a supplier and overseer of payment services.

We welcomed the efforts of the IMF, the World Bank and others in promoting institution-building and the development of local capacity and agreed on the importance of closely coordinating such activities.

Bibliography

Africa Action (2004). 'Africa Action Dismisses "Misdirected" G8 Announcements on Africa'. 10 June. <www.africaaction.org/newsroom/release.php?op=read&documentid=563&type=2> (November 2004).

Alden, Edward (2004). 'Visa Delays Cost Corporate America "More than Dollars 30bn" over Two Years'. *Financial Times*, 2 June, p. 1.

Alden, Edward (2004). 'Washington Launches Border Control Review'. *Financial Times*, 23 April, p. 2.

Alexander, Kern (2001). 'The International Anti-Money Laundering Regime: The Role of the Financial Action Task Force'. *Journal of Money Laundering Control* vol. 4, no. 3, pp. 231–248.

Alldridge, Peter (2001). 'Are Tax Evasion Offences Predicate Offences for Money Laundering Offences?' *Journal of Money Laundering Control* vol. 4, no. 4, pp. 350–359.

Allison, Graham (2004). 'Loose Nukes: The Eight Spoke Loudly, and Did Little'. *International Herald Tribune*, 12 June.

Allison, Graham, Karl Kaiser, and Sergei Karaganov (2001). 'The World Needs a Global Alliance for Security'. *International Herald Tribune*, 21 November.

Alworth, Julian and Donato Masciandaro (2004). 'Public Policy: Offshore Centres and Tax Competition—The Harmful Problem'. In D. Masciandaro, ed., *Global Financial Crime: Terrorism, Money Laundering, and Offshore Centres*, pp. 181–217. Ashgate, Aldershot.

Anderson, James E. and Eric van Wincoop (2003). 'Gravity with Gravitas: A Solution to the Border Puzzle'. *American Economic Review* vol. 93, no. 1, pp. 170–193.

Annan, Kofi (2003). 'Secretary-General's Remarks to Open the Meeting of the G8 Contact Group on Food Security in Africa'. New York, 5 March. <www.un.org/apps/sg/printsgstats.asp?nid=272> (November 2004).

Antholis, William (2001). 'Pragmatic Engagement or Photo Op: What Will the G8 Become?' *Washington Quarterly* vol. 24, no. 3, pp. 213–226.

Arrow, Kenneth J. (1962). 'Economic Welfare and the Allocation of Resources for Invention'. In R. R. Nelson, ed., *The Rate and Direction of Inventive Activity*, pp. 609–626. Princeton University Press, Princeton, NJ.

Artis, Michael and Sylvia Ostry (1986). 'International Economic Policy Coordination'. Chatham House Paper 30, Royal Institute of International Affairs. London.

Atwood, J. Brian, Robert S. Browne, and Princeton Lyman (2004). 'Freedom, Prosperity, and Security: The G8 Partnership with Africa, Sea Island 2004 and Beyond'. May. Council on Foreign Relations, New York.

Audretsch, David B. (1995). *Innovation and Industry Evolution*. MIT Press, Cambridge.

Audretsch, David B. and Maryann P. Feldman (1996). 'R&D Spillovers and the Geography of Innovation and Production'. *American Economic Review* vol. 86, no. 3, pp. 630–640.

Audretsch, David B. and Max Keilbach (2004). 'Entrepreneurship Capital: Determinants and Impact'. Max Planck Institute for Research into Economic Systems. Jena. <econpapers.hhs.se/paper/esiegpdis/2004-37.htm> (November 2004).

Audretsch, David B. and Paula E. Stephan (1996). 'Company-Scientist Locational Links: The Case of Biotechnology'. *American Economic Review* vol. 86, no. 3, pp. 641–652.

Bailin, Alison (2001). 'From Traditional to Institutionalized Hegemony'. G8 Governance No. 6. <www.g8.utoronto.ca/scholar/bailin/bailin2000.pdf> (November 2004).

Bailin, Alison (2005). *From Traditional to Group Hegemony*. Ashgate, Aldershot.

Baker, Andrew (2000). 'The G7 as a Global "Ginger Group": Plurilateralism and Four-Dimensional Diplomacy'. *Global Governance: A Review of Multilateralism and International Organizations* vol. 6, no. 2, pp. 165–189.

Baliamoune, Mina (2000). 'Economics of Summitry: An Empirical Assessment of the Economic Effects of Summits'. *Empirica* vol. 27, pp. 295–315.

Balls, Andrew (2004). 'G7 Invites China to Discuss Fixed Exchange Rate'. *Financial Times*, 1 October.

Bank for International Settlements (2002). 'BIS Quarterly Review – June 2002 — Statistical Annex'. <www.bis.org/publ/qtrpdf/r_qa0206.pdf> (November 2004).

Banoun, Ray, Derrick Cephas, and Lawrence Fruchtman (2002). 'U.S. Patriot Act and Other Recent Money Laundering Developments Have Broad Impact on Financial Institutions'. *Journal of Taxation of Financial Institutions* vol. 15, no. 4.

Bardacke, Ted (2000). 'Camdessus Seeks Broader G8'. *Financial Times*, 14 February.

Barshefsky, Charline (2000). 'Transcript: Barshefsky Says Deregulation Key to Japan's Recovery'. Transcript of press conference on 'Trade Policy in the U.S.-Japan Relationship, 1993 to 2000, Tokyo, 19 July. <japan.usembassy.gov/e/p/tp-2841.html> (November 2004).

Bayne, Nicholas (1999). 'Continuity and Leadership in an Age of Globalisation'. In M. R. Hodges, J. J. Kirton and J. P. Daniels, eds., *The G8's Role in the New Millennium*, pp. 21–44. Ashgate, Aldershot.

Bayne, Nicholas (2000). 'The G7 Summit's Contribution: Past, Present, and Prospective'. In K. Kaiser, J. J. Kirton and J. P. Daniels, eds., *Shaping a New International Financial System: Challenges of Governance in a Globalizing World*, pp. 19–35. Ashgate, Aldershot.

Bayne, Nicholas (2000). *Hanging In There: The G7 and G8 Summit in Maturity and Renewal*. Ashgate, Aldershot.

Bayne, Nicholas (2001). 'The G7 and Multilateral Trade Liberalisation: Past Performance, Future Challenges'. In J. J. Kirton and G. M. von Furstenberg, eds., *New Directions in Global Economic Governance: Managing Globalisation in the Twenty-First Century*, pp. 23–38. Ashgate, Aldershot.

Bayne, Nicholas (2001). 'The G8's Role in the Fight against Terrorism'. Remarks to the G8 Research Group, Toronto, 8 November. <www.g8.utoronto.ca/speakers/baynenov2001.html> (November 2004).

Bayne, Nicholas (2004). 'Concentrating the Mind: Decision Making in the G7/8 System'. In J. J. Kirton and R. Stefanova, eds., *The G8, The United Nations, and Conflict Prevention*, pp. 21–38. Ashgate, Aldershot.

Bayne, Nicholas (2004). 'G7/G8 Performance from Birmingham to Evian and Beyond'. In M. Fratianni, P. Savona and J. J. Kirton, eds., *Corporate, Public, and Global Governance: The G8's Contribution*. Ashgate, Aldershot. Forthcoming.

Bayne, Nicholas (2005). *Staying Together: The G8 Summit Confronts the 21st Century*. Ashgate, Aldershot.

Bayne, Nicholas and Stephen Woolcock (2003). *The New Economic Diplomacy: Decision-Making and Negotiation in International Economic Relations*. Ashgate, Aldershot.

Beaird, Richard (2003). 'Opening Remarks'. OECD-APEC Forum: Policy Frameworks for the Digital Economy, 14–17 January. Honolulu. <www.oecd.org/dataoecd/19/56/2492657.pdf> (November 2004).

Becker, Gary (1968). 'Crime and Punishment: An Economic Approach'. *Journal of Political Economy* vol. 2, pp. 169–217.

Belenkaya, Marianna (2004). 'G8 Rules Out Solving Middle East Problems'. *RIA Novosti*, 10 June.

Bergsten, C. Fred and Thierry de Montbrial (2003). 'Restoring G8 Leadership of the World Economy: Recommendations for the Evian Summit from the Shadow G8'. Institute for International Economics and Institut Français des Relations Internationales. <www.iie.com/publications/papers/g8-2003.pdf> (November 2004).

Bergsten, C. Fred and C. Randall Henning (1996). *Global Economic Leadership and the Group of Seven*. Institute for International Economics, Washington DC.

Bergsten, C. Fred and Caio Koch-Weser (2004). 'The G2: A New Conceptual Basis and Operating Modality for Transatlantic Economic Relations'. In W. Weidenfeld, C. Koch-Weser, C. F. Bergsten, W. Stützle and H. Hamre, eds., *From Alliance to Coalitions: The Future of Transatlantic Relations*, pp. 237–249. Bertelsman Foundation, Gütersloh.

Betts, Paul (2003). 'Executives Urge G8 to Unite for Growth'. *Financial Times*, 21 May.

Biermann, Frank and Steffen Bauer, eds. (2005). *A World Environmental Organization: Solution or Threat for Effective International Environmental Governance*. Ashgate, Aldershot.

'A Bit of Gallic Grit: U.S. and France Inject Useful Tension into G8 Summitry'. (2004). *Financial Times*, 12 June.

Blomberg, S. Brock, Gregory D. Hess, and Athanasios Orphanides (2004). 'The Macroeconomic Consequences of Terrorism'. *Journal of Monetary Economics* vol. 51, no. 5, pp. 1007–1032.

Blomberg, S. Brock, Gregory D. Hess, and Akila Weerapana (2002). 'Terrorism from Within: An Economic Model of Terrorism'. <econpapers.hhs.se/paper/clmclmeco/2002-14.htm> (November 2004).

Bowen, Harry P., Edward E. Leamer, and Leo Sveikauskas (1988). 'Multicountry, Multifactor Rests of the Factor Abundance Theory'. *American Economic Review* vol. 78, no. 791–809.

Bradford Jr., Colin I. and Johannes F. Linn (2004). 'Global Economic Governance at a Crossroads: Replacing the G7 with the G20'. Brookings Institution Policy Brief 131. <www.brookings.edu/comm/policybriefs/pb131.htm> (November 2004).

Bradford Jr., Colin I. and Johannes F. Linn (2004). 'Ist die G8 noch zeitgemäß? Plädoyer für eine Reform der "Global Economic Governance" mit einer gestärkten G20'. *Internationale Politik* vol. 7, pp. 90–94.

Brainerd, Lael (2004). 'Interview'. 6 February. <www.g8.utoronto.ca/oralhistory> (November 2004).

'Brains Not Welcome Here: The Difficulty of Changing a Policy that Drives Talent Away' (2004). *Economist*, 1 May, p. 30.

Brown, Charles, James Hamilton, and James Medoff (1990). *Employers Large and Small*. Harvard University Press, Cambridge, MA.

Bull, Hedley (1995). *The Anarchical Society: A Study of Order in World Politics*. Columbia University Press, New York.

Bundesanstalt für Finanzdienstleistungsaufsicht (2002). 'Die Bundesanstalt für Finanzdienstleistungsaufsicht untersagt der Dahabshiil das Finanztransfergeschäft'. 19 July. Frankfurt. <www.bafin.de 'Presse & Publikationen: Pressemitteilungen 2002 (Mai - Dezember 2002)'> (November 2004).

Bundesanstalt für Finanzdienstleistungsaufsicht (2003). 'BaFin untersagt Zweigstellen von MoneyNett@Nationalbank das Finanztransfergeschäft'. 18 September. Frankfurt. <www.bafin.de 'Presse & Publikationen: Pressemitteilungen 2003'> (November 2004).

Bundesanstalt für Finanzdienstleistungsaufsicht (2003). 'Jahresbericht 2003'. Frankfurt. <www.bafin.de 'Presse & Publikationen: Publikationen: Jahresberichte'> (November 2004).

Burke, Jason (2004). 'Think Again: Al Qaeda'. *Foreign Policy* May/June. <www.foreignpolicy.com/story/cms.php?story_id=02536> (November 2004).

Bush, George W. (2003). 'President Bush Thanks Germany for Support against Terror'. Remarks to a special session of the German Bundestag, 23 May. Berlin. <www.whitehouse.gov/news/releases/2002/05/20020523-2.html> (November 2004).

Bush, George W. (2003). 'Remarks by the President at the 20th Anniversary of the National Endowment for Democracy'. <www.whitehouse.gov/news/releases/2003/11/20031106-3.html> (November 2004).

Bush, George W. (2004). 'Press Conference of President George Bush after the G8 Summit'. Savannah, GA, 10 June. <www.g8.utoronto.ca/summit/2004seaisland/bush040610.html> (November 2004).

Camdessus, Michel (1998). 'Money Laundering: The Importance of International Countermeasures'. Address to the Plenary Meeting of the Financial Action Task Force on Money Laundering, Paris, 10 February. <www.imf.org/external/np/speeches/1998/021098.htm> (November 2004).

Central Intelligence Agency (2004). 'Nauru: Economy'. World Factbook. <www.cia.gov/cia/publications/factbook> (November 2004).

Central Intelligence Agency (2004). 'Notes and Definitions'. World Factbook. <www.cia.gov/cia/publications/factbook/docs/notesanddefs.html> (November 2004).

Chaffin, Joshua (2004). 'Trapped Inside the Summit's Trouble-Proof Bubble'. *Financial Times*, 3–4 July.

Chandler, Clay (2000). 'In Tokyo, Rich Pay Heed to the Poor as G8 Summit Opens'. *Washington Post*, 21 July, p. A19.

Chirico, Francesco (2001). 'Leaders, Elezioni, Governi e Sistemi Politici: Stati Sovrani e Territori — Democracy Index (al 31/12/200)'. <www.geocities.com/CapitolHill/Lobby/3535/country/list-di.htm> (November 2004).

Choe, Sang-Hun (2004). 'North Korea Threatens to Strengthen Nuclear Development after G8 Statement'. *Associated Press*, 12 June.

Chote, Robert (1998). 'Camdessus Urges G8 to Embrace Other Countries'. *Financial Times*, 9 May.

Cohen, Wesley M. and D. Levinthal (1989). 'Innovation and Learning: The Two Faces of R&D'. *Economic Journal* vol. 99, no. 3, pp. 569–596.

Cohn, Theodore H. (2002). *Governing Global Trade: International Institutions in Conflict and Convergence*. Ashgate, Aldershot.

Commission on the Private Sector and Development (2003). 'Unleashing Entrepreneurship: Making Business Work for the Poor'. Report by Paul Martin and Ernesto Zedillo to the United Nations Secretary General. United Nations Development Programme, New York. <www.undp.org/cpsd> (November 2004).

Cooper, Andrew Fenton (2004). *Tests of Global Governance: Canadian Diplomacy and United Nations World Conferences*. United Nations University Press, Tokyo.

Cooper, Richard N. (1968). *The Economics of Interdependence: Economic Policy in the Atlantic Community*. McGraw-Hill, New York.

Cooper, Robert (2003). *The Breaking of Nations: Order and Chaos in the Twenty-First Century*. Atlantic Monthly Press, New York.

Davies, Glyn (2004). Interview with author. Washington DC, 1 June.

Davis, Kevin E. (2003). 'Legislating against the Financing of Terrorism: Pitfalls and Prospects'. *Journal of Financial Crime* vol. 10, no. 3, pp. 269–274.

Deans, Bob (2004). 'G8 Members Snub U.S. Appeal for Iraq Troops'. *Altanta Journal-Constitution*, 14 May.

Digital Opportunity Task Force (2000). 'First Meeting of the G8 Digital Opportunity Task Force'. 30 November. <www.g8.utoronto.ca/dot_force/summary-nov-00.html> (November 2004).

Digital Opportunity Task Force (2001). 'Digital Opportunities for All: Meeting the Challenge. Report of the Digital Opportunity Task Force (DOT Force) Including a Proposal for a Genoa Plan of Action'. <www.g8.utoronto.ca/summit/2001genoa/dotforce1.html> (November 2004).

Digital Opportunity Task Force (2002). 'Report Card: Digital Opportunities for All'. <www.g8.utoronto.ca/summit/2002kananaskis/dotforce_reportcard.pdf> (November 2004).

Digital Opportunity Task Force (2002). 'Team Report: Human Capacity and Knowledge'. Ottawa, June.

Dodwell, David (1993). 'The Gavel Falls on Most of Uruguay Round'. *Financial Times*, 14 December.

Drazen, Allan (2000). *Political Economy in Macroeconomics*. Princeton University Press, Princeton.

Dunning, John H. (2001). *Global Capitalism at Bay?* Routledge, London.

Enablis (2004). 'Enablis in Brief'. <www.enablis.org> (November 2004).

Enders, Walter and Todd Sandler (2003). 'What Do We Know about the Substitution Effect in Transnational Terrorism?' In A. Silke and G. Ilardi, eds., *Researching Terrorism: Trends, Achievements, Failures*. Frank Cass, Ilford.

English, John, Ramesh Thakur, and Andrew Fenton Cooper (2005). *A Leaders 20 Summit: Why, How, Who, and When?* United Nations University, Tokyo. Forthcoming.

Enright, Michael J. (2000). 'The Globalization of Competition and the Localization of Competitive Advantage: Policies Towards Regional Clustering'. In N. Hood and S. Young, eds., *The Globalization of Economic Activity and Economic Development*, pp. 330–331. Macmillan, Basingstoke.

Errico, Luca and Alberto Musalem (1999). 'Offshore Banking: An Analysis of Micro- and Macro-Prudential Issues'. International Monetary Fund Working Paper No. 99/5. Washington DC. <www.imf.org/external/pubs/ft/wp/1999/wp9905.pdf> (November 2004).

'Europe Daily Bulletin' (1990). *Agence Europe*, 18 July, p. 6.

European Commission (2001). 'Network and Information Security: Proposal for a European Approach'. Communication from the Commission to the Council, the European Parliament, the European Economic and Social Committee, and the Committee of the Regions. <europa.eu.int/information_society/eeurope/2002/news_library/pdf_files/netsec_en.pdf> (November 2004).

European Commission (2004). 'WTO-DDA: EU Ready to Go the Extra Mile in Three Key Areas of the Talks'. Brussels, 10 May. <europa.eu.int/comm/trade/issues/newround/pr100504_en.htm> (November 2004).

European Union (2001). 'Coordination of the Community Immigration Policy'. <www.europa.eu.int/scadplus/leg/en/lvb/l33155.htm> (November 2004).

European Union-Japan Summit (2000). 'Joint Conclusions'. 19 July. <europa.eu.int/comm/external_relations/japan/summit_7_19_2000> (November 2004).

Fauver, Robert (2003). 'Interview'. 13 March. <www.g8.utoronto.ca/oralhistory> (November 2004).

Feldman, Maryann P. and David B. Audretsch (1999). 'Innovation in Cities: Science-Based Diversity, Specialization, and Localized Competition'. *European Economic Review* vol. 43, pp. 409–429.

Ferguson, Niall (2004). 'A World without Power'. *Foreign Policy* no. 143, p. 32–40.

Ferrell, Keith (2003). 'Homeland Security Getting Its House in Order'. *Security Pipeline*, 17 September. <www.securitypipeline.com/news/showArticle.jhtml?articleId=14800063> (November 2004).

Fife, Robert and Anne Dawson (2003). 'Border Stays: Manley'. *National Post*, 23 January, p. A04.

Filippov, Yuri (2004). 'G8 and Vladimir Putin's Personal Result'. *RIA Novosti*, 10 June.

Financial Action Task Force (2000). 'Progress Report on Non-Cooperative Countries and Territories'. 5 October. Paris. <www1.oecd.org/fatf/pdf/PR-20001005_en.pdf> (November 2004).

Financial Action Task Force (2000). 'Review to Identify Non-Cooperative Countries or Territories: Increasing the Worldwide Effectiveness of Anti-Money Laundering Measures'. First Review to Identify Non-Cooperative Countries or Territories, 22 June. Paris. <www1.oecd.org/fatf/pdf/NCCT2000_en.pdf> (November 2004).

Financial Action Task Force (2001). 'Special Recommendations on Terrorist Financing'. Organisation for Economic Co-operation and Development, Paris. <www1.oecd.org/fatf/pdf/SRecTF_en.pdf> (November 2004).

Financial Action Task Force (2003). 'Combating the Abuse of Alternative Remittance Systems: International Best Practices'. 20 June. Paris. <www.fatf-gafi.org/pdf/SR6-BPP_en.pdf> (November 2004).

Financial Action Task Force (2003). 'The Forty Recommendations'. Organisation for Economic Co-operation and Development, Paris. <www1.oecd.org/fatf/40Recs_en.htm> (November 2004).

Financial Action Task Force (2004). 'The Financial War on Terrorism: A Guide by the Financial Action Task Force'. Organisation for Economic Co-operation and Development, Paris.

Financial Action Task Force (2004). 'Members and Observers'. <www.fatf-gafi.org/Members_en.htm> (November 2004).

Findeisen, Michael (2000). '"Underground Banking" in Deutschland: Schnittstellen zwischen illegalen "Remittance Services" i.S.v. Paragraph 1, Abs. 1a Nr. 6 KWG und dem legalen Bankgeschäft (Underground Banking in Germany: The Intersection between Illegal Remittance Services in the Sense of Paragraph ... and Legitimate Banking Activities)'. *Wertpapier-Mitteilung*, no. 43, pp. 2125–2133.

Fitchett, Joseph (2001). 'NATO Unity, but What Next? Allies Unsure of What a Counterterrorism Offensive Might Require'. *International Herald Tribune*, 14 September.

Flynn, Stephen (2004). *America the Vulnerable: How Our Government is Failing to Protect Us from Terrorism*. HarperCollins, New York.

Fowler, Robert (2003). 'Canadian Leadership and the Kananaskis G8 Summit: Toward a Less Self-Centred Policy'. In D. Carment, F. O. Hampson and N. Hillmer, eds., *Canada Among Nations 2003: Coping with the Canadian Colossus*, pp. 219–241. Oxford University Press, Toronto.

Fowler, Robert (2004). 'The Intricacies of Summit Preparation and Consensus Building'. In J. J. Kirton and R. Stefanova, eds., *The G8, The United Nations, and Conflict Prevention*, pp. 39–42. Ashgate, Aldershot.

Fox, William T. R. (1944). *The Super-Powers: The United States, Britain, and the Soviet Union — Their Responsibility for Peace*. Harcourt, Brace, New York.

Frankel, Jeffrey A. (1997). *Regional Trading Blocs in the World Economic System*. Institute for International Economics, Washington DC.

Fratianni, Michele and Heejoon Kang (2004). 'Heterogeneous Distance-Elasticities in Trade Gravity Models'. Kelley School of Business, Indiana University. Unpublished.

Fratianni, Michele and John C. Pattison (2001). 'International Organisations in a World of Regional Trade Agreements: Lessons from Club Theory'. *World Economy* vol. 24, no. 3, pp. 333–358.

G7 (1975). 'Declaration of Rambouillet'. 17 November. <www.g8.utoronto.ca/summit/1975rambouillet/communique.html> (November 2004).

G7 (1985). 'The Bonn Economic Declaration Towards Sustained Growth and Higher Employment'. 4 May. <www.g8.utoronto.ca/summit/1985bonn> (November 2004).

G7 (1986). 'Tokyo Economic Declaration'. 6 May. <www.g8.utoronto.ca/summit/1986tokyo> (November 2004).

G7 (1990). 'Houston Economic Declaration'. 11 July. <www.g8.utoronto.ca/summit/1990houston> (November 2004).

G7 (2000). 'G7 Statement'. 21 July. <www.g8.utoronto.ca/summit/2000okinawa/statement.htm> (November 2004).

G7 Finance Ministers (2001). 'Action Plan to Combat the Financing of Terrorism'. <www.g8.utoronto.ca/finance/fm100601.htm#action> (November 2004).

G7 Finance Ministers (2003). 'Statement of G7 Finance Ministers and Central Bank Governors'. Washington DC, 12 April. <www.g8.utoronto.ca/finance/fm041203.htm> (November 2004).

G8 (1999). 'G8 Communiqué Köln 1999'. 20 June. <www.g8.utoronto.ca/summit/1999koln> (November 2004).

G8 (2000). 'G8 Communiqué Okinawa 2000'. <www.g8.utoronto.ca/summit/2000okinawa/finalcom.htm> (November 2004).

G8 (2000). 'Okinawa Charter on Global Information Society'. Okinawa, 22 July. <www.g8.utoronto.ca/summit/2000okinawa/gis.htm> (November 2004).

G8 (2002). 'G8's Africa Action Plan'. <www.g8.utoronto.ca/summit/2002kananaskis/africaplan.html> (November 2004).

G8 (2002). 'The Kananaskis Summit Chair's Summary'. <www.g8.utoronto.ca/summit/2002kananaskis> (November 2004).

G8 (2002). 'Statement by the Leaders: The G8 Global Partnership against the Spread of Weapons and Materials of Mass Destruction'. <www.g8.utoronto.ca/summit/2002kananaskis/arms.html> (November 2004).

G8 (2003). 'Co-operative G8 Action on Trade'. Evian, 2 June. <www.g8.utoronto.ca/summit/2003evian/trade_en.html> (November 2004).

G8 (2003). 'Implementation Report by Africa Personal Representatives to Leaders on the G8 Africa Action Plan'. Evian, 1 June. <www.g8.utoronto.ca/summit/2003evian/apr030601.html> (November 2004).

G8 (2004). 'G8 Action Plan: Expanding Global Capability for Peace Support Operations'. Sea Island, 10 June. <www.g8.utoronto.ca/summit/2004seaisland/peace.html> (November 2004).

G8 (2004). 'G8 Leaders Statement on Trade'. Sea Island, 9 June. <www.g8.utoronto.ca/summit/2004seaisland/trade.html> (November 2004).

G8 (2004). 'G8 Secure and Facilitated International Travel Initiative'. Sea Island, 9 June. <www.g8.utoronto.ca/summit/2004seaisland/travel.html> (November 2004).

G8 (2004). 'Partnership for Progress and a Common Future with the Region of the Broader Middle East and North Africa'. Sea Island, 9 June. <www.g8.utoronto.ca/summit/2004seaisland/partnership.html> (November 2004).

G8 Foreign Ministers (2002). 'G8 Foreign Ministers' Progress Report on the Fight against Terrorism'. Whistler, BC, 12 June. <www.g8.utoronto.ca/foreign/fm130602b.htm> (November 2004).

G8 Foreign Ministers (2002). 'G8 Recommendations on Counter-Terrorism'. Whistler, BC, 13 June. <www.g8.utoronto.ca/foreign/fm130602f.htm> (November 2004).

G8 Lyon Group (2002). 'The G8 Lyon Group'. <www.auswaertiges-amt.de/www/en/aussenpolitik/vn/lyon_group_html> (November 2004).

G8 Research Group (2004). 'What Is the G20?' <www.g8.utoronto.ca/g20/g20whatisit.html> (2004 November).

G20 (2004). 'G20 Members'. <www.g-20.mre.gov.br/members.asp> (November 2004).

Ghemawat, Pankaj (2001). 'Distance Still Matters: The Hard Reality of Global Expansion'. *Harvard Business Review* vol. 79, no. 8, pp. 137–147.

Ghemawat, Pankaj (2003). 'Semi-globalization and International Business Strategy'. *Journal of International Business Studies* vol. 34, no. 2, pp. 138–152.

Gill, Stephen (1999). 'Structural Changes in Multilateralism: The G7 Nexus and the Global Crisis'. In M. Schechter, ed., *Innovation in Multilateralism*. St. Martin's Press, New York.

Glaeser, Edward L., Hedi D. Kallal, José A. Scheinkman, et al. (1992). 'Growth of Cities'. *Journal of Political Economy* vol. 1000, pp. 1126–1152.

Global Information Infrastructure Commission (1995). 'GII Commission Inaugural Meeting'. World Bank, 11–12 July. Washington DC. <www.giic.org/events/ann1.asp> (November 2004).

Golob, Stephanie R. (2002). 'North America Beyond NAFTA? Sovereignty, Identity, and Security in Canada-U.S. Relations'. *Canadian-American Public Policy* vol. 52 (December), pp. 1–44.

Goodman, Matthew (2004). 'The G8 Should Start Opening to China'. *Financial Times*, 3 June.

Govindarajan, Vivay and Anil K. Gupta (2001). *The Quest for Global Dominance*. Jossey-Bass/Wiley, San Francisco.

Graham, Robert and Peter Spiegel (2003). 'Chirac Talks to Bush but Chilly Relations Remain'. *Financial Times*, 16 April.

Grant, Charles (2003). 'Transatlantic Rift: How to Bring the Two Sides Together'. July. Centre for European Reform, London.

Gray, John (2003). *Paul Martin: The Power of Ambition*. Key Porter, Toronto.

Grimes, Christopher (2004). 'Universities Hit by "Unwelcoming" Visa Rules'. *Financial Times*, 29 April, p. 1.

Gruber, William, Dileep Mehta, and Raymond Vernon (1967). 'The R&D Factor in International Trade and Investment in the United States'. *Journal of Political Economy* vol. 75, pp. 20–37.

Hajnal, Peter I. (2002). 'Civil Society Encounters the G7/G8'. In P. I. Hajnal, ed., *Civil Society in the Information Age*. Ashgate, Aldershot.

Hampton, Mark P. and John Christensen (2002). 'Offshore Pariahs? Small Island Economies, Tax Havens, and the Re-configuration of Global Finance'. *World Development* vol. 30, no. 9, pp. 1657–1673.

Hannan, Michael T. and John Freeman (1989). *Organizational Ecology*. Harvard University Press, Cambridge, MA.

Hart, Michael, François Bar, and Robert Reed (1992). 'The Building of the Internet: Implications for the Future of Broadband Networks'. *Telecommunications Policy* vol. 16 (November), no. 666–689.

Hart, Michael and William Dymond (2001). 'Common Border, Shared Destinies: Canada, the United States, and Deepening Integration'. Centre for Trade Policy and Law. Ottawa. <www.carleton.ca/ctpl/borders/hartdymondweb.htm> (November 2004).

Held, David (1995). *Democracy and the Global Order: From the Modern State to Cosmopolitan Governance*. Stanford University Press, Stanford.

Hirschkorn, Phil (2003). 'New York Remembers 1993 WTC Victims'. CNN, 26 February. <edition.cnn.com/2003/US/Northeast/02/26/wtc.bombing> (November 2004).

Hirschman, Albert O. (1980). *Exit, Voice, and Loyalty*. Harvard University Press, Cambridge, MA.

Hodges, Michael (1999). 'The G8 and the New Political Economy'. In M. R. Hodges, J. J. Kirton and J. P. Daniels, eds., *The G8's Role in the New Millennium*, pp. 69–74. Ashgate, Aldershot.

Hodges, Michael R., John J. Kirton, and Joseph P. Daniels, eds. (1999). *The G8's Role in the New Millennium*. Ashgate, Aldershot.

Hofmann, Alexander (2004). 'Pazifikinsel Nauru: Paradies vor der Pleite'. *Frankfurter Allgemeiner Zeitung*, 22 April.

Holder, William E. (2003). 'The International Monetary Fund's Involvement in Combating Money Laundering and the Financing of Terrorism'. *Journal of Money Laundering Control* vol. 6, no. 4, pp. 383–387.

Horrigan, Michael W. (2004). 'Employment Projections to 2012: Concepts and Context'. *Monthly Labor Review* vol. 127, no. 2.

'How Immigrants Keep the Hive Humming' (2002). *Business Week*, 24 April.

Igarashi, Aya (2004). 'Japan Makes G8 Presence Felt'. *Yomiuri Shimbun*, 10 June.

Ikenberry, John (1988). 'Market Solutions for State Problems: The International and Domestic Politics of American Oil Decontrol'. *International Organization* vol. 42, no. 1, pp. 151–177.

Ikenberry, John (1993). 'Salvaging the G7'. *Foreign Affairs* vol. 72 (Spring), pp. 132–139.

Ikenberry, John (1998/99). 'Institutions, Strategic Restraint, and the Persistence of American Postwar Order'. *International Security* vol. 23 (Winter), pp. 43–78.

Ikenberry, John (2001). *After Victory: Institutions, Strategic Restraint, and the Rebuilding of Order after Major Wars*. Princeton University Press, Princeton.

Information Society Website (1995). 'G7 Information Society Conference'. 25–26 February. Brussels. <europa.eu.int/ISPO/intcoop/g8/i_g8conference.html> (November 2004).

International Food Policy Research Institute (2004). 'Funding Africa's Farmers'. *IFPRI Forum*, March, pp. 1, 10–12. <www.ifpri.org/pubs/newsletters/ifpriforum/if200403.htm> (November 2004).

International Labour Organization (2001). 'World Employment Report 2001: Life at Work in the Information Economy'. Geneva. <www.ilo.org/public/english/support/publ/wer/index2.htm> (November 2004).

Jachimowicz, Maia and Deborah W. Meyers (2002). 'Temporary High-Skilled Migration'. Migration Information Source. <www.migrationinformation.org/USfocus/display.cfm?id=69> (November 2004).

Jacobs, Jane (1969). *The Economy of Cities*. Random House, New York.

Jaffe, Adam B. (1989). 'Real Effects of Academic Research'. *American Economic Review* vol. 79, no. 5, pp. 957–970.

Jayasuriya, Dayanath (2003). 'Money Laundering and Terrorism Financing: The Role of Capital Market Regulators'. *Journal of Financial Crime* vol. 10, no. 1, pp. 30–36.

Jeannet, Jean-Pierre (2000). *Managing with a Global Mindset*. Pearson Educational, London.

Jervis, Robert (1986). 'From Balance to Concert: A Study of International Security Cooperation'. In K. A. Oye, ed., *Cooperation under Anarchy*. Princeton University Press, Princeton.

Johnson, Jackie (2001). 'Blacklisting: Initial Reactions, Responses, and Repercussions'. *Journal of Money Laundering Control* vol. 6, no. 3, pp. 211–225.

Johnson, Jackie (2001). 'In Pursuit of Dirty Money: Identifying Weaknesses in the Global Financial System'. *Journal of Money Laundering Control* vol. 6, no. 1, pp. 122–132.

Johnson, Jackie and Y. C. Desmond Lim (2002). 'Money Laundering: Has the Financial Action Task Force Made a Difference?' *Journal of Financial Crime* vol. 10, no. 1, pp. 7–22.

Jonquières, Guy de (2003). 'Poorer Countries Are Likely to Be the Biggest Losers from the Unexpected Breakdown in the Doha Round'. *Financial Times*, 16 September, p. 21.

Kay, Adrian (1998). *The Reform of the Common Agricultural Policy: The Case of the MacSharry Reforms*. CAB International, New York.

Keesing, Donald B. (1966). 'Labor Skills and Comparative Advantage'. *American Economic Review* vol. 56, pp. 249–258.

Keesing, Donald B. (1967). 'The Impact of Research and Development on United States Trade'. *Journal of Political Economy* vol. 75, pp. 38–48.

Kenen, Peter B., Jeffrey R. Shafer, Nigel L. Wicks, et al. (2004). 'International Economic and Financial Cooperation: New Issues, New Actors, New Responses'. Centre for Economic and Policy Research, London. <www.cepr.org/pubs/books/cepr/booklist.asp?cvno=P171> (November 2004).

Keohane, Robert O. and Joseph S. Nye (1977). *Power and Interdependence: World Politics in Transition*. 1st ed. Little, Brown, Boston.

Keohane, Robert O. and Joseph S. Nye (1989). *Power and Interdependence*. 2nd ed. HarperCollins, New York.

Keohane, Robert O. and Joseph S. Nye (2001). *Power and Interdependence*. 3rd ed. Longman, New York.

Kirton, John J. (1989). 'Contemporary Concert Diplomacy: The Seven-Power Summit and the Management of International Order'. Paper prepared for the annual meeting of the International Studies Association, 29 March–1 April. London. <www.g8.utoronto.ca/scholar/kirton198901> (November 2004).

Kirton, John J. (1993). 'The Seven Power Summits as a New Security Institution'. In D. Dewitt, D. Haglund and J. J. Kirton, eds., *Building a New Global Order: Emerging Trends in International Security*, pp. 335–357. Oxford University Press, Toronto.

Kirton, John J. (2000). 'United States Foreign Policy and the G8 Summit'. Lecture given at the Faculty of Law, Chuo University, Tokyo, 6 July. <www.g8.utoronto.ca/g7/scholar/kirton20004> (November 2004).

Kirton, John J. (2001). 'The G7/8 and China: Toward a Closer Association'. In J. J. Kirton, J. P. Daniels and A. Freytag, eds., *Guiding Global Order: G8 Governance in the Twenty-First Century*. Ashgate, Aldershot.

Kirton, John J. (2001). 'The G20: Representativeness, Effectiveness, and Leadership in Global Governance'. In J. J. Kirton, J. P. Daniels and A. Freytag, eds., *Guiding Global Order: G8 Governance in the Twenty-First Century*, pp. 143–172. Ashgate, Aldershot.

Kirton, John J. (2002). 'Embedded Ecologism and Institutional Inequality: Linking Trade, Environment, and Social Cohesion in the G8'. In J. J. Kirton and V. W. Maclaren, eds., *Linking Trade, Environment, and Social Cohesion: NAFTA Experiences, Global Challenges*, pp. 45–72. Ashgate, Aldershot.

Kirton, John J. (2003). 'After Westphalia: Security and Freedom in the G8's Global Governance'. In T. Noetzel and M. Lerch, eds., *Security and Freedom: Foreign Policy, Domestic Politics, and Political Theory Perspectives*. Nomos, Baden-Baden.

Kirton, John J. (2004). 'Explaining G8 Effectiveness: A Concert of Vulnerable Equals in a Globalizing World'. Paper prepared for the International Studies Association conference. Montreal, 17–20 March. <www.g8.utoronto.ca/scholar/kirton2004/kirton_isa_040304.pdf> (November 2004).

Kirton, John J. (2004). 'The G8 and Energy'. Unpublished manuscript.

Kirton, John J. (2004). 'Getting the L20 Going: Reaching Out from the G8'. Paper prepared for a workshop on 'G20 to Replace the G8: Why Not Now?', sponsored by the Brookings Institution, Institute for International Economics, and the Centre for Global Governance, 22 September. Washington DC.

Kirton, John J. (2005). 'Towards Mulitlateral Reform: The G20's Contribution'. In J. English, R. Thakur and A. F. Cooper, eds., *A Leaders 20 Summit: Why, How, Who, and When?* United Nations University, Tokyo. Forthcoming.

Kirton, John J. and Joseph P. Daniels (1999). 'The Role of the G8 in the New Millennium'. In M. Hodges, J. J. Kirton and J. P. Daniels, eds., *The G8's Role in the New Millennium*, pp. 3–17. Ashgate, Aldershot.

Kirton, John J. and Radoslava Stefanova, eds. (2004). *The G8, The United Nations, and Conflict Prevention*. Ashgate, Aldershot.

Kissinger, Henry, Lawrence H. Summers, and Charles Kupchan (2004). 'Renewing the Atlantic Partnership'. Council on Foreign Relations, Washington DC. <www.cfr.org/publication.php?id=6871> (November 2004).

'Koizumi Flies Asian Flag'. (2004). *Taipei Times*, 12 June.

Kokotsis, Eleanore (1999). *Keeping International Commitments: Compliance, Credibility, and the G7, 1988–1995*. Garland, New York.

Lee, Dwight R. (1988). 'Free Riding and Paid Riding in the Fight against Terrorism'. *American Economic Review* vol. 78, no. 2, pp. 22–26.

Levitt, Theodore (1983). 'The Globalization of Markets'. *Harvard Business Review* May-June, pp. 92–102.

Lewis, Flora (1991–92). 'The G7 1/2 Directorate'. *Foreign Policy* no. 85, p. 25–40.

Lucas, Robert E. (1988). 'On the Mechanics of Economic Development'. *Journal of Monetary Economics* vol. 22, pp. 3–39.

Lucas, Robert E. (1993). 'Making a Miracle'. *Econometrica* vol. 61, pp. 251–272.

Marshall, Alfred (1920). *Principles of Economics*. 8th ed. Macmillan, London.

Masciandaro, Donato (1998). 'Money Laundering Regulation: The Micro Economics'. *Journal of Money Laundering Control* vol. 2, no. 1, pp. 49–58.

Masciandaro, Donato (1999). 'Money Laundering: The Economics of Regulation'. *European Journal of Law and Economics* vol. 3 (May), pp. 245–240.

Masciandaro, Donato (2000). 'The Illegal Sector, Money Laundering, and Legal Economy: A Macroeconomic Analysis'. *Journal of Financial Crime* vol. 2, pp. 103–112.

Masciandaro, Donato, ed. (2004). *Global Financial Crime: Terrorism, Money Laundering, and Offshore Centres*. Ashgate, Aldershot.

Masciandaro, Donato (2005). 'Could Sticks Become Carrots? Money Laundering, International Black Lists, and Offshore Centres'. *Finance India*.

Masciandaro, Donato (2005). 'False and Reluctant Friends? National Regulation, International Compliance, and Non-Cooperative Countries'. *European Journal of Law and Economics,* forthcoming.

Masciandaro, Donato and Allessandro Portolano (2003). 'It Takes Two to Tango: International Financial Regulation and Offshore Centres'. *Journal of Money Laundering Control* vol. 6, no. 4, pp. 311–331.

Masciandaro, Donato and Allessandro Portolano (2004). 'Financial Policies: Offshore Centres and Competition in Regulation — The Laxity Problem'. In D. Masciandaro, ed., *Global Financial Crime: Terrorism, Money Laundering, and Offshore Centres*, pp. 125–179. Ashgate, Aldershot.

May, Bernhard (2004). 'The World Economic Summits: A Difficult Learning Process'. In J. Detlev, ed., *The United States and Germany in the Era of the Cold War, 1968–1990: A Handbook*. Cambridge University Press, New York.

McCallum, John (1995). 'National Borders Matter: Canada-U.S. Regional Trade Patterns'. *American Economic Review* vol. 85, no. 3, pp. 615–623.

Minter, Walter (2004). 'USA/Africa: Peacekeeping Repackaged'. *AfricaFocus Bulletin*, 10 June. <www.africafocus.org/docs04/us0406a.php> (November 2004).

Mitchell, Daniel J. (2002). 'U.S. Government Agencies Confirm that Low-Tax Jurisdictions Are Not Money Laundering Havens'. *Journal of Financial Crime* vol. 11, no. 2, pp. 127–133.

Mitton, Roger (2004). 'China Odd One Out in WMD Issue'. *Straits Times Interactive*, 10 June.

Miyake, Kuriko (2001). 'G8 Concludes Tokyo High-Tech Crime Meeting'. CNN, 21 May. <archives.cnn.com/2001/TECH/internet/05/31/g8.cyber.crime.idg> (November 2004).

Morse, Edward and James Richard (2002). 'The Battle for Energy Dominance'. *Foreign Affairs* vol. 81, no. 2, pp. 16–31.

'N. Korea Threatens to Strengthen Nuke Development after G8 Statement'. (2004). *Associated Press*, 13 June.

National Telecommunication and Information Administration (2000). 'Falling Through the Net: Toward Digital Inclusion'. United States Department of Commerce. <www.ntia.doc.gov/ntiahome/fttn00/contents00.html> (November 2004).

Nau, Henry (2004). 'Interview'. 7 May. <www.g8.utoronto.ca/oralhistory> (November 2004).

Nelson, Richard R. and Sidney G. Winter (1974). 'Neoclassical vs. Evolutionary Theories of Economic Growth: Critique and Prospectus'. *Economic Journal* vol. 84 (December), pp. 886–905.

Norgren, Claes (2004). 'The Control of Risk Associated with Crime, Terror, and Subversion'. *Journal of Money Laundering Control* vol. 7, no. 3, pp. 201–206.

Nunn, Sam and Michele Flournoy (2004). 'G8 Leaders Need to Move against Terrorism'. *Newsday*, 9 June.

Nye, Joseph S. (2002). *The Paradox of American Power: Why the World's Only Superpower Can't Go It Alone*. Oxford University Press, New York.

O'Brien, Timothy (2004). 'Senators Raise Doubts about Banks' Antiterror Measures'. *New York Times*, 4 June, p. C3.

O'Neill, Jim and Robert Hormats (2004). 'The G8: Time for a Change'. Global Economics Paper No. 112. Goldman Sachs, New York. <www.gs.com/insight/research/reports/report15.html> (November 2004).

Ohmae, Kenichi (1985). *Triad Power: The Coming Shape of Global Competition*. The Free Press, New York.

Organisation for Economic Co-operation and Development (1998). 'A Borderless World: Realising the Potential of Global Electronic Commerce'. Organisation for Economic Co-operation and Development, Paris.

Organisation for Economic Co-operation and Development (2000). 'E-Commerce: Implementing the Ottawa Taxation Framework Conditions'. Report to Ministers, C/MIN (2000)9. <www1.oecd.org/subject/mcm/2000/e_comm_ott.pdf> (November 2004).

Organisation for Economic Co-operation and Development (2003). 'Implementation of the Ottawa Taxation Framework Conditions: The 2003 Report'. Paris. <www.oecd.org/dataoecd/45/19/20499630.pdf> (November 2004).

Organisation for Economic Co-operation and Development (2003). 'Privacy Online: OECD Guidance on Policy and Practice'. Paris. <www1.oecd.org/publications/e-book/9303051E.PDF> (November 2004).

Organisation for Economic Co-operation and Development (2004). 'Chair's Summary'. OECD Ministerial Council Meeting, Paris, 13–14 May.

Ostry, Sylvia (1991). 'Canada, Europe, and Economic Summits'. In C. H. W. Remie and J.-M. Lacroix, eds., *Canada on the Threshold of the 21st Century: European Reflections upon the Future of Canada*. John Benjamin Publishing Company, Amsterdam.

Ostry, Sylvia (2002). 'Globalization and the G8: Could Kananaskis Set a New Direction?' O. D. Skelton Memorial Lecture, Queen's University and the Department of Foreign Affairs and International Trade.

Owen, Henry (1997). 'Defending the G7'. *International Economy* vol. 11, no. 1, pp. 30–34.

P8 Senior Experts Group (1996). '40 Recommendations to Combat Transnational Organized Crime'. April, Paris. <www.auswaertiges-amt.de/www/de/ infoservice/download/pdf/vn/g8_recommandations.pdf> (November 2004).

Panitchpakdi, Supachai (2004). 'Ministerial Support Must Be Translated into Geneva Progress'. Opening Remarks, Trade Negotiations Committee, 30 June. <www.wto.org/english/news_e/news04_e/tnc_30june04_e.htm> (November 2004).

Penttilä, Risto E.J. (2003). *The Role of the G8 in International Peace and Security*. Oxford University Press, Oxford.

Persson, Torsten and Guido Tabellini (2000). *Political Economics: Explaining Economic Policy*. MIT University Press, Cambridge MA.

Pew Research Center for the People and the Press (2004). 'A Year after Iraq War: Mistrust of America in Europe Ever Higher, Muslim Anger Persists'. <people-press.org/reports/display.php3?ReportID=206> (November 2004).

Pollack, Andrew (1993). 'Summit Breathes Life into World Trade Talks'. *International Herald Tribune*, 8 July.

Porter, Michael E. (1990). *The Competitive Advantage of Nations*. Free Press, New York.

Preston, Ethan M. (2003). 'The U.S. Patriot Act: New Adventures in American Extraterritoriality'. *Journal of Financial Crime* vol. 10, no. 1, pp. 104–116.

'Prospects for 2003 College Graduates: Your Life' (2003). *USA Today (Magazine)*, May 2003. <www.findarticles.com/p/articles/mi_m1272/is_2696_131/ai_101497527> (November 2004).

Putin, Vladimir (2004). 'Speech of Vladimir Putin at a Meeting with James Wolfensohn'. 20 January, Novo-Ogaryovo. <www.worldbank.org.ru/ECA/Russia.nsf/0/BFAB4D0DA09470D4C3256E240038E659> (November 2004).

Putnam, Robert (1994). 'Western Summitry in the 1990s: American Perspectives'. *International Spectator* vol. 29, no. April-June, pp. 81–94.

Putnam, Robert and Nicholas Bayne (1984). *Hanging Together: Co-operation and Conflict in the Seven-Power Summit*. 1st ed. Harvard University Press, Cambridge MA.

Putnam, Robert and Nicholas Bayne (1987). *Hanging Together: Co-operation and Conflict in the Seven-Power Summit*. 2nd ed. Sage Publications, London.

Raum, Tom (2004). 'Bush Says He Doesn't Expect New NATO Troops in Iraq'. *Associated Press*, 10 June.

Reuter, Peter and Edwin M. Truman (2004). *Chasing Dirty Money: The Fight against Money Laundering*. Institute for International Economics, Washington DC.

Rider, Barry A. K. (2002). 'Weapons of War: The Use of Anti-Money Laundering Laws against Terrorist and Criminal Enterprises'. *International Journal of Banking Regulation* vol. 4, no. 1, pp. 13–31.

Rider, Barry A. K. (2003). 'Financial Regulation and Supervision after 11th September, 2001'. *Journal of Financial Crime* vol. 10, no. 4, pp. 336–358.

Romano, Roberta (1985). 'Law as a Product: Some Pieces of the Incorporation Puzzle'. *Journal of Law, Economics, and Organisation* vol. 1, no. 2, pp. 225–283.

Romano, Roberta (1993). *The Genius of American Corporate Law*. AEI Press, Washington DC.

Romano, Roberta (1999). 'Corporate Law and Corporate Governance'. In G. Carroll and D. J. Teece, eds., *Firms, Markets, and Hierarchies: The Transaction Cost Economics Perspective*. Oxford University Press, New York.

Romer, Paul M. (1986). 'Increasing Returns and Long-Run Growth'. *Journal of Political Economy* vol. 94, no. 5, pp. 1002–1037.

Rose, Andrew K. (2000). 'One Money, One Market: The Effects of Common Currency on Trade'. *Economic Policy* vol. 30 (April), pp. 9–45.

Rose, Andrew K. (2003). 'Which International Institutions Promote International Trade?' Data set. <faculty.haas.berkeley.edu/arose/RecRes.htm#Software> (November 2004).

Rotenberg, Marc (2003). 'Global Forum on Information Systems and Networks Security: The Role of Civil Society'. Oslo, 13–14 October. <www.oecd.org/dataoecd/25/19/17842138.pdf> (November 2004).

Rugman, Alan M. (1994). *Foreign Investment and NAFTA*. University of South Carolina Press, Columbia, SC.

Rugman, Alan M. (2000). *The End of Globalization*. Random House, London.

Rugman, Alan M. (2004). *The Regional Multinationals*. Cambridge University Press, Cambridge.

Rugman, Alan M. and Joseph R. D'Cruz (2000). *Multinationals as Flagship Firms: Regional Business Networks*. Oxford University Press, Oxford.

Rugman, Alan M. and Alina Kudina (2002). 'Britain, Europe, and North America'. In M. Fratianni, P. Savona and J. J. Kirton, eds., *Governing Global Finance: New Challenges, G7 and IMF Contributions*, pp. 185–196. Ashgate, Aldershot.

Rugman, Alan M. and Alain Verbeke (2004). 'A Perspective on Regional and Global Strategies of Multinational Enterprises'. *Journal of International Business Studies* vol. 35, no. 1, pp. 3–18.

'Russian Leader Promises "No Begging" from IMF' (2000). 7 February. Russian Public TV (BBC Monitoring).

Russian National Internet Channel (2004). 'James Wolfensohn: Vsemirny bank I Rissiya stali zrelymi druziami (James Wolfensohn: World Bank and Russia Are Mature Friends)'. 20 January. <www.rfn.ru/cnews.html?id=14802&tid=1503&sid=4> (November 2004).

Russian National Internet Channel (2004). 'Rossiya ispol'zovala lish chast' kreditov Vsemirnogo banka (Russia Used Only a Part of World Bank Credits)'. 20 January. <www.rfn.ru/cnews.html?id=14806&tid=1503&sid=4> (November 2004).

Sachs, Jeffrey (1998). 'Global Capitalism: Making It Work'. *Economist* 12 September.

Sandler, Todd, John T. Tschirhart, and John Cauley (1983). 'A Theoretical Analysis of Transnational Terrorism'. *American Political Science Review* vol. 77, pp. 36–77.

Schaetzel, J. Robert and Harald B. Malmgren (1980). 'Talking Heads'. *Foreign Policy* vol. 39, no. 2, pp. 130–142.

'Schroeder Backs China'. (2004). *Straits Times*, 11 June.

Schumpeter, Joseph A. (1911). *Theorie der wirtschaftlichen Entwicklung: Eine Untersuchung über Unternehmergewinn, Kapital, Kredit, Zins und den Konjunkturzyklus*. Duncker und Humbolt, Berlin.

Schwarzenberger, Georg (1959). *Hegemonial Intervention: Yearbook of World Affairs*. Stevens & Son, London.

Schwegmann, Christoph (2001). 'Modern Concert Diplomacy: The Contact Group and the G7/8 in Crisis Management'. In J. J. Kirton, J. P. Daniels and A. Freytag, eds., *Guiding Global Order: G8 Governance in the Twenty-First Century*. Ashgate, Aldershot.

Shea, Andrew (2001). 'Border Choices: Balancing the Need for Security and Trade'. Conference Board of Canada, October. <www.conferenceboard.ca/documents.asp?rnext=61> (November 2004).

'Short-Sighted: Visas and Science' (2004). *Economist*, 8 May, p. 13.

Shultz, George P. (1993). *Turmoil and Triumph: My Years as Secretary of State*. Scribner's, New York.

Skantze, Pernilla (2003). 'European Cyber Security'. OECD Global Forum on

Information Systems and Network Security: Towards a Global Culture of Security. <www.oecd.org/dataoecd/53/43/17979495.pdf> (November 2004).

Smeyser, W.R. (1993). 'Goodbye, G7'. *Washington Quarterly* Winter, pp. 15–28.

Smith, Craig S. (2004). 'Europe's Chief on Terrorism to Reassure U.S. on Efforts'. *New York Times*, 10 May, p. 6.

Smith, Marcia S., John D. Moteff, Lennard G. Kruger, et al. (2001). 'Internet: An Overview of Key Technology Policy Issues Affecting Its Use and Growth'. 31 January. CRS Report for Congress. <www.4uth.gov.ua/usa/english/tech/reports/98-67.pdf> (November 2004).

Solow, Robert M. (1956). 'A Contribution to the Theory of Economic Growth'. *Quarterly Journal of Economics* vol. 70, pp. 65–94.

State University Higher School of Economics (2004). 'Organizatsia ekonomicheskogo sotrudnichestva i razvitia (Organisation for Economic Co-operation and Development)'. Moscow. <www.hse.ru/science/isiez/texts/oesr.doc> (November 2004).

Stephens, Gina (2000). 'The Roots of the New Consensus: The United States and the Transformation of the G8 System'. In J. J. Kirton and J. Takase, eds., *New Directions in Global Political Governance: The G8 and International Order in the Twenty-First Century*, pp. 237–247. Ashgate, Aldershot.

Subcommittee on Immigration and Claims of the Committee on the Judiciary (1999). 'Immigration and America's Workforce for the 21st Century'. Hearing before the House of Representatives, 21 April 1998. <commdocs.house.gov/committees/judiciary/hju58001.000/hju58001_0f.htm> (November 2004).

Talbott, Strobe (2002). *The Russia Hand: A Memoir of Presidential Diplomacy*. Random House, New York.

Tanzi, Vito (2000). *Policies, Institutions, and the Dark Side of Economics*. Edward Elgar, Cheltenham.

Teather, David (2004). 'China and India Groomed for Membership'. *The Guardian*, 11 June.

Torday, Peter (1993). 'Hurdles Stand in Way of Deal'. *Independent*, 8 July.

United Nations General Assembly (2000). 'Crime Prevention and Criminal Justice: Report of the Ad Hoc Committee on the Elaboration of a Convention against Transnational Organized Crime'. A/55/383. 2 November.

United States Embassy in Tokyo (2003). 'U.S.-Japan Joint Statement on Cyber Security'. 9 September. <japan.usembassy.gov/e/p/tp-20030909d2.html> (November 2004).

United States Trade Representative (2004). 'Zoellick Embarks on Global Push to Make Strong Progress on Doha Negotiations'. 8 February. <www.ustr.gov "Press Room"> (November 2004).

Van Cleef, Carol (2003). 'U.S. Patriot Act: Statutory Analysis and Regulatory Implementation'. *Journal of Financial Crime* vol. 11, no. 1, pp. 73–101.

Wallace, William (1984). 'Political Issues at the Summits: A New Concert of Powers?'

In C. Merlini, ed., *Economic Summits and Western Decisionmaking*. St. Martin's Press, London.

Wallace, William (2001). 'Europe, the Necessary Partner'. *Foreign Affairs* vol. 80, no. 3, pp. 16–35.

Wasescha, Luzius (2003). 'Trade Policy Message to Ministers from the Chairman of the Trade Committee'. Council Meeting at the Ministerial Level, Organisation for Economic Co-operation and Development, Paris, 29–30 April. <www1.oecd.org/subject/mcm/2003/mcmtrade.PDF> (November 2004).

Wasserman, Miriam (2002). 'Dirty Money'. *Regional Review* Q1. <www.bos.frb.org/economic/nerr/rr2002/q1/dirty.htm> (November 2004).

White House (1997). 'A Framework for Global Electronic Commerce'. 1 July. <www.technology.gov/digeconomy/framewrk.htm> (November 2004).

White House (2002). 'Securing America's Borders Fact Sheet: Border Security'. 25 January. <www.whitehouse.gov/news/releases/2002/01/20020125.html> (November 2004).

White House (2004). 'Fact Sheet: Broader Middle East and North Africa Initiative'. Sea Island, 9 June. <www.g8.utoronto.ca/summit/2004seaisland/fact_mena.html> (November 2004).

World Bank (2004). 'Annual Report 2004'. World Bank, Washington. <www.worldbank.org/annualreport/2004> (November 2004).

World Economic Forum (2003). 'Global Digital Divide Initiative'. <annualmeeting.weforum.org/site/homepublic.nsf/Content/Global+Digital+Divide+Initiative.html> (January 2003).

World Trade Organization (2003). 'Joint Statement'. Supachai Panitchpakdi, Director-General of the World Trade Organization, Horst Köhler, Managing Director of the International Monetary Fund, and James Wolfensohn, President of the World Bank group, WTO General Council meeting on coherence, Geneva, 13 May. <www.wto.org/english/news_e/pres03_e/pr341_e.htm> (November 2004).

World Trade Organization (2004). 'Round-the-Clock Meetings Produce "Historic" Breakthrough'. DDA July 2004 Package, Meeting Summary 31 July. <www.wto.org/english/news_e/news04_e/dda_package_sum_31july04_e.htm> (November 2004).

Yaniv, Gideon (1994). 'Taxation and Dirty Money Laundering'. *Public Finances/Public Finance* vol. 49 (Suppl), pp. 40–51.

Yaniv, Gideon (1999). 'Tax Evasion, Risky Laundering, and Optimal Deterrence Policy'. *International Tax and Public Finance* vol. 6, no. 1, pp. 27–38.

Yip, George (2002). *Total Global Strategy II*. Prentice-Hall, Upper Saddle River, NJ.

Index